GOTH CHIC

a connoisseur's guide to dark culture

Edited by Paul A. Woods

gavin baddeley

PLEXUS, LONDON

This book is dedicated to Lady M. – the finest familiar a fellow ever had –
who made her final descent during the composition of this tome.
Save me a place by the fire – I'll be along presently . . .

All rights reserved including the right of
reproduction in whole or in part in any form
Copyright © 2002, 2006 by Gavin Baddeley and Plexus Publishing Limited
Published by Plexus Publishing Limited
25 Mallinson Road
London SW11 1BW

British Library Cataloguing in Publication Data

Baddeley, Gavin
       Goth chic : a connoisseur's guide to dark culture. - 2nd ed.
       1. Goth culture (Subculture) – Great Britain – History – 20th century
       I. Title
       306.1'0941

       ISBN-10: 0-85965-382-X
       ISBN-13: 978-0-85965-382-4

Cover and book design by Fresh Lemon
Cover photograph by Nigel Wingrove
Printed in Great Britain by Bell & Bain

Acknowledgements

Goth Chic hasn't had the easiest of births, and a few reluctant midwives deserve a tip of the hat for their involvement in the process. My editor, Paul, who was driven almost as mad by this book as I was. (*I'll edit you back one day, you sonofabitch!*) To my publisher, Sandra, who endured my deadline dodging with restraint. To Bobbie, who dug out some fine old treasures from her album collection and listened to me slag off all her favourite bands without knocking my teeth out. To Bristol Goths past and present, who shared their views and endured my scrutiny without calling the authorities. To Trevor at Nightbreed, Justin at Cold Spring and Marc from Wasp Factory, who struggle to keep a vibrant, independent British Goth scene alive in the face of the indifference of the British media. To Lydia from the Shroud, Myke from the Empire Hideous, Wayne from the Mission, Andy from Nosferatu, and all the other bands who contributed to this book in one way or another. And to all the other individuals who helped in a thousand different ways that are too numerous to detail here – many thanks!

FOREWORD

Gothic. It is more than just a youth subculture, gloomy aesthetic or literary genre. It is a philosophical perspective – a view of the world, in the words of the Irish novelist J. Sheridan Le Fanu, reflected 'In a Glass Darkly'. It is the cosmos in negative, inverted – the strange and eerie are commonplace, while the everyday is somehow uncanny. Here, the dark and threatening have an irresistible allure, while normality and comfort promise only *ennui* and decay. The opposite poles of sex and death are married together in exquisite grotesquerie. Innocence and virtue are treasured only as virgin parchment, upon which the sigils of sin can be written in broad strokes of blood red and midnight black.

It is the twilight world that the manic-depressive Victorian poet James Thomson in between self-destructive bouts of drinking, described in his 1874 epic, *The City of Dreadful Night*. It is a nightmarish netherworld that Thomson used as a metaphor for the hidden hell beneath the surface of both the city and the soul. A century later, journalist Luke Jennings explored this same metaphorical midnight metropolis in a 1999 article for the London *Evening Standard*, with myself as one of his guides. While by day, Jennings wrote, the industrious city represented the 'conscious mind, the city of night represented his subconscious. Like the psyche, however, or any other unregulated region, the city of night was a dangerous and fearful place. Setting apart the hazards of robbery, syphilis and blackmail, the walker of those dark byways could easily come face to face with his true self.'

The city of dreadful night, the shadow of our modern world, is not confined to any time or place. It is fog-haunted Victorian London, trembling beneath the blade of 'Saucy Jack'. It is *fin de siecle* Paris, a glorious bohemian hell of brothels and hashish clubs, where perverts and poets gather to toast their own damnation. It is Berlin in the 1920s, where red-eyed revellers dance and drink in a desperate attempt to drown out the noise of approaching jackboots. It is late twentieth-century Los Angeles, Jim Morrison's 'city of night', a dream factory more adept at manufacturing nightmares. It is a twilight realm with which I have become familiar. I humbly suggest that you join me on my journey into this heart of darkness . . .

Introduction

What is Gothic?

'Gothic' is one of those curious terms we all think we understand – something to do with bats and graveyards. Placed under the microscope, however, it writhes and squirms, proving difficult to pin down.

In the academic world, 'Gothic' has a set of rigid definitions. Tap it in as your keyword on a library database, and you'll be referred to books about the Gothic art and architecture of medieval western Europe. There may be some overlap with the Gothic culture to which this book is devoted – in fifteenth-century 'Dances of Death', woodcuts of cavorting corpses, for example. But glorious medieval cathedrals, or stylised altar paintings of the Virgin Mary have little in common with the mist-wreathed concept of Gothic as a cultural midnight feast.

Our imaginary word-search might also throw up references to the 'Gothic Revival' – the renewal of interest in medieval architecture in eighteenth-century Europe. Some of this is relevant, describing English eccentrics like Horace Walpole and William Beckford, who created atmospheric, mock-haunted abbeys. However, by the mid nineteenth century, Gothic revivalist architecture was assimilated into the everyday, and no less an edifice than Britain's Houses of Parliament was constructed in the Gothic style. While some might contend that evil schemes are hatched there, acceptability by the establishment is clearly not what Gothic culture is about.

Such subversion and reinvention is typical where the Gothic is concerned, and it's unsurprising that the modern Goth subculture is somewhat confused. (As a stylistic point, this book uses the term 'Goth' to refer to the modern underground scene, and 'Gothic' for the broader cultural aesthetic.) 'What is or isn't authentic Goth' is a familiar topic in the subculture's numerous 'zines and websites – many claiming that one sign of true Goths is that they will deny actually being Goths to their dying breath. The very term 'Gothic' has an ambiguity that borders on the chaotic.

This photograph, by Goth fashion house Dark Angel, manifests the Gothic aesthetic in both attire and architecture – and in nostalgia for a darkly mysterious past that never was.

Pretty much since the scene began in the 1980s, the bands most influential to the movement – notably Siouxsie and the Banshees, and the Sisters of Mercy – have vocally disowned the 'Goth' tag. I discussed this paradox with Trevor Bamford, who masterminds Nightbreed, the UK's specialist Goth recording label, and fronts the influential Goth band Midnight Configuration. According to Bamford, 'Goth' is simply whatever Goths themselves are into at a given moment. But this seems too democratic by far: the Gothic aesthetic has always been about outsiders.

On a more contemporary level, I recently attended a 'Goth night' at an alternative music club, where the dancefloor was dominated by industrial and electro music, and people engaged in the kind of energetic dancing common to raves – rather than the slow, ethereal movements familiar from Goth clubs of the 1980s. When 'Gothic' is said to imply an uncanny atmosphere, but the evening finishes with not one but two 'ironic' renditions of a Britney Spears hit, patrons would surely be justified in demanding a refund.

The club-goers were dressed in a suitably eerie array of black leather, fetish-wear and heavy make-up – though offset with psychedelic PVC and colourful hair extensions – and the ambience was more exotic than that of an equivalent mainstream club. But Gothic is much more than an image – it is an aesthetic, a viewpoint, even a lifestyle, its tradition a legacy of subversion and shadow.

The original Goths were a Germanic tribe, who swept into western Europe in the fourth century to carve a kingdom from the decaying remnants of the Roman Empire. As a result, the word 'Gothic' became synonymous with barbarism (a posthumous fate shared by the Vandals, another tribe who troubled the Romans), and the collapse of the Empire, which signalled the advent of the Dark Ages, a turbulent period of war and savagery that eventually settled into the bleak stagnation of the Middle Ages.

The culture and learning of Classical Rome and Greece were gradually rediscovered in Europe from the fourteenth century onwards, in the period known as the Renaissance, that heralded the birth of the modern world. Classical virtues, such as order, beauty and logic, were idealised, but this renewal of interest also unearthed an underground culture in ancient Rome. Excavated ruins revealed buried chambers decorated with erotic or horrific art and sculpture. Half-human, half-goat monsters engaged in orgies with voluptuous maidens, naked prostitutes serviced their clients, while vines and foliage coiled around these scenes as if alive. Archaeologists of the day dubiously concluded that these were man-made caves, or grottoes, used by the Romans for the worship of profane gods.

Works of art or sculpture which emulated the wild and sinister scenes found in such grottoes became known as 'grotto-esque', or 'grotesque', while aspects of the medieval (or 'Gothic') past were seen to be part of this grotesque tradition. Renaissance paintings of Hell, squirming with half-human devils, gargoyles and grinning corpses leering down from mediaeval masonry, shared the grotesque characteristic of being simultaneously fascinating and repellent. (Edgar Allan Poe, the nineteenth-century American author, who was among the greatest exponents of Gothic, later entitled his 1840 collection *Tales of the Grotesque and Arabesque* – 'Arabesque' then implying something strangely ornate in the style of the exotic East, as in William Beckford's tale of Arabian excess, *Vathek*.)

In her study of grotesque art, *Salome and Judas in the Cave of Sex*, Ewa Kuryluk writes: 'Having its origins in the remains of bestial antiquity, the grotesque in turn was to become concerned with the excavation of all that was against the grain, against the canons of religion and the laws of the state, against academic art and sanctioned sexuality, against virtue and holiness, against established institutions, ceremonies and officially celebrated history. The artists of the grotesque unearthed obscure folk legends and secret doctrines and never tired of exploring the obscene and criminal, that which was shadowy, subterranean and macabre.'

'Gothic', as a cultural term, was initially dismissive, reminding people of how the Dark Ages had replaced the classical glories of Rome with barbarity. The eighteenth-century embrace of Gothic, as opposed to classical, style was a self-conscious rebellion against the good taste and good sense of the age. In the same fashion, modern Goths who dress in impractical but elegant

The original Goths of the Dark Ages – a long way from the moody, black-clad hordes who habituate Goth clubs today.

Victorian garb are not demonstrating approval of oppressive Victorian values, but contempt for brash modern aesthetics and an embrace of the nineteenth century's elegance and decorum. It also manifests a passion for the grotesque aspects of the Victorian age, particularly its obsession with elaborate funeral customs – but in the style of camp, rather than straightforward tribute.

'Camp' is an important concept to anyone who wishes to understand the Gothic aesthetic. In 1964, the writer Susan Sontag attempted to define it thus: 'It is not a natural mode of sensibility, if there be any such. Indeed, the essence of Camp is its love of the unnatural, of artifice and exaggeration. It is a particular kind of style. It is the love of the exaggerated, the "off", of things-being-what-they-are-not . . . Camp is the consistently aesthetic experience of the world. It incarnates a victory of "style" over "content", "aesthetics" over "morality", of irony over tragedy . . . Camp taste is, above all, a mode of enjoyment, of appreciation.'

Often associated with homosexuality, the camp persona treats apparently trivial matters with gravity while regarding serious issues light-heartedly. Taken to its logical extreme, camp is a mockery of conventional wisdom, a sophisticated satire of virtue and duty. In terms of today's Goth subculture, an interest in the forbidden and the arcane, a tendency to introspection and sensitivity, nocturnal habits, or any one of a dozen other characteristics considered suspect by mainstream society, can be rendered acceptable by exaggeration to theatrical extremes. If people derisively label you a vampire or a witch, why not take the wind from their sails by adopting the role with relish?

The original Gothic authors of the late eighteenth and early nineteenth century manifested a taste for what one of their number, Horace Walpole, termed the 'gloomth' of Gothic ruins and medieval superstition. It was a kind of perverse nostalgia, and Walpole observed there to be 'no wisdom comparable to that of exchanging what is called the reality of life for dreams. Old castles, old pictures, old histories, and the babble of old people, make one live back into centuries, that cannot deceive one . . .' The world-weary Walpole, tired of his living contemporaries, concluded, 'The dead have exhausted their power of deceiving – one can trust Catherine of Medici now.' (Medici was a sixteenth-century French queen whose name became a byword for dark ambition and ruthless scheming.) Walpole and his imitators typically chose a mythical, camp version of medieval Europe to escape from the society of the day – just as many 21st century Goths choose a darkly mythologised version of the Victorian era for their flights of the imagination, while others are exploring a similarly gloomy, threatening version of the future and styling themselves 'cybergoths'.

Why we should enjoy monstrous things remains a something of a mystery, a mystery which concerned critics of the original Gothic novels. The Gothic novelists found some philosophical justification for their work in a 1756 tract by the politician and philosopher, Edmund Burke, entitled *Philosophical Inquiry into the Origins of Our Ideas of the Sublime and Beautiful*. Burke concluded that there are two opposing ideals: on the one hand, we are attracted to conventional beauty, whose orderliness is associated with classical culture; on the other, we are drawn to what he called 'the sublime', which was wild and daunting and became associated with Gothic culture. A sunny woodland glade might be described as beautiful, while a deserted graveyard during a raging storm exemplifies the sublime. Beauty appeals by pleasing the beholder, while the sublime stimulates by disturbing or overwhelming. 'When danger or pain press too nearly, they are incapable of any delight, and are simply terrible,' wrote Burke, 'but at certain distances, and with certain modifications, they can be, and they are, delightful, as we every day experience.'

Burke's theories fed a growing fashion for the sublime throughout British society in the late eighteenth and early nineteenth century. Middle-class tourists headed for untamed mountainous regions and ruined abbeys, thrilled with the fancy that robbers, spectres or wolves might lurk in the surrounding caves and woodlands. Aristocratic landowners adorned their estates with sinister, mock-medieval Gothic follies, adding a sense of darkly picturesque mystery, while less wealthy enthusiasts devoured the flood of Gothic novels that followed in the wake of Walpole's *The Castle of Otranto*.

The passion for all things Gothic soon crossed the Channel to mainland Europe. In 1832 the French fashion journal, *Flâneur Parisien*, observed, 'We have Gothic dining rooms and Gothic parlours, and now people want the whole building to be Gothic, with dungeons, crenellations, castellations, drawbridges and portcullises.' But, as the trappings of the Gothic movement became fashionable, they also became commonplace and familiar. Gothic novels fell out of fashion and Gothic architecture became less of a guilty pleasure, admired for its qualities of solidity and strength, and for the fact that it was a specifically Northern European style, as opposed to the classical style of Southern Europe. By the mid-nineteenth century, wealthy British patrons who commissioned Gothic buildings felt they were making a patriotic statement rather than a subversive one.

As the subversive power of the original Gothic aesthetic waned, so a new generation of non-conformists emerged in the form of the Romantic movement – a loose grouping with its roots in the

A cardboard cut-out set from a Victorian toy theatre adaptation of Horace Walpole's original Gothic romance, The Castle of Otranto.

eighteenth century. The Gothic and Romantic movements, in many ways, represent two currents in the same dark cultural tide. The most flamboyant of the Romantics – such as the infamous versifying aristocrat George Gordon, Lord Byron – would use the saturnine anti-heroes of Gothic fiction as role models, at the same time putting flesh on the crude scenarios first imagined by Walpole and his imitators.

Horace Walpole's fiction, *The Castle of Otranto*, is generally regarded as the first Gothic Romance. It was published in 1764, initiating a long and influential tradition. Despite this, it's an unimpressive affair. Even a sympathetic reader such as the Gothic Society's Jennie Gray has felt moved to wonder at 'the astonishing degree of influence this weak and rather tiresome fable has had.'

Any modern reader who struggles through this heavily-dated novel will doubtless agree. Walpole explained how it was inspired by a nightmare, in which, 'I thought myself in an ancient castle (a very natural dream for a head filled like mine with gothic story) and that on the uppermost bannister of a great staircase I saw a gigantic hand in armour. In the evening I sat down and began to write, without knowing in the least what I intended to say or relate. The work grew on my hands . . . I was so engrossed with my tale, which I completed in less than two months.'

It reads that way. *The Castle of Otranto* is a tale of political intrigue set in the Middle Ages, with the chief villain, Manfred, attempting to usurp the throne of the mythical Italian kingdom of Otranto. He is hampered by a series of supernatural manifestations, the most striking of which are huge armoured limbs and helmets dropping improbably from the sky to crush or terrify Manfred's family and servants. *The Critical Review*, a contemporary periodical, chided that the 'publication of any work at this time in England, composed of such rotten materials, is a phenomenon we cannot account for.' But the critic was in a minority, and Walpole's strange novel was a minor sensation.

Its chief innovation lay in evoking the contrasting emotions of terror and pity. This use of radical contrast is the hallmark of classic Gothic art: light and dark, good and evil, sex and death. Realism and character development are of little concern compared to effect, and Gothic literature has been marked by this shameless emphasis on style over content. It was a popular recipe, and by 1797 a contemporary commentator observed, '*Otranto* ghosts have propagated their species with unequalled fecundity. The spawn is in every novel shop.'

Gothic tales were referred to as 'romances' to distinguish them from the novel, which was regarded as of a more edifying nature. By way of contrast, a 'romance', was an unashamed work of the imagination, where exciting and entertaining the reader was more important than being realistic or instructive, while 'romantic' was often used as a dismissive term for impractical individuals with their head in the clouds – until it was defiantly adopted by a generation of artists, writers, composers and, above all, poets who revelled in the wistful waywardness that society condemned.

Like Gothic, 'Romantic' is a term that has, over the years, lost much of its edge. Today, the word is almost exclusively associated with flowers, chocolates, moon-in-June lyrics and other sloppy clichés of the love-story genre. The archetypal nineteenth-century Romantic was always associated with passion, but it was not restricted to affairs of the heart – it permeated every aspect of his life, feeding an ethos of political radicalism and sexual liberation. The Romantic was a rebel who saw art and fantasy as his weapons in the revolution against oppression.

According to the Romantic credo, unfettered creativity and individualism were sacred, as opposed to the mainstream values of logical thought and social responsibility. Inward-looking, creative individuals were extolled as the prophets and visionaries of their age, and their art was not perceived as a distraction from the mundane material world but as a blueprint for moving above and beyond its tyranny. Nils Stevenson, road manager for punk standard-bearers the Sex Pistols during their notorious 1976 Anarchy in the UK tour, sees an implicit connection between the rabble-rousing of late 1970s punks and the young Romantics in the early 1800s. In *Vacant*, his diary of the punk years, Stevenson concludes his introduction with a quote from Isaiah Berlin's *The Roots of Romanticism*, which were, according to Berlin, 'the primitive, the untutored, it is youth, life . . . but it is also pallor, fever, disease, decadence . . . the Dance of Death, indeed Death itself . . . turbulence, violence, conflict, chaos, but it is also peace . . . It is the strange, the exotic, the grotesque . . . the irrational, the unutterable . . .' On reflection, this seems to evoke the modern Goth scene more than the punk wave that pre-dated it, and it's perhaps no coincidence that Stevenson went on to manage Siouxsie and the Banshees, the punk mavericks who were instrumental in triggering Goth.

As a generation of rebellious young Europeans adopted Romanticism in the 1840s, they self-consciously smoked the recently invented cigarette at a time when tobacco had gone out of fashion, and drank a powerful form of punch. According to James Laver in his history of style, *Taste and Fashion*, 'the punch-bowl was given a place of honour at every famous Romantic party – orgy, perhaps, would be a better name, for the Romantics spared no effort to make such affairs as macabre as possible by the introduction of death's heads, skeletons, etc., by draping the room in black, and by every manifestation of a somewhat infantile diabolism. There is not much danger in drinking punch for pleasure; but when you drink it on principle in the quantities befitting a blighted being, the effects are likely to be unfortunate, and many a young Romantic drank himself into an early grave.'

In the final decades of the nineteenth century, the darker elements of the Romantic tradition blossomed into the Decadent movement. Romanticism was essentially optimistic, believing the world could be redeemed. Decadence was pessimistic to the point of total nihilism. In his anthology of Decadent writing, *Moral Ruins*, editor Brian Stableford describes the Decadents as 'renegade Romantics' – certainly, the movement shared the Romantic ideals of imagination and individualism, but Decadents did not believe such forces could ultimately save mankind. Essentially, they said, everything's going to hell, so we might as well just try to enjoy the ride as best we can.

Decadents believed only the passing, artificial pleasures of luxury and self-indulgence to be real. While the more scandalous of the Romantics had flirted with narcotics and Satanism, the Decadents wholly abandoned themselves to black magic and druggy debauchery. As with 'Gothic' and 'Romantic', 'Decadent' was a term often used to insult an artist whom a critic felt to be morally bankrupt, and many of the best-known Decadents rejected the label entirely. Ellis Hanson, in his book *Decadence and Catholicism*, observes how, 'the decadents cultivated a fascination with all that was commonly perceived as unnatural or degenerate, with sexual perversity, nervous illness, crime, and disease, all presented in a highly aestheticised context calculated to subvert or, at any rate, to shock conventional morality. Both stylistically and thematically, decadence is an aesthetic in which failure and decay are regarded as seductive, mystical, or beautiful . . . The typical decadent hero is, with a few exceptions, an upper-class, overly educated, impeccably dressed aesthete, a man whose masculinity is confounded by his tendency to androgyny, homosexuality, masochism, mysticism, or neurosis.'

All of which has clear parallels with both the Gothic tradition and the Goth subculture of today. 'Decadence is not a happy state,' observes Stableford in *Moral Ruins*, 'and the Decadent does not bother to seek the trivial goal of contentment, whose price is wilful blindness to the true state of the world. Instead, he must become a connoisseur of his own psychic malaise (which mirrors, of course, the malaise of his society). He is the victim of various ills, whose labels became the key terms of Decadent rhetoric: *ennui* (world-weariness); *spleen* (an angry subspecies of melancholy); *impuissance* (powerlessness).' The movement reached its peak in 1890s Paris, the city becoming a place of pilgrimage and refuge for perverse poets from around the world. The period became known as the *fin de siècle* ('end of the century'), and as tradition insists that the end of a century somehow brings the world closer to the Apocalypse, so the end of the nineteenth century fuelled the wild, feverish excesses of the Parisian scene. (Decadence would later find its twentieth-century mecca in 1920s Berlin, at the same time as Germany gave birth to the Gothic expressionist films that pre-dated the horror movie.)

By the 1980s, the term 'Gothic' was employed to describe a new musical subculture, born from the ashes of the dying punk scene and nurtured on the dandyism of 1970s glam rock –

Charles Baudelaire, the archetypal Decadent poet, wrote verse fixated on whores and vampires. It has been set to music by Christian Death, Dead Can Dance and Diamanda Galas. (Portrait by Alastair.)

which some astute commentators had labelled 'decadent'. Goth rock was the most coherent, widespread manifestation of the Gothic tradition ever. Unlike most equivalent youth cults, like heavy metal or rockabilly, Goth was not centred around a particular musical style, but on an underground movement that assimilated cultural artefacts from the past.

'Over the last 25 years, I have perceived, experienced and participated in "Goth" as emerging from a minor "weirdo fringe" to the fully paid-up and universally-recognised thinking eccentric's subculture,' says Geoff Kayson, of leading Goth jewellery designers, Alchemy. 'As a result of this, a virtual "second Gothic revival" movement has evolved, with competitive instincts inevitably forcing the creative and commercial standards to rise . . . now we not only have a fantastic cornucopia of the highest quality and range of extreme fashion and lifestyle for the hardcore Goth, but, for our sins, Gothic bedsteads and wallpaper in every town high street.'

Musician, Wayne Hussey, was one who attracted the Goth tag, as a result of his roles as guitarist with the Sisters of Mercy and vocalist for the Mission, who enjoyed success in the late 1980s courtesy of their Goth fanbase. Like many who were similarly pigeon-holed – including his erstwhile Sisters band-mate Andrew Eldritch – Hussey actively resisted the label, but, by the turn of the millennium, was impressed by the cult's tenacity. 'It's not just about the music,' he told me, 'it's about a whole lifestyle. There are weekend Goths who just like dressing up – but whatever floats your boat. I love the movie *The Hunger*, for example, while I was never a big fan of *The Rocky Horror Show*. The movement has its own literature, whether it's *Interview with the Vampire* or Edgar Allan Poe. There's the clothes, the make-up, the attitude. It's not just about bands – it's a way of life now for some people.'

Rock journalist Mick Mercer was commissioned to write the first book on the Goth scene, his *Gothic Rock Black Book*, and thus became its earliest historian. He describes the subculture as a 'violently childish dreamworld, involving immense amounts of energy and play-acting . . . Wracked with religious imagery, slippy with sexual inference, Goth onstage is seldom happy. Goth offstage is a hoot. Goth onstage cries, growls and scowls. Goth offstage goes quietly insane and wraps itself in drunken worship, pagan worship, and the loins of psychologically damaged French philosophers.'

As it approached its own 1990s *fin de siècle*, popular culture as a whole was ready to follow the Goths over to the dark side. Brian Stableford, as an authority on Decadent literature, felt

'Gothic' can imply many different things. This photo-portrait of US darkwave duo Lycia parodies Grant Wood's famous 1930 painting American Gothic.

moved to pen an article for the UK Goth 'zine *Bats and Red Velvet* entitled 'News of the Black Feast', in which he notes, 'the end of every century has been marked by a sense of terminus: a *fin de siècle* sensibility which leads particularly sensitive individuals to take sombre delight in the contemplation of darkness and degeneration . . . In our democratic era . . . a Decadent lifestyle is accessible at street level, available to any and all dissenters from middle-class notions of respectability. Its most blatant contemporary manifestation is, of course, the Goth subculture, whose name pays due but ironic homage to the architectural and literary ambitions of Beckford and Walpole.'

Stableford is struck by how the bands Mercer covers in his 1996 Goth encyclopaedia, *The Hex Files*, 'share certain characteristics which link them as securely to the typical concerns of *fin de siècle* culture as to the Goth culture of the 1980s. Their writers give every indication of being widely-read, poetically ambitious and familiar with a wide range of musical styles – styles which they are attempting to combine in a quasi-alchemical fashion.' Stableford compares the scene catalogued by Mercer with the aforementioned Decadent movement, singling out a parallel with the 1884 novel, *A rebours* ('Against Nature'), by the Parisian author, Joris Karl Huysmans. Its main character, Duc Jean Des Esseintes, a witty but world-weary aristocrat, became a role model for nineteenth century Decadents.

A rebours 'represented a new peak in the search for sensation,' observed William Gaunt in his book, *The Aesthetic Adventure*. 'Its hero, Des Esseintes, was an exquisite who lived an artificial life . . . [Des Esseintes] also had a counterpart in literature, the Roderick Usher of Poe's "House of Usher". He had brought, like the demon-driven character of Poe's tale, the cultivation of the senses to the uttermost limits of perversity. He devised for instance a whole orchestra of scents and perfumes. No vice or curiosity was alien to him and his overheated imagination grew, in his rooms from which all outer air and influence was excluded, tropical and monstrous . . . In fact he avoided all natural and external experience and cherished the

The late 1990's Goth culture, pastiched as part of an award-winning campaign promoting Smirnoff vodka. (In true undead style the coolest Goth chick casts no reflection.)

solitary and unusual because what was not nature was art, and art was the only worthy condition of existence.' (More recently, Huysmans' bible of decadence inspired Irish poison-pop experimentalists Fatima Mansions to dub their 1989 debut *Against Nature*, and *avant-garde* 'industrial' musician Magnus Sundström to assume the moniker Des Esseintes for his latest project.)

'The common concerns of the subculture mapped in *The Hex Files* echo common concerns of the countercultures of the 1790s and 1890s,' observes Stableford in 'News of the Black Feast'. 'Goth subculture is expanding to embrace many, if not all, of the issues addressed by Huysmans in *A rebours*: a book which laid before its readers an entire "black feast" of blithe perversities.' Stableford is right in every respect but one – his belief that such 'black feasts' are confined to the final years of a century. It may simply be that the rest of society is more inclined to listen during the *fin de siècle*, giving the impression of a cyclical attraction to darkness, which is in fact more constant.

But it cannot be denied that, as Christoph Grunenberg puts it in an essay in *Gothic*, the catalogue for a 1997 exhibition at the Boston Institute of Contemporary Art, 'Eternal night seems to have fallen over the world and dark is the most fashionable colour in the autumn of the century.

'The subculture of Goth rock, its distinct dress code and lifestyle predate the current revival of a manifestly Gothic aesthetic by almost two decades,' continues Grunenberg, 'its members remaining devoted in their enchantment with death, the macabre and otherworldly. The Goths' romantic look with its strong inclination towards black was successfully appropriated by mainstream fashion several years ago . . . Today, the Gothic in fashion and design has become mass marketable, available courtesy of singer/actor turned designer Cher, whose Sanctuary catalogue offers jewellery, fashion, as well as heavy yet comfortable medievalised furniture.'

Goth counterculture is now manifesting itself at the very heart of mall culture with

Gother Than Thou: evidence of the Goth scene's keen sense of self-deprecating humour – a card game where clove cigarettes and eyeliner are essentials for the ultimate Goth.

increasing virulence. Which returns us to our original enquiry: what *is* Gothic? In one sense, it is the dark undercurrent of everyday existence, a twilight version of the daylight world. In another, it is a welcoming viper's nest of contradictions that has developed through several hundred years of counterculture: Grotesque, Gothic, Romantic, Decadent, Goth.

Gothic is sophisticated barbarism. It is a passion for life draped in the symbolism of death. It is a cynical love of sentiment. It is a marriage of extremes such as sex and death. It uses darkness to illuminate. It believes duty is vain, and vanity to be a duty. It is the compulsion to do the wrong thing for all the right reasons. It is a yearning nostalgia for the black days of a past that never was. It denies orthodox reality and puts its faith in the imaginary. It is the unholy, the uncanny, the unnatural.

But is Gothic merely a pose, as its detractors maintain? Most certainly – but are we not all poseurs at some level? Inevitably, the brilliant, decadent Oscar Wilde put it best, in his Gothic classic *The Picture of Dorian Gray* – a richly sinister Faustian fable set in Victorian London – when he observed, 'Being natural is simply a pose, and the most irritating pose I know.'

Chapter I

The Imp of the Perverse: the Golden Age of Gothic Literature

Musing on the birth of Gothic literature, in the preface to an 1800 anthology entitled *Crimes of Love*, the Marquis de Sade wrote, 'The genre was the inevitable product of the revolutionary shocks with which the whole of Europe resounded. For those who were acquainted with all the ills that are brought upon men by the wicked, the novel was becoming more difficult to write as it was monotonous to read; there was nobody left who had not experienced more misfortunes in four or five years than could be depicted in a century by literature's most gifted novelist. It was therefore necessary to call on hell for aid in the creation of titles that could arouse interest, and to find in the land of nightmare what was once common knowledge from the mere observation of the history of man in this iron age.'

The most powerful of these 'revolutionary shocks' was the French Revolution of 1789, which toppled the aristocracy and sent powerful ripples of chaos and disorder across the map of Europe. And Sade was certainly acquainted with the misfortunes that could befall a man in those turbulent times.

Donatien Alphonse Francois de Sade, dubbed 'the Divine Marquis' by later admirers, is a pivotal Gothic figure. A highly-sexed, high-born French cavalry officer, the diminutive but charming Sade enjoyed whipping and being whipped as well as anal sex with partners of both genders – an exotic, illegal combination only topped by his taste for combining blasphemy and sex, such as inserting communion wafers into his partner's vagina.

In the summer of 1772, one such orgy went badly wrong when the quartet of prostitutes Sade hired fell ill, probably as a result of consuming candy the Marquis had laced with Spanish

An illustration for Edgar Allan Poe's short story 'The Black Cat' by 1890s Decadent artist Aubrey Beardsley.

The terror of the guillotine, imagined by Nigel Wingrove of Salvation Films. According to the Marquis de Sade, such turbulent times inspired the birth of the Gothic novel.

fly (a purported aphrodisiac). A warrant went out for his arrest on charges of poisoning and sodomy, but Sade had already fled. The fact that Sade had taken his wife's younger sister with him as his mistress (adding technical incest to his misdemeanours) outraged his mother-in-law, the formidable Madame de Montreuil, who made the arrest and imprisonment of her scandalous son-in-law a personal priority. In December of that year, Sade was apprehended and began the first of many lengthy periods of incarceration. Indeed, the liberty-loving libertine would spend most of the rest of his days imprisoned in one institution after another, the victim of his own outspoken nature and restless libido, and Madame de Montreuil's unforgiving tenacity.

By 1784, the Marquis was incarcerated in the nation's most notorious gaol – the Bastille. Events orchestrated his release five years later, when the Revolution ousted the aristocratic government and Sade, on the assumption that any enemy of the old regime was a friend of the Revolution, was freed. By nature an outcast, he was soon rejected by the Revolutionary Council as violently as by his aristocratic roots, and Citizen de Sade (as he was now known) again found himself behind bars, accused of conspiring with his blue-blooded peers, a charge exacerbated by his scandalous reputation. Perhaps the most nightmarish episode of his traumatic life was in 1794, when he found himself imprisoned in Picpus hospital prison when the mindless butchery that followed the Revolution, known as 'the Reign of Terror', was reaching its peak.

In a letter from his new prison, Sade, under threat of execution for alleged treason, observed it was 'an earthly paradise, a lovely building, a magnificent garden, choice company, charming women, then all at once the guillotine is set up directly under our windows and they began to dispose of the dead in the middle of our garden ... we buried 1,800 in 35 days.' In a July coup, the zealots responsible for Sade's arrest were themselves guillotined for treason, and in October he was freed once more – though he only enjoyed a final, brief period of liberty before being arrested again for immoral behaviour in 1801. An official report of the time noted that he was 'in a perpetual state of lascivious furore, which constantly compels him to monstrous thoughts and actions.' This time the ageing deviant was confined to a lunatic asylum where he served out the final eleven years of his life. In a marvellously Gothic final flourish, he occupied his time there composing and producing plays, with the cast largely drawn from the asylum's inmates.

The Marquis de Sade's chief legacy is the term 'sadism' – coined twenty years after his death to describe the derivation of sexual pleasure from inflicting pain. But it is not this that concerns us as much as his 'monstrous thoughts', preserved in the form of novels written to ease his boredom while imprisoned and to stave off poverty in his later years. He was also a fan of the new English genre of Gothic romance, though his own self-conscious efforts in the genre are disappointingly bland. It is his other works upon which his notoriety rests, Sade's infamous and often suppressed experiments in pornography – though their dark mood, perverse sexuality, scenes of incest, cannibalism and blasphemy, with exaggerated characters and situations, mark them out as Gothic literature of the most extreme kind.

While once critics condemned them as unspeakably obscene, modern academics display their worldliness by dismissing them as repetitive and dull. However, the repetition and deranged taboo-busting have an almost humorous quality after a while, and much of Sade's writing can be appreciated as smutty satire. The first and most notorious of these works is *The 120 Days of Sodom* (named after the biblical city steeped in sin that became the basis of the word 'sodomy'). Written in secret while Sade was incarcerated in the Bastille, *120 Days* was composed by candlelight and secreted behind a loose brick during the day. It is the tale of four wealthy perverts, all members of the establishment Sade despised, who seclude themselves in an isolated fortress with a cast of whores, madames and innocents in order to indulge every sexual excess and transgression imaginable.

His next two literary atrocities also play with the Gothic theme of innocence in peril, though here the girls were threatened with more than the Gothic novel's traditional 'fate worse than death'. In his related volumes *Justine* and *Juliette*, Sade describe the lives of two sisters faced with improbably extreme ordeals of physical, psychological and sexual abuse. Justine is virtuous, and suffers because of it, while Juliette, who takes to vice like a duck to water, prospers. The subtitles of the twin novels – *The Prosperity of Vice* and *The Misfortunes of Virtue* – highlight their (a)moral context. 'If misery persecutes virtue and prosperity accompanies crime, those things being as one in nature's view,' explained the author, 'is it not far better to join company with the wicked who flourish than to be counted among the virtuous who founder?' Sade goes to Gothic extremes in order to illustrate his 'nice guys finish last' view of the world – particularly in the story of the innocent Justine.

Justine, like all of Sade's most notorious works, is a literary oddity: too brutal and misanthropic to be pornographic; too sexually-fixated and repetitive to be anything else. The trials and tribulations of the virtuous heroine are almost too extreme to take seriously. She saves the lives of several characters, all of whom repay her with betrayal or worse: indeed, Justine is sodomised and whipped with almost tedious frequency (mirroring Sade's own fetishes), and finds herself at the mercy of a wicked gallery of villains. And each, like Justine's evil sister Juliette, knows only profit from his extreme cruelty and selfishness. At the novel's climax, when it finally seems like Justine's blameless character will be rewarded, she is struck by lightning, which passes through her mouth and out of her vagina. Sade's conclusion is that nature – or even God Himself – has nothing but contempt for virtue.

By no means all Gothic fiction was as twisted or as challenging as Sade's dark fantasies. On the contrary, most examples of the genre were cluttered with clumsy moralising, which, with their propagandising the triumph of virtue over vice, went quite contrary to Sade's philosophy. Hugely popular by the end of the eighteenth century, they were remarkably open to parody – most famously by Jane Austen in her satirical novel *Northanger Abbey*, written in 1799. Most ripe for this treatment were those works which also attained the greatest popularity: the novels of Anne Radcliffe.

The picturesque Gothic ruin and the virginal heroine – integral features of the golden-age Gothic romances of Anne Radcliffe and her many imitators.

While she had numerous rivals and imitators (most notably Sophia Lee and Clara Reeve), none came close in popularity to Radcliffe, who formulated the blueprint for the golden age of Gothic literature. Not everyone was so kind. The Marquis de Sade, while enthusiastic about the basic Gothic concept, was unimpressed by her compulsion to debunk all her tales' supernatural elements, lacking as she was the daring that allows the best Gothic literature to endure. The classic example of this is in her best-known novel, *The Mysteries of Udolpho* (1794). Emily, the heroine, discovers something mysterious in a black veil while exploring the damp chambers of crumbling Castle Udolpho. The teasing suspense is maintained for hundreds of pages, until the nervous heroine plucks up courage to peer beneath the veil, revealing 'a human figure of ghastly paleness, stretched at its length, and dressed in the habiliments of the grave. What added to the horror of the spectacle was that the face appeared partly decayed and disfigured by worms, which were visible on the features and hands.' Like all good romantic heroines, Emily faints. The final revelation – that this ghastly corpse is merely a waxwork constructed long ago by monks to frighten sinners – is a cop-out that has disappointed readers for 200 years.

Radcliffe's formula spawned numerous works set in locales and times distant enough to be mildly exotic, virtuous heroines pinballed around cobwebby crypts and sinister castles, swooning or shrieking each time they collided with some ominous vision. Dominating the sprawling plots were villains who undoubtedly offered a mild crackle of erotic menace for the primarily female readership. Unlike real Gothic villains, like the highly-sexed Sade, these fictional scoundrels lived in a universe far too restrained for them ever to inflict the 'fate worse than death' that's constantly threatened. Instead, with tedious reliability, virtue triumphs and vice is vanquished. Radcliffe concludes her 1790 novel, *A Sicilian Romance*, by describing it as 'a singular and striking instance of moral retribution. We learn, also, that those who only do THAT WHICH IS RIGHT, endure nothing in misfortune but a trial of their virtue, and from trials well endured derive the surest claim to the protection of heaven.'

Time has transformed Radcliffe from the leading popular authoress of her day to very much an acquired taste, read largely for academic reasons rather than pleasure. Notoriously reclusive, she cultivated an image as 'the Great Enchantress', but as the new century advanced, as revolutionary idealism was replaced by reactionary anxiety, and male writers tried to regain the heights occupied by women, Radcliffe – former visionary and magician – was reinvented as madwoman and witch.'

In 1810, one Reverend Charles Apthorp Wheelwright issued a poetry anthology containing an 'Ode to Horror', in which horror is personified as a goddess of madness who pursues her victims to the grave – her chief victim being Anne Radcliffe. In case he hadn't made himself explicit enough, Wheelwright added a footnote explaining, that Radcliffe was 'reported to have died under the species of mental derangement, known by the name of the horrors.'

Nobody was more surprised to hear of her demise than Mrs Radcliffe herself. Furthermore, she was perturbed by the common public assumption that those who create dark or disturbing art must themselves be disturbed – although, in her case, as so often in the Gothic arena, there was some truth to this. Having suffered from acute depression – or 'melancholy', as it was then known – throughout her adult life, when Radcliffe died of a fever brought on by a bronchial infection in early 1823, her suffering was compounded by delusions. Ironically, Radcliffe's mysterious private life was more powerfully Gothic than her prose. With meandering plots, cardboard characters and complex (touching on incestuous) revelations as to which characters are related, the Gothic romance resembles nothing so much as a mildly spooky soap opera – more *Days of Our Lives* than *Dracula*.

In the 1960s, Victoria Holt's surprise best-seller *The Mistress of Mellyn* sparked a revival in the Gothic romance genre. Aimed primarily at the female market, these paperbacks were mostly limp and bloodless affairs, more hackneyed romance than Gothic thriller (though a few old classics were reprinted among the anaemic pulp). Perhaps the main contemporary inheritor of Radcliffe's tradition is Virginia Andrews, with her claustrophobic tales of suburban suspense – though the most authentically scary aspect of Andrews is the way her name has been sold as a franchise, allowing her effectively to write from beyond the grave.

The authentic roots of what became the horror genre are to be found with another Gothic author who, unlike the timid Mrs Radcliffe, possessed balls.

The author in question was Matthew Gregory Lewis – known in his day, due to the literary sensation he created, as Matthew 'Monk' Lewis. In his analysis of the Gothic novel, the Marquis de Sade lists Lewis alongside Radcliffe as one of the two pillars upon which the genre stands, describing the former's work as 'superior in all respects to the strange flights of Mrs Radcliffe's brilliant imagination'. Crucially, Lewis' 1796 novel, *The Monk*, never debunks the plot's supernatural elements, nor shrinks from describing the shocking episodes of sex and violence over which his competitors habitually drew a veil. As a modern admirer, Les Daniels (whose 1977 book, *Fear*, remains one of the better histories of the horror genre), noted of *The Monk*: 'A standard history of English literature claims that it exhibits "the perverted lust of a sadist". Can there be a higher recommendation?'

This condemnation is nothing new, as the book has been the target of pious invective since it was first published. Typical was the outraged commentator who condemned it as 'a mass of murder, outrage, diablerie and indecency', or the critic who dubbed the book 'totally unfit for general circulation'. Lewis, by then a Member of Parliament, was sensitive to the scandal. He omitted his name from the first edition, and, threatened with prosecution for obscenity by the Attorney General, substantially toned down subsequent editions. The original, uncensored text was not to be published again for well over a century, when Grove Press, an American publisher notorious for literary erotica and pornography, issued an unexpurgated edition in 1952.

Unsurprisingly, *The Monk* was a hot topic of conversation when it first surfaced – something like the *American Psycho* or *Exorcist* of its day – and was discussed in hushed tones in the coffee-houses, gaming clubs and drawing rooms of fashionable late eighteenth-century England. It tells the story of Ambrosio, a famously virtuous abbot in early seventeenth-century Spain who is seduced by a young beauty called Matilda, later revealed as a demon in human form. In a commendably lurid scene, Matilda flashes one of her breasts at the flustered monk, whereupon, 'A raging fire shot through every limb; the blood boiled in his veins, and a thousand wild wishes bewildered his imagination.'

From thereon Ambrosio quickly slides into a life of vice, black magic and murder, culminating in the rape of his own sister and murder of his mother. When retribution finally catches up with him in the fearsome shape of the Spanish Inquisition, Ambrosio orchestrates his escape by summoning Lucifer himself. But Lucifer taunts the monk with his sins before casting him down to his death from a mountaintop – clearly, here is one Devil who doesn't look after his own. Leading the assault upon *The Monk*, the poet Samuel Taylor Coleridge, echoing organisations like the Society for the Suppression of Vice, condemned the book for shocking episodes 'such as no observation of character can justify, because no good man would willingly suffer them to pass however transiently, through his own mind.' In other words, someone who created something as monstrous as *The Monk* must be a monster himself, an accusation levelled at Gothic artists ever since.

This 'monster', Matthew Lewis, certainly led a life with Gothic overtones (coincidentally, he inherited his parliamentary seat from William Beckford, author of *Vathek*). The spirit of Lewis' brother, Barrington, who died at an early age, was reputed to have haunted him throughout his life. Also, when Lewis set out in 1815 to inspect slave plantations he had inherited in Jamaica, he was dismayed by the brutal conditions under which they laboured and their superstitious belief in Obeah (native witchcraft). He witnessed their tendency toward 'this vile trick of poisoning', and cynically noted how the slaves were more inclined to poison kind masters than cruel ones. (Despite this, he instituted a series of humane reforms on his plantations.) In May 1818, Lewis died aboard ship after suffering an attack of yellow fever. Officially, medicine taken to ease his suffering had the reverse effect and proved fatal – but local gossip had it that he promised to set his slaves free upon his death, and some of the more enterprising slaves decided to speed up the process ('The Misfortunes of Virtue' – to appropriate Sade's subtitle for *Justine*). His burial at sea was suitably Gothic: the weights used to drag his coffin to the seabed slid off, and it bobbed to the surface, his shroud forming a macabre sail that caught the wind, slowly sailing back towards Jamaica.

Like the Marquis de Sade, 'Monk' Lewis was possessed of 'a passion for the macabre', according to one acquaintance, that 'amounted to a mania with him.' But in both cases their literary offences pale into insignificance when contrasted with the horrors of their age – in Sade's case the Reign of Terror, in Lewis' the horrors of slavery. Both men had noble qualities that marked them as Gothic anti-heroes rather than villains.

The acquaintance who commented on Lewis' manias was the notorious Romantic poet Lord Byron. Lewis had visited Byron in 1816, when sexual scandal in England had made the aristocrat an effective exile in the villa Diodati on the shores of Lake Geneva in the Swiss Alps. Also staying with Byron were his physician, Dr Polidori, his lover, Clare Clairmont, his friend and fellow poet, Percy Shelley (himself on the run from creditors and an abandoned wife), and Shelley's young mistress, Mary Wollstonecraft Godwin, and their infant son, William. Lewis entertained the assembled party by telling Gothic tales, which inspired a ghost-story writing competition after he had left.

Matthew Gregory Lewis' 1796 Gothic masterpiece The Monk *has been adapted several times – including this 1972 French film interpretation.*

One of the tales invented for this contest would become a Gothic legend, created not by one of the great poets but by the shy girl they nicknamed 'Dormouse'. Upon marriage that young woman would be known as Mary Shelley, and her story was *Frankenstein*.

Frankenstein was a product of the tempest of narcotics, sexual tension and intellectual fervour at the Villa Diodati in 1816. First published in 1818, by the time Mary Shelley issued her definitive, much-expanded edition in 1831, she was the only surviving member of the party, all the other luminaries fulfilling their destiny to live fast and die young.

It begins in the Arctic, where an explorer comes across a crazed young man named Victor Frankenstein, who tells of the horrors that brought him to that blasted end of the earth. Told in flashback, his experiments into the nature of life lead him to create an artificial man from parts of corpses – but, rather than the beautiful superhuman he had planned, his creation is a malformed giant, and Victor abandons him in disgust. With almost supernatural speed, the Monster develops a level of sophistication and sensitivity, but remains the object of horror and rejection by the human race.

In desperation, the Monster seeks out his creator and begs Frankenstein to build him a mate to relieve his isolation. Victor initially agrees, but, terrified that the two will breed and create a race of monsters, he destroys his second creation. Enraged, the Monster resolves to make his creator share his desolation and loneliness, slaughtering all those near and dear to the medical genius. Frankenstein then sets off in pursuit of his murderous creation, ending at the Arctic wastelands where we first met him. Exhausted, Frankenstein expires, while his creation drifts off into the frozen hell atop an iceberg.

Frankenstein remains the only Gothic novel that has enjoyed almost universal approval from the literary establishment, and more ink has been spilt dissecting and re-evaluating it than any comparable text. Its central figures are composites of a number of archetypal Gothic figures, stitched together to form the enduring creation so familiar to us today. The first is indicated in the novel's subtitle, *The Modern Prometheus*. Prometheus was a Titan (the semi-divine race of giants from Greek mythology) whose defiance of the gods made him a noble symbol of Romantic self-sacrifice. According to legend, he stole the life-giving secret of fire in defiance of the gods. Divine retribution was terrible – according to the most popular version of the myth, the Titan was chained to a rock for all eternity while an eagle pecked at his liver, the organ regrown each morning for the torment to continue. The parallels are obvious: Victor Frankenstein as a Romantic martyr to the thirst for knowledge, punished for his temerity in defying God and trying to create life.

The second archetype is Satan. In the introduction to *Prometheus Unbound*, Shelley drew comparisons between the character of Prometheus and the version of Satan portrayed in John Milton's epic poem, *Paradise Lost*. Milton intended his poem as a dramatisation of the fall from grace of Satan and man, but Satan emerges from the work as a noble villain or sympathetic anti-hero. As an archetypal rebel against divine tyranny, Satan had a great appeal to the Romantics – as he did for the monster in *Frankenstein*, Mary depicting him reading *Paradise Lost* in his doomed efforts to understand humanity. Inevitably, the Monster sees himself as a Satan to Victor's God ('Evil thenceforth become my good,' quotes the despairing creature) –

Romantic poet Lord Byron inspired the archetypal, brooding 'Byronic anti-hero', suggested by this model for the Dark Angel Goth catalogue.

just as Victor's transgressions against divine law make him a satanic figure in the eyes of his own God.

The last archetype evoked is that of Faust, the legendary black magician. Attempts have been made to cast *Frankenstein* as a pioneering work of science fiction, but Victor is more sorcerer than scientist – a 'pale student of unhallowed arts', whose methods owe more to necromancy and alchemy than science. In the Faust legend the sorcerer signs a pact with the Devil in return for power and pleasure, but pays with life and soul, when the powers of darkness demand settlement of the debt. It's a morality tale that appealed to the pious as a warning against ambition and ungodliness, but bolder souls saw in it a noble struggle for knowledge and experience in the face of terrible retribution.

Faust has been reworked and reinterpreted countless times. According to modern Gothic horror writer, Clive Barker, who based three of his stories (*The Damnation Game*, 'The Hellbound Heart' and 'The Last Illusion') on the legend, it's 'one of the important roads in all fantastic literature. At its centre is a notion essential to the horror genre and its relations: that of a trip taken into forbidden territory at the risk of insanity or death.' The Faustian spirit of adventure, Promethean defiance of convention and satanic appetite for freedom engendered early death for both Percy Shelley (in 1822) and Lord Byron (in 1824). In her journal that year, Mary, increasingly depressed and withdrawn, labelled them 'the people of the grave – that miserable conclave to which the beings I best loved belonged.' For her, the selfish pacts Byron and her husband had made with their own demons of freedom and pleasure carried too high a price, and Mary, desolate and isolated, renounced her rebellious past.

Her 'hideous progeny' (as Mary memorably described the creature in her novel) had developed a life of its own, and *Frankenstein* has outlived many of the myths that informed it. Over a century after the novel's completion, the head of the movie industry's Production Code Administration – a devout Catholic named Joe Breen – was very uncomfortable about the Faustian subtext in *The Bride of Frankenstein* (regarded by many as the definitive celluloid *Frankenstein*). 'Throughout the script,' he observed, 'there are a number of references to Frankenstein which compare him to God and which compare his creation of the monster to God's creation of Man. All such references should be eliminated.' So they were, but James Whale's the film's artful director, still included sacreligious imagery: the Monster's captivity in a graveyard, where the mob bind him in cruciform to a wooden stake, clearly parallels Christ's crucifixion.

Today, the metaphor for blind ambition that breaks divine or natural laws is not Prometheus, or Faust, but Frankenstein. His legend is assimilated into the language to such a degree that the science of genetic engineering – an 'unhallowed art' – has been described as unleashing the horror of 'Frankenstein foods'!

Another Gothic archetype took centre-stage in a novel published shortly after *Frankenstein*, which many hail as the last great work of the golden age of Gothic literature. The book was *Melmoth the Wanderer*, written by Charles Robert Maturin, and published in 1820. The myth that informed it was that of the Wandering Jew, a folkloric figure who mocked Jesus as he carried his cross to Calvary, and, for his contempt of divine majesty, was doomed to wander the earth friendless and homeless for eternity. Initially a medieval anti-Semitic myth, the

*Mary Shelley (Natasha Richardson), Claire Clairmont (Myriam Cyr), Lord Byron (Gabriel Byrne)
and Percy Shelley (Julian Sands) in the delirious* Gothic *(1986).*

figure of Ahaseurus, the Wandering Jew, evolved into the Gothic archetype of the ultimate
outcast, a reluctant nomad rejected by both God and man: the Wandering Jew has a walk-on
part in *The Monk*; Percy Shelley makes several references to the character in his works; he
surfaces in waterborne form as the Flying Dutchman, or perhaps even as Captain Ahab in
Herman Melville's 1851 classic *Moby Dick*.

Maturin very nearly invited exile status upon himself with the publication of *Melmoth*.
From a respected family of French Protestants who found refuge in Dublin, he was a
melancholic dandy who the *Dublin University Magazine* recalled as 'eccentric in his habits,
almost to insanity, and compounded of opposites; an inveterate reader of novels, an elegant

Back to the Villa Diodati in Frankenstein Unbound *(1990): Byron (Jason Patric),*
Mary (Bridget Fonda) and doomed Shelley (similarly doomed rock star Michael Hutchence).

preacher, an incessant dancer, which propensity he carried to such an extent that he darkened his drawing-room windows and indulged during the daytime.' His masques and parties were the talk of the town, but he had to resort to two careers in order to pay for his lifestyle. Sadly, those careers – Gothic novelist and Christian preacher – proved profoundly incompatible.

'A dignitary of the Church had called on him in York Street to offer him preferment,' recalled one contemporary. 'He was kept waiting some time, until Maturin entered, dressed in a fantastic dressing gown, reciting passages from his play, his hair stuck over with pens. His guest was so startled that he hastily retired, giving up all idea of promoting a crazy curate.' It is unsurprising that the anti-clerical sentiments expressed by his characters were often believed to be shared by the author.

These sentiments found their greatest expression in his masterpiece. Melmoth is a memorable creation, an amalgamation of Faust and the Wandering Jew who has sold his soul to Satan in return for extended life and supernatural powers. But, on finding himself an outcast, Melmoth searches for someone willing to exchange their place for his. He finds numerous tortured souls, each experiencing a terrible fate, but none of them is willing to trade places with the damned anti-hero. In the course of the baroque narrative, Melmoth becomes acquainted with the central concerns of the Gothic novel, 'accustomed to look on and converse with all things revolting to nature and to man – forever exploring the madhouse, the jail or the Inquisition, the den of famine, the dungeon of crime, or the death-bed of despair.'

Maturin went to his own death-bed in 1824. It is both a tribute to his subversive nature, and a tragedy for fans of Gothic excess, that his son felt it necessary to burn all of his father's papers to protect the family name. He had many admirers, including Lord Byron (who helped finance his extravagant lifestyle), the celebrated French novelist Victor Hugo (author of *The Hunchback of Notre Dame*), and the Parisian Decadent poet Charles Baudelaire (who dubbed *Melmoth* 'that great satanic creation'). Some modern critics cite *Melmoth the Wanderer* as the first true horror novel, relegating *The Monk* to a mere rehearsal for Maturin's masterpiece.

Remembering Maturin, his editor, Alaric Watts, called him 'the most impulsive and eccentric of Irishmen – and that is saying a great deal.' Indeed, nineteenth-century Gothic literature was dominated by Irish authors. Why this was so is difficult to say – perhaps political turmoil (or, as Sade put it, 'revolutionary shocks') inspired writers to morbid and excessive themes (Maturin witnessed the first violent outbreaks of nationalism in his native Dublin, which some believe contributed to his dark moods). Maybe the other disasters that befell Ireland had a dark effect on sensitive souls residing there (Bram Stoker used graphic accounts of an 1832 cholera epidemic in Sligo, heard at his mother's knee, as inspiration for some of his earliest Gothic tales). Perhaps the Irish are, as the stereotype has it, a lyrical people prone to fits of enthusiasm followed by maudlin moods.

Whatever the case, fellow Irishman J. Sheridan Le Fanu certainly matched Maturin for eccentricity – though Le Fanu was as much a recluse as the 'crazy curate' was an exhibitionist. Indeed, such was his self-imposed seclusion from Dublin society that he earned the nickname of 'the Invisible Prince'. Le Fanu's retreat into seclusion was prompted by the death of his wife Susanna in 1858, a tragedy from which he never truly recovered. Her brother-in-law attributed Susanna's demise to an 'hysterical attack' which, it was implied, was the result of religious fanaticism (another strong potential reason for Ireland's Gothic tradition).

Le Fanu's early works were unremarkable historical romances, but, when tragedy made a recluse of him, his tales began reflecting a bleaker world, seen (in the words of his acclaimed 1872 anthology) *In a Glass Darkly*. While comparatively obscure in his day, Le Fanu is now widely recognised as the master of the Victorian ghost story. In some ways it's a perverse accolade, as conventional spectres are largely absent from his work – replaced by supernatural manifestations such as large rats with human faces, crawling hands and an amorphous horror that resembles 'a great mass of corpulence, with a cadaverous and malignant face'.

As a Gothic pioneer, Le Fanu removed his fiction from the traditional exotic locales – ancient castles, haunted crypts, ruined abbeys – into more familiar locations. The unease in his

In Gothic literature, everybody expects the Spanish Inquisition. They became stock villains in classics like Lewis' The Monk, *and* Melmoth the Wanderer *by Charles Maturin (left).*

tales was a product of the contradiction between the familiar and the uncanny, and his rejection of the sprawling style of his predecessors in favour of tighter, more measured prose. As fellow ghost story author E. F. Benson remarked, although Le Fanu's tales would 'begin quietly enough, the tentacles of terror are applied so softly that the reader hardly notices them till they are sucking the courage from his blood.' The other classic element of Le Fanu's style is the ambivalence of the eerie manifestations, which appear to be supernatural, but could be tricks of the mind, making his works the progenitor of modern psychological horror.

Le Fanu is best remembered for 'Carmilla', a novella also featured in *In a Glass Darkly*. The narrator, a young girl living in Austria, takes in a mysterious young lady named Mircalla as a house guest. Mircalla is in reality Carmilla Karnstein, a vampire who, in the form of a black cat, drains the blood of her hosts. 'Think me not cruel,' she tells her victim, 'because I obey the irresistible law of my strength and weakness . . . In the rapture of my enormous humiliation, I live in your warm life, and you shall die – die, sweetly die – into mine. I cannot help it . . .' The story positively shivers with undertones of lesbian passion – published at a time when Queen Victoria (who embodied the repressive *zeitgeist* of her age) reputedly refused to impose the same punitive legislation against lesbians that applied to male homosexuals, because she couldn't believe the fairer sex would engage in anything so unspeakable.

Le Fanu's later fictions work to a nightmarish logic – a dark, dreamlike quality that is unsurprising considering the circumstances under which they were written. According to Le Fanu's son, Brinsley (one of the few people privileged to see the Invisible Prince at work in his latter years), his father would begin a tale by candlelight in bed until he fell asleep. He would then awaken in the middle of the night, by which point the plot and his dreams had become hopelessly entangled, and continue writing. The story was finally finished the following morning, the last seams between fiction and nightmare sewn shut. Le Fanu, who was plagued by a vivid recurrent nightmare, wherein the walls of his house collapsed upon him in his bed, died a year after the publication of *In a Glass Darkly*. The doctor called to pronounce him dead observed wryly, 'I feared this; that house fell at last.'

Dreams play a prominent role in the Gothic world. Indeed, it's difficult to find one significant Gothic artist who has not made delved into the realm of nightmare for inspiration – from Gothic author Horace Walpole to postmodern graphic novelist Neil Gaiman. As a modern psychiatric study postulated, 'nightmares are linked to creativity . . . nightmares mean a person is unable to put his ghosts to rest.' (Some have more trouble waking them – one of the few details known about Anne Radcliffe is her habit of deliberately eating indigestible snacks before bed, in the hope of inspiring nightmares.)

One such inspirational nightmare was experienced on the night of 8 March 1890 after a dinner of dressed crab. It so affected the man who experienced it that he scribbled down the salient details the following morning: 'young man goes out – sees girls one tries – to kiss him not on the lips but throat. Old Count interferes – rage and fury diabolical. [Count says to girls] This man belongs to me I want him.' The dreamer was Bram Stoker, and the nightmare inspired his novel, *Dracula*.

Since its appearance in 1897, the popularity of *Dracula* has elevated its title character to the status of a modern myth of almost unparalleled power. It has also attracted its share of analysis by literary academics, many of whom focus on it as a symptom of its age – emerging as it did at the height of the deeply repressive Victorian era. Its true sexual subtext may have been rather different. Stoker (who, in true Victorian style, had described sex as 'a problem' in an 1890 article) was a married man with one child, though the cliché 'happily married' may be an exaggeration. For, after giving birth in their first year of matrimony, Florence Stoker was reputed to dislike sex intensely.

LeFanu's novella 'Carmilla' has been filmed several times. The Vampire Lovers (1970) was surprisingly faithful, though the lesbian eroticism became more explicit.

Dracula actually gains some of its power from being a resolutely *anti-sex* book. But by trying to make the implied sex horrible, whether the young English lawyer's temptation by Dracula's brides, or Dracula himself despoiling the flower of English womanhood, Stoker managed to make the horrible sexy. Sex did not come to a halt during Queen Victoria's reign (there were certain decrees even that redoubtable lady dared not issue), but it went underground. And in this Gothic underworld the Victorian libido mutated, turning the things that an English gentleman should shun – being thrashed, perfumed Parisian boudoirs, same-sex love – into the guilty foci of fetishism. To this day, England remains the capital for those who delight in 'the kiss of the cane'.

The character of 'the Old Count' was very probably inspired by Stoker's employer, the actor Sir Henry Irving, a pompous theatrical ham, to whom the Irishman declared himself a 'faithful, loyal and devoted servitor'. Irving, who had a diabolical temper and a dominant personality, was a slave-driver. His employer's demands robbed Stoker of his time, energy, and, in some cases, self-respect.

Stoker originally intended setting his vampire novel in Styria, the Austrian region Le Fanu used as the setting for 'Carmilla'. Then, during his extensive research, Stoker came across a reference to a notoriously cruel Eastern European warlord called Prince Vlad V – nicknamed Tepes ('the Impaler'), or Dracula ('Son of the Devil'). He borrowed the tyrant's name for his charismatic villain, and his birthplace of Transylvania (which translates as 'the land beyond the forests') as the main setting for his book.

The story of *Dracula* has been retold so many times, in so many variations (from the blaxploitation Dracula, *Blacula*, to the porn version, *Dracula Sucks*) that most of us are familiar with every aspect of the plot. But Dracula himself has transformed over the years into a satanic smoothie, a parasitic playboy in an opera cape. (There are a couple of exceptions – most notably, oddball cult director Jess Franco's 1970 Spanish production, *El Conde Dracula*, starring Christopher Lee, and Francis Ford Coppola's 1992 adaptation.)

Stoker's Dracula is a mannered, moustachioed warlord, prone to fits of fury – a powerful, but ageing eastern European aristocrat, who grows younger upon the blood of his victims. It is an image that owes something to both the overacted tragic Shakespearean heroes of Henry Irving, and to the few surviving portraits of Vlad Tepes – relaxing among forests of impaled bodies. Stoker portrayed his Prince of Darkness as akin to a military commander, whose tactics were those of contagion and who fought to conquer reservoirs of fresh blood. As opposed to the debonair seducer we are familiar with today, Stoker's original character was closer to a supernatural rapist.

Although Bram Stoker's death certificate (he died in 1912) describes the cause as 'exhaustion', it may also suggest a curious epigram to his story. For 'exhaustion' was reputedly a euphemistic reference to syphilis, used by doctors when they wished to spare grieving relatives the stigma of this debilitating venereal disease. Had Bram caught syphilis (most probably from a whore) in his younger years? It would explain why he regarded sex as 'a problem'. It could also explain Florence's absence of enthusiasm in the *boudoir*. But such thoughts can never be more than speculation, and in the end, by indulging in amateur psychoanalysis we are in danger of draining *Dracula* of its lifeblood. We must make amends by giving the final word to Bram's mother, Charlotte.

Bram Stoker's Dracula *(1992) was the first major film to explicitly draw the connection with medieval tyrant Vlad the Impaler (right, and above played by Gary Oldman).*

Mrs Stoker wrote to her son to congratulate him on the publication of *Dracula* in 1897, claiming the novel 'will place you very high in the writers of the day . . . No book since Mrs Shelley's *Frankenstein* or indeed any other at all come near yours in originality or terror – Poe is nowhere . . . In its terrible excitement it should make a widespread reputation and much money for you.' Allowing for understandable maternal pride, Charlotte Stoker is right in all but two regards: First, sad to say, *Dracula* did not make

Bram the fortune his mother had hoped for him, and second, her dismissal of Poe as 'nowhere' has not been borne out by history.

It's characteristic of the maelstrom of confusion surrounding Edgar Allan Poe that there are 22 different theories surrounding his 1849 death. Most agree, however, with the orthodox version, that it was one of his notorious drinking binges that finally loosened Poe's tenuous hold on life. Details of the maudlin American poet's origins are less ambiguous. He was born in Boston in 1809, the son of two itinerant actors. His father, David Poe, abandoned him, and his mother, Elizabeth, died in young Edgar's presence before he was three years old.

The windswept abbey overlooking the Yorkshire port of Whitby, where Count Dracula disembarks in Bram Stoker's novel. Whitby now hosts the best established British Goth festival.

These traumatic origins prefigure the two major themes of Poe's life: his unhealthy romanticisation of women who were wasting away, and his tendency to theatricality. He lived his life as a performance, unable to resist the temptation to turn any minor crisis into a melodrama. In classic Gothic style, he treated life as a series of roles and masques. The first was chosen for him when he was adopted by a wealthy Virginian merchant, named John Allan, and Edgar began to style himself as the stereotypical Southern gentleman – an impeccably mannered, reactionary *bon viveur*. It was a role he could not sustain, when Allan refused to clear his university gambling debts in 1826. The adoption, never official, was dissolved and, in a familiar Gothic pattern, Poe abandoned orthodox education.

Forced to support himself, Poe adopted a new mask – that of the Romantic poet, observing in a letter to a friend, 'Literature is the most noble of professions.' He even went as far as to imitate the feat of his idol, Lord Byron, who swam across the legendary Hellespont in Greece (though Edgar, not being a European aristocrat, had to make do with the James River in Virginia).

Poe regarded his verse as the most significant aspect of his literary output. Indeed, it was 'The Raven', a sonorous epic of foreboding and loss, that finally made his reputation just four years prior to his death. But his most Gothic works are his short stories (first collected as *Tales of the Grotesque and Arabesque* in 1840), which, alongside his journalistic work, helped maintain the pale American's fragile existence. Poe's first professional sale was 'Metzengerstein' in 1832, a Gothic tale highly redolent of Horace Walpole's *The Castle of Otranto*, wherein the climactic supernatural manifestation is a giant spectral horse.

Indeed, it's unclear as to whether 'Metzengerstein' was intended as a pastiche, or even as a work of black humour. Poe's short stories are roughly divided between tales of Gothic horror and dark satire, but there is a large overlap of tales that are as grim as they are absurd. If they provoke laughter at all, it is of a decidedly nervous nature. Typical is the 1835 tale, 'Berenice', in which the narrator, in a feverish trance, unearths the corpse of his dead love in order to steal her teeth! (Poe later revealed he wrote the story to win a wager with a friend, who bet him he could never sell a piece with such a bizarre plot.)

If there were an authentic face behind Poe's mask, it was a rictus grin. He stared at a malevolent, irrational universe through sad eyes, and decided it was best to take it all as a cruel joke. As Walpole once observed, 'This world is a comedy to those who think, a tragedy to those who feel.' Many of Poe's stories walk this tightrope between comedy and despair, with death (or, indeed, the absence of death, as in the 1844 tale 'The Premature Burial') as the ultimate punchline. As his poem of 1842 observes of existence, 'the play is the tragedy, "Man" / And its hero the Conqueror Worm.'

Poe's literary jokes are seldom funny, and almost by definition sick. They work best as they were originally intended – each short, sharp shock read individually, an excess of Poe almost invariably making his style read as purple parody. He wrote only one novel, *The Narrative of Arthur Gordon Pym of Nantucket* (1838), which reinforces this argument. A deranged adventure story in the Jules Verne mode, it is best read (if at all) as an oddball satire, or for firm evidence that Edgar was drinking far too much even then.

If Poe had a main theme, alongside death, then it was perversity. Not necessarily sexual perversity – though his passion for dead or dying damsels leaves him open to accusations of necrophilia – but 'the primitive impulse of the human heart' to transgress, not just against others but also oneself. A close relative of madness, Poe described it as an 'unfathomable longing of the soul to *vex itself* – to offer violence to its own nature – to do wrong for wrong's sake only.' The exploration of this masochistic urge, that 'Imp of the Perverse', preoccupied Poe and has been a prominent theme in Gothic art ever since.

A contemporary of J. Sheridan Le Fanu, Poe took Gothic literature into even more firmly psychological territory, where almost every eerie manifestation is evidence of mental imbalance rather than an indication of supernatural forces. Poe forces us into the minds of the disturbed and deranged, obliges us to share their vicious circle of flawed logic, until we recoil from a kind of nausea of the soul. By which time it is too late – the kittens are dead, the rival

Closed on Account of Rabies: *an album of Poe's words performed by such luminaries as Gothic diva Diamanda Galas and proto-punk Iggy Pop. The title refers to a theory about Poe's death.*

walled up in the cellar, the sister interred alive – and we are left wondering whether to laugh or cry.

This same Imp of the Perverse haunted Poe's character – and indeed, his characters – which he described as 'constitutionally sensitive – nervous in a very unusual degree. I became insane, with long periods of horrible sanity.'

Charles Baudelaire, the Parisian Decadent poet who did much to establish Poe's reputation in Europe, identified Poe's death by drink as 'almost a suicide – a suicide prepared from an early period. He drank not as a gourmand, but as a savage, with that time-economy altogether American, as if accomplishing a homicidal function.' Whether we accept the orthodox theory that Poe died from alcoholic over-indulgence, or favour one of the more exotic proposals (such as death from hydrophobia), the recorded cause seems appropriate for a man tormented by a fevered imagination: 'congestion of the brain'.

If Baudelaire was ambivalent about Poe's means of dying, he was outraged by the author's post-mortem fate. The administration of Poe's literary estate fell to one Rufus W. Griswold, a literary rival and failed preacher, who some believe to have been mentally ill. This choice of executor was a classic example of Poe's perversity, as Griswold had fallen victim to the acidic pen of 'the Tomahawk Man' (a name given Poe in reference to his frequent written and spoken attacks on rivals). Predictably, he set about destroying Poe's posthumous reputation, depicting him as an 'erratic, cynical and unprincipled' alcoholic degenerate. While an indifferent poet at best, Griswold proved to be a character assassin of great skill – although, ironically, he only served to increase the mystique of his victim.

Baudelaire made arch reference to Griswold's posthumous libels by wondering if American law permitted dogs into graveyards – the executor metaphorically defiling the author's grave. But cats can also reside in churchyards – admirers report that a black feline has taken residence in a tomb adjoining Poe's, 'who seems to stand guard over his grave' – a fitting sentinel for the author of 'The Black Cat', whose eponymous creature is a figure of retribution. Similarly, every year since the 1949 centenary of Poe's death, a mysterious visitor has marked his birthday (19 January) with a midnight tribute, depositing three red roses and a half-empty bottle of cognac on the writer's grave, before disappearing into the night. Poe himself couldn't have written a better ending.

(Poe's disciple, Charles Baudelaire, cultivated his own bad reputation, turning infamy into an artistic statement. 'I let it be known that I had killed my father and eaten him,' he wrote in a letter to a friend, 'and also that I had been allowed to escape from France because of the services I was rendering the French police, AND THEY BELIEVED ME!' While extensive French translations of Poe helped establish his reputation, Baudelaire's masterpiece was his 1857 poetry collection *Les fleurs du mal [The Flowers of Evil]*. In its fevered verse, voluptuous vampires, holy whores and languid lesbians writhe for attention beneath the approving gaze of 'Satan Trismegistus' ['thrice majestic'], as beauty and corruption become inextricably linked. Recognised as a work of genius today, at the time official sanction condemned sections of *Les fleurs du mal* as obscene and blasphemous.)

Poe's posthumous influence continues to grow. In the musical arena, the eerie power of his writings continues to inspire numerous compositions. Modern composer Phillip Glass, progressive rock producer Alan Parsons, and songwriter/experimental musician Peter Hammill have all created major pieces inspired by 'The Fall of the House of Usher' – the classic Poe tale of incest, degeneration and mental collapse mirrored by a disintegrating mansion. It has even lent its title to the Goth band House of Usher – one of a number of manifestations in the modern subculture, including Poe as the unlikely hero of an eponymously titled comic book, written by Jason Asala, wherein he confronts a multitude of demons inspired by an angel who promises to reunite him with his dead wife, Lenore, named after 'the lost Lenore' in 'The Raven'.

During the writing of this book, Tony Lestat, founder member of Goth-punk band Wreckage, was putting together a CD featuring music by Goth and death rock bands on a Poe-based theme. 'Poe for me is a great part of what the "Goth" scene is all about,' Lestat told me. 'Everyone has a different idea of what "Gothic" means, but I relate the most pure aspects of it to the scene that I enjoy . . . For me it's Edgar Allan Poe, Anne Rice [as his appropriated surname suggests], classic movie monsters, dark music, horror movie TV hosts, *Famous Monsters* magazine and living Hallowe'en all year round. That's what death rock is all about (and has been for the last twenty years) and Gothic is simply a more sedate version of that. Death only enters into it as the melancholy from a poetic aspect – which is where Poe comes in . . . He was, I believe, in literary terms, the first true Goth. For those on the Gothic scene who understand all this, the CD is a natural tribute, because Poe's dark world is timeless.'

Poe's greatest influence, however, is on the written word, and few modern macabre writers can pass his shrine without a tip of the hat. Perhaps John M. Ford put it best in his essay for the 1988 anthology, *Horror: 100 Best Books*: 'There isn't anywhere you can go in this overcast, weedgrown, blood-fertilised field of ours that he hasn't been first: the chilly blue-lit corners, the arena of on-stage violence, Poet's Corner, the comedy side-show, the Vale of Things Man Was Not Meant to Know. In the perfumed, moldy halls of horror, he is the doorkeeper, the cartographer, and the resident ghost. (Edgar, now be still: we swiped not from Walpole or Stoker with half so good a will.)'

Chapter II

A Symphony of Shadows: the Golden Age of gothic Cinema

The first tentative steps towards Gothic cinema began in the early twentieth century. In the USA, Gothic literature was occasionally plundered for simple narrative ideas. The first such film worthy of note was *The Avenging Conscience* (1914), directed by the controversial D. W. Griffith, father of the film epic. It uses the storyline of 'The Tell-Tale Heart', Poe's classic short tale of murder and guilt – embellished by scenes from other *Tales of the Grotesque and Arabesque* – to illustrate the anti-hero's belief that existence is 'a long system of murder'. But Gothic cinema's true origins lie in Germany, which became renowned for the production of *schauerfilme* ('shudder films') between her humiliation in World War I and the rise to power of the Nazis in the 1930s.

For the same sense of despair that inspired wild decadence among the elite in Berlin also created an appetite for screen nightmares among the less privileged. Appropriately, the distinctive approach borrowed from the fine arts, theatre and literature by *schauerfilme* was that of expressionism – in which atmosphere, mood and psychology were more important than realism. Of particular significance in the history of Gothic cinema was *The Golem* (1914), based on an old Hebrew legend, whereby a clay man was animated by ancient cabalistic rites to defend the Jewish community. Remade in the 1920s, it was one of the first films seen by an infant Vincent Price, and caused the horror icon to wet his pants with fear, a perfect initiation into the world which he would make his own.

But the 1919 film, *The Cabinet of Dr Caligari*, is the definitive expressionist picture, described by one critic as a 'madman's vision of the world'. Its surreal plot concerns a sinister

Lon Chaney as Hollywood's first vampire in London After Midnight *(1927). As a grotesque hoax, his character was less influential than later, more seductive bloodsuckers.*

hypnotist, named Caligari, who exhibits the sleepwalker Cesare at a town fair, claiming that his quasi-comatose charge can predict the future. Cesare predicts death for a customer, then Caligari fulfils such prophecies by sending the somnambulist out after dark to murder those he has warned.

With its themes of madness and brainwashing, *The Cabinet of Dr Caligari* was inspired in part by the experiences of its co-writer, the Austrian poet Carl Mayer, who had been wounded serving in World War I and sent for psychiatric assessment after challenging his

Expressionistic German classic The Cabinet of Dr Caligari *(1919). Its sets and make-up suggest an internal world where madness reigns.*

superiors. For Mayer, Caligari represented the mad leaders who sent the compliant masses – represented by the sleepwalking Cesare – out to kill and be killed in the Great War. The British distributors issued a statement about 'the strangest motion picture ever made' that could be read as a manifesto for expressionist cinema: 'It may add to your appreciation to know something of the aims of the producers. They believed that the screen could be made something more than a mere medium for the exact photographic reproduction of conventional stories . . . In every scene there is a special setting made and painted by hand, which fits the mood of the action that is taking place. You will see Cesare, the sleep-walker, floating down the street that seems to have been ripped from some nightmare – a street of misshapen houses with brooding windows, streaked by dagger strokes of light and darkened by blots of shadow . . .'

Nosferatu (an archaic central European word for vampire), released in 1922, was the first major vampire film. Horror author Ramsey Campbell also identifies it as the first film made with the sole intention of frightening the viewer. A number of texts mistranslate its subtitle as 'A Symphony of Shadows' – ironically, a far better description of the movie than the accurate translation, 'A Symphony of Shudders'. Graf Orlock, the title monster, is a bald, rat-like vampire, who leaves the plague as his calling card – in many ways closer to the original, repulsive vampire of folklore than the seductive, post-*Dracula* bloodsuckers of pop culture.

Max Schreck as the undead Graf Orlock in Nosferatu *(1922) – a Gothic 'Symphony of Shadows'.*

The title role was taken by an actor calling himself Max Schreck (Klaus Kinski reprised the role in Werner Herzog's heavily atmospheric, if ponderous, 1979 remake), to whom an air of mystery still clings. Indeed, Schreck was a stage name, being German for 'dread' or 'fear'.

The inevitable axis between the Gothic *schauerfilme* and the emergent Third Reich was made flesh in the curious form of adventurer and best-selling author Hanns Heinz Ewers. Ewers specialised in Gothic tales thick with sadism, cynicism and exotic degeneracy. His most successful, *Alraune* (1911), was a scandalous but popular novel, in which a vampiric super-bitch is bred by mating the worst whore in Berlin with Germany's vilest sex criminal, his seed obtained from a corpse after the 'father' had been executed. It was filmed several times (in 1918, 1928, 1930 and 1952), while Ewers wrote a number of scripts for *schauerfilme* such as the 1913 reworking of the Faustian 'pact with the devil' myth, *The Student of Prague*.

Ewers was also politically active, an early member of the Nazi Party and acquaintance of

Adolf Hitler. He shared the Nazi fascination with blood – though to them it was a symbol of racial purity, while Ewers fixated on the erotic overtones of drinking it in novels like the 1922 *Vampire*. More damaging for Ewers, however, was his conviction, expressed in *Vampire*, that Jews could be good Germans, better even than Aryans. This was too much for the Nazi State, and in the 1930s his books were condemned and banned as 'decadent'. Their author was declared an 'unperson' and died in 1943.

Even before the outbreak of World War II, expressionist film-making had gone into sharp decline. Many of Germany's most talented *schauerfilme* makers, such as *Nosferatu* director F. W. Murnau, crossed the Atlantic to the US, where American audiences valued realism over atmosphere. Unsurprisingly, many emigrants were Jewish, and the movie-industry community of Hollywood was founded primarily by Jewish expatriates pursuing the American dream.

Watching *schauerfilme* today, for all their dreamily atmospheric qualities, they fail to engage – let alone frighten – in the way they were originally intended to. Technical tricks, such as speeding up footage of the vampire Orlock, look more comical than disturbing. While still viewed as a milestone by film students, *The Cabinet of Dr Caligari* never had the explosive impact on world cinema that enthusiasts had predicted in the early 1920s – though shadowy *schauerfilmen* were still to guide the future of Gothic screen horror.

Expressionist *schauerfilme* live on today outside the world of cinema, in the Goth subculture. Because they have no soundtracks, they've proven popular as projected backdrops at Goth clubs and gigs (including performances by Goth author Caitlin Kiernan's former band, Death's Little Sister). In 1996, English Goth electronic duo In The Nursery released an album of music to accompany *The Cabinet of Dr Caligari*. (The same film inspired the visual imagery of Bauhaus, who many regard as the first Goth rock band.) The title *Nosferatu* was also adopted as a band name by one of the most successful British Goth bands, who make heavy use of horror-movie melodramatics and sound samples (though obviously not from the silent *schauerfilme*).

In the silent age of Hollywood, there was little to rival the darkness of the *schauerfilme*. One notable exception came in the form of Hollywood's first real sex goddess, Theda Bara. Her adopted name was an anagram of 'Arab death', and suggests the exotic menace that was the sultry actress's trademark. She helped popularise the term 'vamp' to describe a fatally-seductive woman – death and sex combined in one irresistible package. Bara specialised in playing 'La Belle Dame Sans Merci' – such as *Salome* (1917) and *Cleopatra* (1918) – embodied by Keats in his famous poem of that name. In her 1914 starring debut, *A Fool There Was*, based on the poem 'The Vampire' by Rudyard Kipling, she memorably cast rose petals over the drained body of a dead lover, laughing 'Kiss me, my fool!' A true Goth babe, she wore purple make-up to emphasise her pallor, was rumoured to have occult powers, and received guests while stroking a snake in a chamber thick with incense smoke.

But things were not all that they seemed. As Kenneth Anger later wrote in his book *Hollywood Babylon*, which celebrated the depravity beneath the movie industry's wholesome image, 'Theda Bara was always good for a laugh. The colony [Hollywood] knew that the fatal vamp, being sold to the rubes as a French-Arab demon of depravity born beneath the Sphinx, was in truth Theodosia Goodman, a Jewish tailor's daughter from Chillicothe, Ohio, a meek goody-two-shoes.'

The term 'horror' had yet to be coined to define a genre, and silent Hollywood only had one male star who successfully explored Gothic themes. Lon Chaney had a perverse head-start in his profession in the form of two deaf-mute parents, requiring him to express himself in mime from an early age. He became particularly popular with directors, because his acting skills and talent with make-up allowed him to assume more than one role in a film (even murdering himself in one production), earning Chaney the epithet 'the Man of a Thousand Faces'.

His breakthrough movie was the lavish 1923 screen adaptation of Victor Hugo's *The Hunchback of Notre Dame*. Chaney powerfully conveyed the pathos of the deformed hero from beneath a punishingly heavy, self-applied costume, which included a straitjacket. The promotional catch-phrase 'Don't step on it – it might be Lon Chaney' soon entered popular usage, a smart-ass tribute to the actor's ability to change not just his face but his whole form.

His most celebrated performance was the title role in *The Phantom of the Opera* (1925), for which Chaney conceived an even more agonising make-up. Wires made his eyes bulge and nostrils flare in a skeletal grimace, as Erik, the deformed composer who broods vengefully in the catacombs beneath the Paris Opera House. 'He suffered you know,' the film's cinematographer later recalled, adding that the wires made Chaney 'bleed like hell.' The director, Rupert Julian, understood the importance of the dramatic build-up, leaving Chaney masked for most of the movie and only revealing his 'accursed ugliness' in a climactic unmasking scene near the end.

Theda Bara as the original Gothic femme fatale in Cleopatra *(1917). Egyptian exoticism has influenced Goth style, in the wearing of heavy kohl eye make- up and the use of the mystical ankh symbol.*

This shock remains one of the classic moments in cinematic history, and caused an impressionable young Robert Bloch – who later became one of America's premier horror novelists – to piss his pants. (With Bloch at *The Phantom* and Price at *The Golem*, there was scarcely a dry seat in the house in American movie theatres during the 1920s.)

Chaney's dedication to his art was frighteningly perverse. The term 'masochistic' crops up again and again in descriptions of the tortuous costumes and make-ups he adopted – often against medical advice – to achieve the disfigurements and malformations required for his specialist roles. Indeed his apparent delight in agonising ordeals is suggestive of the performance artists who inflict pain on themselves, with whips, needles or branding irons, at today's clubs like London's Torture Garden. Chaney never played supernatural roles – his characters may have been monstrously deformed or disfigured, but they were essentially human, and the films that made him famous were melodramas with Gothic overtones. In 1927, however, Chaney's most frequent collaborator, Tod Browning, took the first tentative step in the direction of pure Gothic horror with *London After Midnight*. Chaney starred as a vampire (its title changed, bizarrely, at the insistence of British censors to *The Hypnotist*, the original title since adopted as the name of one of America's most popular Goth bands). It featured Chaney in typically extreme make-up: shark-like rows of teeth and bulging eyes, which made it difficult to speak or see, an incongruous fright wig and beaver-skin top hat, altogether a more deliriously-ghoulish interpretation than subsequent cinematic vampires. But *London After Midnight* lacked the courage of its convictions. In true

The Phantom (Lon Chaney) makes a dramatic entrance to the Paris Opera's costume ball disguised as Edgar Allan Poe's Red Death, in The Phantom of the Opera *(1925).*

Scooby Doo style, in the final reel Chaney's bloodsucker reveals himself as a detective disguised as a vampire in order to frighten some criminals into confessing. Browning implausibly claimed the story's (dubious) 'plausibility increased, rather than lessened, the thrills and chills.'

However, the director had been discussing adapting *Dracula* for the screen with Chaney for some time, and had no intentions of deflating the supernatural classic with any rational explanation. According to *The New York Times*, 'Chaney had a full scenario and a secret make-up worked out even at that early date, but Browning held out for a talkie.' The advent of the 'talkies' in the late 1920s had brought the careers of many stars to an abrupt end, as their voices failed to match their visual charisma. Lon Chaney suffered no such problems. In 1930 he remade one of his earlier silents, *The Unholy Three*, showing the same vocal versatility he had displayed visually, undertaking no less than three 'voice reproductions' – an old woman, a young girl and a parrot. But fate evidently never intended the silent screen's master of the macabre to interpret fiction's greatest Gothic villain. In the summer of 1930, throat cancer silenced Chaney's voice – and then the actor himself.

Universal Pictures had bought the rights to a hit stage production of Bram Stoker's *Dracula* in 1927. In the title role was an Hungarian immigrant, named Bela Lugosi, who played the vampire count with green make-up and an opera cape, resembling, as one unkind critic observed, 'an operatically inclined but cheerless mortician'. Perhaps unsurprisingly, Universal bosses were less than enthusiastic about transferring the Hungarian from stage to screen – not least because Lugosi spoke almost no English, and thus had to learn his part phonetically. This undoubtedly required a great deal of self-discipline, but with that strong will came a large dose of obstinacy which hampered the East European throughout his tragic career.

Fans flocked to see Lugosi's spine-tingling performance. 'It was the embrace of Death their subconscious was yearning for,' the actor later explained. He had been chosen for the role because the play's producers believed his swarthy foreign appearance and thick accent would add to the sinister repellence of his character. In reality, he had the opposite effect on sections of the audience, particularly women. 'Death,' Lugosi explained, was 'the final triumphant lover.'

Even more explicitly, in an interview entitled 'The Feminine Love of Horror' for a US movie magazine, the actor mused on his character's sexual allure. America's women were, he said, 'unsatisfied, famished, craving sensation, even though it be the sensation of death.' It would be easy to dismiss such amateur psychiatry as vainglorious hype (and suspiciously articulate hype, coming from a man who spoke little English), were there not ample evidence of Lugosi's magnetic power over women. He married five times, though each tryst ended in disaster often because of another woman. During the theatrical run of *Dracula*, the 'other woman' was none other than Clara Bow. Now largely forgotten, during the late 1920s Bow had been one of Hollywood's hottest sex symbols, known as the 'It Girl'. Clara went beyond her screen persona as a thoroughly modern, jazz-loving good-time girl, and became known for an even more insatiable off-screen appetite for men, booze and parties. In *Hollywood Babylon*, Kenneth Anger salaciously reports how Ms Bow liked to service an entire American football team during her drug-fuelled weekend gang-bangs.

This frantic self-indulgence concealed a tragic past which biographer David Stenn described as 'Brooklyn Gothic'. As a child she had been mercilessly abused by her alcoholic mother, eventually using her vivacity and beauty to escape the ghetto via the magic of the movies. By the time she met Lugosi in 1927, while her star was reaching its zenith in the Hollywood constellation, she still carried a little of that darkness within her. One lover recalled how, instead of merely kissing, she would bite his lips until they bled. When she spurned him, the lovestruck sap tried to cut his wrist so the blood dripped over a photo of his lost belle. In response, she called a press conference to mock his botched attempt, observing that he should have used a gun.

Bela Lugosi was only one of a string of lovers taken by Clara, but the contrast between these icons of sex and death is striking – and must have caught the attention of Universal, who finally agreed to let Lugosi take the title role in their big-screen *Dracula*. By the time it went into production, Clara Bow's star had begun falling earthward. In 1930 her private secretary sold the story of Clara's sex-and-drugs lifestyle to a tabloid paper, horrifying the public. The advent of sound did Ms Bow no favours either, her harsh Brooklyn accent clashing horribly with her enchanting looks, and audiences abandoned their erstwhile idol in droves. In 1931 she was confined to a lunatic asylum after a breakdown, the first of numerous such interludes, which signalled a tragically Gothic end to her meteoric career. That same year *Dracula* was released and made its title character – and the man who portrayed him – into a household name. Though criticised today as ponderous and anaemic (it contains only one trickle of blood – from a cut finger), the film shocked many.

For modern film historians it's surprising that *Dracula* ever got made at all. From the start of production it was in trouble. Studio heads, suspicious of such an unusual project, did not lavish funds on the film and corners were cut. Browning, without Chaney in the lead, evidently lost interest early on. His trademark cobwebs are much in evidence in Castle Dracula where, in an effective moment, the Count appears to walk through a web without disturbing it, and the crypt-like hall was also infested with rats, bats and, bizarrely, armadillos. But after the atmospheric opening scenes, the film becomes increasingly pedestrian, and some suggest Browning spent more time drinking than directing.

Directorial duties increasingly fell to Karl Freund, a German cinematographer who had worked on the very first (unofficial) Dracula movie, Murnau's *Nosferatu*. Disappointingly, Freund shot the largely-unaltered stage play with a static camera, with many vital scenes verbally described by a cast with a tendency to over-act wildly, which, while appropriate to the stage, comes over as inappropriately camp on the big screen. To add to the confusion, Freund spoke little English, and Lugosi delivered his phonetically-memorised lines in an unearthly fashion that has, nevertheless, proved very influential. Hungarian has become the clichéd sound of the vampire ever since – even though Transylvania is actually in Romania, a region with a very different accent. Even Lugosi's look – slicked-back black hair and an opera cape – became the public image of Dracula, despite its difference from his appearance in the original novel. Perhaps it was Lugosi's intense identification with the role, which verged upon possession, that gave such power to his interpretation – witnesses recall him stalking the set, pulling poses in mirrors and announcing, 'I *am* Dracula.' Today, it might be regarded as method acting. Back then, people wondered whether he was mad.

Bela Lugosi with Carroll Borland in Mark of the Vampire *(1935). Borland's image provided an early prototype for the classic Goth chick look.*

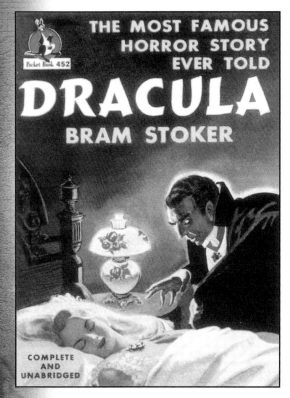

THE MOST FAMOUS
HORROR STORY
EVER TOLD

Pocket Book 452

DRACULA

BRAM STOKER

COMPLETE
AND
UNABRIDGED

Even when Bela Lugosi's career went into freefall, his portrayal of Dracula remained definitive – as suggested by this 1947 paperback cover for Stoker's novel.

But whether *Dracula's* appeal lay in some perverse psychological death-wish among Lugosi's female fans, the unambiguous chills of watching a supernatural demon on-screen, or the novelty of a Hollywood picture using expressionist techniques, Universal knew they had a fresh phenomenon on their hands. Gothic cinema had arrived in America, and a new term was coined for the films that followed in *Dracula's* wake. In 1931, the 'horror movie' was born.

Hollywood had a profitable new genre to exploit, and Universal quickly went into production on an adaptation of Mary Shelley's *Frankenstein*. But did the studio have a new Lon Chaney to front the project? They soon had cause to doubt Bela Lugosi's suitability, when the actor began displaying signs of *prima donna* contrariness. He didn't like the part of the Monster because it had no lines – perverse for an actor to whom language presented a major problem – and insisted he should devise his own make-up if he were to undertake the role. Edward Van Sloan, who had played the vampire hunter, Van Helsing, in *Dracula*, memorably mocked Lugosi's concept as looking 'like something from *Babes in Toyland*'. Studio bosses evidently agreed, and abandoned the idea of casting Lugosi – though Van Sloan's talents were called on again.

Elsewhere, it was all change. The director was an up-and-coming English ex-pat, named James Whale, who learned his craft staging plays while a PoW in World War I. He employed his friend Colin Clive, a twitchy Englishman, to play the driven Frankenstein. Whale found his Monster in the Universal canteen, in the form of yet another ex-pat – a bit-part actor named Boris Karloff, who specialised in playing thugs and heavies. Karloff (whose real name was William Henry Pratt) had a grim tombstone of a face and a gently ominous, lisping voice to match. But, as the Monster was a non-speaking part, it was his appearance that interested Whale.

The job of making Mary Shelley's concept flesh fell to Universal's make-up wizard, Jack P. Pierce. Pierce took his work very seriously, complete with a surgeon's smock donned to effect his transformations. 'I did some research in anatomy, surgery, criminology, ancient and modern times, and electrodynamics,' Pierce revealed. 'I discovered there are six ways a surgeon can cut the skull, and I figured Dr Frankenstein, who was not a practising surgeon, would take the easiest. That is, he would cut the top of the skull off, straight across like a pot lid, hinge it, pop the brain in, and clamp it tight. That's the reason I decided to make the Monster's head square and flat like a box, and dig that big scar across his forehead, and have metal clamps hold it together. The two metal studs that stick out the side of his neck are inlets for electricity – plugs.'

The procedure was arduous – taking three-and-a-half hours to apply every morning and an hour-and-a-half to remove, echoing, if not equalling, the ordeals Lon Chaney had subjected himself to. Significantly, however, Karloff still had the freedom of facial and bodily expression to communicate real pathos, making the Monster more than a mere walking corpse or murderous robot. Even though Karloff would always credit Pierce with the success of the creation, it was his expressionistic performance that made the Monster so memorable. Indeed, the first sight of the Monster, as he walks backwards through a dungeon doorway, then slowly turns around, grimacing, one eye rolling back in his socket, rivals Chaney's unmasking scene in *The Phantom of the Opera* as one of early Gothic cinema's most powerful shocks.

Time and familiarity have substantially diluted this effect, but there were reports of screaming and fainting at a 1931 test screening. Worried that their new shocker might be a little too effective, Universal made a few last-minute cuts to soften the impact: in particular, a scene where the Monster is playing with a little girl who throws flowers into a stream, before, with clumsy over-enthusiasm, he throws in the girl herself. This troubling scene was cut so that the little girl was last seen floating flowers with the Monster – before appearing later in the arms of her father, bedraggled and dead. Ironically, this suggested the Monster may have done something even worse to his playmate, giving the 'deflowering' motif very sinister connotations. But despite this, the offending scene was not restored to completeness and coherence until the 1980s.

Universal had another hit on their hands and a fitting successor to Chaney in the shape of Boris Karloff – soon dubbed 'Karloff the Uncanny'. For a time Lugosi and Karloff enjoyed equal billing, but Karloff's superior acting skills and easier temperament saw him eclipse his rival, as Lugosi's career began a steady decline. Meanwhile, Whale was prevailed upon to direct a follow-up to his Gothic masterpiece, *The Bride of Frankenstein* (1935). It is a rare example of a sequel surpassing its predecessor, highly regarded by both 'serious' film critics and fans of Gothic cinema.

The story loosely adapts the second part of the original novel, where Frankenstein undertakes a doomed attempt to build a mate for his Monster. The title role of the 'bride' was taken by Elsa Lanchester, yet another English performer, who also played author Mary Shelley for a silly prologue set at the Villa Diodati. The make-up Pierce devised for the female Monster – a surgical gown, bandages and shock of vertical black-and-white hair – may not be as iconic as his design for Karloff, but it still shows up at costume parties and has inspired more than one adventurous Goth chick.

Completing Whale's repertory of ex-pat limeys was Ernest Thesiger, who very nearly steals the show as Dr Septimus Pretorius. Thesiger himself was something of a Gothic grotesque – albeit a charming one, who enjoyed both needlework and the smell of drains. Blue-blooded, brittle, effeminate and cultured, he claimed to possess sorcerous powers and delighted in attending costume balls ostentatiously disguised as the spirit of Death. Thesiger's gin-swigging Pretorius proves himself far madder than Frankenstein, confessing to the doctor's wife, 'Sometimes I wonder if life would not be much more amusing if we were all devils, and no nonsense about angels and being good.' He also kidnaps the new 'bride of Frankenstein' to coerce her reluctant husband into helping him build a mate for the Monster, so he can breed a new race of 'Gods and monsters!' A witty, weird and curiously inhuman scarecrow, Pretorius casually eats his supper from a sarcophagus lid after robbing the grave. ('I rather like this place,' he observes.)

Gothic camp personified, Thesiger's performance is instrumental in propelling the film into the territory between outrageous morbidity and pitch-black comedy. Sadly, the same arch gallows humour that characterised much of director James Whale's best work also marked his death: Whale drowned himself in his swimming pool in 1957, leaving a book on his bedside table entitled *Don't Go Near the Water*.

Meanwhile, back in the 1930s, Universal was joined by a number of other Hollywood studios, all increasingly aware that, while this new horror genre might be distasteful, it was a vital money-spinner as the economic depression threatened to send them out of business. Newspapers joined church groups, women's organisations and sundry other busy-bodies and do-gooders in lamenting the growth of the horror film. But the almighty dollar spoke louder than they did, and audiences continued to pay to escape from the everyday misery of their lives into the world of Hollywood Gothic.

Following his success with *Dracula*, Tod Browning set out to shock America the following year with *Freaks*. He succeeded all too well. The film appalled test audiences and was quickly suppressed by MGM, the studio that produced it. *Freaks* suffered a 30-year ban in Britain, and was championed only by fans of forbidden film, before being belatedly recognised as a masterpiece.

Karl Freund, Browning's cinematographer on *Dracula*, was given his own picture to direct in the bandaged form of *The Mummy* (1932) – employing expressionistic style while Karloff gave a sensitive and understated performance as

Hollywood created the Frankenstein Monster we know and love today – seen here in a poster from Germany, birthplace of the horror film.

the ancient Egyptian brought back from the grave by love, adding another monster to the Universal menagerie. Lugosi hammed it up in *Murders in the Rue Morgue* (1932), the tale of a sadistic scientist that owed more to *The Cabinet of Dr Caligari* than the Poe short story on which nominally it was based. 1934 saw another purported Poe adaptation which bore even less resemblance to its supposed inspiration – nevertheless, *The Black Cat* is a cult classic. It was directed by Edgar G. Ulmer – another German veteran of *schauerfilme* – and inspired in part by the scandalous activities of Aleister Crowley. Ulmer's widow later recalled that her husband 'had a dark side to his character that was unbelievable. It took me years to dig under and find the "why" of it. You couldn't use the word "crazy" in his presence; it would petrify him . . . he always worked in shadows.'

Whatever the 'why' of Ulmer's dark side, he directed Karloff and Lugosi together in their first collaboration – one of the grimmest Gothic pictures of the entire period. Indeed, it's difficult to imagine how anyone could film *The Black Cat* without recourse to the word 'crazy': the devil-worshipping Karloff (as Hjalmar Poelzig – a tribute to the great expressionist architect Hans Poelzig) matches wits with old rival Lugosi (as Vitus Werdegast – which translates as 'life becomes a guest') in a bizarre Bauhaus-style mansion heavy with a miasma of perversion and death. In the bleak finale, driven mad by his thirst for vengeance upon the man who betrayed him and stole his wife (in a necrophiliac flourish, Karloff keeps her dead body in a glass coffin, and, to add a dash of incest, has married her daughter), Lugosi skins Karloff alive.

As the 1930s wore on, Tod Browning sought to make amends for the scandal of *Freaks* by remaking the safe *London After Midnight* as *Mark of the Vampire* (1935), with Lugosi as the fake vampire, while Dracula had a daughter (1936) and Frankenstein had a son (1939). *Dracula's Daughter* is a low-budget affair which has its admirers. But the plot originally mooted sounds far more intriguing than the film that was actually made. 'The use of a female Vampire instead of a male gives us the chance to play up SEX and CRUELTY legitimately,' raved original screenwriter John L. Balderston, who had previously co-written the Broadway adaptations of *Dracula* and *Frankenstein*, and written the screenplay for Universal's *The Mummy*. In particular, he proposed having the title character keep control over her fellow female bloodsuckers, and draw blood from young men, using whips, chains and other sado-masochistic equipment. Instead, Universal made a far less daring picture with the title character as a sad, doomed figure – albeit one with strong lesbian overtones – rather than an undead dominatrix.

In 1941 Universal released *The Wolf Man*, completing their cast of classic monsters, and signalling the end of the Golden Age of Hollywood Gothic. It starred Lon Chaney's son – who reluctantly changed his name from Creighton Chaney to Lon Chaney, Jr. to profit from his father's legend – as Larry Talbot, a hapless American in a hokey Hollywood version of Wales, cursed to become a werewolf. In a telling reflection on his declining career, Bela Lugosi, who originally anticipated the lead, was relegated to a supporting role as a gypsy werewolf. The scenes where Chaney wakes up, unable to remember what bestial atrocities he's committed the night before, play well as a parody of awakening after a heavy night's drinking and wondering if apologies are due for one's behaviour. Indeed, many of Chaney, Jr.'s colleagues remember an actor prone to heavy drinking, giving his performance an extra edge. (When Britain's Hammer studios made their werewolf movie, *The Curse of the Werewolf*, twenty years later, they cast Oliver Reed in the title role, an actor also legendary for his alcoholic binges.)

Pierce's make-up for *The Wolf Man* was not among his best work. Using a selection of materials including yak hair, he created a monster that looked more like a rabid teddy bear than a wolf. Nonetheless, the public accepted it as the 'authentic' appearance of a werewolf, alongside aspects of werewolf lore that had little to do with occult tradition – the werewolf of myth being a human being that transforms into a large wolf, while more authoritative

The appearance of The Bride of Frankenstein *(1935) was based on Ancient Egyptian queen Nefertiti. Her vertiginous hairstyle has sometimes been emulated by punk and Goth girls.*

historical accounts stress that the werewolf never truly changed shape, but was possessed by a bestial spirit. The werewolf of European folklore voluntarily transformed using enchanted pelts or magic potions, but remained vulnerable to normal weapons. Under the new Hollywood rules, werewolves were hairy, fang-faced men who caught the 'disease' from the bite of another werewolf, transformed according to the phases of the moon, and were only vulnerable to silver weapons. It's interesting to note how all this has become ingrained in the popular consciousness (as also happened with the vampire), indicating how films have become the primary source of folklore in the modern age.

The 1940s saw a steady decline in the horror movie, both in terms of quantity and quality. British censors, long disapproving of the genre, used World War II as an excuse to ban them for the duration, on the declared ground that 'the dreadfuls were not good for general film audiences where there was so much wartime horror,' according to industry paper, *Variety*. With a ruthlessness that would impress any vampire, Universal drained the last drops of profit from its horror franchises in increasingly cynical, second-rate outings. Monsters which had made grown men faint a decade before were now familiar enough to appeal to an unsophisticated adolescent audience.

Karloff gave up his role as the Frankenstein Monster, while Chaney, Jr. donned the boots and bolts for 1942's *The Ghost of Frankenstein*. Lugosi, in one of a humiliating number of climbdowns, also adopted the role he so contemptuously rejected a dozen years before for *Frankenstein Meets the Wolfman* (1943) – a cynical 'title fight' picture that smacked of desperation and lacked Gothic atmosphere. More multi-monster pile-ups followed – *House of Frankenstein* (1944), *House of Dracula* (1945) – each more threadbare than the last, as Universal treated both its audience and its roster of monsters with increasing contempt.

While a lean time for Gothic cinema, the 1940s did produce some atmospheric pictures of note – in particular, those produced for RKO studios by Russian-born Val Lewton, who made more of a mark on his movies than the directors he commissioned. Low-key in the extreme – indeed, pretty short on scares – Lewton preferred unease to horror, leaving the audience afraid of shadows or suggestions of the macabre, rather than any concrete manifestation. Among his most successful works were *Cat People* (1942), about a girl who believes she will turn into a big cat if sexually aroused, because of a medieval curse upon her ancestors (remade in 1981 with Natassia Kinski, an antithetical version as explicit as the original was subtle); *I Walked with a Zombie* (1943), which somewhat improbably transplanted Charlotte Brontë's pastiche Gothic romance *Jane Eyre* to a Caribbean plantation, complete with walking dead; and *The Seventh Victim* (1943), which posits a devil-worshipping cult in contemporary Greenwich Village – though they're a pretty innocuous bunch who apply peer pressure to persuade members to commit suicide, rather than conduct gory sacrifices of their own.

The increasing popularity of television in the 1950s had Hollywood running scared. The cinema industry's concerns took on concrete form in the oddball 1953 British satire, *Meet Mr Lucifer* – in which comedian Stanley Holloway, made over to resemble a cut-price Lugosi, reveals that TV is 'an instrument of the Devil' sent 'to make the human race utterly miserable.' One of cinema's more pro-active responses was to employ gimmickry. Universal's *The Creature From the Black Lagoon*, filmed in 3-D in 1954, was a dubious late entry to Universal's monster menagerie. The humanoid 'gill-man' of the title was more a science-fiction creature than a classic Gothic grotesque, reflecting an increasing trend.

Movie monsters in the 1950s were more likely to come from outer space, or to be the product of radioactive mutation, than to hail from the graveyard. This development reflected increasing unease among the American public about the Cold War. Threats to the nation's security no longer came from the Old World of Europe, the classic Gothic setting, but from the Soviet foe in the East – manifested in the form of concerns about losing the space race, and the possibility of nuclear war.

Traditional Gothic was rehashed in 3D in the 1953 *House of Wax*. (Ironically, director André de Toth only had one eye, so he could never experience the 3D effect.) This remake of 1933 chiller *The Mystery of the Wax Museum* concerned the museum's owner, horribly scarred in a fire. Unable to replace his models because of his injuries, he takes to murder to fashion new mannequins. As a modest success, it was most significant in launching one of the twentieth century's foremost Gothic icons, its star, Vincent Price. Price displayed his devilish sense of fun during the publicity campaign. In a wax museum near Anaheim, California, he took the place of a wax figure of himself in a display replicating the film. 'I was standing in a menacing pose with a hypodermic needle,' recalled Price. 'As the people came closer to look, I squirted water from the needle at them.'

Gloria Holden captivates all around her as Dracula's Daughter *(1936). The most ambiguous of* femmes fatales, *the Countess's story has an explicit lesbian subtext.*

The other hallmark of 1950s horror was the emergence of studios specialising in low-budget exploitation. (In 1948 an American court ruling had opened up the market for film production and distribution, previously monopolised by the big Hollywood studios.) Short on finance, but long on enthusiasm and inventiveness, the theory was simple – make a movie cheaply enough, promote it aggressively enough, and it was bound to turn a profit. Few were more enthusiastic or inventive than William Castle, the producer-director, whom author Mark Thomas McGee hails as 'the King of Showmanship', in *Beyond Ballyhoo*, his history of 'Motion Picture Promotion and Gimmicks'. Castle couldn't afford expensive processes like

Bela Lugosi (standing), with exploitation director Ed Wood (right), in the twilight of his career. In 1956, Lugosi was buried in the Dracula cape that made him famous.

3D, so he had to find cheaper ways to lure unsuspecting customers to view his less-than-epic productions. To spice up the unremarkable thriller, *Macabre*, in 1958, for example, Castle arranged for all patrons to be insured against dying of fright while watching the film. His next gimmick, 'Emergo', was a large plastic skeleton which was winched across the cinema during the follow-up to *Macabre*, *House on Haunted Hill* (1958).

Castle's subsequent picture, *The Tingler* (1959), is generally considered to be his masterpiece (at least among those who would give him the time of day). The story was a bold, if bizarre, effort that boasts the distinction of being the first ever film to feature an LSD trip. Vincent Price plays a doctor who's discovered fear is caused by a small crab-like creature which attaches itself to the spine, and can only be repelled by screaming. He finds a perfect experimental subject in the shape of a deaf-mute girl who cannot scream, and thus becomes a host for the 'Tingler' of the title.

Of course, the real star was the gimmick – in this case 'Percepto', whereby cinema seats were wired up with buzzers. During the film, a Tingler gets loose in a cinema and starts crawling up someone's leg. As Price advised, 'Ladies and gentlemen, please do not panic. The Tingler is loose in the cinema . . . Scream, scream for your life!', the projectionist flicked a switch to give a mild shock to a few patrons.

The Aurum Encyclopedia of Horror credits *The Tingler* with starting the trend for audience participation that led to the 1975 Goth favourite *The Rocky Horror Picture Show*. This oddball musical combines satire of golden-age horror and 1950s science fiction movies with songs inspired by the rock 'n' roll music of the time. For the rock 'n' roll era had seen the birth of the teenager as a recognised demographic, at the same time that the car became an indispensable part of American life. This adolescent audience was a godsend for the poverty-row studios. Drive-in movie theatres sprung up all over the US, where watching the movie was secondary to other activities such as making out or drinking – making for an undemanding audience.

The studios responded with incredibly cheap films that didn't so much insult the intelligence as take it outside and beat it to death with a shovel, on themes that appealed to teens (rock 'n' roll, drag racing, monsters). By the late 1950s, Hollywood Gothic had been reduced to clumsy metaphors for adolescent angst in drive-in fodder like *I Was a Teenage Werewolf* (1957) and *I Was a Teenage Frankenstein* (1957). Lycanthropy served as a parody of the teenager who had begun growing hair in strange places and experiencing mood swings, while the man-made monster exhibited a complexion worse than any acne-ridden youth – and could truly claim that his father didn't understand him.

Many of those who relish the popular culture of the 1950s include these fun-but-feeble films – alongside rock 'n' roll, quiffs and hot rods – as part of the lurid era's kitsch appeal. Psychobilly, Goth's in-bred cousin, is exemplified by such long-lived bands as the USA's Cramps (who recorded a song entitled 'I Was a Teenage Werewolf') and the UK's Meteors, who got much of the juice for their psychotic rocky horror from 1950s drive-in movies. US death rock pioneers the Misfits, one of the few such acts to incorporate 1950s-style crooning into their style, have also recorded numerous songs inspired by horror movies from this period.

In 1978, the Misfits called their independent record label Plan 9 – a reference to the 1959 science fiction-horror film *Plan 9 from Outer Space*. Originally entitled *Graverobbers from Outer Space* (also a reasonable summary of the plot), it is the *meisterwerk* of one Edward D. Wood, Jr., a director whose best efforts make his poverty-row rivals look akin to cinematic genius Orson Welles (an idol of Wood, ironically enough). Genre fans had long been happy to allow *Plan 9* – alongside other efforts such as *Bride of the Monster* (1956) and *Night of the Ghouls* (1959) – to slip into obscurity. The plots are incoherent and the scripts surrealistically inept, the acting manifestly wooden just as the sets are obviously cardboard. But the dubious distinction of being labelled 'the worst film of all time' in the successful 1980 book *The Golden Turkey Awards*, by film critics, the Medved brothers, brought *Plan 9* – already acquiring an unlikely reputation as a cult movie – into the spotlight.

Wood's closest connection to authentic Gothic, however, was his close friendship with Bela Lugosi. Lugosi was one of a freak-show repertory of actors the director had assembled for his deranged movies: popular horror movie hostess Vampira, notoriously inaccurate TV psychic Criswell and a 400-pound bald Swedish wrestler, named Tor Johnson. By this point Lugosi was struggling with alcohol and morphine addiction, and his career could sink no further. In Wood's *Glen or Glenda* (1953) he appears as the narrator, who tells the hero beware 'the big green dragon that sits on the steps and eats little boys!', and crowing his descent into absurdity, at one point has stampeding buffalo superimposed over his face, while intoning 'Pull the string! Pull the string.' He died in 1956, and, according to his last request, was buried in the costume of Dracula, the role that had brought him stardom a quarter of a century before.

By the middle of the twentieth century, with the first ever horror-movie star buried, it looked like Gothic cinema was going the same way.

Fittingly, Lugosi rose from the grave for one last role. After he died a few days into the shooting of *Plan 9 from Outer Space*, the ever-resourceful Wood used what little footage he had and replaced him with a chiropractor who bore almost no resemblance, having the man hold

Juvenile delinquency, the moral panic of the 1950s, given trash-Gothic form in I Was a Teenage Werewolf *(1957) – immortalised by original psychobilly band the Cramps.*

a cape in front of his face. It's typical Wood – somewhere between a touching tribute and a cynical cash-in, a triumph of hopeless optimism over common sense. For some, that kind of blind vision remains inspiring.

Meanwhile, Vincent Price had resolved to make a horror movie he could be proud of. When the prolific drive-in director Roger Corman raised an uncharacteristically healthy budget for a new project in 1960, the stage was set for a revival of American celluloid Gothic.

CHAPTER III

EVERY COVER WAS BLACK:
Modern Gothic & the Horror Genre

When America began her march to global dominance, 'Gothic', as a European generic label, seemed outdated. New terminology was needed to describe the genre that sought to unsettle its audience. That new generic label was 'horror' – first used to describe the flood of Hollywood films that begain in 1931 with *Dracula*. Horror is a utilitarian term that upset some of the authors it sought to define, placing their work near the bottom of the literary heap, beneath science fiction but (just) above pornography.

But it's a mistake to try to reject the label. Genre fiction is not only different in intent, but, in this writer's opinion, more potent than any self-conscious efforts of the literary establishment. Some modern Gothic artists have been bothered by the connotations of 'horror', which suggests revulsion and disgust. The accomplished film actor Christopher Lee, who made a career (and, he complained, became typecast) playing satanic villains such as Count Dracula, is a typical example. In conversation with the author, he described his horror films for Hammer Studios as 'Pantomime, fairy stories, fantasies – that's how I've always looked at them. Compared to what we've had to put up with for the past twenty years they're pretty mild.' And Lee is right, in a way – the appeal of Hammer horror for modern fans has a lot to do with period charm. But these same films were condemned as hideously graphic by critics during their 1950s-70s heyday.

Similarly, the classic Victorian fairy stories of the Brothers Grimm were indeed grim, but were trimmed of gore and violence for the twentieth-century nursery audience. In turn, however, the Grimms had already excised sexual references from the folk tales they retold, regarding it as inappropriate for the infants of the nineteenth century. These days, it's more familiar to hear the originators of a genre scapegoating those who have tried to exceed their own efforts. Ramsey Campbell, one of the most respected names in horror literature, has observed the phenomenon, telling fellow horror author Douglas E. Winter, 'It seems peculiar to this field that a number of practitioners, particularly when they stop writing it themselves, decide that nothing else worthwhile is being written.'

This same hypocrisy has led to more prissy horror authors drawing imaginary lines to divide them from the more disreputable elements of the genre. The implication is not only that those lost souls on the other side of the line are morally bankrupt, but that anyone who writes material that is so horrible must also be a 'bad' writer per se. In recent decades this debate has been addressed in various terms: 'quiet' versus 'loud' horror; 'psychological' versus 'splatter'. 'Gothic' is generally seen as synonymous with the more dignified end of the genre, but this is a modern idea that doesn't bear scrutiny. For the Gothic is, at root, about extremes of experience and an appetite for excess.

The Gothic aesthetic has always been about subversion, about turning everything on its head. I spoke to Steve Matthews, co-creator of the *Urban Gothic* TV series and no mean student of the literary roots of the genre, about what it meant in the year 2001. 'The real elements of horror that endure – the elements that link Matthew Lewis [author of *The Monk*] with the modern horror film and the "Goth scene" itself – are nothing to do with the props and sets,' observed Matthews. 'Horror has to be slightly disreputable. Consider how common it is that horror storytellers distance themselves from the subject. Many Gothic novels are based on constructions of books within tales within manuscripts, a perfect reflection of horror's real place in a vernacular tradition. Anybody spotted the similarity between a character in *Melmoth* "finding" an old manuscript and the film-makers in a recent block-buster "finding" a set of film cans in the woods?'

Efforts to gentrify the genre go right back to the twin pillars of Gothic fiction, Anne Radcliffe and Matthew 'Monk' Lewis – with the latter obliged to censor his masterpiece to avoid prosecution. But while *The Monk*, Lewis' exercise in excess, is read and enjoyed in its restored, uncensored form today, Radcliffe's moralistic ramblings are only of interest to a few feminist literary historians. Foreshadowing later squeamishness, Radcliffe was keen to distinguish between 'terror', the emotion supposedly evoked by her books, and 'horror', which she condemned. According to Radcliffe, terror 'expands the soul, and awakens the faculties to a higher degree of life,' while horror 'contracts, freezes and nearly annihilates them.' Horror is associated with disgust, terror with the less negative reaction of awe – or, put another way, 'good Gothic' is psychological, engaging the mind, while 'bad Gothic' is visceral, affecting us in an altogether more primitive fashion. It's a very hazy distinction. More seductive is the distinction expressed by Oscar Wilde in the preface to *The Picture of Dorian Gray*: 'There is no such thing as a moral or immoral book. Books are well written or badly written. That is all.'

Certain Gothic manifestations have long enjoyed a degree of respectability, particularly those which originated in the British Empire during its latter glory days. The classic ghost story, traditionally enjoyed at Christmas, is a quintessentially British strain of horror – characterised by strange footsteps down long, wooden-panelled libraries at midnight, mysterious women in black who disappear into the mist in ornate cemeteries, horse-drawn hearses and crumbling mansions that hide ancestral secrets in hidden chambers. Critics traditionally regard the ghost story's golden age as the Victorian era, but its recognised master, Montague Rhodes James, was active well after Queen Victoria's death in 1901.

In *Fear*, Les Daniels describes James as 'an isolated toiler in his own literary graveyard,' but all of the foremost ghost story writers of the early twentieth century – such as Oliver Onions and E. F. Benson – were, like James, evoking the spirit of a bygone age. (J. Sheridan Le Fanu, one of the few authors associated with the classic ghost story actually active during Victoria's reign, owes most of his posthumous fame to a twentieth-century revival instigated by M. R. James.) The American Gothic author H. P. Lovecraft, concluded his 1927 essay, *Supernatural Horror in Literature*, with a chapter on 'The Modern Masters', ending with a discussion of M. R. James, who, he said, was 'gifted with an almost diabolic power of calling horror by gentle steps from the midst of prosaic daily life'. While Lovecraft wrote that James had 'developed a distinctive style and method likely to serve as models for an enduring line of disciples,' he was pretty much alone in regarding him as the future of horror fiction. For most critics, James was a delightful anachronism who evoked the quaint chills of yesteryear.

Lovecraft's opinion may have been influenced in part by wishful thinking. As a contemporary of Lovecraft, James (who died in 1936 – one year before the American) led a life the Anglophile New Englander would have envied. A product of the privileged worlds of Eton and King's College, Cambridge, James spent his life serving these institutions as a scholar, at King's, then a Provost, at Eton. Both shared a love of history and antique tomes, but while Lovecraft could merely dream about them, James was paid to become an expert on medieval manuscripts and apocryphal texts at Cambridge University.

Neither author showed much interest – either in their lives or fiction – in women. But while Lovecraft felt obliged to make the awkward effort to marry, James didn't attract any undue attention by remaining a lifelong batchelor. Though Lovecraft could affect to be a gentleman and disdain any interest in commercialism, he could only do so by living a frugal lifestyle that was anything but genteel. By way of comparison, James, well paid by academia, could dismiss his stories as idle diversions composed to tell his friends and students round a roaring fire at Christmas. On the subject of the supernatural, Montie (as his friends called him) remained resolutely sceptical but open-minded.

Not everyone was convinced by M. R. James' casual attitude. Friends talked of Montie's susceptibility to eerie atmospheres and 'Celtic sense of the unseen' – though very English and inherently rational, he championed the work of more superstition-bound writers like Sheridan Le Fanu. He confessed that his interest in the unknown was inspired by a childhood incident: 'I chanced to see a Punch and Judy set, with figures cut out in cardboard. One of these was the Ghost. It was a tall figure habited in white with an unnaturally long and narrow head, also surrounded with white, and a dismal visage. Upon this my conceptions of a ghost are based, and for years it permeated my dreams.'

Colleagues recall how the well-liked academic continued to be plagued by nightmares throughout his adult life. Just as his Victorian predecessor Le Fanu deliberately worked his dreams into his fiction, James' 'Punch and Judy set' duly surfaced in his 'Story of a

Disappearance and an Appearance'. Like Le Fanu, James made comparatively little use of 'traditional' ghosts, preferring to employ ill-defined horrors that reach from the shadows of the past, glimpsed − or more often touched − only long enough to know there is something unearthly afoot. The same dreamlike logic informs both writers' work, where the mundane and everyday slowly distort, the irrational gradually shifting from the corner of one's eye to dominate the whole field of vision.

When talking about writing ghost stories, James emphasised that it was important to establish a recognisable, even reassuring setting before the author unsettled the reader, using contrast to heighten the effect. These settings − picturesque cathedrals, college reading rooms, quaint 'olde worlde' inns − may have been familiar to James, but to an increasing number of readers it represented a disappearing world. For much of his British readership, the nightmares James offered

'A Jamesian ghost': inspired by the stories of M. R. James and rendered by Dave Carson, one of the UK's leading contemporary Gothic artists.

were as reassuring as they were unsettling, evoking an age of moral certainties when − as the cliché has it − 'the sun never set on the British Empire'. But, during James' lifetime, the cast-iron confidence of the nineteenth century would lie twisted on the Western Front of World War I, alongside a confetti of human corpses. Next to the nightmare of mass-produced murder and mustard gas, M. R. James' Yuletide spectres belong to a more refined age. It's a dark but dignified era, to which some still pay tribute in Goth nightclubs, where the men deck themselves in top-hats and frock-coats, and their consorts in midnight-black Victorian wedding gowns, signalling a longing for the cobwebbed romanticism of days gone by.

While some were sheltered from the horrors of World War I − like James, in his haunted world of Victorian gentility − few could ignore the conflict that plunged most of the globe into midnight darkness. A young British artist and writer named Mervyn Peake applied to be an official war artist in World War II, but was rejected by the Government − a disaster for both parties, as he succeeded in accidentally burning down an army facility before being invalided out due to nervous collapse in 1942. Seemingly a sucker for punishment, in the final months of WWII Peake was one of the first Allied civilians to visit Belsen concentration camp and witness the horrors of the Nazi Holocaust for himself, committing them to paper in his sketchbook.

His experiences furnished Peake with a rich source of disturbing images, but he was no stranger to the dark side. Born in 1911 in China, the son of a missionary, Peake's formative years were spent in the otherworldly wonder of deprivation, beauty and decay that characterised the declining Chinese Empire. These experiences appeared to blend in his mind with the traumatic war years, resulting in the novel *Titus Groan* (1946), the first of a trilogy that continued with *Gormenghast* (1950) and *Titus Alone* (1959).

Titus was the trilogy's hero, heir to the castle of Gormenghast. He is as eccentric as his name suggests, as are the other resident grotesques – with names like Irma Prunesquallor, Lord Sepulchrave and Nanny Slagg – whom Peake manages to render both as grim caricatures and convincing personalities. But the focus of the books is the castle itself, Gormenghast, a vast, crumbling edifice that holds the characters trapped, like some ancient spider that has entangled them all in a web of meaningless customs and insanely complex rituals. In *Gormenghast*, the Gothic castle that dominated golden-age Gothic literature became a world unto itself, where all the distracting themes of innocence and romance are forgotten, and we are left with madness and degeneration.

Into this stagnant Gothic arena arrives Steerpike, a lowly kitchen boy, who worms his way up Gormenghast's rigid pecking order using cunning and deceit, before being confronted by Titus for his crimes. On the surface Steerpike is a villain, although he is as sympathetic as most of the trilogy's characters, and without his subversive influence, it is unlikely Titus would ever have escaped the terrible gravity of his castle and all of its mindless traditions. In *Titus Alone* he strikes out and discovers a world, much like our own, where Gormenghast is but a legend. Titus initially resolves to return to the gloomy halls of his ancestors, but at the last minute he turns back 'for he carried his Gormenghast within him.' Just as it seems Peake – who many believed had never recovered from the horrors he witnessed in the concentration camps – always carried Belsen within him.

Next to the Gothic claustrophobia of the preceding volumes, *Titus Alone* is taut and fast-paced. In part, this reflects the author's state of mind, affected by the degenerating health which prevented him from completing the final part of the trilogy to his satisfaction. Peake was finally hospitalised with Parkinson's Disease in 1962, until his death six years later.

Critical response at the time was mixed: some distinguished figures lauded Peake's startling achievement, but most regarded *Gormenghast* as too dark, relegating his trilogy to the ghetto of the horror novel or into the shadow of another fantasy trilogy, J. R. R. Tolkien's popular, quasi-medieval *The Lord of the Rings*. As Ramsey Campbell – one of numerous contemporary horror authors who hail Peake's trilogy as a masterpiece – observes, 'the high fantasy guys seem to find [Peake] disturbing because of his violence and sense of the macabre.' Perhaps his work contained messages people didn't want to hear. There are echoes of the dying British Empire in the decadent, absurdly formal halls of Gormenghast. The world was moving on, but the British remained frozen in class-bound traditions that began to topple, along with many other comfortable nineteenth-century assumptions about European civilisation, after the World War II.

As cultural power shifted across the Atlantic, the births of two men straddled the threshold of the twentieth century, two men who would become legendary in the new genre of American Gothic (or 'horror'). Both of our subjects – whom we'll call Howard and Eddie – were classic momma's boys, brought up in an overbearingly feminine environment, in which they were told, in no uncertain terms, that it would have been better if they'd have been little girls. Indeed, Howard was told by his eccentric mother that he *was* female, up until the age of six, and dressed in little girl's clothes. Both found escape in colourful books and lurid magazines, an appetite that increased as they grew up.

Both Howard and Eddie were raised in such stifling environments that neither man can be said to have matured in the conventional sense. Howard's biographer, L. Sprague de Camp, describes him as having adolescent characteristics 'in his thirties, more than a decade after he had ceased to be an adolescent. In some respects, such as the sexual and the monetary, he never did mature.' Eddie's development was arrested even earlier. In both cases, when their domineering mothers died it hit these vulnerable men like a thunderbolt. Howard describes the death of his mother when he was 32 – and had still never left home – as 'an extreme nervous shock'. Eddie's response to the death of his own mother, just before his fortieth birthday, is not recorded, but was doubtless even more intense. In both cases, the trauma caused the

Steerpike dominated the all-star BBC TV adaptation of Gormenghast *(2000) – a somewhat disappointing version that downplayed the book's darker elements.*

chinks in their already fractured personalities to yawn wide open.

For one man – New Englander Howard Phillips Lovecraft – that shock contributed to him becoming the most influential author of twentieth-century Gothic fiction. The other – Edward Gein, the Wisconsin 'ghoul' – responded by perpetrating the most notoriously Gothic crimes in American history. Lovecraft was able to cope with his bizarre background because he had a powerful, versatile intellect, while Gein appears to have bordered upon the retarded. But the similarities between the characters are striking, and the twentieth-century horror genre cannot be understood without some acquaintance with these two fragile American eccentrics.

H. P. Lovecraft was born in 1890 in Providence, Rhode Island, where he spent almost the whole of his life. Although he reluctantly left his beloved New England home town on occasion, Lovecraft was happiest as a recluse. His chief excursions were those of the mind – whether via the extensive correspondence he maintained with numerous correspondents (composing around 100,000 lengthy letters) or the books he consumed voraciously from an early age. Part of the reason for this was his over-protective mother, Sarah, whom Lovecraft's friend August Derleth described as 'a psychoneurotic, determined to shelter her son from the rigours and dangers of life'. Like many children obliged to spend long periods indoors, Lovecraft developed a lively inner life. He fancied himself a Roman citizen, an eighteenth-century English gentleman, or, most significantly, an Arabic wizard named Abdul Alhazred.

Death and madness attended Howard from an early age. His father was committed to a mental asylum when he was just three and died five years later. When the boy was six his grandmother died, a trauma that, he would later recall, 'plunged me into a gloom from which I never really recovered . . . I began to have nightmares of the most hideous description, peopled with things which I called "night-gaunts" – a compound word of my own coinage.' The oppressive care Sarah had taken with her sickly son blossomed into full-blown hypochondria. The adult Howard displayed a tendency to collapse if exposed to mildly chilly temperatures, complained of regular headaches and dizziness, and a fear of odd things such as seafood and dogs (like so many of those of a Gothic disposition, however, Howard was a cat-lover).

Meanwhile, Sarah herself suffered a nervous collapse, requiring hospitalisation in 1919. Howard struggled to cope, but seeing himself very much as an old-style gentleman, had always regarded selling his literary efforts as beneath him. However, his mother's hospital bills were mounting, so he compromised by charging to revise (often extensively) other people's work – his chief source of income throughout his life. When his mother died in 1921, the desolate Howard found himself at a crossroads.

Like the French Decadent poet Charles Baudelaire he found a guide in Edgar Allan Poe, whom he dubbed 'God of Fiction'. If Poe, another poverty-stricken American with pretensions to being a gentleman, could sell to fiction magazines, then Lovecraft felt he could follow suit. In 1922 he began selling stories to a periodical entitled *Home Brew*. The following

year, a new title called *Weird Tales* was launched. Judging it sufficiently literary to be worthy of his efforts, Lovecraft began an unstable but enduring association with the classic pulp magazine.

Poe may also have influenced him in affairs of the heart although anyone looking to that tragic, unrequited lover for guidance was clearly asking for trouble. Love was a subject of which Lovecraft had confessed himself 'quite ignorant!' in a 1919 letter. Nevertheless, in the early 1920s he began courting a pretty fellow writer named Sonia Greene. But it was love Lovecraft-style:

New England eccentric H. P. Lovecraft, whose fictional worlds of 'crawling chaos' and 'eldritch horror' cast a shadow over twentieth-century Gothic.

he took her to his favourite local spots, like the Providence graveyard, where Poe had (unsuccessfully) courted the poetess Sarah Helen Whitman, in the 1840s, and read her passages from his idol's works. While on a break in Massachusetts, Howard encouraged Sonia to write a Gothic tale, praising the results so warmly that she kissed him suddenly upon the lips. Lovecraft, who hadn't been kissed since infancy, went white as a sheet. But, despite such awkward moments, the romance progressed, and in 1924 they married.

The couple moved to New York, where his wife had opened a hat store, but the store failed and the move proved a disaster. There was an element of racism in Lovecraft, which reached its most strident pitch when he described New York City as 'a babel of sound and filth' overrun by a plague of degenerate immigrants. This attitude also erupted in his tale 'The Horror at Red Hook', which reads in parts like weird Gothic propaganda for the American Nazi Party (the source of some domestic strife, not least because his wife was Jewish).

Lovecraft had become a big favourite with *Weird Tales* readers, so the publisher offered him the editorship. But it would have involved moving to Chicago, so he turned down the offer. Howard yearned for his Providence home, and in 1926, Sonia suggested he return, effectively ending the marriage – for Lovecraft's old-fashioned, overbearing aunts would not have a female member of the family 'in trade' locally, yet the couple could not have survived without Sonia working. He had thrown away his only chance of a normal relationship and a regular job, choosing instead to hurl himself back into the maternal embrace of his aunts and the reclusiveness of his Providence study. There, with curtains drawn day and night, all of his darkest fantasies were recorded in prose, posthumously establishing the reclusive New Englander as, in the words of Stephen King, 'the twentieth century horror story's dark and baroque prince'.

While dream plays a cardinal role in the creation of Gothic art, few have worn this inspiration on their sleeve as prominently as H. P. Lovecraft. A number of his tales take place almost exclusively in 'the Dreamlands'. The 'night-gaunts' that haunted his childhood nightmares came home to roost as faceless, winged demons, and ominous dreams were woven into stories almost unaltered – indeed one 'short story' published posthumously ('The Evil Clergyman') was actually just a description of a nightmare taken from one of Lovecraft's lengthy letters.

Poe's literary influence was most obvious in earlier material, and though classic Gothic themes – incest, cannibalism, insanity – are evident, in Lovecraft's hands they take on a new, distinctive form. Paranoia – that distinctive late twentieth-century 'form of awareness' that found its most popular recent manifestation in *The X-Files* – looms large in his world. But the conspiracy hinted at in Lovecraft's work is infinitely more appalling than any alien or Masonic plot for world dominance. It is a vast, subhuman, primeval cult, whose activities threaten to send the cosmos spinning into dreadful chaos. The deities these degenerates worship, and wish to conjure out of hibernation, known simply as 'the Great Old Ones', are the embodiment of what Lovecraft called 'cosmic horror'.

Significantly, in an increasingly godless century, Lovecraft disdained the folkloric figures of Christian culture, such as vampires and werewolves, and abandoned traditional Gothic archetypes like the Wandering Jew or Faust. In a sense, he was the first important post-Christian Gothic writer, jettisoning the spectres of the past in favour of something bewilderingly formless, and appallingly vast, that lurks at the threshold of tomorrow and dwarfs the quaint myths of the Bible. In Lovecraft's paranoid vision, every scholar with a passion for the past, every white-coated scientist planning the future, is potentially destined to bring ruin not just to himself, but to the whole human race – even tearing apart the fabric of reality itself.

'We live on a placid island of ignorance in the midst of black seas of infinity,' wrote Lovecraft, 'and it was not meant that we should travel far. The sciences, each straining in its own direction, have hitherto harmed us little; but some day the piecing together of disassociated knowledge will open up such terrifying vistas of reality, and our frightful position therein, that we shall either go mad from the revelation or flee from the deadly light into the peace and safety of a new dark age.' These words are taken from one of his most popular tales, 'The Call of Cthulhu' (1926) – named after the demonic octopoid entity, the best known of Lovecraft's gaggle of 'Great Old Ones', at the centre of 'the Cthulhu Mythos'. Cthulhu lies dreaming on the floor of the Pacific Ocean, while other malevolent gods lurk patiently in the endless cold wastes of space or, more suggestively, 'Not in the spaces we know but between them.'

As the passage suggests, Lovecraft was dealing with very modern horrors. At a time when America looked forward to a bright future courtesy of scientific progress, the self-professed outsider, H. P. Lovecraft, suggested such a path would lead to waking nightmares beyond the imagination. In the same way Gothic writers of the past had challenged the traditional faith of Christianity, so Lovecraft created a Frankenstein myth for the scientific age (indeed, some see 'The Colour Out of Space' – one of his best stories – as predictive of the horrors of radiation). Alongside this was another equally modern anxiety – that of insignificance. Lovecraft reduces the human race to a tribe of ants on a trivial planet that will be obliterated by a callous universe, not out of malice but because, in the grand scheme of things, we are all but irrelevant.

Lovecraft has never been short of critics to point out his literary shortcomings. His characters are weak – breathless cardboard scholars, whose curiosity has taken them too far – and speak in unconvincing dialogue. This is not, however, his greatest failing. Despite a great fondness for adjectives, when it actually comes to the climactic act of describing a story's ultimate horror, Lovecraft becomes tongue-tied. Everything is 'unspeakable', 'indescribable', 'formless' or 'unnameable'. Some critics have observed that if Lovecraft, as a horror writer, could not find the vocabulary to describe horrible things, then maybe he had not found his true vocation.

Paradoxically, this gives us a clue as to why an author with such obvious limitations has had such an impact: Surrealists have hailed him as an authentic visionary; occultists portray him as the unwitting prophet of forgotten gods; hippies embraced his 'cosmic horror' as a dark prototype for psychedelia; thrash-metal bands looked to him as the source of 'cool' new monsters with which to populate their lyrics. In the ultimate tribute to his influence, 'Lovecraftian' is now an established adjective in the Gothic culture to describe something so weird as to be sanity-threatening.

Lovecraft's secret is sincerity, his creative madness leaking through the pages like the 'crawling chaos' he describes. It seems born of Lovecraft's very real fear that the insanity which claimed both his mother and father was destined, via heredity (and 'degenerate blood' was a recurring theme in his work), to destroy him too. And madness is the end that awaits his most unfortunate heroes, a fate far worse than the messy murders, mutilations and eviscerations that he passes over with comparative restraint. H. P. Lovecraft made a deal of sorts with madness, exorcising it via fiction that chimes resonantly with those sensitive enough to appreciate just how flimsy the illusion we call sanity can be.

Not all such pacts with the demons of inner darkness have a positive outcome. Twenty years after Lovecraft's death from cancer in 1937 (another form of 'crawling chaos'), Edward Gein, a handyman in the tiny Wisconsin town of Plainfield, was arrested by the local police. The revelations that followed his apprehension deserve Lovecraftian adjectives such as 'unspeakable' and 'indescribable'. Gein was found responsible for the cold-blooded murder of two women, and the exhumation of the bodies of upwards of a dozen others. But it was his motivation that was truly disturbing, a leap into the irrational that would have made Sigmund Freud choke on his cigar.

On that fateful winter's day in 1957, in the shed by Gein's squalid farmhouse, police

Satirical US presidential election campaign material issued by Chaosium. Their role-playing game, The Call of Cthulhu, *brought H. P. Lovecraft to a new generation.*

officers found the woman who ran the local store hanging upside down, gutted like a deer. Inside the Gein house was a selection of human body parts used as materials for home furnishing and costumes fashioned from the skin of cadavers. Perhaps most disturbing were a belt made of nipples and a box containing a collection of nine disembodied vaginas.

For many of the reporters who covered the story, the facts of the case were not just unspeakable, but in 1950s America, unprintable. The same grotesque quality, however, that made the press reticent ensured that the story would get out, if not by official reportage, then via the Chinese whispers of rumour and gossip. The murders were discussed in bars, children made Gein the subject of sick jokes known as 'geeners', while teenagers made the twisted handyman into a bogeyman in fireside ghost stories. In this fashion Ed Gein wormed his way into the popular consciousness, transformed from a simple-minded local handyman into an American Gothic legend.

Though this psycho-sexual slice of twentieth-century taboo seems a million miles from the comparative restraint of Poe's tales, the 'imp of the perverse' was made foetid flesh in Gein. Characteristic Gothic themes lay at the twisted heart of his case: incest (Gein's unrequited love for women who resembled his domineering mother); necrophilia (that lust was sated with the corpses of other dead women); masks (the facial masks he constructed from human skin). Cannibalism was also suggested (a human heart was found in a coffee pot atop his stove), although Gein denied it.

Gender bending was Gein's real speciality, however, and he took it to ritualistic extremes, becoming a kind of 'skin transvestite'. Draping himself in costumes fashioned from the flesh of bodies he had exhumed, complete with female sexual organs, he would dance beneath the moon beating a human skin-and-bone drum. Recent commentators have seen some kind of improvised shamanic rite in this bizarre behaviour. Even in the most extreme of today's fetish clubs, however, Ed's exuberant performance might have given pause for thought. The Gothic theme of madness obviously also looms large in the Gein case, and it didn't take the courts long to commit him to a Wisconsin lunatic asylum where he lived quietly until his death 27 years later.

This was not, of course, the end of the story. The 'Jack the Ripper' murders of 1888 had exposed the underbelly of the British Empire at the height of its power, a viper's nest of depravity and vice in London, at the Empire's very heart. Ed Gein's atrocities, taking place as America geared up for world domination in the optimistic 1950s, suggested a seething mass of repressed horror beneath its facade of small-town conformity. If, as graphic novelist and occultist Alan Moore has suggested, the Ripper murders prefigured the following hundred years, perhaps Gein's crimes fulfil a similar quasi-mystical role for the transgressions at the end of the twentieth century.

In his pulp fiction-style autopsy of the legend, *Ed Gein – Psycho!*, true crime obsessive Paul A. Woods observes, 'What simultaneously appals and enthrals is that the things he did just don't seem possible. The imagery of his crimes is dredged up from some surreal nightmare: the skin suit, the flesh furniture, the bone ornaments. Ed Gein was extracting the primal desires from the darkest parts of his psyche and making them solid. His own home was littered with the foul daydreams of his subconscious, made nightmarishly visible.'

Harold Schechter is the New York English professor whose book, *Deviant*, is the classic factual study of the Gein case. 'The really significant thing about Gein is that, in a sense, he Americanized horror,' says Schechter. 'Before Gein and the films that sprang from the obsession with this case, the monsters that populated horror films were always foreign in some way. They either came from Transylvania, Egypt or outer space. With Gein you really got the beginning of a very specifically American kind of horror.'

That 'American kind of horror' is, of course, still with us. Buffalo Bill, the skin-stealing serial killer in *The Silence of the Lambs*, published in 1989, owes much to Gein. This smash hit, which made serial-killer thrillers acceptable mainstream entertainment, was written by Thomas Harris – 'a nineteen-year-old trainee crime reporter when the Gein story broke,' observes Paul Woods.

According to Woods, 'Between the *Time* and *Life* magazine articles in the late 1950s, and

Ed's death in 1984, so little was written on the factual elements of the case that it amounted to some kind of moratorium by the forces of "good taste". The Gein case survived as a guilty secret in America's closet – proof that the 'golden age' of the 1950s harboured something unspeakable, and that loving your mother was not always the sign of a good boy. It first came knocking at the door of popular culture in 1959, creating an overnight sensation.

Robert Bloch was a 41-year-old writer who, at the time of the crimes, happened to be living in a Wisconsin town just 40 miles from Gein's home. Bloch was a friend and admirer of H. P. Lovecraft, and imitated his idol's style in his early work. The two had even 'killed' each other in print: Bloch made Lovecraft the ill-fated hero of his 1935 Cthulhu Mythos tale 'The Shambler from the Stars' (after receiving a mock-permission letter from his mentor, authorising Bloch to 'portray, murder, annihilate, disintegrate, transfigure, or otherwise manhandle' him); in good-natured revenge, Lovecraft despatched Robert Bloch (in the form of 'Robert Blake', though with his full Milwaukee address) in 'The Haunter of the Dark'.

By the 1950s, however, Bloch had found his own voice. While his 1934 tale for *Weird Tales*,

Ed Gein, a true-life icon of American Gothic, inspired a musical tribute from British psychobillies the Meteors and a fictionalised 1974 biopic, Deranged *(below).*

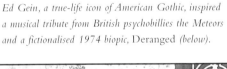

'The Feast in the Abbey', had earned notoriety for its explicit depiction of cannibalism, Bloch emerged from beneath his mentor's shadow with the 1943 short story 'Yours Truly, Jack the Ripper'. Authentically chilling, it depicts the Victorian serial killer as a superhuman butcher immune to the ravages of time. In a sense the message was accurate, inasmuch as the spectre of serial murder continues to haunt the modern world.

'I knew very little about the Gein case per se,' observed Bloch of the relative restraint of local press coverage, 'and nothing whatsoever about him, except that he was a 50-year-old man, a respected citizen for his entire life. He had been a baby-sitter; he gave people little gifts (of 'venison') [Gein is rumoured to have given human flesh to neighbours] . . . I was amazed that Gein could conduct himself without anyone suspecting the truth. I said, "There's a book here!"' That book, published in 1959, was *Psycho*, which, Bloch mordantly observed, 'made me neither rich nor famous, but it gradually invested me with a certain small amount of notoriety.' Others are more assertive in their praise. Horror author and voodoo expert, Hugh Cave, calls *Psycho* 'a milestone in horror fiction' that took the genre 'from then to now in one big scary leap.' Most of the book's notoriety actually came courtesy of the 1960 film, which proved the most lucrative movie in the horror genre to date. It was lent legitimacy by the director, British master of suspense, Alfred Hitchcock (who also made a Ripper film called *The Lodger* way back in 1926), but the impact of *Psycho* was due to its anti-hero, Norman Bates: a nice quiet man who happens to kill women at the behest of his dead mother. This twist – that the monster could be living next door and look just like you – shocked audiences in an increasingly impersonal world, as twentieth-century horror began to substitute psychiatry for the supernatural.

By now over 200 years old, Gothic literature enjoyed a widespread popular revival in the purer form of 'horror' fiction in the 1970s. As Clive Bloom observes in his introduction to the book *Gothic Horror*, entitled 'Death's Own Backyard', 'It was gothicism, with its formality, codification, ritualistic elements and artifice (its very origins as an aesthetic outlook and *literary* condition first and foremost), that transformed the old folk tale of terror into the modern horror story.'

Modern Gothic-horror authors had to struggle ever harder to create the intensity of sensation their readers craved, in a market changed forever by the lurid progeny of Bloch's *Psycho*. British author, Ramsey Campbell, was one of the most distinctive. Like so many twentieth-century horror writers, he began by writing Lovecraft pastiches (most notably, the 1969 Cthulhu Mythos story 'Cold Print') before perfecting his own style. Campbell's nightmare fiction manifested echoes of his unhappy Liverpool childhood. His father and mother split when he was young, but remained in the same house, a situation made even more bizarre by his father's determination never to communicate with his young son. The elder Campbell became an unseen presence in the house – an indistinct voice, nocturnal footsteps – and a source of formless fear to young Ramsey. Later, when the younger Campbell came home from work, his father would hold the door from inside to make sure they never came face-to-face.

Subsequently, his mother began slowly losing her sanity, becoming convinced she was being talked about on the radio, or that disembodied heads were staring at her from inside vases. Only after her death in 1982 did Campbell begin to appreciate that the themes dominant in his fiction – alienation, dwindling sanity, paranoia – were those that dominated his youth. His novels have a hallucinatory quality that Campbell has compared to experiments with LSD – though this is the stuff of bad trips that leave permanent psychological scarring. His writing has been described as psychological – as opposed to supernatural – horror, but, as Campbell has observed, in many ways it is impossible to distinguish between the two. The frightening thing about madness is that psychotic hallucinations (or, if you like, paranormal manifestations) feel just as real, perhaps more so, than anything else going on around the victim.

Beginning with Lovecraft pastiches in the short story collection, *The Inhabitant of the Lake and Other Less Welcome Tenants* (1964), Campbell's distinctive stylistic tics – disintegrating reality, dysfunctional families, deviant or repressed sexuality – have remained constant. *The Face that Must Die* (1979), his second novel, is a first-person serial-killer narrative, written before Thomas Harris popularised the subject with his Hannibal Lecter novels, and considerably grimmer in tone. *Obsession* (1985) gives a distinctive Campbell take on the old adage 'Be careful what you wish for', as four friends confront the sanity-threatening consequences of their desires becoming reality by virtue of a bizarre supernatural agency. (The same idea lies behind the classic 1902 ghost story by W. W. Jacobs, 'The Monkey's Paw'.) *The Hungry Moon* (1986) depicts an ancient horror gradually unleashed on an isolated English village by the unthinking actions of a fundamentalist Christian preacher. His most recent novel is *Silent Children* (2001), a return to serial-killer territory. For the 1990s saw Campbell increasingly marketed as a crime author – a reflection of the greater respectability afforded those writers who remove the supernatural element from their examinations of the dark side. Ramsey Campbell has also been criticised for creating too many selfish and unsympathetic characters, for reflecting a world too bleak for most tastes, for demanding too much of the reader with prose that describes a disintegrating reality. Certainly, the commercial horror market that took off in the mid-1970s never really took to Campbell, who remains, like the

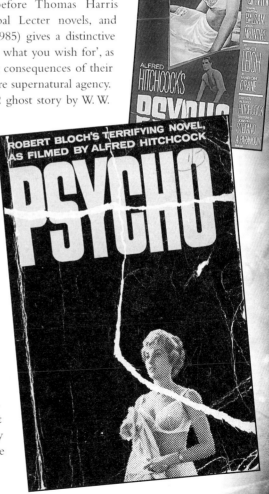

creeping insanity in one of his stories, a disturbing background presence, his brand of desolate unease and distorted reality far from cinematic.

Perhaps inevitably, American authors whose novels could fulfil the visual demands of Hollywood came to dominate the Gothic horror market from the 1970s onward. It's no exaggeration to say that the man who single-handedly launched the modern horror boom was Stephen King. The sheer scale of the success of *Carrie*, his 1974 breakthrough novel and subsequent 1976 film, changed the whole nature of the genre. As John Nicholson observed in his essay 'Scared Shitless' (for the 1993 anthology *Creepers*), commercial developments led to changing attitudes: 'By the 1980s horror had become big business. Here was a viral infection spreading out of control! In the late 1960s it had been like belonging to a secret society to admit you read horror. Few publishers and fewer shops bothered . . . By the 1980s horror was on every paperback list and in every town. Horror had its own section, even a livery: every cover was black.'

But did the 'secret society' who enjoyed the guilty pleasures of horror fiction really want their lodge doors flung open to the general public? American horror author, Whitley Streiber (author of the vampire novel, *The Hunger*, adapted for the screen as a Goth favourite in 1983, and controversial 'non-fiction' account of alien abduction, *Communion*), once described his eager initiation into horror, via black-and-white monster movies and comics in the 1950s: 'I realised that it was forbidden and despised; by reading it I declared myself to the world as a rebel, a member of a secret cabal of screwed-up kids who were cheerful at funerals, who giggled when ordered to say a prayer at the sound of an ambulance siren, who weren't above putting a dead rattlesnake in bed with their sister to see if the *EEEYAAAHHH*s scattered across EC comics were accurate renderings of the sound of horror.'

It would be interesting to know if Streiber (born in 1945) would have chosen musical or sartorial methods of rebellion had he been born a generation later. Were the young people devouring EC comics in the 1950s akin to the tribe of lost souls who found escape via bands like Bauhaus and clubs like the Batcave, three decades on? Interestingly, Streiber's words are taken from a book about Stephen King (*Kingdom of Fear*) – did it occur to Streiber that King, whom he admires, was responsible for shattering his treasured 'secret cabal' by turning horror into a mainstream product?

In an equally revealing talk given at Billerica Public Library in New England in the early 1980s, King labelled horror 'as Republican as a banker in a three-piece suit. The story is always the same in terms of development. There's an incursion into taboo lands, there's a place where you shouldn't go, but you do. And the same thing happens inside: you look at the guy with three eyes, or you look at the fat lady, or you look at the skeleton man or Mr Electrical, or whoever it happens to be. And when you come out, well, you say, "Hey I'm not so bad. I'm all right. A lot better than I thought." It has that effect of reconfirming values, of reconfirming self-image and our good feelings about ourselves . . . it appeals to teenagers – the two things go together because teenagers are the most conservative [people] in American society.' Which may be news to many teenagers.

What King says about horror fiction is certainly true of his own style – conformists have always scapegoated misfits in order to make themselves feel better – but another kind of horror exists that prefers the twisted occupants of the tent to those nice, ordinary folk who come to mock. In the 1960s the term 'freak' was adopted as a positive term by the counterculture, and much of the ethos of the Goth subculture has been based upon making the badge of outsiderdom a proud rejection of conventional society. It's a theme central to modern Gothic horror, and prominent in the work of Anne Rice.

While King was by far the most successful entrant into the 1970s horror arena (indeed, arguably the most successful storyteller of all time), Rice demands attention for her 1976 hit novel, *Interview with the Vampire*, which sent profound waves across the horror genre. A brief comparison of King and Rice throws light on both the mainstreaming of horror and its relationship with the Gothic aesthetic. *Interview with the Vampire* is the first of *The Vampire Chronicles* – an ongoing series of novels that explores the undead, from their roots in ancient history to the present day. Significantly, Rice tells her narrative from the point of view of the vampires themselves, making them into seductive anti-heroes. The archetype of the seductive, Byronic anti-hero had been immortalised in the figure of Count Ruthven, the title character of John Polidori's *The Vampyre* back in 1819 – but no author had ever embraced the part of the vampire to the same extent, or so successfully, as Rice.

In a 2000 interview for *Wicked* magazine, Rice opined, 'They [the vampires] are obvious metaphors for the outsider, the outcast, or that part of us that always feels like an outsider. And they are a metaphor for the predator in all of us.' In King's novel *'Salem's Lot*, the vampire, Kurt Barlow, is a repellent child-killer, monstrous and inhuman in almost every respect. By way of contrast Rice's bloodsuckers are darkly romantic fantasy figures, *Wicked*'s Chandra Palermo describing her central character, Lestat, as a 'courtly velvet-clad Adonis with as insatiable a lust for knowledge and *haute couture* as for life-sustaining blood'.

King lives in small-town Maine, the pine-tree state, whose very ordinariness feeds his creative talents – 'New York isn't America, L.A. isn't America. *This* is America,' he recently told *The Observer*. Rice remains bound to New Orleans, a spicily-decadent gumbo of a city where lust, death, pleasure and the scars of America's slave-owning past bubble just beneath the surface. Arguably, this steamily-exotic place is the capital of American Gothic, and it's certainly become a mecca for the nation's Goth contingent. While King remains resolutely engaged in the present, with occasional forays into the 1950s and '60s, the fruits of Rice's painstaking historical research have become an increasingly prominent facet of her work.

King is naturally not without his defenders. 'If by some odd chance the people of the future read,' observed Whitley Streiber, 'and they want to learn about America in our time – not the history, but the smell and taste and feel of it – they will certainly turn to Stephen King for guidance.' But mainstream America remains a deeply alien environment to 'the secret cabal of screwed-up kids' to which Streiber once belonged. For many such kids, Anne Rice's shadow world – where outcasts are elegant anti-heroes and ordinary people mere cattle – is an appealing refuge. Her books have played a significant part in the development of the Goth subculture, both feeding off each other like mutually dependent bloodsuckers.

The secretary of the Vampyre Society – the British club for aficionados of the undead – spoke to me in 1997 about the impact of Rice on the Gothic and vampire scene: 'She's changed the angle on vampirism. Before her popularity, we didn't get as many Romantic types who dressed in eighteenth-century and Victorian costume joining. We have younger members who don't know life before Anne Rice, as it were. She's well-loved, but not exclusively.'

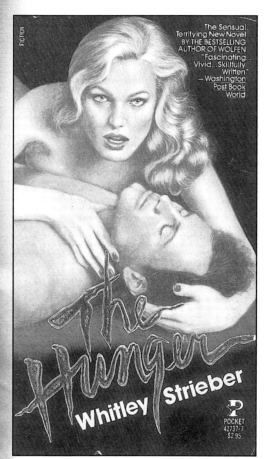

Whitley Strieber's erotic vampire novel The Hunger – *filmed in 1983 as a Goth cult movie featuring David Bowie and Goth-rock pioneers Bauhaus.*

Indeed, in *Udolpho*, journal of the Gothic Society, John Walton penned a broadside entitled 'The Trouble with Anne Rice'. Walton's charge is that Rice makes reference to giants of literature and philosophy – such as Shakespeare and Sartre – while 'the quality of her work is unable to sustain the allusions she makes.' In Walton's view, Rice is a pseudo-intellectual, a poseur. The modern horror novelist can't win: write plain-speaking, populist horror, like King, and be accused of churning out trash; write evocative, romantic horror, heavy with historical and literary allusions, like Rice, and be accused of rising above your station.

These critiques of Rice clearly sting – she makes no secret of her desire to be regarded as an author of literary fiction. Perhaps this explains why some members of the Goth subculture tends to reject Rice as 'softcore' Gothic. The Gothic must subvert to survive. It must feed upon taboos. Gothic horror maintained its outcast status during the 1980s, therefore, by making a 'big scary leap' on the same scale as when the case of Ed Gein entered the public domain.

The new movement was first identified at the 1986 World Fantasy Convention, held in Providence, Rhode Island, as a tribute to the city's famous son, H. P. Lovecraft. But while Lovecraft had found certain horrors 'indescribable', the new aesthetic was all about refusing to avert your gaze from even the most unendurable sights. The debate was initially about 'quiet' versus 'loud' horror – in the loud corner, very vocal indeed, was the American author David J. Schow.

Schow had decided that the graphic horror being produced by the genre's hip, hungry, young writers needed a buzzword. 'Cyberpunk' had already been coined to describe the cool, pessimistic new wave of science fiction that would usher in an age of computer-generated alternative realities. Half in jest, Schow suggested horror's savage new generation should be defined as 'splatterpunks'. The term stuck, but, in the same way 'Gothic' itself had once been a dismissive term for anything barbaric and tasteless, 'splatterpunk' was often used as an insult to authors who favoured sex, savagery and shock. Many of the authors themselves were dubious about embracing such a provocative label, just as many of the dark 'alternative' bands of the golden age of Goth-rock disdained 'Goth' as a restrictive pigeonhole.

Nevertheless, a loose coalition of writers formed – with Schow and the double act of John Skipp and Craig Spector at its black heart – who were dubbed 'the splat-pack'. More than one commentator observed that the shades and black leather-clad splat-pack looked more like a mean Goth-biker rock combo than a group of authors (in fact, Skipp and Spector were also musicians) and there was a danger of style overtaking substance. In 1990, author and film critic Paul M. Sammon attempted to define the movement in *Splatterpunks: Extreme Horror*, an anthology of short stories by various candidates (albeit often reluctant ones) for the splat pack, tail-ended with an essay by the editor entitled 'Outlaws', which examined the whole phenomenon.

Sammon traces the roots of this 'outlaw' fiction to literary terrorists such as the Marquis de Sade and Decadent poet Charles Baudelaire. The splatterpunk generation had been brought up beneath the mushroom cloud of Cold War paranoia, on a diet of explicit horror movies like *The Exorcist*, angry rock music like the Dead Kennedys, hardcore porn like *Deep Throat*. They were a kind of Generation XXX – cynical, streetwise and insatiably curious, writers who, according to Sammon, 'understand the allure of outrageousness. They are the epitome of black humour, stand-up comics for the apocalypse. And their fiction sweeps across the page like hot actinic searchlights, probing the darkest corners of our souls.'

The movement's many critics dismissed it as 'carnography' – exploiting gore and violence just as pornography exploits sex and desire. But splatterpunk wasn't just about sticking a needle in the eye of taboos about sex, violence, child abuse, cancer or whatever else, it was about a determination to gaze upon the world in all of its glorious horror and unspeakable beauty. It was about rebellion, youth and excitement, replacing horror's traditional clichés with references to today's trash culture in the form of TV shows, fast food and rock music. 'These stories carry profound subtexts,' Sammon insisted, 'harrowing insights into our own sick and shining twentieth century. Within every evisceration you will find humour's darkest entrails; beside every seeming adolescent gross-out, the most serious adult concerns.'

Gothic is a living tradition, and splatterpunk surely deserved its place at the table (even if its table manners could use some work). 'The Father of Splatterpunk', David J. Schow, was also the movement's most energetic polemicist via his witty 'Raving and Drooling' column for 'gorehound bible', *Fangoria*. Schow's strengths as an author lie in his ability to change tempo – from scenes of stomach-churning gore to moments of heart-rending sentimentality. Seldom is this more evident than in his co-written screenplay for Goth celluloid icon, *The Crow*. The film is harsher, arguably sharper than its comic-book source, with its black-leather chic, vivid violence, and the Goth-industrial soundtrack replacing the comic's literary references.

Just behind Schow in the line-up of splatterpunk's 'usual suspects' was the dread duo of Skipp and Spector. While they wrote powerful, howling prose, they've inappropriately been compared to Stephen King on account of the fierce morality that insists good triumph over evil after a bloodthirsty struggle. The best example is in their 1987 novel, *The Cleanup* – the tale of how a loser musician is gifted with supernatural power that he uses to set the world to rights, until he realises his 'gift' comes at a terrible price (another update of the 'careful

what you wish for' plot of 'The Monkey's Paw'). In one scene set in New York's Central Park, seemingly based on the infamous 'wilding' case that shocked the city in the late 1980s, the hero transforms himself into a pretty jogger in order to ensnare a pair of rapists. When his attackers pounce, he fatally brands one with the legend 'Rapist', and transforms the other into a nubile woman, challenging 'her' to make it home in an act of savagely poetic justice.

Perhaps their greatest contributions to splatterpunk are *The Book of the Dead* (1989) and *The Book of the Dead 2: Still Dead* (1992). Featuring the genre's darkest stars, these pioneering splatterpunk showcases were based loosely around the world created in director George Romero's classic trilogy of zombie

Interview with the Vampire: Anne Rice (left) was initially dismayed at the 1994 casting of Tom Cruise as Lestat and Brad Pitt as Louis – seen here feasting on a barmaid.

movies – *Night of the Living Dead* (1968), *Dawn of the Dead* (1979), *Day of the Dead* (1985) – where the dead revive as shambling corpses who crave human flesh. The first of the gory trilogy caused a stunned Robert Bloch to wonder, 'What's going to come out of those people who think that *Night of the Living Dead* isn't enough?' *The Book of the Dead* answered Bloch's rhetorical question. The editors' introduction, 'On Going too Far, or, Flesh Eating Fiction: New Hope for the Future', pleaded an articulate case for splatterpunk. 'We, the inhabitants of the latter half of the twentieth century, ride a razor's edge,' observed Skipp and Spector. 'A new dark age beckons on the one side. A renaissance, on the other. If there is any hope for the future, it must rest on the ability to stare unflinchingly into the heart of darkness.'

If Skipp and Spector (and indeed David Schow, in the 1988 cinema-themed horror anthology *Silver Scream*) show the influence of explicit horror movies on splatterpunk, then Clive Barker provides evidence of the influence of pornography. The multi-talented Englishman was described as the 'patron saint' of splatterpunk after the publication of his remarkable six-volume *Books of Blood* (1984-6), anthologising graphic tales of copulation and evisceration. Talking to Douglas E. Winter in the 1980s, Barker declared, 'There is a very strong lobby that says that you can show too much. Wrong. Not for me. You can never show too much. I'm sitting there with my popcorn and my enthusiasm, and I'm saying "Come on, man, do it for me. Whatever you want to do, *do it*."' He described his aims to *Film Threat* magazine, in 1989, as not being simply to unsettle his readers or audience, but to 'subvert them, throw over their ideas about the status quo, throw over their ideas about sexuality, throw over their ideas about death.'

Barker's chief technique lay in exploring the territory between abnormality, sexuality and death. 'Sex is about a little madness – how often is horror about madness?' he said to Winter. 'Sex is about a little death – how often is horror about death? It's about the body – how often is horror about the body?' In plain terms, this translated into surreal stories with a particular focus on transformation (particularly between genders) and perverse sexuality (particularly sadomasochism). If Skipp and Spector's *Book of the Dead* took things further than zombie director George Romero ever could, then Barker's *Books of Blood* created bizarre scenarios that would shock the most jaded porn director.

While Anne Rice offered up her elegant vampires as icons of sensuous seduction, Barker's demons were a harsh, riskier version of the Gothic vision. The Cenobites, from his story 'The Hellbound Heart', were immortalised in his film *Hellraiser* (1987) – angels of agony for a new breed of Goths who made the move from nightclubs like the Batcave to fetish clubs like the Torture Garden, adopting sadomasochism as a transgressive fashion statement. If the Goth subculture of the 1980s were influenced by the vampire chic of Rice's decadent anti-heroes, in the next decade Barker's marriage of pleasure and pain became a much more powerful theme.

By the last decades of the twentieth century, respected writers like Angela Carter – and the academics who studied them – began to give a certain respectability to Gothic fiction, which, as she noted, had 'not been dealt with kindly by the literati'. That this situation has slowly been changing over the last twenty years is due in no small part to Carter's own 'profane' gothic tales of 'mirrors; the externalised self; forsaken castles; haunted forests; forbidden sexual objects,' and her revisionist fairy tales, where dream logic exposes the very adult horrors hiding in her haunted woods and ghostly castles.

Carter recaptured the savagery and darkness of the original fairy story, removed by subsequent generations who considered such material threatening to childhood innocence. In the 1979 anthology *The Bloody Chamber*, folk tales like 'Little Red Riding Hood' and 'Bluebeard' were re-interpreted as tales of lust, blood and coming-of-age, transplanted from the world of 'once upon a time' to more familiar locales. Perhaps Carter's most modern spin was to turn them into myths of feminine empowerment, where the female prey turn the tables on their male predators: Red Riding Hood tames the rapacious wolf; the wife-murdering anti-hero Bluebeard is slain by his mother-in-law.

In analysing the Gothic genre, Carter described its main themes as 'incest and cannibalism. Characters and events are exaggerated beyond reality to become symbols, ideas, passions. Its style will tend to be ornate, unnatural – and thus operate against the perennial human desire to see the word as fact. Its only humour is black humour. It retains a singular moral function – that of provoking unease.'

In 1991, an anthology entitled *The New Gothic* was published to spotlight some of those seen as the leading lights of the modern Gothic genre. Alongside a story by Angela Carter is a piece by Ruth Rendell (a British psychological crime writer whose narratives can be unusually bleak) concerning an old woman descending into panic on a London underground train. Joyce Carrol Oates was an obvious contributor, her 1980 philosophical novel, *Bellefleur*, hailed in academic circles as *the* classic of modern American Gothic. The novel follows the fortunes of six generations of the Bellefleur dynasty, from the early 1800s onwards. This is not, however, a Waltons-style all-American family, but a vision of the formation of modern America through a dark lens. The publisher's blurb describes members of the family such as 'a baby, Germaine – the heroine of the novel – who is born with the lower half of her male twin protruding from her abdomen; [and] a female vampire who, in her girlhood had a passionate but doomed affair.'

Peter Straub, one of America's more subtle horror novelists, also made a contribution to *The New Gothic*, as did Anne Rice – albeit half-heartedly, offering an excerpt from *The Vampire Chronicles*. Perhaps Rice's reticence was wise. *The New Gothic* falls short of the claim that it 'reanimates – and reinvents – the genre of Mary Shelley and Edgar Allan Poe'. Essentially backward-looking, the anthology feels self-conscious, anaemic, aimless, trapped between genre and literary fiction.

Nevertheless, there were other writers, like Oates, who crossed bookstores from the shameful shadows of the horror section to the general fiction shelves, using the newly respectable 'Gothic' or 'Decadent' tag as a passport. Among the most interesting of these is Patrick McGrath, co-editor of *The New Gothic* and a talent in his own right with darkly delightful novels such as *The Grotesque* and *Dr Haggard's Disease*. McGrath lists Gothic greats such as Matthew Lewis, J. Sheridan Le Fanu and Bram Stoker as literary influences, while his fiction travels from claustrophobic, Peake-style fantasies to grim historical sagas, via the lunatic fringes of reality.

It doesn't take a psychiatrist to identify the origins of McGrath's fiction of obsession, hate and perversion. In an interview with *Udolpho*, the author revealed a childhood rooted in the

Gothic, devouring the long-running *Pan Book of Horror Stories* anthologies before discovering Poe at the age of twelve. An oddball child (or perhaps ' a member of a secret cabal of screwed up kids'), his hobbies were keeping snakes and collecting toilet chains. 'But my father's work – he ran Broadmoor [the UK's most notorious facility for the criminally insane] for 25 years – was the strongest influence on my developing imagination,' explained McGrath. 'The men and women he treated had all, while insane, committed violent and often bizarre crimes. So while I was still young I was introduced to extreme forms of human behaviour, and the curiosity and fascination inspired by this early exposure to madness has served me from the very start of my career as a writer.'

While McGrath is the modern author to whom the term 'Gothic' is most readily applied, the distinction of being thought a modern 'Decadent' belongs to David Madsen. Madsen's debut, *Memoirs of a Gnostic Dwarf*, takes the reader back to Renaissance Rome. But instead of immersing himself in the artistic and intellectual achievements of this golden age, Madsen conjures a world very much of the body, which a *Sunday Times* critic described approvingly as 'scatological and bloody . . . grotesque, fruity and filthy'. The follow-up, *Confessions of a Flesh Eater*, also attracted surprising plaudits for its contemporary tale of a highly-sophisticated misogynist named Orlando Crispe, whose preoccupation with the sensuality of flesh leads him to cannibalistic excesses. The spirit of Ed Gein is not only alive and well, but appears to have got himself a college education.

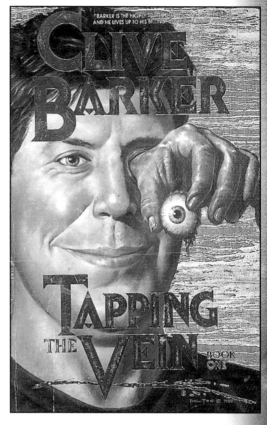

Clive Barker's groundbreaking Books of Blood *were adapted into graphic novel form as* Tapping the Vein.

In 1991, that same spirit gate-crashed the environs of mainstream literature in the form of Bret Easton Ellis' *American Psycho* – depicting brutal serial murder in parodically-explicit detail. This work of carnography was camouflaged as a critique of consumerist society, and succeeded in maintaining its author's high profile through controversy. The jury is still out as to its literary value, but as a personal aside, this writer can testify to a disturbing number of women who privately confess they find it a 'sexy book'. This twisted erotic subtext is (one hopes) coincidental, but in the case of another, superior exploration of serial murder it's far nearer the surface. Poppy Z. Brite's 1996 *Exquisite Corpse* is based upon her fascination with two gay serial killers – the American Jeffrey Dahmer and the Englishman Dennis Nilsen –

combined with her erotic interest in male homosexuality. The novel is breathtakingly perverse, fictionalising Dahmer and Nilsen as romantic cannibals, the only possible vindication being Wilde's dictum that books can only be judged as to whether they are 'well written or badly written'. In these terms, Brite's book passes with flying colours while Ellis' is a more dubious proposition.

One of the many charges laid at splatterpunk's door was misogyny – despite the fact that, in splatterpunk fiction, *everybody* is a candidate for dying viscerally and violently. But one of the flaws of Paul M. Sammon's *Splatterpunks* anthology was a dearth of female contributors – only two among seventeen writers – which didn't reflect the increasing number of women working in the field. It also strengthened the argument that splatterpunk had little to do with true Gothic, which has always had a powerful, even dominant, feminine aspect.

Of the two women included, Nancy A. Collins debuted in 1989 with her novel *Sunglasses After Dark*, which introduced the character of Sonja Blue and attained a level of cult status. Like Anne Rice, Collins was based in New Orleans and happily exploited the erotic overtones of the legend. But Sonja Blue is more Punk than Goth – a vampire bitch turned vampire-hunter, willing to get her hands dirty (and bloody) in ways Rice's dark dandies would never consider. Collins emphasises that much of her output fits the Southern Gothic mode of American literature, which addresses degeneracy and insanity rather than the supernatural, but she represents an axis where Deep South decadence meets a far more abrasive, streetwise attitude.

Sammon corrected the gender imbalance of his first anthology with the 1995 follow-up *Splatterpunks II: Over the Edge*, which predominantly showcased female talent. By this point, however, splatterpunk was a spent movement that, like its punk rock namesake, burned itself out in a few short years with the heat of its own intensity. (Clive Barker, for one, had long since moved on from horror to the 'magic fiction' first signalled by his 1987 novel *Weaveworld* – although his 2001 novel, *Coldheart Canyon*, which evokes a Barkeresque idea of Hollywood invaded by Hell, is something of a return to fearsome form.) But *Splatterpunks II* at least allowed Sammon to rectify the omission of Poppy Z. Brite from the first collection, by including the typically weird, warped and wonderful piece 'Xenophobia'. Brite retrospectively resisted attempts to portray her as the leading female light of the splat-pack. 'Splatterpunk doesn't exist,' she observed dismissively. 'Writers only form "movements" when they're drunk, and I gave up drinking. However, I do love the fact that a lot of women are now writing visceral, erotic horror.'

Like Rice and Collins, Brite exploded upon the scene with a vampire novel, the 1992 classic, *Lost Souls*. Written and located, naturally, in New Orleans, and dealing with the undead in a highly eroticised fashion, it begged comparisons with Rice's Gothic milieu and Collins' punk attitude. Again, as with splatterpunk, Brite was keen to distance herself from these comparisons. Brite wrote *Lost Souls*, she later intimated, while 'involved with the Gothic/deather subculture at the time – the music, the clothes and make-up, the affinity for graveyards, the bloodletting. That was what I wanted to write about, and vampires are an essential icon of that culture. These kids are beautiful, alienated, at once craving wild experiences and romanticising death. Is it any wonder they identify with vampires?'

*Angela Carter's Gothic fairytales were brought to the big screen by
Neil Jordan as* The Company of Wolves *(1984).*

The book plays out to a soundtrack of Gothic-industrial sounds like the Cure and Nine Inch Nails, while its title refers to a fictional Goth band that has the misfortune to encounter a nomadic clique of vampires. These are significantly different bloodsuckers to Rice's cultured creatures of the night – pierced and tattooed wild children, amoral Goths who, in the absence of the restraints imposed by mortality, lose themselves in the pursuit of pleasure.

One of the many interesting aspects of *Lost Souls* – indeed, of much of Brite's work – is the almost total absence of female characters. In direct contrast to the gentle lesbian archetype of Le Fanu's sapphic vampire 'Carmilla', Brite's bloodsuckers are almost as intent on sucking sperm as the red stuff, and graphic homosexuality rears its head with a regularity that borders on comedy. If the sex scenes had been heterosexual, there's little doubt critics would have treated the self-indulgent eroticism less charitably – as it was, it earned her an award nomination for 'gay, lesbian, bisexual and transgendered writing' by the Lambda Literary

Foundation. Much homo-eroticism is implicit in the world of Anne Rice, and she enjoys considerable success in the growing gay market, but in Brite's world it's unrepentantly explicit. If Anne Rice is softcore Goth for the romantically-inclined, then Poppy Brite is hardcore for the post-splatterpunk generation.

Brite's follow-up to Lost Souls, *Drawing Blood*, was, despite its title, not a vampire novel. Instead it focuses on a house haunted by the memories of a bloody crime – though, as the house is occupied by a gay couple, again cocksucking is more prevalent than bloodsucking. One particularly interesting theme introduced in the novel is that of hacking and cyberspace – which were becoming increasingly dominant in the Goth subculture, reflected in those who had begun referring to themselves as 'cybergoths'.

Unsurprisingly, Poppy Z. Brite maintains an impressive presence on the web, not least via the Pandora Station (Pandora being the woman in Greek mythology whose curiosity unleashed chaos and horror into the world) – a 'Pleasurecraft of Renegade Sex Goddesses' she shares with two other female authors who also write 'visceral, erotic horror'. Together, they help mark out the direction of Gothic literature in the 21st century. The second member of the trio, Caitlin Kiernan, first began making waves in 1998 with her debut novel, the award-winning *Silk*, and a series for the Vertigo Comic imprint, entitled *The Girl Who Would Be Death*. The latter was based loosely upon

Neil Gaiman's *Death*, although the character never appears. As Kiernan explains, it was 'not so much a story about Death as it is a story about those whose *lives* have became entangled with her effects on the world,' and the author never falls into the trap of making the story a simple pastiche or tribute. Instead, she creates an evocative tale of occult obsession set against the now familiar backdrop of New Orleans drinking dens. Kiernan describes her style as 'goth*noir*', and her growing status was confirmed the following year, when Clive Barker contributed photos to an illustrated limited edition of *Silk*, while she composed a musical accompaniment CD. *Silk* also won Kiernan an award from the International Horror Guild.

Kiernan, like Brite, has roots in the Goth subculture, and sang with a band called Death's Little Sister (another tribute to Gaiman's Death character) based in Athens, Georgia during 1996-7. 'I think we were the only Goth band Athens had ever seen, at least since the eighties, and there were a lot of confused faces in the crowd,' she recalled of their Hallowe'en debut performance. 'We had these two huge jack-o'-lanterns burning on stage and *The Cabinet of Dr Caligari* playing on a big screen behind us. People actually seemed scared of us. But at least nobody booed.'

The third member of the Pandora triumverate is Christa Faust, who also appears in Paul Sammon's *Splatterpunks II* anthology. 'She has worked as a 25-cent peep girl, exotic dancer, tarot card reader, performance artist, and panhandler,' explains her truncated biography. 'Currently she sings backup for Skipp and Spector's band Blood Brothers [the side-project that split when the Skipp-Spector writing partnership broke up in 1993]. Throw in some underground comics, some weird flicks, and some loud raunchy music and you have Faust's literary DNA.'

Ms Faust is also married to the founder of the splatterpunk movement, David Schow. In familiar splatterpunk fashion, she explores the territory between sex and death – not only in her fiction, but also in her dayjob. For, after working as a stripper and becoming interested in sadomasochism and bondage, Faust became a professional dominatrix. More recently she has taken the helm of the Gothic erotica website *Necromantic Online*, featuring 'original lascivious fiction' and 'fearless non-fiction on erotic topics ranging from eroticism in horror movies to necrophilia'. All of which may seem a long way from the work of Mary Shelley, let alone Anne Radcliffe (although the Marquis de Sade may have felt quite at home).

Count Dracula, the character conceived out of Victorian repression, however, remains the most powerful Gothic icon. Stoker created the undead lord as a personification of predatory sexuality, surrounded by his life-sucking brides who embody a fear of feminine power. But perspectives have changed. In a 1995 article entitled 'Love Bites', in the fetish-fashion journal *Skin Two*, J. Sebastian Blockley muses on the significance of the male vampire 'as a misunderstood hero . . . because of his action as a "liberating" force for females: an affirmation that it is not wrong to be proactive and sexually voracious. In *Dracula* it may well be that the sexually dominant female is meant to be feared and overcome, but we no longer read it in that way . . . This appears to be borne out by the dress code of modern female Goth "cultists"; they never choose the innocent submissive virgin (Mina) role to complement their male counterpart's "Dracula": they step out as equals, their vampy elegance signifying some imagined past aristocratic code (defiant Lucys).' A new generation of creatures of the night is emerging for the new millennium, confident in their power over sex and death. At the same time, Gothic literature has never been as dangerous or exciting.

Chapter IV

Stay Tuned For Terror

Gothic Television & Radio

How significant is the cathode-ray tube to a culture that idolises the past, yearns for an era of candlelight and shadow and an escape from the artificial glow and 24-hour surveillance culture in which we now live? In his book, *Gothic*, Richard Davenport-Hines is in little doubt as to TV's significance to the aesthetic today, dubbing it 'the most important medium for gothic infiltration'.

'Televised histrionics belong in the gothic tradition,' he argues, 'afternoon talk-shows, with their carefully-staged, emotionally intensive demonising, most significantly construct gothic villains whose transgressions sustain an unspeakable cycle of despoilation and ruin. The difference between Ann Radcliffe's villains and Oprah Winfrey's is that, in modern America, when villains confess publicly, they disavow responsibility.' *Oprah* as Gothic? Only if one accepts that anything with any dark content at all, or any element of staged theatricality, is Gothic. More typically, talk shows have been instrumental in drumming up the moral panics that scapegoat society's outsiders and misfits, such as members of the Goth subculture.

In direct contrast to the Gothic aesthetic, which revels in dark secrets and mystery, television is a conformist medium that simplifies and demystifies in order to explain the world. Despite this, TV's insatiable appetite for material ensured it would plunder Gothic culture. But in the folksy, conservative world of TV, even pop-horror author, Stephen King, is outrageously exotic. He's written TV scripts, and evidently disliked the experience, dubbing

Buffy (Sarah Michelle Gellar), the MTV generation's favourite vampire slayer, meets Dracula, that grandaddy of them all, portrayed as a byronic young Goth.

Elvira may have bigger pumpkins, but Vampira – whose Goth gal look was inspired by the underground fetish magazines of the day – was the original horror hostess.

television 'the endless gobbler of talent . . . the hungry maw, the bottomless pit of shit.' On a slightly more conciliatory note, King concedes, 'television has really asked the impossible of its handful of horror programs – to terrify without really terrifying, to horrify without really horrifying, to sell audiences a lot of sizzle and no steak.'

Much has changed since King wrote those words in 1981, and perhaps we will look back on the 1990s and early 21st century as the golden age of small-screen Gothic. *Danse Macabre*, King's personal survey of horror in the mass media, begins in the 1950s, when Hollywood was worried that competition from television would spell financial ruin. The two media actually developed a symbiotic, rather than combative, relationship – it was radio that suffered from the rise of television.

Once home to a host of programmes, radio is now reduced to begging for commercial scraps from TV's table. King, born in 1947, observes that he is 'of the last quarter of the last generation that remembers radio drama as an active force – a dramatic art form with its own set of reality.' He remembers families gathering around the radio in the same way people subsequently gathered around the TV set, often to be thrilled and chilled by Gothic drama.

Radio was especially well suited to genres that required an active imagination, such as Gothic horror – the only limitations being the imaginative capabilities of the radio dramatist and his audience. While film has to show us demons, radio need only suggest them. As Stephen King put it, 'radio deposited to that bank of imagination rather than making withdrawals.'

Perhaps the early radio series remembered with the greatest fondness is *The Shadow*, which ran from 1930 to 1954, the golden age of radio drama. It began as a series of unrelated crime stories. The title character, originating from the pulp magazines, provided continuity as narrator. In 1937, however, a young Orson Welles took up the role of the Shadow, making him the show's protagonist, while a menagerie of monsters was added to the roster of bad guys. The Shadow was a creepy crime-fighter with strange powers learned in the Orient, most notably 'the hypnotic power to cloud men's minds so they cannot see him'. In the tradition of the Gothic comic-book heroes who succeeded the pulps, such as the Batman, the Shadow is as frightening as the villains he opposes. 'Who knows what evil lurks in the hearts of men? The Shadow knows!' he would declare with a gale of unnerving laughter, leaving a distinct ambiguity about what lurked in his own heart.

Most Gothic radio series consisted of self-contained horror plays, introduced by a regular host. Probably the first of these anthology shows was *The Witch's Tale*, which promised 'weird blood-chilling tales told by Old Nancy, the Witch of Salem, and Satan the wise black cat'. The show opened in 1931 – the same year Universal Studios discovered horror as a lucrative new film genre. Stars of this new genre, like Boris Karloff and Peter Lorre, also found employment as radio actors in ghoulish shows such as *Inner Sanctum Mysteries* (1941-51) and *Suspense* (1942-62). The real star of *Inner Sanctum*, however, was its host, Raymond Johnson – known to rapt listeners simply as Raymond. The show's trademark opening was a squeaking door that slammed shut again at the play's shock ending, with a mockingly insincere wish that the audience have 'pleasant dreams '. Many credit Raymond as the prototype of the sardonic horror host, a gleefully sinister archetype now familiar to readers of horror comics and viewers of TV horror shows.

Most radio connoisseurs maintain that the best of the bunch was *Lights Out*, created by writer Arch Oboler, which ran from 1934-47. Stephen King attributes the series' success to Oboler appreciating radio drama's main strengths and applying them to the horror genre: 'the mind's innate obedience, its willingness to try to see whatever someone suggests it see, no matter how absurd.' The most powerful aspect of Oboler's shows was their explicit horror, evoked long before gore could be realised effectively on screen. 'Some of the appalling mental images were created by the simplest means,' recalls David J. Skal in *The Monster Show*. 'Sizzling bacon held up to the microphone became the sound of electrocution. Broken bones were simulated by cracking spareribs with a pipe wrench. Squishy cooked pasta could conjure cannibalism. Oboler's innovative use of sound effects to create terror and suspense was without equal – not surprising, since he pioneered many of those techniques himself.' As these disturbing scenes were only suggested, they were obviously products of the listener's own mind. Critics had a tough job attacking *Lights Out*, when the writer could legitimately point out that anyone who 'saw' anything truly disturbing had ultimately created the scene for themselves.

By the 1950s the heyday of radio drama was over. The more successful Gothic horror shows made a bid to move with the times and onto the small screen – *Lights Out*, *Inner Sanctum* and *Suspense* were all produced as TV series – but none could echo the atmospheric intensity of their radio days. Significantly, *Inner Sanctum*'s sardonic host, Raymond (now played by Paul

McGrath), chose to stay off-camera, while the show's trademark squeaking door, as Stephen King observes, 'certainly was horrible enough – slightly askew, festooned with cobwebs – but it was something of a relief, just the same. Nothing could have looked as horrible as that door *sounded.*'

Gothic radio drama didn't die in the 1950s, but it slumped into a dignified semi-retirement. The earliest efforts to reproduce the success of radio Gothic on the small screen were handicapped by tiny budgets, sparse sets and not-very-special effects. Threadbare productions like *Hands of Murder* (1949-51) and *Tales of the Black Cat* (1950) were pioneering curiosities. *Alfred Hitchcock Presents*, which started in 1955, mostly featured the porcine English director introducing, with ironic detachment, the murder mysteries he was best known for on the big screen. But the show did make occasional forays into the Gothic, such as 'Speciality of the House' – which dealt with an exclusive club for gourmets with a penchant for human flesh (the same story, penned by Stanley Ellin, was later dramatised for radio in *The Price of Fear*).

More satisfying from a Gothic perspective was *Thriller* (1960-2), which employed the charms of horror-movie icon Boris Karloff. Karloff was then in his twilight years and suffering from chronic arthritis – dating back to wearing the punishing Frankenstein Monster costume in the early 1930s – but nevertheless maintained the dedication to his craft that made him so well-loved. *Thriller* too began as a vehicle for orthodox crime stories, but hit its stride adapting the classics of supernatural fiction published by pulp magazines like *Weird Tales* in the 1920s and '30s. The cream of the creeps was the oddly-titled 'Pigeons from Hell', from the original short story by Robert E. Howard – a pen pal of H. P. Lovecraft, best known for creating *Conan the Barbarian*. 'Pigeons from Hell' is a bayou-bound haunted house story, where two brothers are forced to seek shelter in an apparently deserted mansion when their car breaks down. But they aren't alone and find themselves stalked by an inhuman horror known as 'the Zuvenbie'. 'The atmosphere is supremely creepy,' enthuses *The Penguin Encyclopedia of Horror and the Supernatural*, 'the scene in which a man wakes in a deserted mansion to a weird trilling and sees his companion stalking stiffly down a set of stairs through bars of moonlight clutching a gore-clotted hatchet is one of the most hair-raising moments in horror literature.' In the hands of *Thriller*'s producers, 'Pigeons from Hell' also became one of the most hair-raising hours in horror television.

But ironically, Gothic culture's greatest impact on TV came from the small screen's taming of its most venerable icons. Titans of terror like Count Dracula and Frankenstein's Monster became kitsch heroes for children. Bram Stoker's demonic vampire, was gradually transformed into the amiable foam-rubber Count who teaches kids arithmetic on *Sesame Street*. Children nagged their parents to buy them cloyingly-sugary breakfast cereals like Count Chocula and Frankenberry. Such a radical transformation could only have been achieved via the trivialising influence of television.

In 1958, Universal Pictures, desperate once more for cash, licensed 52 of their old horror pictures for syndication on the small screen. Released as *Shock Theatre*, the series introduced a whole new generation to the black-and-white Gothic classics of Universal's golden age. It was hosted by one John Zacherle, a presenter with a background in radio, who took to the screen

The Addams Family – *cartoonist Charles Addams' dysfunctional nuclear unit, as brought to the primetime TV audience. Morticia Addams was a Goth chick prototype.*

first as 'Roland', and then 'Zacherly', a cadaverous character resembling a mortician, who practised his craft on himself. Zacherly became a cult figure among the young, making hugely popular personal appearances, releasing the hit single 'Dinner with Drac', and even running a mock presidential campaign.

While many of the movies revived for *Shock Theatre* justified their revival, many more were of a dubious quality, and Zacherly made his name enlivening the duller flicks with madcap antics. He used laughably cheap props, such as a cauliflower for a brain in a mock transplant skit, and a largely non-existent cast of support players – his dead wife, referred to as 'My Dear', was represented by a small coffin with a stake protruding from it. In addition, Zacherly parodied the more sub-standard movies in the series. With his mordant sardonicism, he clearly owed much to *Inner Sanctum*'s Raymond – although he took the whole thing to new levels of hysteria and indignity.

If Zacherly's spiritual Goth-father was radio pioneer Raymond, then the horror-show host's metaphorical mother must surely be TV's original funereal *femme*, Vampira. While Zacherly took the whole of America by storm, Vampira remained in the Los Angeles area and never hit the big time – but she would ultimately be far more influential than John Zacherle's walking cadaver. Vampira was the creation of Finnish-born beauty Maila Nurmi, who invented the character to present the horror-movie slot on the Californian KABC-TV network a full four years before *Shock Theatre* made its debut. As the prospect of a successful Hollywood acting career was diminishing fast, Nurmi put everything into the character. She fashioned her ferocious nails from heavy black plastic, and underwent a harrowing programme of what amounted to body-modification in order to achieve her striking 38-17-36 figure. Most punishingly, she wore home-made corsets made from rubber inner tubes – massaging papaya powder (the main constituent of meat tenderiser) and cold cream cocktail into her midriff just to get into the constrictive garment.

David Skal recalls her stunning on-screen entrance with evident warmth: 'From the impossible waistline swelled the cartoon bosom of a sex goddess, barely contained by the stiletto neckline plunge of a formfitting, tattered black rayon cocktail dress. The figure slinked past a floor-standing candelabra, fixed its gaze on the camera like a cobra seeking its prey. Three-inch-long black nails seemed to drip, rather than grow, from the ends of her fingers. Her eyebrows arched and loomed like boomerangs from beyond the grave. Nearing the camera, she raised talon-like fingers to serpentine hair. And then she screamed – a piercing banshee's wail of anguish.'

I met Maila Nurmi in 1993, and asked her about the origins of her Goth archetype character. 'The Dragon Lady in [the comic strip] *Terry and the Pirates* inspired it,' explained the charming veteran actress. 'A lot of the inspiration came from Disney as well – the Evil Queen in *Snow White*, for example. Then there was Theda Bara and Norma Desmond in *Sunset Boulevard* – all of this seeped into me, melded and came out as Vampira. I loved it when the lighting men gave me cadaverous features – I love cadaverous things. I was trying to be the most beautiful woman in the world. I knew that I was naturally quite ugly and the challenge was to try and hide my ugliness behind all of this artifice. I did meet with some success because I still receive mail saying how beautiful they thought Vampira was.'

There was a level of eroticism to the character – she might take a bubble bath in a boiling cauldron, for example – that lent Vampira a necrophilic sexiness that appealed to an adult audience. Nurmi has also credited the legendary underground fetish magazine of the 1950s, *Bizarre*, as an influence, for its images of domination and bondage. In effect, Vampira, midway between a vampire and a dominatrix, was the first walking, talking pop-culture version of the Decadent *femme fatale*. She was also a powerful prototype for the modern Goth babe, predating the subculture's adoption of fetish-wear as fashion by over three decades.

Vampira was a sensation on her Hollywood debut in 1954. Never out of costume, her morbid celebrity got her into the most exclusive clubs and restaurants, and she was instantly recognised beneath her black parasol, cruising the streets of LA in a Packard convertible.

She struck up a friendship with James Dean, then a struggling young actor, who appeared in one of her sketches to be disciplined by Vampira in dominatrix-librarian mode. On the surface it was an unlikely relationship. But Dean, who was to become Hollywood's angst-ridden eternal adolescent, had a death fixation that evidently found fulfilment in Vampira's company. It wasn't to last. Nurmi became embroiled in a dispute with her employers over the rights to the Vampira character, and the studios turned their collective back on the sinister sex kitten.

As Vampira's star began falling and his own began to rise, the self-obsessed Dean also turned his back on his erstwhile friend, publicly dismissing her as 'a cartoon', implying he had hoped she might possess some authentic occult powers but had been disappointed. Subsequent events give an ironic twist to Dean's petulance. Desperately trying to keep her career alive, Nurmi posed for some pin-up pictures in the famous Forest Lawn cemetery. She sent one of the shots, with her posed on the edge of a grave, to Dean, inscribed with the legend, 'Having a wonderful time – wish you were here.' He never received it – an employee, interpreting the black joke as a threat, confiscated the photo shortly before Dean died in a 1955 car wreck. The tabloid papers maintained he was also the victim of a curse by the 'black madonna', Vampira, producing the graveyard photo as evidence, its inscription suitably altered to read, 'Darling come join me!'

Such unwelcome media attention did nothing to rescue her ailing career and, in 1956, she reached the bottom of the Hollywood pile when she 'starred' in Ed Wood's *Plan 9 from Outer Space* (not to be released for another three years). For her part, Vampira only appeared for a few scant minutes and refused to speak any of the absurd lines Wood had written for her. Like co-star, Bela Lugosi, who died early in production, Nurmi gave birth to a Gothic creation she just couldn't escape. Asked to a Hallowe'en party by an admirer decades later, she forcefully declined with the bleak lament, 'My whole life has been a Hallowe'en party!'

Nevertheless, Nurmi's ghoulish sex kitten lives on. She was portrayed in Tim Burton's 1994 Oscar-winning *Ed Wood* biopic by Burton's then fiancee, Lisa Marie. More controversially, in the 1980s an actress named Cassandra Peterson took to the small screen as Elvira, a horny horror hostess reminiscent of Vampira. Just how reminiscent she was became the subject of a court battle, when Nurmi tried to sue Peterson for breach of copyright. It's easy to feel sympathy for the ill-fated Maila Nurmi, but Elvira is distinctly more sassy and less sepulchral than Vampira (and even more cartoonishly top-heavy). Nurmi was unsuccessful, and Elvira continues to go from strength to strength, with comic books, albums and her second film, *Elvira's Haunted Hills*, slated for a 2002 release. The official Elvira costume rated as the most popular female rental in the US over the Hallowe'en period in 2000, proving that she truly is America's favourite Mistress of the Dark.

Maila Nurmi's entry into her lifelong Hallowe'en party began with a high-profile 1953 LA costume ball, where she won first prize for her outfit. She was dressed as Morticia, a character from the popular Charles Addams cartoons that featured in the *New Yorker* magazine between 1932 and the author's death in 1988. The humour in Addams' cartoons was unremittingly black – often verging on sick – but something about the gleeful gloominess of his style allowed him to get away with a catalogue of subversion. A family of dysfunctional Gothic deviants served as the focus for the ghoulish gags: pouring boiling oil on carol singers, attracting vultures onto their bird table with bones, and generally leading the lifestyle of the wholesome American nuclear family in total reverse, revelling in misery, mayhem and morbidity.

The Munsters – *the first TV couple to be portrayed sharing a bed.*
(See how happily Herman holds his candle – though Lily looks a little flustered!)

Nurmi had hoped that cartoonist Addams might spot her at the ball, and be inspired by the possibility of bringing his creations to life on the screen. Instead, the attention of studio executives that evening gave birth to her creation Vampira, who Nurmi made more sexual and less cadaverous than Morticia for fear of legal action by Addams. His cartoons would eventually come to life in the following decade as *The Addams Family* TV show, which ran between 1964-6.

The Addams Family had a doppelganger in the form of *The Munsters*, a series with an almost identical premise and lifespan on the networks. While *The Addams Family* used Addams' cartoons as a starting point, *The Munsters* was centred upon a family of camped-up versions of Universal's classic monster menagerie, featuring a goofy Frankenstein's Monster for a father, a gone-to-seed vampire count as grandpa, and a lycanthropically-inclined little boy. Both shows were essentially one-joke wonders: both cashed in on the contrast between the Gothic creatures who assume they are normal and the shocked responses of ordinary American families. *The Addams Family* was somewhat more sophisticated, with a less overtly supernatural, more depraved clan as its focus, but neither series exactly qualifies as a classic.

But *The Addams Family*'s catchy, finger-clicking theme tune sticks like a hook in the brain, and the show retains a special place in the affections of many Goths – there's even a British Goth band named after the show (though minus a 'd' – presumably for copyright reasons). The relationship between the show and the Goth scene is an ambivalent one – whistling the theme is a 'witty' way for straight people to mock anybody dressed in gloomy or Gothic attire. For all that, a film version of *The Addams Family* broke box office records in 1991 by grossing more in its first three days than any other movie on a non-holiday weekend – the chairman of Paramount Productions describing the appeal of the characters as that of 'the original dysfunctional family'.

Dark Shadows was originally inspired by the surprise success of Victoria Holt's 1962 novel, *The Mistress of Mellyn*, and the numerous Gothic romances that appeared in its wake. Initially aimed at the housewives who made up the vast majority of Holt's readership, *Dark Shadows* soon became a bigger success with younger viewers, whose lively imaginations were open to its outlandish plots. The focus of this Gothic soap was the Collins family – notably the vampire, Barnabas, although most other members of the clan also suffered from supernatural curses. *Dark Shadows* was almost *The Munsters* or *The Addams Family* played straight. Werewolves, ghosts and other familiar Gothic horror stand-bys proliferated in a period drama disdained by adult purists ('laughably cheapjack saga,' sneered one horror critic) and embraced by young fans. Jonathan Frid, the classical actor who took on the role of Barnabas Collins, became an overnight sensation – a Gothic heartthrob who made an impact on the emerging libido of many budding children of the night. Such erotic overtones were not confined to male members of the cast. In *Retrohell*, the nostalgia bible for Generation X, contributor Pleasant Gehman waxes lyrical on the show's appeal, particularly the 'ultrasexy vampires' of both genders.

'The opening features spooky, unearthly music (I think it had a theramin on it, or at least that's what it sounded like) and a grainy film of waves crashing on a desolate, rocky beach,' reminisces Gehman. 'There were all sorts of sexy, cleavage-heaving women fainting in tight-bodiced dresses, and lots of carnal love bites to the neck, flashing capes, people getting bricked up into walls, evil laughter, and always a cliffhanger on Fridays. *Tiger Beats* and other teen mags were full of the cast because they were so damn good-looking (Quentin looked kind of like Adam Ant, if I recall correctly). The show came on from 4.00-4.30, so everyone would rush home from school, gather in the living room, pull down the shades so it was real dark, and get the shit scared out of them.'

Another eager young viewer was Boyd Rice, who later became an industrial music pioneer with his militant noise project, Non, and one of the foremost figures in Anton LaVey's Church of Satan. Rice, who has cited *Dark Shadows* as a formative influence on his life, described it in a recent conversation with Chad Hensley of Goth.Net as a 'Wagnerian television show where every day there was death, resurrection, and blood. What they would usually do is introduce a character that was really evil, like Barnabas Collins. He was a vampire that was a really cruel son of a bitch. Everybody loved him. The producers realised they had to keep him in the show but tone him down because he was the most popular character. So then, they had to bring in other characters that were pure evil like Nicholas Blare and, later on, a ghost named Quentin who would get kids to play a game where they had to try to murder their father.'

The man behind *Dark Shadows* was producer Dan Curtis, who in many ways did for Gothic television what Arch Oboler had done for the genre on radio – produce relatively high-quality material that overcame (or at least largely disguised) the medium's many limitations. Curtis followed *Dark Shadows* with a less romantic, more contemporary and downbeat exercise in Gothic. *The Night Stalker* was made for TV in 1971, scripted by reliable veteran horror scribe Richard Matheson, from an original story by Jeff Rice. It broke records with its viewing figures, and ABC quickly commissioned a follow-up movie, *The Night Strangler*, and then a series to exploit the movie's success.

The series was entitled *Kolchak – The Night Stalker* after its hero, a dogged yet cynical reporter in a battered straw hat played by Darren McGavin. In the first movie, he discovers that a spate of murders in Las Vegas are actually the work of a vampire, while the follow-up has him tracking down an immortal serial killer who dwells in a subterranean city beneath the streets of Seattle. In each case, the authorities are dismissive of Kolchak's outlandish claims and obstructive of his investigations, preferring to cover up evidence of supernatural threats rather than risk panic or their own credibility.

Kolchak didn't keep at it for that long – the series limped along for one 1974 season before descending ratings inspired the network to plunge a stake through its heart. The monsters included werewolves, witches, dinosaurs, and even a headless motorcyclist ('one of the most tasteless programs ever done for network TV,' according to Stephen King) – an endless weekly parade that made the show increasingly implausible to the average viewer. Perhaps more significantly, however, the creative duo behind the two Kolchak movies – director-producer Dan Curtis and writer Richard Matheson – were absent from the series.

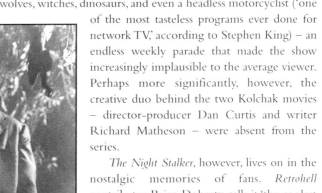

The Night Stalker, however, lives on in the nostalgic memories of fans. *Retrohell* contributor Brian Doherty calls it 'the coolest shit I'd ever seen on network TV circa 1974, and it still is as far as I'm concerned.' The most influential fan was one Chris Carter. 'I just remember being scared out of my wits by that show as a kid,' recalls Carter, 'and I realised that there just wasn't anything scary now [the 1990s] on television.' It inspired him to create

Barnabas (Jonathan Frid, left) and Quentin (David Selby) – respectively, a vampire and a ghost/werewolf were unlikely heart-throbs from Gothic soap opera Dark Shadows.

his own series featuring regular characters investigating supernatural phenomena against a background of official denial and cover-ups – *The X-Files*.

In addition to *The Night Stalker*, in the 1970s Dan Curtis adapted a number of classic Gothic novels as one-off movies for the small screen, such as *The Picture of Dorian Gray* and *The Strange Case of Dr Jekyll and Mr Hyde*. The latter starred Hollywood villain, Jack Palance, who also took the lead in Curtis' 1973 *Dracula*, which re-united him with scriptwriter Richard Matheson. While it has its fans, the 1977 British production of *Count Dracula* by the BBC, starring the sinisterly sophisticated Louis Jourdan, is a superior adaptation of Bram Stoker's novel and something of an epic at nearly three hours (billed by the BBC as 'a Gothic romance'). Connoisseurs, however, prefer the comparatively modest and obscure Anglo-Canadian 1975 adaptation of E. F. Benson's classic Victorian vampire tale, 'Mrs Amworth'. The title character is a three-centuries-old vampire, slyly spreading corruption through a tranquil English village, evocatively realised in a half-hour special that was to have been the first of a series entitled *Classics Dark and Dangerous* (sadly never made).

Kolchak: The Night Stalker – *one of TV's more unlikely crusaders against evil, though Darren McGavin's dishevelled reporter partly inspired* The X-Files.

Had it ever left the drawing board, perhaps the series might have been as good as *Supernatural*, the show which occupies a dark place in this writer's heart. Screened in 1977 by the BBC, this slice of pure Gothic ran for a sinfully short eight episodes. Though based on original scenarios, the series was very much a Victorian period piece. The atmospheric linking scenario ran as follows: 'During the final years of the last century, there still stood a mansion in Limehouse, to the east of London, known as the House on the River. Here men with bizarre tastes would meet once a month in order to terrify each other by means of true stories of horror and the supernatural. Those story-tellers who failed to impress the assembly were – it is said – never seen again. Those who succeeded were permitted to join . . . the Club of the Damned!' Each week a prospective member would try to impress the wealthy degenerates with all the familiar figures from the Gothic tradition.

The debut episode, 'Dorabella', dealt with two young men in fevered pursuit of the title character, a beautiful creature with whom one of them has become besotted. She is, of course, a vampire, and the show might have had little to distinguish it, had it not contained striking, even shocking, scenes that lifted it above most equivalent Gothic drama. The trail of fly-covered corpses that the eerily elegant *femme fatale* leaves in her wake and the blasphemous 'wedding', where Dorabella is joined with her drained, damned suitor by a special ring studded with a gold thorn, causing a crimson rivulet to gush down his arm. These images have remained with me ever since I saw the show over twenty years ago.

Supernatural was televisual evidence that the British are still the masters at staging traditional Gothic. Hammer Films had excelled in the Gothic field during the late 1950s and the 1960s, existing in happy symbiosis with small-screen entertainment. One of Hammer's first forays into the genre that made them internationally famous was adapted from a popular 1940s Gothic-horror radio show, *The Man in Black*. The saturnine Valentine Dyall played the title role, introducing anthologised tales of terror both for the radio and for the 1950 cinematic version. According to Jonathan Rigby in *English Gothic*, the film 'showcases a number of motifs which were to become staples of Hammer's future product – a damsel in distress, a prominently displayed coffin, a chase through the woods, an exhumation in a crypt, a moodily-lit seance and a climactic return from the dead.' The same year, Dyall also played sinister Ripper suspect, Dr Fell, in Hammer's *Room to Let*, originally a BBC radio play.

The real turning point for the studio, however, came in 1955 when they released *The Quatermass Xperiment* (retitled *The Creeping Unknown* in the US), adapted from a highly successful BBC TV series. The plot dealt with a rocket that returns to earth, its only surviving passenger infected with an alien contagion that gradually mutates him into a formless horror. While ostensibly part of the science-fiction boom that eclipsed the horror genre in the 1950s, critics were in little doubt which genre it belonged to, the *News Chronicle*'s reviewer describing it as 'the best and nastiest horror-film that I have seen since the war'.

Audiences were similarly enthusiastic, and Hammer resolved to take their biggest gamble to date, investing in a comparatively lavish production of pure Gothic horror: *The Curse of Frankenstein*, a runaway success upon its 1957 release. In the wake of their highly successful first Frankenstein film, the studio entered a partnership with Columbia TV in the US to make a series entitled *Tales of Frankenstein*. The partnership didn't work out, and only a pilot episode was made, 'The Face in the Tombstone Mirror', which remains, tantalisingly, locked in a vault somewhere. Hammer's second transatlantic TV collaboration was more successful, a seventeen-part 1968 series entitled *Journey into the Unknown*. Creatively, it was another disappointment, however, with Hammer's trademark lurid Gothic sanitised and Americanised to please the networks.

The British studio's third and final TV horror effort, *Hammer House of Horror*, was also their best. Broadcast in 1980 in thirteen parts, Hammer managed to update their traditional Gothic horror to a contemporary milieu – something they conspicuously failed to do in their final years as a movie studio in the 1970s – while delivering just enough blood and eroticism to satisfy the audience. Classic horrors were transplanted to 1980s England in the form of vampires ('The Carpathian Eagle'), witches ('Witching Time') and werewolves ('Children of

The horror hostess lives! Curvaceous Halloween camp personified in the buxom form of Elvira (Cassandra Peterson), mistress of the dark.

the Full Moon'), the latter carrying a satisfying charge of black humour.

The most disturbing episode was 'The Mark of Satan', the last to be transmitted. Its original scenario depicted a hospital porter infected with a mysterious, demonic virus, caught from the blood of a lunatic who committed gory suicide with a bone drill. It blurred the barriers between the supernatural and schizophrenia to a truly disturbing extent, until reaching a sickeningly inevitable climax. Ingenious twists-in-the-tail, and a disorientating tendency to question reality distinguish the best of *Hammer House of Horror*.

The truth is out there: The X-Files' FBI Agents Mulder and Scully, who made TV sex symbols of actors David Duchovny and Gillian Anderson.

The 1980s produced no shortage of horror product from American TV studios, of varying levels of quality and originality. Attempts were made to turn profitable film franchises into small-screen successes: *Freddy's Nightmares* tried to exploit the popularity of the *Nightmare on Elm Street* movies with an anthology series hosted by bogeyman, Freddy Krueger, between 1988-90. Meanwhile the *Friday the 13th* TV series used the movie title without lowering itself to borrow any elements from the plotless stalk-and-slash films themselves.

On a more original note, *Tales from the Darkside* exploited the talents of some of the horror genre's best-known and most bankable names – most notably, George A. Romero, the director of the *Living Dead* (or 'Anubis') trilogy, and Stephen King. Despite penny-pinching budgets, the half-hour horror stories attracted respectable viewing figures mainly on account of their macabre glee, staying on the air for four seasons between 1983-88.

The black comedy and bloodthirsty irony of the 1950s' EC horror comics were clearly a big inspiration, and that mean-spirited mirth was directly mined for a series directly based on one of the original EC titles, *Tales from the Crypt*. Running for seven mostly successful seasons, between 1989-96, it featured the comic's Crypt Keeper as its sarcastic skeletal host. An endearingly creepy animatronic creation, the Crypt Keeper became a minor horror icon in his own right, and shared the stage at a number of Hallowe'en events with fellow horror host, Elvira – the ultimate Gothic kitsch double-act. Ultimately, many of the shows in *Darkside* and *Crypt* are pretty good considering their low budgets and production-line schedules. But their relentlessly tongue-in-cheek approach and simplistic (or sometimes nonsensical) stories meant that even the best episodes had an unmistakably throwaway quality. If Gothic television was to survive into the 21st century, it needed to start producing some serious material.

The renaissance of Gothic TV began in 1993, in the shape of *The X-Files*. Despite trimmings from the science fiction and crime genres, at heart *The X-Files* is a horror show. Its signature image is one of impotent torchlight, struggling vainly to illuminate claustrophobic spaces that contain some inexplicable threat. 'The truth is out there' runs the program's slogan – with the powerful subtext that you might be happier not to know this particular truth.

As already stated, the connections between the ill-fated 1970s *Night Stalker* TV series and *The X-Files* are seminal. Series supremo, Chris Carter, had the benefit of studying *The Night Stalker* with hindsight and trying to learn by its ultimate failure. 'I saw what the limitations were,' he observes. 'I think having a "monster of the week" reduced the longevity of the storytelling capabilities. I thought there was a wide world of weird science, paranormal phenomena, and other stories to tell that were best explored by people who had a reason to explore them, and who actually could effect some outcome.'

However, while Carter stated in pre-publicity that 'about half the time these [episodes] are going to play out as either hoaxes or traditional cases that appear to have paranormal aspects to them,' in the first three seasons there was only one case that could have feasibly been a hoax. Similarly, while 'weird science' and paranormal phenomena might give *The X-Files* a more scientific veneer, the series still operates on the terms of the classic monster movie. *The X-Files* succeeds because the writing is consistently inventive in a medium saturated by bland, or outright moronic, programming. Michael Lange, who directed a number of episodes in the first series, may have been slightly grandiose in describing the show as 'an intellectual exercise', but it has never been allowed to slide into self-parody in the way that *The Night Stalker* quickly did.

The X-Files, with its overwhelming subtext of government cover-up and conspiracy, also has its finger very firmly on the paranoid pulse of the millennial era. Star David Duchovny describes the show as 'very nineties, because everything is left in doubt. There's no closure, no answers . . . Obviously it's tapping into something the nation wants. I think it has to do with religious stirrings – a sort of New Age yearning for an alternate reality and the search for some kind of extrasensory god. Couple that with a cynical, jaded, dispossessed feeling of being lied to by a government, and you've got a pretty powerful combination for a TV show.' This antsy vision of modern America is also the happiest marriage between the Gothic aesthetic and the mainstream thrills necessary for television success.

The limitations of *The X-Files* are exemplified in the episode that is arguably closest to the traditional Gothic style, and actually involves the Goth subculture as a plot device. '3' was screened in the second season, and deals with a trio of killers known as the Trinity, who have a fetish for drinking blood. Mulder's pursuit of the murderers takes him to a mythical Los Angeles Goth club, known as Club Tepes. Screenwriter Glen Morgan remembers a lot of resistance among hardcore fans to the idea of an episode featuring vampires. 'My feeling is, "Why not?"', said Morgan. 'We did the [mythic Native American] manitou last year, and that's essentially a werewolf, and they [the fans] hated that too.' Perhaps *X-Files* devotees need the quasi-scientific veneer of aliens and ESP to be able to accept its fantastic scenarios.

If mainstream audiences have imposed some limitations, then the network executives in charge of maintaining broadcasting standards have imposed more. Again, this was particularly evident in '3'. 'In starting to do research, I began to find out about these people who felt it was a sexual fetish to ingest blood,' recalls Morgan. 'Obviously the standards people, say "Huh? What the . . ." I think we caved in on too many points to the standards people. In the first draft it was a really kinky, erotic episode. It lost that . . .' Conversely, some of the show's Goth fans took exception to what they felt was the reinforcement of popular myths associating the Goth scene with evil deeds and criminal deviance.

The other 1990s TV show to thrust Gothic themes to prominence was, of course, *Buffy the Vampire Slayer*, a program which has become just as big a cultural phenomenon as *The X-Files*. *Buffy* had an unusual genesis, beginning as a 1992 film starring Kirsty Swanson in the lead role, opposite blond heavy Rutger Hauer's violin-playing vampire. The film was really a one-joke wonder, crossbreeding the air-headed high-school movies popular in the 1980s with a classic horror-film scenario, to create an incongruous clash between the midnight forces of Gothic evil and the sunny world of Californian Valley Girls.

Only the most potent media mystic could have predicted that, five years later, the formula would prove to be the ratings smash of the late 1990s. As well as a new cast, a change of mood and tempo helped transform *Buffy* into a huge small-screen success. The comedy elements became more low-key, mostly dry one-liners from the heroine, and the show began to explore, rather than just parody, the high-school world represented by Sunnydale. Part of the show's success can be attributed to the way it explores teen issues, while maintaining pace and tension with displays of butt-kicking and supernatural pyrotechnics.

Buffy enjoys a large Goth following. Indeed, none other than Mick Mercer, at one point promised to abandon Goth music in favour of the series. 'My favourite programme ever,' enthuses Mercer, 'this stuns me more than any one individual band ever has!' At best, however, *Buffy* is Goth-lite. Most of the Gothic elements that draw connoisseurs to the genre – decadence, deviance, death – are mere window-dressing for the show's prime-time themes of teen trauma and adolescent angst, if they're there at all.

Nevertheless, the enormous success of *Buffy the Vampire Slayer* and *The X-Files* prove that there continues to be cash in creepiness. Both shows have spawned further Gothic offerings on the small screen, many of them significantly darker than their predecessors. *Angel* – the *Buffy* spin-off featuring the vampire slayer's reformed, undead boyfriend – is certainly more Gothic than its sunnier Sunnydale progenitor. David Boreanaz, in the title role, has the brooding good looks and tormented soul of a classic Gothic anti-hero – particularly in comparison to wholesome Sarah Michelle Gellar (a spokeswoman for Maybelline cosmetics) as Buffy. *Angel*'s plot is also darker – with the lead character attempting to redeem past sins by combating evil on the mean streets of Los Angeles – but is ultimately a classic private detective vehicle with Gothic flourishes.

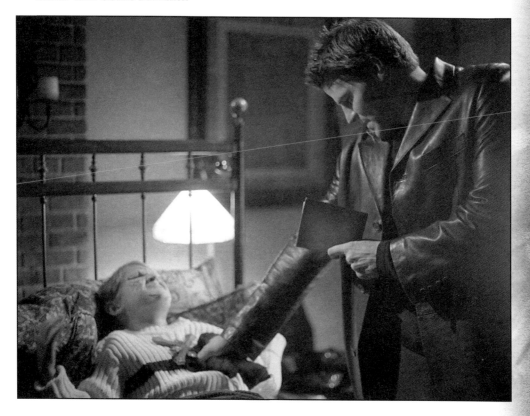

Angel *(David Boreanaz) – seen here performing an exorcism – is a centuries-old vampire with a conscience, an undead hero with his own* Buffy *spin-off TV series.*

In 1997, Chris Carter tried to create a darker companion to *The X-Files* that addressed the pre-millennial angst instrumental in that show's success. The series went under the obvious title *Millennium*, and starred Lance Henriksen as Frank Black, a government operative, whose psychic powers make him a natural (albeit reluctant) choice to track down serial killers. Henriksen is a magnetic and naturally unnerving performer (strangely reminiscent of Boris Karloff), but audiences preferred the sexual friction of the Mulder and Scully partnership, and this, combined with the show's unremittingly grim tenor, meant that *Millennium* was not destined to become a similar phenomenon to *The X-Files.*

Several other Gothic crossover series were superior in many respects to *The X-Files* and *Buffy*, but too dark or offbeat to make the leap into the mainstream. *American Gothic* (1995-6) created a Gothic soap opera without the outrageous period camp that had turned some people off Dan Curtis' *Dark Shadows*, with Gary Cole as satanic Sheriff Lucas Buck, holding an isolated South Carolina community in a grip of fear. *Brimstone* (1998-9) featured Peter Horton as Zeke Stone, an unjustly-damned cop, sent back from Hell by Satan himself to recapture 113 escaped evil souls. As a Gothic detective series, *Brimstone* occupied much the same territory as *Angel*, but was edgier and nastier than the slick *Buffy* spin-off. Goth cinematic favourites, *The Hunger* and *The Crow*, also made it to the small screen (1997-9 and 1999 respectively), and in both cases they achieved cult audiences before impatient network schedulers put them on ice.

It is perhaps too easy to mourn the passing of such shows, rather than marvelling that they ever got made at all in the ruthlessly bland world of television. This survey of small-screen Gothic began by wondering whether TV could ever prove a suitable medium for Gothic drama. The conclusion: 'No – but it's somehow wormed its way in there anyway.' And dark oddities continue to surface upon the cathode-ray tube. My personal favourite is the British series, *Urban Gothic*, its two seasons screened on Channel 5, the UK's smallest terrestrial network, in 2000-1. Filmed on a very modest budget, *Urban Gothic* is full of energy and invention, young flesh and fresh blood, that lend it a welcome dose of unpredictability and postmodern street-smarts. Its stated intent is to bring 'British horror out of the Hammer museum and onto the streets of London – the pubs, the council estates, the Soho drinking clubs . . . It's two fingers up to Buffy and her prom queen sisters. It's horror on heat, on drugs, where anything can happen and being young and pretty won't save you.'

It has taken enough risks with its two series of thirteen episodes each to stay fresh, while having a firm grounding in the Gothic tradition. When we spoke in early 2001, producer and co-creator, Steve Matthews, told me that he and screenwriter, Tom de Ville (only 23 when the series started, and a member of the Goth subculture), 'felt that that bizarre, extraordinary ragtag collection of brilliance – Hammer – had left a legacy not properly understood by many of those working in the genre since. Most British screen horror since has relied too much on recollections of the stylistic idiosyncrasies of the brand. Creaky sets, cheesy costumes, unabashed melodrama . . . the junk aesthetic has an enduring camp-kitsch appeal.'

Urban Gothic is wildly uneven, and takes creative gambles that don't always pay off. Such willingness to take chances is all but unheard of in television, but it's integral to the cutting edge of Gothic horror. 'Digging deep into the archetypes to find their power anew was always the plan for *Urban Gothic*,' says Matthews. 'The horror story itself, from way back before the Gothic movement, has had a particular shamanistic place in the culture . . .'

Keith-Lee Castle as Rex, the post-modern playboy vampire in the 'Vampirology' episode of cult British TV series Urban Gothic.

Chapter V

Morbidity, Putrefaction & Pain:

The modern horror movie

A young boy was growing up in the dull environs of 1960s suburban California. As he later recalled for the British magazine, *Fear,* 'When I was young I had these two windows in my room, nice windows that looked out onto the lawn, and for some reason my parents walled them up and gave me this little slit window that I had to climb up on my desk to see out of . . . To this day I've never asked them why . . . So I likened it to that story by Poe where the person was walled in, buried alive so to speak.'

The young boy's name was Tim Burton. In many ways the stereotypical quiet, thoughtful boy, Burton was not bookish – preferring the Gothic horror films produced in nearby Hollywood to Gothic novels. 'The Vincent Price ones spoke specifically to me for some reason,' he told *Fear.* 'Because of growing up in an atmosphere which was perceived as nice and normal but I had other feelings about. These movies were a way to acknowledge these feelings, and I think that's why I responded so much to certain Edgar Allan Poe themes.' These claustrophobic themes included premature burial – the perennially unhealthy obsession of the 1960s Poe adaptations starring Price, where young Burton discovered the morbid poet second hand.

Twenty years later, Burton paid tribute to these films in his own first production, a six-minute animated short entitled *Vincent* (1982). The film is clearly semi-autobiographical – by his own admission the director was something of a morbid child, and the title character looks

Gothic character actor Vincent Price in the 1973 camp classic Theatre of Blood.

The face of Vincent Price dominates the promotional art for director Roger Corman's classic 1964 adaptation of Poe's 'The Masque of the Red Death'.

suspiciously like an animated infant Burton, pale, slender and delicate, wide expressive eyes staring from beneath an unkempt halo of black hair. Echoing with quotes from Price's horror films, as well as passages from the original Poe tales and poems, *Vincent* combines the visual style of the expressionist classic, *The Cabinet of Dr Caligari*, with the anarchic verse of Dr Seuss' *Cat in the Hat*. Vincent stalks the fog-bound night searching for victims, keeps bats and spiders as pets, and conducts insane experiments with his dog. Finally, Poe-style obsessions – particularly premature burial – assail young Vincent before he is overcome. 'And my soul from out that shadow that lies floating on the floor, shall be lifted nevermore,' the narrator concludes, quoting from Poe's 'The Raven'.

The narrator was actually Vincent Price, whom Burton persuaded to voice this animated tribute to himself. Price's first Poe adaptation with director Roger Corman was made in 1960. Price came relatively late to the horror genre, with a long career on the stage and in mainstream Hollywood behind him (he first signed to Universal in 1938). He was originally recruited as a potential romantic leading man, but, despite his good looks and undoubted acting talent, it never happened. The problem was that Price, with his suave upper-class St Louis accent (which many mistook for English), and reputation as a wine connoisseur, gourmet and art expert, was too sophisticated for audiences who preferred square-jawed, straight-talking heroes who communicated with their fists. Cultured *bon viveurs* like Price were more likely to be regarded with suspicion than admiration.

Significantly, the last serious effort to establish Price as a matinee idol was in the 1946 film, *Dragonwyck*. Price's character, Nicholas Van Ryn, is a romantic lead, but he is also a brooding, cruel, drug-taking anti-hero in the classic Gothic mode. By the 1950s, Price found himself cast in increasingly sinister roles such as those he undertook for William Castle, developing his mastery of what one critic later referred to as 'the poetry of evil'.

So when director Corman was looking for a star for his projected adaptation of 'The Fall of the House of Usher' (billed as 'Edgar Allan Poe's classic tale of the ungodly . . . the evil'), Price was the obvious choice. Obvious, but not cheap. The film was budgeted at $270,000 (no fortune even then, but nearly three times Corman's usual shoestring budget), 'a large part of which went to the actor I wanted for the part of Roderick Usher: Vincent Price,' Corman later wrote in his autobiography. 'It was the most money AIP [American International Pictures – Corman's regular employers] had ever gambled on a film.' The film was also a gamble in several other respects: it departed from the monster-movie model he had followed so successfully in the 1950s; it concentrated on the psychological rather than the supernatural;

and it didn't have a monster (the kids, complained AIP, liked monsters). 'The house is the monster,' Corman reassured the studio, inserting a line for Price about the house 'breathing' to bolster this dubious premise.

Corman had been a fan of Poe since his schooldays, introduced to the writer as required reading. AIP were unconvinced that teenagers would want to watch something that reminded them of homework, but, based on the director's record for turning a profit (Corman titled his autobiography *How I Made a Hundred Movies in Hollywood and Never Lost a Dime*), gave the project the green light. Corman's progression from the cheap-and-cheerful exploitation movies of the 1950s to the Hollywood Gothic of the 1960s is equated by Stephen King with the transformation of a caterpillar into a butterfly.

Price was an inspired choice for the lead, his voice pitch-black and smooth as molasses, with a whisper of bat's wings – pure Gothic poetry. Beneath the surface, Corman 'felt audiences had to fear the leading man but not on a conscious, physical level based on strength. I wanted a man whose intelligent but tormented mind works beyond the minds of others and who thus inspires a deeper fear.' This same psychological emphasis characterised Corman's preparation for the film. He decided 'to use Freud's theories to interpret the work of Poe' and applied contemporary psychiatric mumbo-jumbo, even booking sessions with therapists to discuss the story.

The German directors of expressionist *schauerfilme*, 40 years before, had drawn on psychiatric theory when filming their silent nightmares. Similarly, Corman's twisted, almost insanely Gothic set designs embody the maelstrom of madness at the heart of *House of Usher*. Corman was initially reluctant to film any exterior shots that might break up the movie's surreal atmosphere, but then he heard there had recently been a forest fire nearby, and raced over to film the movie's opening scene there. 'It was great,' the director recalled. 'The ground was grey with ash; the trees were charred black. And we threw a little fog in to add some effect. I got exactly what I wanted: to not show green grass, leafy trees, or any other organic signs of life. This film was about decay and madness.'

The film achieved the rare balancing act of pleasing both thrill-seeking audiences and highbrow critics. The latter appreciated Richard Matheson's literate script, Corman's inventive direction and Price's carefully overstated performance. The former savoured the shameless morbid theatricality and intimations of taboo themes – incest, necrophilia – which the movie, as a costume drama based (loosely) on a literary classic, could safely address. More importantly, Roger Corman's *House of Usher* hailed the revival of Hollywood Gothic.

In the age-old Hollywood tradition, AIP encouraged Corman to milk his winning formula for all it was worth. In the following four years, he directed another seven films in what became known as 'the Poe cycle'. Alongside Vincent Price, Corman employed a number of very talented professionals who went on to become legends in their own right: Jack Nicholson, Hollywood's wisecracking madcap, learned his trade playing romantic leads against sinister anti-heroes Price and Boris Karloff; director Francis Ford Coppola helped Corman behind the camera, which he later described as 'a fabulous opportunity'; cinematographer Nicolas Roeg – who gave *The Masque of the Red Death* (1964) its lurid, almost psychedelic vibrancy – went on to become a controversial and acclaimed arthouse director.

Among the most important members of the repertory was horror author, Richard Matheson, who took script-writing duties on most of the films. Matheson is best remembered for his classic 1954 vampire novel, *I Am Legend*. A clever spin on a familiar theme – regarded by some as the first truly modern take on the undead – it depicts a world overtaken by vampires, with its hero, Robert Neville, venturing out by day to stake the undead who besiege him by night. It gradually dawns on lone crusader Neville that he has become the monster and the undead are his victims. (The novel was filmed twice – with Vincent Price as the title

Price, as Poe's M. Valdemar, putrifies rapidly – to the horror of screen stalwart Basil Rathbone, in Corman's Tales of Terror *(1962).*

role in *The Last Man on Earth*, 1964, and Charlton Heston as *The Omega Man*, 1971.)

Matheson's creativity was stretched on the Poe films, as Price observed: 'The problem is it's very difficult to turn a short story like "The Pit and the Pendulum" or a poem like "The Raven" into a long picture. The stories had to be expanded to fit the movies. What Roger tried to do was express some of the psychology of Poe's characters, and imbue our movie versions with the spirit of Poe. Richard Matheson . . . captured the essence of Poe.' That essence became a formula, wherein a cocktail of Poe's preoccupations – incest, insanity, inbreeding, necrophilia, sadism, disease, decay and a veritable squadron of malevolent black cats – characterised the overripe Gothic melodrama.

The Pit and the Pendulum (1961) featured Price as Nicholas Medina, a man obsessed with the crimes of his father, a sadistic member of the Spanish Inquisition, and the torture chamber at the heart of the family castle. *The Premature Burial* (1962) followed, with Ray Milland, a fading matinee idol, as a Victorian medical student terrified of being buried alive. For *Tales of Terror* (1962), Matheson adapted a trilogy of Poe short stories – 'Morella', 'The Black Cat' (meshed with 'The Cask of Amontillado') and 'The Facts in the Case of M. Valdemar'. Price appears in all three, and is joined by Peter Lorre, a Hungarian-born actor, who made a name playing simpering creeps and pathetic villains.

Tales of Terror leavened its horror with gallows humour. By this point Corman was tiring of the formula, lamenting in his autobiography how filming 'those Poe films on dimly lit gothic interior sets' was in danger of sending him 'as nutty as Roderick Usher'. But AIP still demanded Poe pictures. So Matheson, who declared he had 'had it up to the eyeballs with all the heavy torture and burial stuff,' scripted a parody of the previous entries in the cycle. One more horror veteran, in the welcome shape of ageing icon, Boris Karloff, joined Price and Lorre for *The Raven* (1963).

Set in medieval England, Price and Karloff are rival sorcerers engaged in a duel of magic, with Lorre as a wizard who has crossed Karloff and was turned into the raven of the title as a result. It has precious little else to do with the poem that allegedly inspired it – a situation that evidently irked the raven brought on set to play the transformed Lorre. Jack Nicholson, the film's romantic lead, recalled that 'the raven we used shit endlessly over everybody and everything . . . My whole right shoulder was constantly covered in raven shit.'

The next entry, *The Haunted Palace* (1963), took the title of a Poe poem, but was really based on a story by that other master of American Gothic, H. P. Lovecraft. 'I made some gestures towards bringing some Poe into it,' Corman maintains apologetically, 'but it was really primarily Lovecraft and it was slightly misleading advertising.' The film was based on a novella from the Cthulhu Mythos, *The Case of Charles Dexter Ward*, about a man possessed by the spirit of his evil ancestor, who had been burnt at the stake as a warlock. Price starred as both evil ancestor and unsuspecting descendent, with assistance from a refugee from the Universal menagerie – ex-*Wolfman* Lon Chaney, Jr.

Corman's penultimate Poe project was his best. *The Masque of the Red Death* (1964) merged two Poe tales – its namesake and 'Hop Frog' – for its Gothic saga of perversion, pestilence and devil-worship set in medieval Italy. Price plays Prince Prospero, named after Shakespeare's charismatic magician in *The Tempest*, a decadent Satanist who invites all of his wealthy friends and followers to a grand party in his castle, as the plague known as the Red Death is ravaging his kingdom. The film is full of arresting images, from the hallucinatory tour through the different coloured chambers (in which Nicolas Roeg makes masterful use of Technicolor – proving that expressionism doesn't have to be in black-and-white), to the climactic masked ball of the film's title. (Some experts on the Goth subculture claim that the ethereal, hand-writhing dance popular in Goth clubs in the late 1980s and early 1990s – termed 'taffy-pulling' because its waving arm movements resemble someone making old-fashioned toffee – was initially inspired by the eerie dance in *Masque*'s ballroom scene.)

Utilising sets scavenged from better-financed productions (the *ABC Film Review* described them as having 'the shocking authenticity of the frightful cult of Satanism'), *The Masque of the Red Death* looks wonderful. Price is, as ever, a dark joy to behold and there is a sexy performance from horror stalwart Hazel Court, as Juliana, Prospero's equally degenerate mistress. *Time* magazine ungallantly observed that her cleavage could be employed

The films of Vincent Price cultivated a Gothic disposition in young fans like Tim Burton – who fictionalised his obsession in the 1982 animated short Vincent.

to 'sink the entire works of Edgar Allan Poe and a bottle of his favorite booze at the same time' – certainly the scene where she brands that ample bosom with an inverted cross, in an attempt to please her man, is Gothic kinkiness of the highest order.

Film historian, Bruce Lanier Wright, dubbed *The Masque of the Red Death*, 'One of the high-water marks of modern Gothic cinema . . . ambitious, original, uneven, sometimes pretentious and ultimately brilliant.' Other critics have compared it favourably with arthouse classic, *The Seventh Seal* (1957) – the Swedish film about a medieval knight who plays chess with Death, that first brought director Ingmar Bergman to international prominence. 'Had [*Masque*] been shot in a foreign language and subtitled, it would probably still play at art and revival houses today,' *Cinefantastique* magazine observed with justified cynicism. Corman himself described his masterpiece as his most 'philosophical' horror film: 'We were dealing with the plague, and it was fear of death *per se*, not fear of any violence.'

AIP demanded more Poe adaptations from Corman, though he felt he was 'wearing out on the series'. He completed the cycle with *The Tomb of Ligeia* in 1964, with Price in the lead in black wig, top hat and antique wraparound shades. The plot is the familiar Freudian cocktail of gathering madness and barely repressed perversion in a picturesque Victorian Gothic setting. Some aficionados regard it as Corman's most polished Poe adaptation – others think *The Tomb of Ligeia* is a little tired and confused. Certainly, Corman knew when it was time to quit. When, in the time-honoured fashion, the Gothic mansion burnt to the ground at the movie's climax, he turned his back on Edgar Allan Poe, signalling an end to his short but significant role in the development of Gothic cinema.

If embarking on a series of comparatively lavish Gothic films in 1960 had been a gamble for AIP, it was a carefully calculated one. Two years previously, the surprise hit of the year had been a low-budget movie from a small British studio, an exercise in full-colour Gothic. For Hammer Films – in many ways the British equivalent to AIP, as producers of cheap programme-fillers aimed at undemanding audiences – had plundered the golden age of European Gothic literature which proved so profitable for Universal Pictures 25 years earlier.

As Jonathan Rigby observes of Hammer's return to classic Gothic, in his book, *English Gothic*, 'the first shot involved Baron Frankenstein cutting down a bird-pecked highwayman from a wayside gibbet. The world-wide resurgence of horror began with this simple, but entirely appropriate gesture.' The film was *The Curse of Frankenstein* (1957), which established the studio as world leaders in period chillers and its two stars as horror icons to stand alongside AIP's Vincent Price: Peter Cushing, who played Baron Frankenstein (the studio had elevated the good doctor to the aristocracy), and Christopher Lee, as his ill-fated creation. Hammer completed their winning line-up with Terence Fisher, who would direct much of the studio's Gothic horror, and Jimmy Sangster as screenwriter. Fisher was unafraid to imbue Gothic horror, by now regarded as quaintly old-fashioned, with a visceral charge, returning to the twisted and perverse spirit of seminal classics such as Lewis' *The Monk*. (*The Curse of Frankenstein* was also the first British horror movie filmed in gloriously gory colour.) Film journalist Andrew Mangravite claimed Sangster 'took Mary Shelley's Romantic dishrag and raised him to the Gothic pantheon of demon-heroes where Melmoth, Ambrosio and Vathek dwell.'

Sangster's Baron Frankenstein was wholly devoid of the gentlemanly actor Peter Cushing's warmth and humanity. The actor's own research for the part took him first back to the original Mary Shelley novel, then to investigating the theoretical background to the Baron's experiments. The latter led him to consult his family doctor who, Cushing recalled, 'spent about an hour explaining how to transplant a brain'. 'When we first started, Frankenstein was trying to do the impossible,' Cushing told *House of Hammer* magazine in 1978. 'Then transplants began to be shown on the television and we thought that would be the end of the doctor [Frankenstein], with his crude do-it-yourself surgery. But he is more popular than ever.'

'He is not evil, but a man obsessed by what he is trying to achieve by any means that will justify the end,' Cushing concludes, applying characteristic generosity to his role almost to the point of an apologia. For Frankenstein employs not only grave-robbing and the mutilation of the dead – depicted with unprecedented frankness – but cold-blooded murder. If not actively evil, Cushing's Frankenstein is icily focused to the point of inhumanity, and the actor portrayed his obsessive ambition with chilling conviction.

The Baron became the focus for sequels, unlike the Universal Frankenstein series, where the Monster provided continuity. While Cushing would vary emphasis – sometimes rendering a more sympathetic character, motivated ultimately by a desire to aid mankind, rather than plain egotism – his Frankenstein is always possessed of a clinical callousness and frighteningly single-minded drive. As such, he embodies all of our fears about the scientists we now allow to 'play God' with our future.

Lee took the role of the Creature only once, unsurprisingly, considering he had to undergo a painstaking make-up which made him resemble 'a road accident' according to one critic. Despite these trying circumstances, Lee gave a powerful performance, portraying the Creature as what Cushing described as 'a spastic child', albeit one possessed of great strength and rage. In this fashion, like Karloff's ultimately pathetic Monster, Lee's angry, oversized infant – as sad as he is frightening – only served to emphasise the cold rationalism of his very grown-up creator.

The critics, however, felt little pity for either the Creature or the film. 'We all survived to go on to yet more horrid things,' Lee reflected in his autobiography, *Tall, Dark and Gruesome*. 'Before any further projects could be realised, however, there was an unexpectedly horrid experience for all of us, when the press saw it and gave it a venomous reception. "Disgusting"

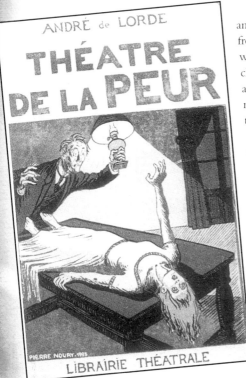

ANDRÉ de LORDE

THÉATRE DE LA PEUR

PIERRE NOURY. 1928

LIBRAIRIE THÉATRALE

The Grand Guignol theatre's explicit gore and violence – as in the plays of 'Prince of Terror' André de Lorde – preceded, and were outmoded by, Hammer horror.

and "Grand Guignol" were the two milder epithets from that quarter of the entertainment world which is hardly famous for keeping its own nose clean. However, the wounds they caused had the appearance of being dealt in private, because nobody heeded them and the crowds flocked to the picture in millions.'

The Grand Guignol was a Parisian theatre, founded in 1897, that hosted nightly programmes of short comedy and horror plays. Its name became a by-word for the gruesome and macabre. *Time* magazine, in 1947, described the theatre as 'a quaint little Gothic chapel. Inside, carved cherubs and two seven foot angels smile down from the black-raftered vault at a nightly round of vile murders, manglings and assorted acts of torturing, fang-bearing, acid-throwing.' The Grand Guignol finally closed its doors in 1963, unable to cope with direct competition from the cinema, then becoming increasingly graphic in its depiction of bloodshed – courtesy of the influence of Hammer studios.

Christopher Lee's next part for Hammer was the title role of the 1958 *Dracula* (US: *Horror of Dracula*), an obvious move, which reunited Lee and Cushing as stars and Fisher and Sangster on directorial and writing duties.

Cushing played the vampire's nemesis, Dr Van Helsing, with an iron will that, despite the actor's wiry frame and gentle demeanour, made him a credible adversary to the embodiment of raw evil. He even made Van Helsing, previously portrayed as a bookish academic, something of a man of action – notably in the finale, which is emblematic of the way Hammer pumped new blood into the moribund Gothic genre.

'I suggested that it was always a good idea to have some sort of almost Douglas Fairbanks scene – to have a jolly good leap or a jump,' Cushing told *House of Hammer*. Originally, Van Helsing was to take out a crucifix and use it to force Dracula into the sunlight – the kind of low-key ending you might expect from one of Universal's more lackadaisical efforts. At Cushing's instigation, the scene was changed so he raced along a banqueting table, leapt off to yank down some curtains, then improvised a cross using two candlesticks in order to drive his undead foe into the pool of sunlight where he crumbles into dust.

But this time the show belonged to Christopher Lee, who played the vampire count. Like it or not – and in many ways the actor most certainly did not – Lee was born to the role. As he concedes in his autobiography, 'At the same time I was being made [1922], so was *Nosferatu*, otherwise *Dracula*, in the great silent version by the German F. W. Murnau.' Lee's father was the archetypal English officer – heavily decorated in World War I and an accomplished hunter and sportsman. His mother belonged to the Carandini family, an ancient, aristocratic Italian dynasty that could trace their bloodline back to ancient Rome (were it not for the law of primogeniture – whereby titles pass through the male line – Lee would have been a real-life count). This background, which combined traditional English values with foreign nobility, made him something of an outcast in both worlds during his youth. Efforts to fit in were not helped by his height – Lee shot up to six feet four inches at a time when many men were nearly a foot shorter.

It was a mixture that would also complicate his acting career, when he struggled to find work in the British film industry. 'They were terrified that people would shift their attention to me because I towered over most of the British leading men,' he told me when we spoke in 1997. More damagingly, perhaps, although he was handsome, impeccably mannered, if a little imperious, and possessed of a fine, deep voice, there was something inescapably 'foreign' about Lee, while the domestic audience demanded heroes who were as English as a bowler hat. So, like Price, whose sophistication alienated American audiences, Lee found his career steering obstinately towards celluloid villainy.

Part of the secret of his success in playing Count Dracula lay in the way he deliberately ignored Bela Lugosi's 1931 performance, going instead to the 1897 Bram Stoker novel. After reading it twice, he drew upon those characteristics of the infamous vampire with which he could personally identify: 'his extraordinary stillness, punctuated by bouts of manic energy with feats of strength belying his appearance; his power complex; the quality of being done for but not undead; and by no means least the fact that he was an embarrassing member of a great and noble family.'

The other main characteristic, which the gentlemanly Lee omits, is sexual magnetism. While Lugosi's Count was considered hot stuff in the 1930s, few later fell for his sepulchral charms. By way of contrast, Lee gave the world a savagely seductive creature – a wolfish aristocrat as opposed to Lugosi's undead lounge lizard. 'The vampire's bite is his kiss,' Lee observed, 'and in sexual language, a kiss is often the prelude to a bite. And blood is the symbol of virility.' Lee's Dracula became the archetypal outsider-as-sex-symbol, attracting a legion of fans and admirers.

Lee was also the fiercest critic of his own portrayal of the vampire count, though much of the venom beneath the surface is still reserved for the scriptwriters. 'I was always fighting, during all of the Hammer Dracula films over the years, to retain Stoker's original character and above all the lines,' he told me. 'I kept on saying "Why do you write these stories and try and fit the character in, why not take Stoker's original, use the lines he wrote, and build a story around that? If you want to make a different story, by all means, but use his lines where appropriate." They almost never did.

'The Hammer version is completely incorrect visually. The only thing they did was to dress me, more or less, in black. I did in fact make another version in 1970 called *Count Dracula* [Jess Franco's Spanish production], which was a really disastrous film for a large number of reasons. I actually am, I think, the only actor to have ever played Dracula on film as Stoker described him – an old man with white hair and a long white moustache dressed entirely in black from head-to-foot without a single speck of colour. I did that for *Count Dracula*, but not in any of the Hammer films.'

Hammer's infidelity to the Stoker novel was only one factor in the actor's increasing antipathy towards his most successful role. While he may have ignored Lugosi's interpretation of Dracula, Lee was obviously aware of the Hungarian's tragic career where the Count's cape, both professionally and literally, became his shroud. Or, as Lee put it in his autobiography, the role brought 'the blessing of Lucifer, the third and final nail in my coffin. Count Dracula might escape, but not the actors who played him.'

Not all of the actors who found fame in Gothic cinema wanted to escape the typecasting that Lee resented. Boris Karloff, who remained active in the genre until his death in 1969, was always grateful of the employment the horror genre gave him over the years. 'An extraordinary thing about Boris was his gratitude for *Frankenstein*,' said his friend Vincent Price. 'He had great pride in it, even though it was something that plagued him his whole career.' Price himself clearly enjoyed his villainous roles, while Peter Cushing was pragmatic. 'I don't mind being a horror film star,' he reflected. 'To object would be like socking a gift horse in the face.' Thus, while Lee refused to reappraise his role as Count Dracula for eight years, Cushing began work on *The Revenge of Frankenstein* (1959) almost at once.

The critic for the UK's *Observer* newspaper dubbed the film a 'vulgar, stupid, nasty and intolerably tedious business,' adding, 'I want to gargle if off with a strong disinfectant, to scrub my memory with carbolic soap.' Happily, the public didn't share his weird sense of personal hygiene and the film was a success – connoisseurs regarding this sequel as superior to *The Curse of Frankenstein*. Hammer would make a further five Frankenstein features, all but one featuring Cushing as the fanatical Baron (the exception, *Horror of Frankenstein*, starred Ralph Bates, whom Hammer were then grooming as a new Gothic leading man. Bates portrayed the Baron as an immoral playboy with a passion for science in this 1970 production, featuring much black comedy amidst the dissection tables and open graves).

Cushing also reprised his vampire-hunting role for *Brides of Dracula* (1960). When Lee stubbornly refused to revisit the role of Dracula, however, the studio were forced to look elsewhere for their aristocratic bloodsucker – settling on actor David Peel to play the vampiric Baron Meinster. The absence of Lee's potent presence has led many Hammer cultists to overlook *Brides of Dracula*, but Peel gave us a more decadent vampire, an effetely evil undead mother's boy. 'Blonde and beautiful,' wrote Jonathan Rigby, 'Meinster is an androgynous figure straight out of [decadent artist] Aubrey Beardsley or Oscar Wilde; indeed Peel's own sexual preferences were the target of tabloid sniggering at the time of the film's release' (critics have since theorised that Meinster is himself one of the *Brides of Dracula*, the Count never appearing in the movie).

Universal had originally threatened to sue if the Creature make-up for *The Curse of Frankenstein* owed anything to Karloff's Monster make-up for their 1931 *Frankenstein*. After the success of *Curse*, however, the studios entered a working relationship, allowing Hammer free rein to plunder the Universal back catalogue. In the title role of *The Mummy* (1959),

Christopher Lee brought a charge of predatory eroticism to his vampire count. In Dracula Has Risen from the Grave *(1968), he is about to neck with a nervous Veronica Carlson.*

Christopher Lee typically gave the bandaged horror a much greater physical presence and vitality than the dreamily-ponderous Universal version. 'I only kill three people,' Lee observed, 'and not in a ghastly way. I just break their necks.' But there certainly are ghastly moments — particularly when Lee, as the Ancient Egyptian Kharis, has his tongue cut out before he is mummified and buried alive.

Dr Jekyll and Mr Hyde got the Hammer treatment (*The Two Faces of Dr Jekyll*, 1960), as did the werewolf legend (*The Curse of the Werewolf*, 1961), and, there was also a Hammer *Phantom of the Opera* (1962) starring Herbert Lom. They even contributed fresh creations, such as serpentine *femme fatales, The Gorgon* (1964) and *The Reptile* (1966), but overall, by the late 1960s, Hammer's plots and screenplays were becoming formulaic, while budgets were

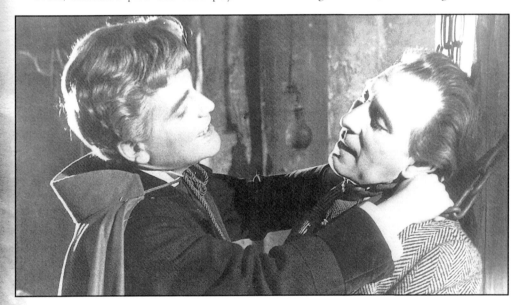

Baron Meinster (David Peel) in mortal combat with Van Helsing (Peter Cushing),
Hammer horror's hero, in this climactic scene from Brides of Dracula *(1960).*

shrinking. When Christopher Lee finally agreed to don the black cloak again in 1966, for *Dracula — Prince of Darkness*, it was with reservations. While his performance is magnificent, the actor, in protest at the weakness of his lines, confined himself to snarling and hissing.

Hammer made five more Dracula pictures with Lee — *Dracula Has Risen from the Grave* (1968), *Taste the Blood of Dracula* (1969), *Scars of Dracula* (1970), *Dracula AD 1972* (1972) and *The Satanic Rites of Dracula* (1973). All have their admirers — *Dracula Has Risen from the Grave* is a personal favourite of Tim Burton — and all are pure pleasure to fans of Hammer Gothic. But the series was displaying signs of a studio in crisis, desperate to update their winning formula.

Lee cites the last two entries in the cycle as the final nails in the coffin of Hammer's Dracula franchise, and – by extension – their whole Gothic output. In *Dracula AD 1972*, the studio endeavoured to breathe new life into their bloodsucker by dragging him out of his natural Victorian environment into swinging-seventies London. Inevitably, the film had dated before it even reached the screen, and any toothsome Gothic flourishes are overwhelmed by the hilariously cringe-worthy 'hip' dialogue and fashions. Gothic was never designed to be groovy.

The Satanic Rites of Dracula also uses a modern setting, although this time the Count has become an evil megalomaniac intent on wiping out humanity, whom Lee describes as a cross between legendary recluse, Howard Hughes, and James Bond villain, Dr No. He dismisses the film as an unintentional parody, though it isn't nearly as bad as its star believes – and Lee finally got his wish of delivering some original Stoker dialogue, before refusing point-blank to play the character for Hammer again.

The cycle's main director, Terence Fisher, has been accused of latent misogyny in his work, largely because the influence of evil transforms virtuous virgins into rapacious vamps. In true Victorian style, good girls are frigid and only bad girls can indulge their libidos. The heroes in these films are either actual clergymen, or like Cushing's Van Helsing, so driven by their crusade as to seem effectively celibate. Most strikingly, the most horrific scenes often show these servants of God meting out punishment to the women who have given themselves over to sin. Horror movie regular, Barbara Shelley, is transformed from a prim, nervous wife into a dark sexual predator by the bite of the vampire in *Dracula – Prince of Darkness*. The scene where a group of monks 'free' her from her 'curse' by hammering a stake through her heart has been compared to gang-rape by proxy by more than one horrified critic.

Critics have been inclined to see this as Fisher equating female sexuality with evil. A more perceptive interpretation might be to wonder whether the good-versus-evil struggles at the centre of his films is more complex than first appears. Certainly, the hot embrace of sin seems more appealing than sterile Victorian virtue, to the point where one wonders if it is Cushing's fanatical crusaders who are the true villains rather than Lee's demonic seducers. For it is in the very nature of all Gothic art to invert convention, celebrate sin, and turn outcasts into anti-heroes – whether or not the artists concerned consciously intend to do so.

Christopher Lee as Count Dracula, with nubile admirers, in a 1970s publicity shot. Goth icon Siouxsie Sue named the young Chris Lee as one of her personal sex symbols.

Certainly, the generation who gorged on Hammer's crimson feasts were drawn to the monsters rather than the monster-hunters. Those of us who grew up on these films, in the late 1960s and early 1970s, were excited by this subversive edge. It offered a mythic, romantic yet deliciously villainous past, more tempting than the asinine pop-modernity of the swinging sixties or the phoney worthiness of the burgeoning New Age. Ingrid Pitt, an actress who worked for the studio during this period, evoked the world of Hammer when we spoke in 1998, describing how 'you think you see something and you don't, and there are different shades of darkness beneath moonbeams, and subtle sounds that play tricks with your senses. All of these tingling, teasing feelings of anxiety and fear have disappeared in modern horror films which just throw things in your head. It's shocking, but not titillating at all.'

This almost sado-masochistic blend of fear and titillation was vital to Hammer's appeal – one that Ingrid Pitt played no small part in creating. Both the studio's fans and its critics often focused on the overflowing, low-cut period gowns of the actresses Hammer employed. Many of the ladies concerned were not quite as heavily over-endowed as legend suggests, their cantilevered costumes serving to emphasise the bosomy charms they did possess. Nevertheless, compared to the competition – fashionably flat-chested waifs like Twiggy, or the bra-less earth mothers of the hippie counterculture – Hammer's buxom sex symbols were heady stuff indeed.

Naturally, as the Gothic aesthetic has always respected feminine power, women were not merely victims in the Hammer universe. As films became more sexually daring, and feminism became more of an issue, Hammer were bound to make their own 'girl power' statement. It emerged in a series of films that became known as the 'Karnstein trilogy', after the surname of the lead bloodsucker in J. Sheridan Le Fanu's 1872 novella of vampiric lesbianism, 'Carmilla': *The Vampire Lovers* (1970), *Lust for a Vampire* (1971), and *Twins of Evil* (1971) – alongside the similarly themed *Countess Dracula* (1970).

These movies were Hammer's last fresh attempts to recapture their diminishing audience, and certainly their most potent blend of sex and horror – although they are pretty tame to modern eyes. Most critics were less than generous to these films, dismissing them for their shameless exploitative appeal. But for those of us who like the idea of beautiful, nocturnal nymphs nipping nipples rather than necks in a sumptuous Gothic setting, it's possible to forgive a multitude of sins (such as the brief scene in *Lust for a Vampire* where you can clearly see one of the camera crew).

For the first entry in the series Hammer employed Polish actress Ingrid Pitt as undead seductress, Carmilla Karnstein. 'As a woman I was incredibly lucky that Hammer gave me predatory roles,' Pitt told me, 'because all the women before me in Hammer films had been victims. I don't think it's good to be a victim because people don't remember victims, they only remember the villains who perpetrate the crimes. As Christopher Lee had played it to perfection as Dracula, I wanted to play it to perfection too.' Just as Lee's good looks were considered 'too foreign' for leading roles, so Pitt's East European beauty was thought too exotic to play romantic leads. But the mainstream's loss was Gothic cinema's gain, and just as Lee made a lupine ladykiller, so Pitt gave us a feline female of the species. 'If I'd known as much about vampirism then as I do now, it probably would have killed my performance totally,' says Pitt, 'because there's a prevailing innocence over the film, including my character Carmilla. She had a sort of loving vileness about her, an evil that was quite undeliberate, quite gentle and loving, which was what made her so dangerous.'

Ingrid Pitt's second stint as a bloodthirsty Goth babe was in *Countess Dracula*. It was something of a crossbreed, not least because the director, Peter Sasdy, wanted to make a Gothic historical drama, while the studio demanded a more traditional horror picture. Inspired by Valentine Penrose's book, *The Bloody Countess*, it recounts the life and crimes of the real-life Transylvanian Countess Erzebet Bathori (better known by the westernised name Elizabeth Bathory). Accused of murdering over 600 young girls, Penrose's decadent history claims the Countess killed not just to satisfy sadistic lesbian urges, but also because she believed that, by invoking black magic, it was possible to use virgin blood as an elixir of youth.

Pitt delivers another magnetically erotic performance, noting affectionately in her *Bedside Companion for Vampire Lovers* how the film benefited from 'wonderful sets, fabulous costumes, a story that would peel tiles off a mortuary wall and a prime director.' There was, however, a 'problem with the blood. It seemed a bit ridiculous to me that I exposed everything for a blood-bath then prodded fairly futilely at the jiggly bits with a practically dry sponge. I wanted to have the virgins strung up overhead, have their throats cut and let the gore shower over me. That's what Erzebet Bathori, the character the film was based on, did. If only!'

Polish actress Ingrid Pitt became the new 'horror from Hammer' in 1970, creating a voluptuous female counterpart to Christopher Lee's horror heartthrob.

Lust for a Vampire cast Swedish beauty Yutte Stensgaard in the role of Carmilla Karnstein, while *Twins of Evil* featured twin brunette bombshells, Madeline and Mary Collinson, in the title roles. All of the ladies made credible undead temptresses, but lacked the strange intensity Pitt brought to her interpretation.

These films were the exotic swansong of Hammer horror. Recent years have seen a renewed interest in the humble British horror movie of the 1970s, especially among cult film fanatics, who maintain that, far from being in crisis, Gothic celluloid enjoyed a brief golden age. Hammer may have been on their last legs, but other UK studios – most notably Amicus

– were producing some fine contemporary Gothic, predominantly in the anthology format, which featured several stories in one movie. Sex-and-violence-oriented exploitation director Peter Walker took advantage of loosening censorship to produce memorably nasty, squalidly kinky movies like *House of Whipcord*, 1974, and *House of Mortal Sin*, 1975. Even Vincent Price, that most American of Gothic icons, made some of his best movies in the UK in the 1970s,

British-born horror heroine Barbara Steele gets nailed by Italian Gothic, in Mario Bava's
The Mask of Satan *(aka* Black Sunday*, 1961).*

such as the two *Dr Phibes* films – *Abominable* in 1971, and *Rises Again* in 1972 – and the camp Shakespearean shocker, *Theatre of Blood*, 1973.

Ingrid Pitt's only true rival for the crown of cinema's Goth Queen came in the reluctant form of Barbara Steele, whom Tim Burton describes as 'one of the only real horror goddesses'. 'She has a great otherworldly quality,' notes Roger Corman, 'her bone structure, her face, the way of movement.' Corman cast her opposite Vincent Price in *The Pit and the Pendulum*, confirming Steele's place in the pantheon of Gothic legends. It was a status first established when the actress starred in the 1960 Italian cult hit *Black Sunday* (aka *The Mask of Satan*) in which she played both the vampire villainess, Asa, and the heroine, her virtuous descendent Katia, her unorthodox good looks suggesting both erotic vulnerability and smouldering evil. (There is something of the sinister china-doll about Steele's appearance, akin to the otherwordly good looks that established Christina Ricci as an equally reluctant Gothic sex symbol three decades later.)

Black Sunday was directed by Mario Bava, and clearly influenced by the Hammer style of

Gothic – although fans maintain that Bava's efforts are superior to their inspiration. Bava is one of a number of Italian directors who turned out horror films from the 1960s to early 1980s, now established as cult favourites among connoisseurs of cult movies. Typically, Italian horror is more explicit and visually stylish than its British or American counterparts, though plots are often incoherent and derivative, acting is wooden and the scripts less than lyrical. Other giants of Italian horror include Lucio Fulci, who specialised in garish gore, and Dario Argento, whose show-stopping set-pieces created a cult of admirers.

The Italian horror movies of the 1960s dwelt upon Gothic taboos which most American and English studios would not dare address. In her follow-up to *Black Sunday*, *The Terror of Dr Hichcock* (1962 – the 'T' removed from 'Hitchcock' for fear of legal action from the English director), Steele played the second wife of a doctor, whose first wife died while engaged in perverse sex. The good doctor could only get it up if his partner feigned death – or, 'The candle of his lust burnt brightest in the shadow of the grave,' as the promotional blurb put it. Strong stuff in the 1960s! 'I liked doing all of those scenes that had these forbidden aspects to them,' Steele later confessed, 'Necrophilia, incest, all these kinds of repressed emotions.'

Despite this, Steele resented the way the success of her perverse Gothic persona – the 'predatory bitch goddess' as she put it – eclipsed her other work. For a long time she avoided talking about her 1960s horror films, and denied ever having seen any of them. Only recently has she come to terms with her Gothic past, calling the films' appeal 'a mystery', but theorising that fans 'sense something in me, and maybe what it is that they sense is some kind of psychic pain. Some kind of childhood grief. Some kind of isolation and some unresolved pain.' As if to seal her reconciliation with her iconic status, Steele accepted a leading role in the brief early 1990s revival of small-screen Gothic soap opera *Dark Shadows*.

By way of contrast, the earthier Ingrid Pitt has always embraced cult acclaim. 'If you're famous for doing a certain type of role, that shows you've done it well, so why revile it?' she told me. Indeed, the multi-talented actress has now written several books on Gothic themes, and appears regularly in a number of British vampire and Gothic magazines, penning features for the likes of *Bite Me!*. She was also given a cameo role in 'Vampirology', the second episode of the UK TV series *Urban Gothic*: a postmodern tale of the undead in modern London filmed as a mock documentary, its lead character, Rex, a cool but sleazy vampire, struck dumb with admiration for his screen idol when he glimpses her in a restaurant.

This admiration is shared by *Urban Gothic*'s scriptwriter, self-confessed Goth Tom de Ville. 'When I was a kid, the Hammer girls were the epitome of desire,' de Ville told alternative culture magazine, *Meltdown*. 'One of the ways that I first got into horror was through an old book of horror movies that was in my library at school, which I used to flick through all the time. There was something about the way the women looked which doesn't exist today. It was something unique, and Ingrid was the queen of them in a way.'

Consciously or otherwise, the Goth babes in low-cut, but elegant funereal gowns, and their consorts in morbid period garb, borrowed heavily from the sumptuous imagery all Hammer horror fans had absorbed in the previous decade. This classic Gothic look saw its heyday as an underground fashion statement in the Goth clubs of the late 1980s. More recently, as Goth rock has been increasingly eclipsed by sampling, electronic beats and synthesiser-based sounds, it has been accompanied by a tendency towards a more futuristic-

One of Hammer's Twins of Evil *(1971), Madeline Collinson.*
(Not to be confused with her identical sister Mary, who refused to disrobe on-screen.)

fetishistic look dubbed 'cybergoth'. Many Goths, however, remain true to their traditional roots – such as Nosferatu, one of the most popular UK Goth bands, boasting old-school spooky aesthetics. When I spoke to lead guitarist and founder member, Damien de Ville (no relation to Tom), in 1991, he confirmed, 'stylistically, and in dress, we do take a lot of inspiration from Hammer films . . . We used to have intros to most of our songs at live shows, but we found it broke the set up too much. We've used a lot of different horror films for that before – Hammer movies, a lot of Vincent Price talkovers which usually fit in with the mood of the lyrics.'

Regardless of late successes such as the Karnstein trilogy, by the early 1970s Hammer's days were clearly numbered. Many date the beginning of the studio's terminal decline as early as 1968 – the year it received the Queen's Award for Industry. Not everybody, however, celebrated the studio's decade as leaders in the horror market – newspapers like *the Daily Worker* lamented their 'spectacular rise to power and prosperity through ten years of trading in morbidity, putrefaction and pain.'

   In 1968, two horror films appeared that challenged Hammer's supremacy in the genre. *Night Of The Living Dead* came from the commercial underground, a shoestring-budget American film that took the drive-in market by storm – and, as far as many young horror fans were concerned, blew away Hammer's cobwebs forever. The other film actually earned enough critical approval to win an Academy Award (for best supporting actress). *Rosemary's Baby* was faithfully adapted from a best-selling novel about urban Satanism by Ira Levin. Ironically, its producer was William Castle, whose gimmick-laden Gothic horrors hadn't impressed the critics at all back in the 1950s.

Castle, however, had been convinced by his backers to hand the director's chair to an up-and-coming young European, Roman Polanski. Despite his diminished role, Castle maintained that his involvement in the movie led to him suffering from an unspecified curse, which culminated in his hospitalisation with acute uremic poisoning. He became convinced that 'the story of *Rosemary's Baby* [is] happening in life. Witches, all of them, casting their spell' and of 'becoming one of the principal players' in a horrific drama that was spilling off the screen into reality. Castle's paranoia can only have intensified when he found out that the film's soundtrack composer had been admitted into the same hospital with a freak head injury that was soon to prove fatal.

It would be easy to dismiss Castle's claims as a case of Hollywood's greatest showman, never off-duty, taking advantage of his illness to promote his latest project even while in hospital. Certainly Roman Polanski, the film's Polish-born director, called the claims 'ridiculous'. But Polanski was himself at the centre of a vortex of dramatic events playing out between cinema and the occult. In an 'illustrated history of cursed movies', *Hollywood Hex* author Mikita Brottman, dedicates two out of seven chapters to the coincidences, curses and calamities that have attended Polanski's career. But even Brottman fails to detail fully the numerous strange myths and omens that haunt the films of Polanski before and after *Rosemary's Baby*.

Like fellow Pole Ingrid Pitt, Polanski's earliest years were blighted by experiences of the Nazi occupation in the early 1940s. 'I come from a background which should have slanted me towards the macabre. I was born into the biggest horror show of the century, the brutalities of the Nazi regime, and anything after that was like a walk on the banks of the Euphrates,' wrote Pitt in the autobiographical intro to her *Bedside Companion*. She was able to channel her traumatic past into a healthy appreciation of the Gothic. Polanski was not so fortunate – not least because the future still had further horrors in store for him: the brutally sadistic murder of his heavily pregnant wife in 1969, at the hands of a loosely knit band of hippies dubbed 'the Manson Family', after Charles Manson, their acid-guru leader.

Polanski first rose to prominence making a series of claustrophobic, twisted psychodramas in the early 1960s, before filming a full-blown Gothic horror movie in 1967 – variously titled *Dance of the Vampires* or *The Fearless Vampire Killers*, with the subtitle *Pardon Me, but Your Teeth Are in My Neck*. This flippancy gives a sense of the film's chief weakness, as Polanski balked at making a straight Gothic horror, diluting his film with a series of gags that turn it into a cheesy Hammer parody. Despite this, some scenes rise above the puerile humour to attain a certain morbid magnificence, like the climactic vampire ball of the film's title (although it owes much to a similar undead masque in the 1962 Hammer horror, *Kiss of the Vampire*).

The female lead in Polanski's *Dance* was his achingly beautiful, red-headed wife, Sharon Tate, playing what the script described as 'a sacrifice to Lucifer' – falling victim to the vampires of the title. Meanwhile, in San Francisco, a young hippie girl called Susan 'Sadie' Atkins had secured a job working for Anton LaVey's Church of Satan in a lurid publicity stunt entitled 'The Topless Witches Revue'. Atkins, employed to emerge semi-nude from a coffin as a vampire, would later be one of the quartet of bloodthirsty hippies who broke into Tate's Hollywood home in August 1969, butchering the actress and four of her friends. Atkins reputedly licked blood off the knife she used to murder Tate. That same night, the hippie-hating LaVey claimed he had placed a curse upon the whole movement.

Back in 1967, Polanski was researching *Rosemary's Baby*. He employed LaVey as a consultant, used him in publicity, and even featured him in the film. LaVey plays the Devil in the notorious satanic rape scene, although his many detractors dispute this, claiming the Devil costume was far too small for a full-grown man. Despite, or perhaps owing to, its ambivalence towards its subject matter, *Rosemary's Baby* was a big hit, critics and audiences alike thrilling to Polanski's chilling but unsensational approach to the birth of the Antichrist. For some critics his style was too downbeat, *Film Quarterly*'s reviewer complaining that the Satanists in the film weren't 'frightening, but an absurd lot, rather like a small far-out California religious

Roman Polanski with his wife Sharon Tate, in Gothic parody The Fearless Vampire Killers *(1967). Tate later fell victim to the horror of the 1969 Manson massacres.*

sect.' It's a description that could just as easily have described Manson's rag-tag crew, who seemed more pathetic than threatening until they bared their teeth in 1969.

Whatever one makes of all the striking coincidences and occultic synchronicities, Polanski was traumatised by his loss and resolved to throw himself into his work. Deciding that 'a comedy, a horror film, or a thriller were out of the question,' his chosen project was very surprising. For Polanski decided to make a cinematic adaptation of William Shakespeare's most Gothic work, *Macbeth* (1971), a bloody play which those in the theatrical world believed to be 'cursed'. The Polish director chose to bring the horrific aspects to the fore in a version which some still condemn as too graphic. It's impossible to watch without being seized by parallels between the action on screen and the murders that blighted the director's life just a few months before.

Polanski banned discussion of the tragedy on set, but alluded to it himself on at least one occasion. It was hardly surprising – although there is nothing in the play identical to the events of Polanski's personal tragedy, the similarities would send a shudder down any spine. The addled Manson family had considered trying to save Polanski's child by performing an improvised caesarian section, sinisterly echoing the birth of Macduff, Macbeth's bane, who was himself 'from his mother's womb / Untimely ripp'd.' Even Polanski implicitly recognised the connections. When the critic, Kenneth Tynan was employed to revise Shakespeare's text for filming, he was particularly concerned about the scene portraying the murder of Macduff's infant child. 'A difficult moment came when I questioned the amount of blood that would be shed by a small boy stabbed in the back,' wrote Tynan, 'Polanski replied bleakly, "You didn't see my house last summer. I know about bleeding."'

Newsweek's reviewer observed, 'parallels between the Manson murders and the mad, bloody acts of these beautiful, damned Macbeths kept pressing themselves upon the viewer, as though Shakespeare's play has provided Polanski with some strange opportunity to act out his own complicated feelings about mystic ties, blood, evil and revenge... All that is good here seems but a pretext for close-ups of knives drawing geysers of blood from the flesh of men, women and children. No chance to revel in gore is passed up,' concluding that Polanski's *Macbeth* is a 'work of art – in the same manner of Buchenwald, Lidice and, yes, the Manson murders.'

But before the murders introduced real-life melodrama into his career, the fact that a European arthouse director like Polanski received big-budget backing to undertake a horror picture, and that the results made a great deal of money, changed Hollywood's attitude to the genre. During the 1970s, for the first time since the 1930s, studios spent big bucks and hired established names to make horror movies like *The Exorcist* (1973) and *The Omen* (1976). Both were satanic paranoia pictures like Rosemary's baby, both won Oscars, and both made substantial profits, *The Exorcist* being the most successful horror film up to that point.

But both also represented a move away from atmospheric Gothic into more polished mainstream territory – without *Rosemary's Baby's* religious ambivalence, they turned Christian parables into horror fables. Polanski would not return to the Gothic arena until 1999 with the release of *The Ninth Gate*, another satanic thriller. Despite the presence of Gothic-romantic leading man Johnny Depp, however, *The Ninth Gate* is disappointing. Perhaps Polanski has finally banished his creative demons.

Night of the Living Dead (1968) shared *Rosemary's Baby's* downbeat feel, this time taken to documentary extremes, and *Macbeth's* unflinching attitude to bloodshed, but not, thankfully, for those concerned, the eerie parallels between life and art. Made in Pittsburgh by director, George A. Romero, and co-writer, John Russo, as their micro-budget debut, the film was originally reviled by most critics as an obscenity, although the benefit of hindsight would later establish it as a classic of cinematic art.

The response of noted critic Roger Ebert gives an idea of the impact this modest production had on unsuspecting audiences. 'The kids in the audience were stunned,' wrote Ebert of a matinee performance. 'There was almost complete silence. The movie had long ago stopped being delightfully scary, and had become unexpectedly terrifying. A little girl across

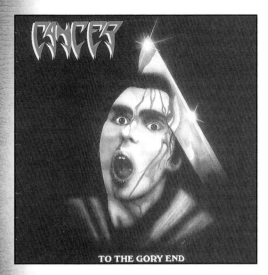

To the Gory End *by British death-metal band Cancer.*
The cover depicts a scene from George A. Romero's
1979 zombie-splatter classic Dawn of the Dead.

the aisle from me, maybe nine years old, was sitting very still in her seat and crying.

'I don't think the younger kids really knew what hit them. They'd seen horror films before, but this was something else. This was ghouls eating people – you could actually see what they were eating. This was little girls killing their mothers. This was being set on fire. Worst of all, nobody got out alive – even the hero got killed.'

As the disturbed critic suggests, the film's powerful impact was acheived not just by its casual attitude to graphic gore, but also by its nihilistic inversion of genre conventions. The hero, played by black actor Duane Jones, makes mistakes and meets an anti-climactic fate that is bleak in its absurdity, as he is casually shot by the gung-ho rescue party, who mistake him for one of the flesh-eating undead. As Kim Newman observes in *Nightmare Movies*, his history of the modern horror movie (which begins in 1968, in tribute to *Night of the Living Dead*'s importance), 'English gothic cinema was fatally wounded by the bullet in Duane Jones's head.' That act of shocking violence signalled the death knell for Hammer's sumptuous, low-budget period pieces, just as much as high-budget competition from the big studios made them seem redundant in the 1970s.

This wave of visceral tension gained further momentum several years later, when the story of Edward Gein began to bleed into pop culture and inspired a decidedly disreputable movie – 1974 midnight-matinee sensation, *The Texas Chainsaw Massacre*. The film opens with a prologue that assures the audience that what follows is based upon a true story – it isn't, but the film's cannibalistic family of inbred, skin-draped rednecks are not wholly without factual basis. 'My relatives that lived in a town close to Ed Gein told me these terrible stories,' director Tobe Hooper told *Clive Barker's A-Z of Horror*, 'these tales of human-skin lampshades and furniture. I grew up with that like a horror story you tell around a campfire. I didn't even know about Ed Gein, I just knew about something that happened there that was horrendous. But the image really stuck.' *The Texas Chainsaw Massacre*, like *Night of the Living Dead*, is regarded as a landmark, either as a new low of graphic exploitation or a bold Gothic foray into America's bloody heart of darkness, depending on how strong your stomach happens to be.

Romero didn't follow up his own traumatising debut until 1979, with *Dawn of the Dead*, which followed the descent of civilisation into chaos under the onslaught of cannibalistic walking cadavers. While *Dawn of the Dead* is certainly grim and graphic, its comical, almost slapstick, elements are increasingly evident. The film works on several levels: concealed beneath its flesh-eating facade is a very sick comedy, and some astute social commentary. After legal wrangling, John Russo released *Return of the Living Dead,* his alternative *Night of the Living Dead* sequel, in 1985. It arrived at much the same time as Romero completed his 'Anubis' trilogy (after the ancient Egyptian god of the dead) with *Day of the Dead* – perhaps the most nihilistic and harrowing of the three, with little to distract from its central theme of desolation and decay. A journalist in a Richmond, Virginia paper dubbed the film 'a cesspool of vile filth produced by a sick mind for sick-minded people who delight in seeing viscera rawly ripped out of bodies, eaten and sucked on by deformed zombie extras'.

By way of contrast, *Return of the Living Dead* upped the sick humour quotient to create a feast of ghoulish fun, with a soundtrack featuring death rock favourites, such as the Cramps and the Damned. The same subcultural chic is apparent in the casting: with a gang of bored punks as the protagonists – most memorably Linnea Quigley, as punk slut Trash, fantasising about being eaten alive as she strips off, before 'Partytime', by death rock pioneers 45 Grave, kicks off on the soundtrack and the zombies attack. Both films are underrated, although Russo's anarchic enthusiasm for blending guilty giggles with gore was more indicative of the trend towards horror-comedy in the 1980s.

While *Night of the Living Dead* created a new monster in the form of the cannibalistic zombie, the other creature that dominated late twentieth-century horror cinema was the serial killer – or at least a heavily-fictionalised version of this real-life horror. While one could argue that Alfred Hitchcock's 1960 *Psycho* initiated the trend, the real pioneers were John Carpenter's 1978 hit, *Hallowe'en,* and Sean Cunningham's hugely successful 1980 hack-job, *Friday the 13th.* Between the two of them, they launched the 'stalk-and-slash' sub-genre – films featuring masked killers who brutally murder a series of teens in increasingly inventive and absurd ways. Not only were the killers unstoppable, but the films generated seemingly endless vapid sequels, much to the dismay of critics and horror purists alike. Perhaps they misread these plotless wonders – certainly they read too much into them.

The preponderance of vulnerable, naked, female flesh in these films was not a comment against promiscuity, or an

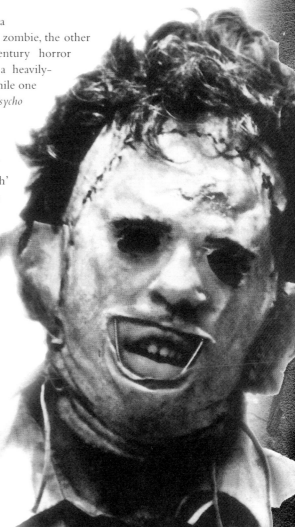

Gunnar Hansen as cannibalistic simpleton Leatherface in The Texas Chainsaw Massacre *(1974). This dripping slab of American Gothic was supposedly inspired by the case of Ed Gein.*

expression of rampant misogyny – it was just because the predominantly young male audience liked looking at tits and ass as well as gory set-pieces. The real ancestors of the stalk-and-slash flick were not in Gothic cinema, but in the slapstick movies of days gone by. The murders were just extreme versions of the cruel mishaps that befell the likes of Charlie Chaplin and Harold Lloyd in the heyday of silent cinema, only now stand-bys like ladders and buckets had been replaced with chainsaws and machetes. When mainstream Hollywood got around to satirising the sub-genre with movies like *Scream* (1996), it seemed woefully unaware that no-one – cast, crew or fans – had ever taken these films seriously anyhow.

The *Nightmare on Elm Street* films (initiated in 1984) are the most Gothic of the stalk-and-slash series – with a dominant dream theme, a comparatively complex villain in Freddy Krueger, and a willingness to address taboos. (The film also featured Johnny Depp's big-screen debut.) Freddy is a child-killer, maybe even a paedophile – not something Hollywood would usually tackle. Even here, Krueger is closer to a crazed vaudeville comedian than Count Dracula, and most 'splatter movies' – as gore-heavy, low-budget offerings became known – are at best quasi-Gothic, lacking sophistication and style, substituting quick shocks for atmosphere or unease.

By the 1980s, splatter was addressing a new core audience, whose bible was the magazine, *Fangoria*, and whose heroes were the special effects artists who created the gore that defined their sub-genre. The unchallenged king of viscera is Tom Savini. A school-friend of George Romero, Savini was slated to work on *Night of the Living Dead* but was called up for service in Vietnam instead. He partially attributes his success to his experiences there, claiming, 'the severed heads or the body parts have to be real to me. I have to get the same feeling that I had when I saw the real gore in Vietnam as a photographer.'

Later, Savini established his reputation with special effects for *Dawn of the Dead* and *Friday the 13th*. Just as, in the 1980s, the drive-in monster movies of the 1950s-60s inspired many death rock bands, and the Gothic horror output of Hammer and AIP in the 1960s-70s helped inspire the Goth subculture, so the splatter movies created by Savini and friends in the 1970s-80s created a generation of 'gorehounds', who, in the 1990s, formed the extreme heavy metal scene that became the core of a new underground. Most overtly, these gore-obsessed death metal bands would often dedicate their frantic, brutal guitar compositions to favourite splatter films. Although there's little in common between their frenzied world of video viscera and the dark elegance of the Goth scene, just as the Gothic romances of Anne Radcliffe are worlds apart from the celluloid creations of George Romero, they share the same roots. By the end of the 1990s, the subcultures would crossbreed to create the popular hybrid of Gothic metal.

Splatter movies arose partly in response to the new video market that emerged in the early 1980s. Just as drive-ins had created a demand for sensational but shabby productions in the 1950s, so the introduction of the VCR to living rooms across the world created a new market for cheap chillers. Most of the horror films that exploited this new market were primitive at best and did little to enrich the Gothic aesthetic. But, just as in the 1950s, there were a few real gems to be found among the bargain-basement dross.

The most significant was director Sam Raimi's deranged 1983 masterpiece, *The Evil Dead*. A witty rollercoaster ride stuffed to capacity with shocks and laughs, the film makes up for its paucity of plot and characterisation by giving the audience virtually no space to breathe. Ash, the film's hapless hero (played with peerless hysteria by Bruce Campbell), is trapped in an isolated log cabin, where he is besieged by a delirious barrage of demonic manifestations. (The forces of evil are unleashed by an ancient book called *The Necronomicon* – a wry nod to H. P. Lovecraft, who invented the tome as the unholy bible of his Cthulhu Mythos.) In the 1987 sequel, *Evil Dead II*, Raimi perfected what Max Méténier, founder of the Grand Guignol theatre, described as the 'hot and cold showers' of horror and humour, each designed to emphasise the effect of the other. Just as the stalk-and-slash flick's true ancestor was slapstick, so Raimi's *Evil Dead* films owe as much to the violence of Warner Brothers cartoons as they do to the Gothic aesthetic. Bruce Campbell's monster-hunter, Ash, bears greater resemblance to the mistreated Wile E. Coyote of the *Roadrunner* cartoons than he does to Van Helsing.

The Babysitter Murders, *an album by English Goth band Brother Orchid, borrowed the original title of the 1978 film* Halloween *and its cover image from the film's poster.*

A more conventional marriage between traditional Gothic and 1980s splatter was achieved by director, Stuart Gordon, best known for his free-wheeling adaptations of H. P. Lovecraft's short stories. The first of these, *Re-Animator* (1985), takes an unpromising Lovecraft tale and turns it into a gloriously sick black comedy that deals with the outrageous possibilities created by a re-animating fluid that wakes the dead. Who knows what old-fashioned H.P. would have made of the exuberant tastelessness? A highlight is the sight gag, when the re-animated villain places his severed cranium between the naked heroine's legs, 'giving her head'. Lead actor, Jeffrey Combs, as mad scientist Herbert West makes a fitting successor to Ernest Thesiger's camped-up Dr Pretorius in the 1935 classic, *The Bride of Frankenstein*. Gordon was evidently aware of the parallel, dubbing his 1990 *Re-Animator* sequel *Bride of Re-Animator*.

More serious use of similar source material was displayed in 1987's *Hellraiser*, a film both written and directed by horror's *enfant terrible*, Clive Barker, based on his story 'The Hellbound Heart'. The result was a new take on the legend of Faust, a tale of the quest for ultimate experience – total pleasure and pain – which plunges the seeker into the realm of the Cenobites. These leather-clad, sadomasochistic demons subject themselves and their victims to an eternal torment of exquisite agony with a range of exotic techniques. *Hellraiser* quickly became a cult success, establishing Barker as a unique and disturbing voice with a new audience, and generating a series of sequels along with a range of merchandise.

Most of this merchandise centred around the lead Cenobite, who became known as Pinhead, because of the matrix of nails that covered his pale cranium. This icon of horror – like the film itself – stood head and shoulders above *Friday the 13th*'s Jason or the wisecracking

Freddy Krueger. As Barker observes of his most notorious creation in *The Hellraiser Chronicles*, a book about the movie series: 'where, I am regularly asked, does this nightmare [Pinhead] come from? Well, I've already made mention of the sadomasochistic elements, which reflect my own long-standing interest in such taboo areas. Associated with that milieu is the punkish influence, which makes Pinhead the Patron Saint of Piercing.'

'Somebody once asked me what the main difference was between the Hammer *Dracula* and Francis Ford Coppola's, and I said, "About $50 million,"' Christopher Lee dryly told me in 1997. (The actual budget was more like $40 million.) 'The other difference is that for the Hammer films we depended on performance, nowadays it's all special effects and make-up – it's all done for you.' Coppola's film *Bram Stoker's Dracula* (1992) initiated a traditional Gothic revival in Hollywood during the 1990s. Inevitably, not everybody was impressed by this big-budget take on the genre – especially hardcore horror fans, who had been disdained by the mainstream for so long that they decided they preferred it that way.

The film's clichéd romantic angle was derided as 'Mills and Boon Gothic,' by cult movie afficionado, Stefan Jaworzyn. Mina Harker (Winona Ryder), a comparatively minor character in the novel, became the focus of the film as a reincarnation of the Count's long dead love. One of the most clichéd plot devices in the Gothic genre, it was hackneyed when used way in Boris Karloff's 1932 film, *The Mummy*. Victorian author, H. Rider Haggard, had made use of the plot device in his 1886 dark adventure-fantasy, *She*, in which Ayesha, an immortal white African empress, falls for an English explorer who is the reincarnation of her long-dead lover. It might be forgivable, were it not for Coppola's well-publicised determination to deliver a faithful adaptation of the original Stoker novel, as emphasised by the film's title. But the high budget demanded that Coppola toe the Hollywood line, obliging him to include a love story at the film's core in despite its absence from the original novel.

Still, this darkly romantic appeal is nothing new. Bela Lugosi's 1931 *Dracula* was billed as 'The story of the strangest passion the world has ever known!', and released on Valentine's Day. According to promotional copy, Christopher Lee's *Dracula* was 'The Terrifying Lover who died – yet lived!' Even the 1922 *Nosferatu* – sometimes credited as the most faithful adaptation – has its monstrously ugly vampire lured to his death by the self-sacrificing heroine, out of love for her husband. Coppola's addition of a love affair between Count Dracula and Mina may be heavy-handed, but it's far from a fatal flaw. While the film deviates from Stoker's novel in other ways, it was inevitable that a lengthy Victorian novel would not reach the big screen unaltered.

But many of Coppola's innovations work well: the prologue, where he makes an explicit link between the Count and his historical inspiration, Vlad the Impaler, is powerfully exciting, as is the simultaneous establishment of the vampire's immortality as an outcome of his war with God. Gary Oldman's Count is a bold variation on the Lugosi/Lee cliché, and while Keanu Reeves, as the English hero, is clearly out of his depth, the decision to cast cult rhythm 'n' blues songwriter Tom Waits as the deranged Renfield more than compensates. (according to some reports, Lux Interior, frontman with psychobilly legends, the Cramps, provided vampire screams for the film). Overall, the film has a bold visual style that truly looks like a Hammer movie might have done if they had access to Columbia Pictures' bottomless coffers, and deservedly won Oscars for its costumes and make-up with a further nomination for art direction.

In the end, just as many horror films are revered as classics despite their low budgets, so perhaps a Gothic romance like *Bram Stoker's Dracula* encountered prejudice because of its high budget. Horror fans suckled on splatter barked that it was too slushy, students of the old Hammer school dismissed it as too flashy, but other filmgoers, myself included, enjoyed a sexy new spin on an old Gothic myth. In fact, *Bram Stoker's Dracula* was the highest-grossing vampire movie ever made, although it only retained this record for two years.

With such a success to his name, it's unsurprising that Coppola sniffed around the Gothic library for another property to film – settling upon the obvious follow-up in *Mary Shelley's Frankenstein* (1994). This time he took only production duties, vacating the director's chair in favour of acclaimed English Shakespearean actor Kenneth Branagh, who also took the lead as Victor Frankenstein. Legendary method actor Robert De Niro played opposite Branagh as his creation, with Helena Bonham Carter as Frankenstein's fiancée, Elizabeth. Once again, as indicated by the title, the film trumpets its fidelity to the source novel – although Branagh appeased contemporary mores by presenting Elizabeth and Victor as 'two equal partners', with Bonham Carter's character even reprising her role post-mortem as the Monster's prospective mate.

According to Branagh, he saw the story 'as less a horror film than a larger-than-life Gothic fairy

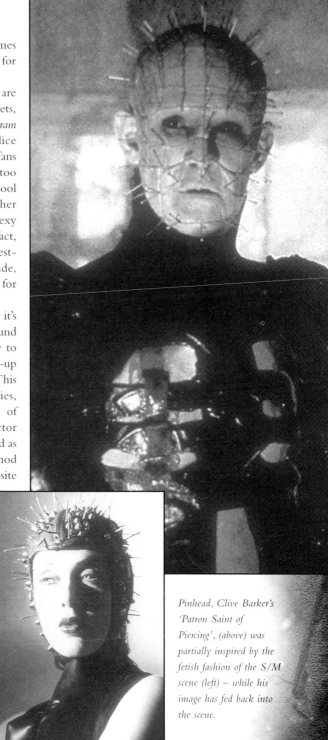

Pinhead, Clive Barker's 'Patron Saint of Piercing', (above) was partially inspired by the fetish fashion of the S/M scene (left) – while his image has fed back into the scene.

tale'. This is revealing, in that many enthusiasts of the genre are already aware that horror movies *are* Gothic fairy tales, albeit ones that retain their gore as opposed to the sanitised versions of today. Branagh's desire to distance his production from the horror genre is a clue as to why *Mary Shelley's Frankenstein* doesn't really work – the film is ashamed of its heritage, too anxious to protect its respectability as a literary adaptation. Like *Bram Stoker's Dracula*, the high budget ensures that it boasts lavish visuals, but the high-profile actors that come with such a hefty bankroll seem somehow out of their depth. De Niro isn't bad as the Creature, but he's no Karloff; Branagh is competent as Frankenstein, but nowhere near as compelling as

Jonathan Harker (Keanu Reeves) falls under the deadly spell of the Count's brides in Bram Stoker's Dracula *(1992).*

Peter Cushing. This film, far more than *Bram Stoker's Dracula*, illustrates Christopher Lee's contention that Hammer's low-budget shockers shone because they 'depended on performance'. While *Mary Shelley's Frankenstein* has all the requisite anatomical parts, its creator, Branagh, never really manages to bring it to life.

By way of contrast, another Gothic epic released the same year seemed dubious in conception but was beautifully realised. Anne Rice's *Interview with the Vampire* (1994) had been an obvious cinematic project since it became a publishing phenomenon in 1976, but it took nearly twenty years to come to fruition. Early signs were not promising – particularly the decision to cast bankable heartthrobs Tom Cruise and Brad Pitt as the lead vampires, Lestat and Louis, which alarmed many devotees of *The Vampire Chronicles*, as well as the author herself, who was vocal in her disapproval. But the director was Neil Jordan, who had adapted

Angela Carter's *The Company of Wolves* (1984) for the big screen a decade before, now a Goth classic. Crucially, just as he recruited Carter to help him bring her story to the screen, he employed Rice on scriptwriting duties for *Interview with the Vampire*. The results speak for themselves. Rice was even more public in her endorsement of the finished product than she had previously been about her reservations, eating her words in double-page ads. Cruise surprised just about everyone who had endured his performances in dross, such as *Top Gun*, by delivering a potent performance as Lestat. Pitt, if not so much of a revelation, at least looked suitably lost and confused as the angst-ridden vampire, Louis. The film vividly brought to life Anne Rice's romantic vision of doomed immortality, stealing the crown from *Bram Stoker's Dracula* as the most successful vampire picture ever made.

The year 1994 proved the high-water mark for Hollywood's Gothic vogue. Jack Nicholson essayed another of cinema's great creatures of the night in *Wolf*. There is something unmistakably lycanthropic about Nicholson's screen persona, but the film ultimately lacks the courage of its convictions – unable to decide whether it's a straight Gothic thriller or a self-consciously clever metaphor for the beast within.

In 1999 Universal's last great monster shambled in, bringing up the rear, in *The Mummy*. An enjoyable if empty-headed, effects-heavy action romp, *The Mummy* (and its similarly-successful sequel) owes more to the Indiana Jones films than Karloff's original and appeared to signal an end to Hollywood's *fin de siecle* Gothic revival.

The turn of the millennium brings us back to Tim Burton, the alienated California boy who, in 1999, created one of Gothic celluloid's instant classics in *Sleepy Hollow*. Burton had served his apprenticeship at Disney studios in the 1980s, where he made his proposed Gothic children's book, *Vincent*, into an animated short. While a clear indication of talent – winning awards at a number of independent film festivals – Disney were unsure what to do with *Vincent*, and quietly shelved it. The next year, Burton was allowed to make his first live-action film, a similarly mischievous 35-minute short entitled *Frankenweenie*. The MPAA objected to the 'tone', and awarded it a PG rating – which was death according to Disney, who demanded G pictures – and *Frankenweenie* was consigned to limbo like its predecessor.

Frankenweenie tells the story of ten-year-old Victor Frankenstein, who lives in suburbia and re-animates his dog Sparky as a scars-and-stitches monster after the unfortunate creature is run over. The film prefigured many of Burton's future preoccupations. It also attracted enough positive attention within the industry to secure Burton his first full-length feature project, outside of Disney's rigid guidelines, and later, to enable him to direct his first truly Burtonesque feature, the 1988 *Beetlejuice*.

Beetlejuice is a Gothic supernatural-comedy, with a level of energy and inventiveness that bemused many critics just as it delighted Burton's new fan cult. An exaggeratedly nice couple called the Maitlands die in a car wreck, and are forced to try to haunt the awful yuppie Deetz family who move into their home. The trouble is, the fresh arrivals are so vacuously trendy that they find the Maitlands' haunting an amusing feature of the house. Fortunately, the 'newlydeads' find an ally in the youngest member of the Deetz family, daughter Lydia (Winona Ryder), a Goth. Through Lydia the Maitlands employ the title character (Michael Keaton), a sleazy supernatural slimeball who specialises in 'exorcisms of the living'.

Logic and plot development are sacrificed in the name of Burton's distinctive vision, which blends the surrealistically garish colour of cartoons with the disorientating aesthetics of silent expressionist horror films. *Beetlejuice* is a dizzying fairground hall of mirrors, filled with the director's playful subversion. One of the film's central gags is about the ultimate taboo – Burton explaining that he 'always had it in mind to poke fun at death, and it was a case of what kind of people to put in here? Let's have a guy who's been in a shark attack, a skin diver with a shark on his leg. So we'd come up with sketches like the magician's assistant who's been sawed in half, or a guy who's been burnt to death while smoking in bed.'

It was another surprise money-spinner, and scored an Oscar for the effects team – vindicating Burton's belief that filmgoers would tolerate a little more weirdness than Hollywood gave them credit for. He was rewarded with the director's chair on Warner Brothers' big-budget *Batman* (1989). However, the director was clearly uncomfortable with the level of hype and attention surrounding such a high-profile production, and for his next film returned to something closer to his heart.

Edward Scissorhands (1990) had its roots in a drawing Burton made as a child: 'It came subconsciously and was linked to a character who wants to touch but can't, who was both creative and destructive.' In many ways, this is a reworking of the Frankenstein story as a modern suburban fairy tale. His 'monster' is just as childishly innocent and more obviously vulnerable than previous versions, a slender creature who looks rather like Burton himself. Despite lacking any physical bulk, however, he is dangerous because of the blades adorning his hands instead of fingers. For Edward was left unfinished by his creator (Vincent Price, in his final role), who is, nonetheless, a sympathetic character and certainly not the villain of the piece.

That distinction falls upon the eerily ultra-normal suburbanites, who live in the pastel houses surrounding the Gothic castle in which Edward is created. Here Burton draws strong parallels between the mob of villagers who would storm Frankenstein's castle and the conformist mob mentality at work beneath the surface of suburban America. 'I was always fascinated by that,' he confirms, 'and how the parallel between suburban life and a horror movie was really closer than you think.'

Winona Ryder starred as the love interest, an ordinary girl who sees the beauty beneath Edward's freakish exterior. Burton cast against type, Ryder's own personality reputedly being closer to the Goth misfit she played in *Beetlejuice* than to the clean-cut innocent of *Edward Scissorhands*. 'She responds to this dark material,' he observed, 'and I thought the idea of her as a cheerleader, wearing a blonde wig, was very funny.' Playing opposite her in the title role was Johnny Depp, entering into a highly productive working relationship with Burton. Burton could see in the rising star the same elements that had appealed to him in horror icons like Vincent Price, Christopher Lee and Peter Cushing: a mysterious, penetrating intelligence, inner turmoil, and an aloofness to the other characters with which the director could identify. But Depp's good looks were conventional enough to afford him pin-up status. In effect, Depp – erroneously 'perceived as dark and difficult and weird', according to Burton – was to become mainstream Hollywood's first Gothic teen idol. Indeed, *Entertainment Weekly* would later call Depp and girlfriend Christina Ricci (who also made her first cinematic waves in a Burton film, *Sleepy Hollow*) 'the [Spencer] Tracy and [Katharine] Hepburn of the Goth set'.

Winona Ryder as archetypal teen Goth girl Lydia – with Michael Keaton as the lecherous eponymous spectre in Tim Burton's Beetlejuice *(1987).*

After this self-indulgent slice of vintage Burton, it was time for the director to return to a (comparatively) conventional project, the sequel to his smash hit, *Batman*. While directing the exceedingly Gothic *Batman Returns* (1992), Burton handed over an idea he had been toying with since his Disney days, *Tim Burton's The Nightmare Before Christmas*, to director Henry Selick. The result is a charming, stop-motion animated musical, with a ghoulishly celebratory tone to delight the lightest of hearts and the blackest of souls.

Expressing the sentiment of Goths everywhere, Burton explained, 'Hallowe'en has always been the most fun night of the year. It's where rules are dropped and you can be anything at all. Fantasy rules. It's only scary in a funny way. Nobody's out to really scare anybody else to death. They're out to delight people with their scariness, which is what Hallowe'en is all about and what *Nightmare* is all about.' Ostensibly a children's film, Burton has been surprised by the wide variety of people who have taken it to their hearts, noting how he saw somebody who worked at Carnegie Hall wearing a *Nightmare Before Christmas* watch.

Burton's two tributes to the trashy monster movies of the 1950s followed, *Ed Wood* (1994) and *Mars Attacks!* (1996) – both are excellent, but neither was a great box-office success or overtly Gothic in tone. But his next project made a fitting Gothic finale to the first century of celluloid, ghoulishly embellishing a folksy short story written by Washington Irving in

1820. *Sleepy Hollow* (1999) is Burton's most perfectly realised picture; his first full-blooded period Gothic horror movie. In it he publicly repays the genre that inspired him to make films with cameo roles for Christopher Lee and Michael Gough – a talented supporting actor at Hammer, and star of producer Herman Cohen's horror 'B'-flicks *Horrors of the Black Museum* (1959) and *The Black Zoo* (1963).

Burton also borrowed Hammer's distinctive Gothic look from 30 years before. In particular, he strove to imitate Hammer-style expressionism, which the director describes as being like recreating 'the inside of somebody's head, like an internalised state externalised' – making even outdoor locations look like prepared sets to achieve the film's otherworldly atmosphere.

Johnny Depp takes the lead as Ichabod Crane – a stubbornly rationalist New York detective struggling to impose reason upon an obstinately supernatural case. It is a role in which Peter Cushing would have been marvellous, as Burton himself conceded (Cushing died in 1994 – following Burton's mentor Vincent Price, who died the previous year. Christina Ricci is the romantic lead – a role that 30 years earlier would have gone to Barbara Steele. The resemblance between the two actresses is intriguing – as is their determination not to be pigeon-holed as Gothic horror stars. Christopher Walken, too, is exhilarating as the Headless Horsemen – a natural role for the young Christopher Lee (seen here as the stern burgomaster who sends Crane on his mission).

Sleepy Hollow revives the classic period Gothic of Hammer and Corman – not strictly as it was, but even better than fans fondly remember it. It is appropriately tasteful grave-robbery, allowing us one last glance at these faded glories before the coffin lid of twentieth-century Gothic slammed shut for good.

In 'Creepshow', a 2001 cover feature for UK newspaper *The Guardian's* entertainment guide, critic Joe Queenan hails the arrival of a new wave of scary movies that favour a foreboding atmosphere over shock and violence. *The Sixth Sense*, the surprise hit film of 1999, began this cycle and went on to become the most successful horror movie ever made, entering the outer reaches of the ten top-grossing movies of all time. This modern Gothic chiller, about a young boy who believes he can speak with the dead, is subtle, intelligent and unusually downbeat. It found a low-budget equivalent in *The Blair Witch Project*, a mock-documentary about three young film-makers who disappear in the woods while investigating a local legend about a witch. Made on a shoestring budget of just $40,000, *The Blair Witch Project* took over $29,000,000 in its first weekend, making it the most successful independent movie ever made.

'Since these two films debuted in 1999, they have sparked a gradual resurgence of the unabashedly creepy film,' writes Queenan, 'where the audience is kept in suspense for long stretches of the movie and the body count is not especially high. Like *The Sixth Sense*, films such as *What Lies Beneath* and *The Haunting* (a disappointingly flashy remake of the subtle 1963 classic, based on Shirley Jackson's novel, *The Haunting of Hill House*) centre on ghosts who are desperately trying to contact the living in the hopes of vindication, revenge or emotional peace.'

All of these pictures have more in common with the Gothic ghost-story tradition than the gross-outs familiar to horror movie audiences of the last few decades. Indeed, their plots could quite easily have been written by the godfather of the ghost story, M. R. James, had he lived in the final years of the twentieth century rather than those of its opening. The focus of Queenan's feature is *The Others*, a haunted house film set in the 1940s that he describes as 'easily one of the most claustrophobic movies of all time'. The other titles he previews, however, hark back to the Gothic atmosphere from a very modern perspective – *Session 9*, for example, features a team of asbestos-removal specialists who unleash something nasty while treating a derelict lunatic asylum.

Those other Gothic standbys – the vampire and the werewolf – have also entered the 21st century in style. The Canadian-made *Ginger Snaps* (2000) uses the werewolf as a metaphor for menstruation, the Ginger of the title being a Goth-misfit teenager (played by Katharine Isabelle) going through changes that turn out to be more than the standard hormonal 'curse', with only her oddball sister Brigette (Emily Perkins) to help her. 'I got this ache,' Ginger explains, 'and I thought it was for sex, but it's to tear everything to fucking pieces!' Incidentally, the same theme use of lycanthropy as a metaphor for menstruation appears in the classic *The Company of Wolves*, and even in the song 'Wolf Moon' by sardonic Goth-metal band, Type O Negative.

Shadow of the Vampire, another critically acclaimed low-budget 2000 release, brings the story of Gothic celluloid full circle. A fictionalised account of the making of the 1922 German film, *Nosferatu*, it postulates that Max Schreck, the actor who played the eponymous vampire, really was a member of the undead, recruited by director F. W. Murnau in an obsessive quest for authenticity. Willem Defoe is uncanny as the inhuman Schreck, stalking the lovingly recreated expressionistic sets that blur the distinction between celluloid and reality, like some kind of giant shaven rodent. Like *Ginger Snaps*, *Shadow of the Vampire*'s central conceit is comic, but played with such skill and seriousness that its black humour just adds to the atmosphere of menace, wonder and dread.

Indeed, director, Elias Merhige, uses vampirism as an underlying metaphor for what he sees as the strange power of film. He depicts Murnau as just as much of a monster as the vampire he employs, a 'psychic vampire' who beguiles and then drains his actors, offering them a strange immortality at an awful price. As Merhige told *Wicked* magazine, '*Shadow of the Vampire* really became a vessel for a lot of things that I've been thinking about for years in terms of the metaphysics of what moviemaking is... it's almost a kind of sorcery that takes place.'

In true Goth style, Christina Ricci resented her 'Goddess of Gothic' tag: 'I was called [a] Goth. People made me sound weird . . . Someone dark, different . . .'

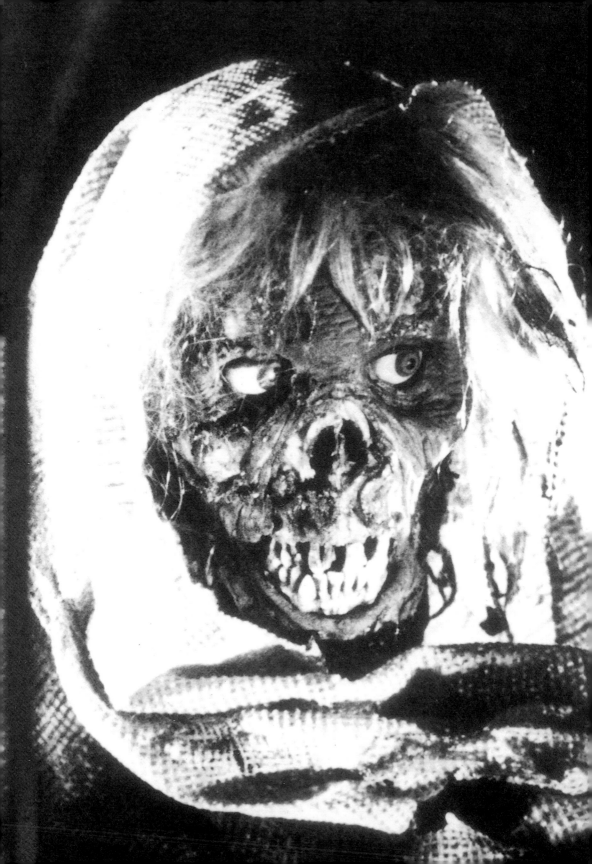

Chapter VI

The Seduction of the Innocent: From Shilling Shockers to Graphic Novels

When book publishers began shunning the Gothic novel in the early nineteenth century, it lived on in poorly printed periodicals. Some, such as the Gothic chapbooks (cheap and cheerful folded paper booklets), and Gothic bluebooks (referring to the colour of the cover rather than any erotic content), were digest-sized mini-novels. Others, like the later 'penny dreadfuls', 'penny bloods' and 'shilling shockers', ran episodic stories. These gaudy publications were born of new technology that allowed affordably ugly books to be printed, and Gothic creativity to survive when fashion removed it from the mainstream.

Typically, unscrupulous publishers would commission works borrowing characters, titles, even authors' names, from hit Gothic novels, distilling hundreds of pages into a few episodes. While Gothic novels were only affordable to the upper classes and, via lending libraries, to the middle classes, these periodicals were aimed at the working man and woman. They were crack to of the Gothic novel's powdered cocaine, but they probably contributed more to working-class literacy than any educational program.

Foremost among their contributors was George W. M. Reynolds, who, in his time (he died in 1879), was a more popular author than Charles Dickens. Dickens sometimes made use of Gothic story elements (although, given the starvation wages paid to Reynolds and his contemporaries, they were actually closer to the poor that Dickens described). Reynolds' greatest successes were a trilogy of horror sagas: *Faust* (1846), *Wagner the Wehr-wolf* (1847) and *The Necromancer* (1857). The first was a loose adaptation of the Faust legend; the second was one of the first 'wehr-wolf' stories in English, about a pact with the devil signed by Faust's

The host of Creepshow *(1982) – a tribute to EC horror hosts the Crypt Keeper, the Vault Keeper and the Old Witch, by horror specialists George A. Romero and Stephen King.*

apprentice that turns him into a werewolf once a month. The title character of *The Necromancer* is Lord Danvers, a medieval rogue, who also signs a demonic pact he can only escape if he finds six virgins willing to be sacrificed in his place. Sadly, the lascivious Lord falls one short of his target.

Reynolds' chief competition came from one of the first vampire stories, *Varney the Vampire* – a sensation that ran to 220 chapters during its 1845-7 serialised publication. *Varney* has largely disappeared into obscurity, and even its authorship is now disputed (ascribed variously to two writers named James Malcolm Rymer and Thomas Peckett). But it is not without its admirers – the Gothic Society's Tina Rath made a spirited defence of this much-maligned but little-read epic of hackwork in her *Udolpho* article 'The Unknown Vampire'. Rath, who first came across the Victorian villain, incongruously enough, in a Christmas anthology when she was only eight or nine years old, observes how Varney was, 'my first vampire, and as they say, you never forget your first.'

Varney the Vampire created a halfway house between the repulsive revenant of tradition and the familiar satanic smoothie of modern folklore. The author introduces the bloodsucker of the title thus: 'The figure turns around and the light falls upon the face. It is perfectly white – perfectly bloodless. The eyes look like polished tin; the lips are drawn back and the principle feature next to those dreadful eyes is the teeth – the fearful looking teeth – projecting like those of some wild animal, hideously, glaringly white and fanglike. It approaches the bed with a strange gliding movement. It clashes together the long nails that literally appear to hang from the finger ends.' Overwritten? Probably. Overwrought? Certainly. But so is much of Dickens' classic fiction, and popular demand never insisted he extend one of his efforts to 220 chapters.

By the early twentieth century, printing technology allowed the production of even cheaper, uglier periodicals aimed at a younger, less affluent market than more reputable publications. These became known as 'pulps' (due to the dismal quality of the paper used) and concentrated on genre fiction – crime, science fiction, fantasy and, of course, Gothic horror. Popular titles included *Famous Fantastic Mysteries*, *Terror Tales* and *Horror Stories*, most disappearing into the obscurity that claimed Varney and friends. One title that has survived, albeit somewhat erratically, is *Weird Tales* – returning from the grave six times over a 75-year period, mutating from pulp

magazine to paperback book-sized periodical and back again. Founded in 1923, it survived in its original incarnation for a remarkable run of 32 years. A major reason for its longevity was the policy of not patronising the reader, commissioning stories of sophistication and craftsmanship. This encouraged submissions from some of twentieth-century Gothic's most talented authors, providing a readership and income (though a slender one), for giants in the field, such as H. P. Lovecraft and Robert Bloch.

The golden age of the pulps was long over by the time *Weird Tales* first folded in 1954, but Gothic horror magazines still appear from the underground, featuring talented writers and artists who are more than just the latest Stephen King clone. Recent periodicals of note have included *Iniquities* – this writer's favourite, though now defunct, a platform for some of the finest exponents of the mid-1980s splatterpunk sub-genre. *Phantasm* is the bastard son of *Iniquities*, which also went the way of all flesh in early 1998 while *Bloodsongs* is originally from Australia, blending fearsome fiction with interviews and features on horror-related films and music. *Grue* is notable for quality, cutting-edge explicitness and editorial connections to the Church of Satan. And *Cemetery Dance*, which began as a college hobby in 1988, has now grown into a specialist horror publisher.

The tradition of lurid illustrations for the Victorian penny dreadfuls, often folding out of the inside cover, was continued in the pulps. The magazines' artists are the unsung heroes of pulp's golden age. But this confirmed to the minds of critics that such works were fit only for children and the lower classes, and the belief that words and illustration could not compliment each other continued to be held by the blinkered majority.

When the pulps went into decline it wasn't because there was no appetite for Gothic fantasy, but rather that toothsome new horrors had emerged to satisfy that appetite. The new form was sequential art, or 'comics' – stories told in panels of pictures with the text relegated to bubbles of dialogue, and boxes containing commentary at the head or foot of the illustration. From the start, comics were not just regarded as the poor relation of literary fiction, but as the idiot cousin nobody talked about. Only a few enlightened souls appreciated how comics could appeal to people who didn't want to be told what to read, and who would have otherwise, in all probability, read nothing at all.

Comics first appeared as fillers in American newspapers at the start of the twentieth century – 'the funny papers' – but were published in their own right in the 1930s and '40s. These 'funnies' were often heavy with the Gothic standards of black humour and camp, and borrowed heavily from their rivals in the pulp genre. Where magazines like *Weird Tales* had enjoyed success with spooky sleuths like Seabury Quinn's popular Jules de Grandin, (a Hercule Poirot-style detective who specialised in the supernatural), comic publishers went one better with heroes who fought crime from beyond the grave, like the Spectre, the Spirit, the Wraith, Mr Justice and Sergeant Spook.

More subversive were Gothic *femmes fatales* like Madame Satan and the Black Widow, supernatural seductresses who provided erotic thrills alongside chills as they reaped the souls of the sinful. The Black Widow was formerly the psychic, Claire Voyant, before a 'maddened client' murdered her, allowing the devil to recruit her as a dark angel of vengeance who killed with a kiss. (The irresistible moniker, Claire Voyant, has since been adopted by a Californian

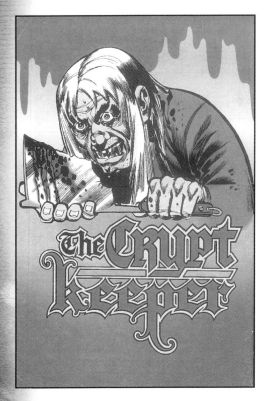

The original Crypt Keeper, on the cover of EC Comics' reprint of their Vault of Horror.

'ethereal power pop' trio, with a growing Goth following.) Madame Satan contaminated as many souls as she culled, when this 'black corrupt soul of a beautiful woman' took employment under the Prince of Darkness. Exploitative misogynist trash, or trashy celebration of feminine power? At least they were entertaining *Gothic* trash.

No comic-book approached the legendary status of the *Weird Tales* pulp until, in 1950, three new titles were launched – *Tales from the Crypt*, *Vault of Horror* and *Haunt of Fear*. They were published by EC, ('Entertaining Comics') under the ownership of William Gaines, an enthusiast who sought to address 'a new trend' in the market. Instead of an ongoing series, each title consisted of anthologies of short stories with a wise-cracking horror host (the Crypt Keeper, the Vault Keeper and the Old Witch) to give them a coherent identity. The main innovation was in the level of graphic gore, still pretty strong by today's standards. EC historian E. B. Boatner explains how the stories 'opened new vistas of death from sources previously unimagined by the reader. Victims were serial-sectioned by giant machines, eaten by ghouls, devoured by rats – from inside and out – pecked by pigeons, stuffed down disposals, skewered on swords, buried alive, dismembered and used as baseball equipment, hung as living clappers in huge bells, made into sausages and soap, dissolved, southern fried, hacked up by maniacs in Santa Claus suits and offed in unusually high percentages by their wives or husbands.' Qualms about the comics' gruesome nature were addressed by EC's policy of ensuring that those on the receiving end were fully deserving of their fates. (Although the sheer severity of their 'punishments' suggested a ghoulish sense of irony as much as any authentic moralism.) But this overt theme of poetic justice – and, indeed, the ironic black humour running beneath it – went largely unnoticed by EC's censorious critics.

EC provided a welcome, witty beacon of darkness in the white-bread world of 1950s America. Fondly recalled as a paradise of security and certainty by some conservative elements, the 1950s was also an era of Cold War paranoia and sterile conformity. And it was an atmosphere ripe for witch-hunts. In the political arena, Senator McCarthy launched his hunt for imaginary 'reds under the bed', while, in the social sphere, panic-mongers warned of the threat to American society from juvenile delinquency. Comics, particularly horror comics, quickly came into the firing line, as dubious 'experts' like the psychiatrist, Dr Frederic Wertham, blamed them for corrupting American youth.

As David J. Skal observes in his 'Cultural History of Horror', *The Monster Show*, 'Wertham's evidence for his claims was purely anecdotal, rather like Senator Joe McCarthy's knowledge of communists in government. Wertham eschewed the professional journals to make his case in the popular press – women's magazines often helped to spread his alarm – and his crusading culminated in a best-selling book, *Seduction of the Innocent*, published by Rhinehart in 1954.' It's an entertaining read – particularly the sections Wertham sees idealised homosexuality in Batman's relationship with the Boy Wonder (his bare legs and 'discreetly evident' genital region promoting homosexuality), damns romance comics as ads for prostitution, and portrays Wonderwoman as a man-hating lesbian – which would seem to tell us more about Wertham's psychosexual preoccupations and personal agenda than it does about the comics he found so indecent and provocative.

It looked to be a clash of the titans – Dr Wertham's populist pseudo-science versus William Gaines' popular Gothic thrillers. In 1950, a total of 50 million comic-books had been printed, around a quarter of which were horrific in content. Over half of the readership was adult, but this wasn't something Wertham was keen to emphasise. It's a familiar pattern – reactionaries, eager to wield the censor's scissors, always claim they're protecting the young and innocent. (It would be repeated in 1984, appropriately enough, when, in another attack on the horror genre, British conservatives and Christians used similar tactics to push draconian video-censorship laws through Parliament.)

Back in 1954, William Gaines found himself defending EC before the senatorial Subcommittee to Investigate Juvenile Delinquency. 'It would be just as difficult to explain the harmless thrill of a horror story to a Dr Wertham as it would be to explain the sublimity of love to a frigid old maid,' observed Gaines of his persecutors. But Capitol Hill was full of 'frigid old maids', unable to understand this 'harmless thrill', and far more morally destitute than the material they condemned. In a scenario echoed by the PMRC 'porn rock' hearings three decades later, comics were held up as a scapegoat and obliged to adopt a 'voluntary' censorship system. The music industry was slick and well-established enough in the 1980s to shrug off such an attack, cynically adopting its 'Parental Advisory' stickers, but comic publishers were not so fortunate when they were saddled with a new 'Comics Code'.

The Code made it clear there was no longer any place for Gothic horror in the world of comics, with strict proscriptions on the treatment of religion or sex in any form. In particular, the second section of 'General Standards' took a rigidly anti-Gothic stance:

No comic magazine shall use the word 'horror' or 'terror' in its title.

All scenes of horror, excessive bloodshed, gory or gruesome crimes, depravity, lust, sadism, masochism shall not be permitted.

All lurid, unsavory, gruesome illustrations shall be eliminated.

Inclusion of stories dealing with evil shall be used or shall be published only where the intent is to illustrate a moral issue and in no case shall evil be presented alluringly nor so as to injure the sensibilities of the reader.

Scenes dealing with, or instruments associated with walking dead, torture, vampires and vampirism, ghouls, cannibalism, and werewolfism are prohibited.

Unsurprisingly, EC's horror titles quickly went out of business, as did their competitors and imitators, and the industry was devastated. Some publishers managed to turn this holocaust to their advantage, using more wholesome characters to establish dominance of the market. DC Comics were particularly successful, with their hero Superman's devotion to 'truth, justice and the American way'. In attempting to prevent 'the seduction of the innocent', Wertham had effectively strangled the medium in its cradle.

He also put the final nails into the coffin of the struggling horror pulps, whose distributors were now very reluctant to touch anything vaguely horrific. They didn't, however, disappear without any struggle. Science fiction author Ray Bradbury had cut his teeth writing for *Weird Tales*, having several of his early efforts adapted by EC. The young Bradbury saw worrying echoes of Nazi book-burning in this contemporary attack on freedom of speech, and responded in his fiction. In the short story 'Usher II', a futuristic Poe-loving author invites a group of censors to his mansion on Mars, where they are despatched in appropriately macabre ways. The novel, *Fahrenheit 451*, however, was his ultimate statement on the matter. A futuristic work attacking censorship, it was named after the temperature at which books supposedly start to burn (this title was later adopted as a name for a mid-eighties New York Goth band, fronted by Athan Maroulis, who went on to form popular dark industrial act Spahn Ranch).

In the late 1960s (a decade outwardly as liberal as the fifties had been conservative), a few bold souls tried to revive the spirit of EC's glorious headlong charge into Gothic bad taste. Most notable were Warren Publications, who entered the Gothic fray in 1958 with the horror movie periodical, *Famous Monsters of Filmland*, a juvenile-oriented romp through Hollywood horror that retains a place in the hearts of aficionados as the archetypal monster magazine. *Creepy*, *Eerie* and *Vampirella* all followed in the 1960s: comics that used their larger format and absence of colour to avoid the attentions of the Comics Code Authority by dubiously claiming to be 'magazines'. The first two were horror anthologies (introduced by ghoulish horror hosts, Uncle Creepy and Cousin Eerie) that owed too much in flavour to their EC predecessors to possess the same morbid freshness, although they did introduce fans to the likes of definitive Gothic illustrator, Berni Wrightson. *Vampirella*, as the title reflects, was inspired by Roger Vadim's hip and kinky 1968 space opera, *Barbarella* – itself based upon a French comic – although *Barbarella*'s heroine had been transformed into a tacky, top-heavy, semi-clad bloodsucking anti-heroine from another planet. Nevertheless, *Vampirella* set enough adolescent hormones racing to inspire a recent revival of the title. Less derivative were the titles published by Warrens skidrow rivals, Skywald. Their three titles, *Psycho*, *Scream*, and *Nightmare*, were more intense. Furthermore, they did not resort to the ghoulish chumminess relied on by Warren's material to create what editor, Alan Hewetson, described as 'the horror mood'.

In 1971 the repressive Comics Code was relaxed, although it still remained laughably puritanical. Over the ensuing decade, the two giants of the US comic-book scene gently began to test its restrictions: Marvel launched the *Dracula*, *Werewolf* and *Frankenstein* comic titles, alongside bloodier, black-and-white magazine-format counterparts, again designed to

Michelle Pfeiffer as the feline fetishist Catwoman, in Tim Burton's Batman Returns *(1992).*

circumvent the censorship regulations. The monsters, in true Gothic style, were portrayed as sympathetic anti-heroes rather than figures of fear (Marvel also introduced quasi-Gothic characters into their regular colour superhero titles, like the vampire villain, Morbius, and the lycanthropic Man-Wolf, although this pair were supposedly created by science rather than the supernatural). In the meantime, DC comics followed up their overtimid anthology titles, *House of Mystery* and *House of Secrets*, by bringing the peculiar *Swamp Thing* shambling onto the USA's news stands.

By the 1980s it was becoming clear that there were more still more dollars in darkness to be had. While Reaganite America was in its own way just as reactionary as the 1950s, the attentions of self-appointed censors were focused on music. In a familiar Gothic fashion, interest among the Marvel comic readership shifted from the hero to the anti-hero. Foremost amongst these were the metal-clawed beserker, Wolverine, the era's most savagely popular protagonist; Ghost Rider, a demonic skull-headed biker who set fire to the souls of the damned and the Punisher, an anti-heroic Vietnam vet in a skull-motif costume who was originally envisaged as a villain because of his mercilessly bloody war on crime. All became 'hot' characters.

The most significant development, however, came from Marvel's rival DC, with one of their oldest characters. Since his creation in 1939, Batman had always been DC's darkest hero. Aside from the sinister overtones of his bat costume (adopted to frighten criminals, who were 'a superstitious, cowardly lot'), Batman wasn't motivated by justice or decency so much as – like the Punisher – a private quest for vengeance against those who had slain his family, a vendetta which blossomed into a crusade against all lawbreakers. Overwhelming, self-destructive vengefulness is a powerful Gothic theme. To match the darkness of the Batman, even darker villains were required, and his foes were not subject to the usual motivations of greed or egotism so much as pure psychotic malevolence.

A popular but stupid 1960s TV spin-off had all but drained the character of his dark overtones. When in the 1980s the trend was reversed by a groundbreaking title that set the comics world alight, the shadow of Dr Wertham was finally dispelled, five years after his death in 1981. In *The Dark Knight Returns*, writer and artist, Frank Miller, updated and re-invented Batman as a twisted shell haunted by his violent past. His final nemesis comes in the form of Superman, reduced by blind patriotism into a puppet for a proto-fascist President Reagan. Signalling a dark new dawn in the comics world, this 'graphic novel' – the term coined to describe an original book-length work – announced the form's newfound maturity.

Miller has since advanced the medium still further. The best of his current projects is *Sin City*: a *noir* thriller with many Gothic elements, not least its brutality and nihilism. The metropolis of the title, abbreviated from 'Basin City', is an urban hell presided over by corrupt officials and perverted priests. The only check on their excesses are the ruthless whores who rule the vice trade and damaged, dangerous loners like Marv, a delusional psychopath with a heart of gold. In traditional Gothic style orthodox authority becomes the villain, while the saga's heavily-flawed heroes are all social outcasts. It's a hell of a ride, inspiring an unofficial soundtrack by sado-masochistic industrial rockers the Genitorturers.

The Batman character was taken to his Gothic extreme in the 1989 graphic novel, *Arkham Asylum*, penned by Scottish author-playwright Grant Morrison and illustrated by Dave

McKean. McKean's distinctive style — haunted collages of sepia photographs, obscure diagrams and luxuriant painting — has subsequently seen him become one of modern Gothic's foremost artists, while *Arkham Asylum* is one of the relatively rare instances where he imprints his vision on an entire project. The title is a clue to the universe in which this remarkable work takes place — the name Arkham is borrowed from H. P. Lovecraft, and the asylum of the title is home to many of Batman's lunatic foes. As the tale progresses, we begin to suspect that Batman is as dangerous and deranged as any of the grotesque killers whom he pursues.

If these treatments re-Gothicised the Batman for comic fans, then cinematic adaptations did the same for the general public. As the director of the 1989 big-screen *Batman* (and its 1992 sequel, *Batman Returns*), Hollywood maverick Tim Burton was an inspired choice. The film is as close to a compromise between Gothic atmosphere and mainstream acceptability as is possible. Big names queued up to play the villains in Burton's ultra-Gothic Gotham City: the Joker was a role Jack Nicholson was born to play; Danny DeVito turns the potentially pathetic Penguin into an authentic grotesque and Michelle Pfeiffer's Catwoman is a PVC fetishist's wet dream on legs. Burton also dropped in a couple of Gothic in-jokes. Batman's butler Albert is played by Michael Gough — a stalwart of British horror movies from the 1950s to the early '70s — and the evil tycoon in *Batman Returns* is called Max Shreck: the name borrowed from the silent German horror actor who starred in 1922's *Nosferatu*, the first major vampire movie. In the most direct nod to the Goth subculture, Burton also secured the services of proto-Goth pioneers Siouxsie and the Banshees for the soundtrack.

If *Batman* fed Gothic aesthetics into comics, the Goth subculture would in turn borrow from the comics medium. A prime example is writer Jamie O'Barr's *The Crow*. It is a tale of a young man, brutally tortured and murdered alongside his fiancée, who returns from the grave possessed by the vengeful spirit of the eponymous black bird. It wears its Gothic colours with pride, quoting verse from Decadent poets, such as Arthur Rimbaud, and lyrics from Goth-rock pioneers, including the Cure and Joy Division. Its anti-hero, Eric, combines the looks of both Batman and his nemesis, the Joker, and acts like the bizarre love-child of these two enemies: both a vengeful vigilante and a wise-cracking psychopath. O'Barr's avenger, however, appeared in 1989, years before Frank Miller gave Batman his Gothic makeover.

'God had had his elbow on my neck my whole life,' O'Barr reflected bleakly, 'like I was being tested to see how much I could put up with.' The final 'test' was the death of a close personal friend, mown down by a drunk driver in the early 1980s. 'I wanted someone to pay for all this anger and pain that I was going through,' he told the *Clive Barker's A-Z of Horror* TV show, 'and that was essentially where the story of *The Crow* came from. That was the genesis of it.'

The first issue, debuting in 1989, was dedicated to singer Ian Curtis of Joy Division — who hanged himself while deeply depressed nine years before. Lead character Eric's hairstyle owed much to Cure lead singer Robert Smith, his face recalled the angular androgyny of Bauhaus vocalist/Goth icon Pete Murphy, while his physique and movement were borrowed from Iggy Pop, the proto-punk animal in all his sinuous unpredictability. (Wild man Iggy was initially supposed to take the role of the psycho named 'Funboy' in the film version of *The Crow*, but later appeared instead as the villainous Curve in the 1996 sequel *Crow 2: City of Angels*.) This grim Goth-rock vibe was enhanced when the character was adapted for the big screen in 1994. Director Alex Proyas, best known for rock videos, explained how he used stark blacks and whites to lend the film 'a dark, expressionistic look. It's a very aggressive style, driven by rock and roll music. I wanted to have that raw, frenetic energy of the industrial rock we have on the soundtrack' – performers included Goth-industrial favourites Nine Inch Nails and My Life With The Thrill Kill Kult, who also perform in the film's nightclub sequence.

Scripting duties went to David J. Schow, orignator of the controversial splatterpunk genre

The ill-fated Brandon Lee contemplates the grave, as the title character in the 1994 movie adaptation of The Crow.

that brought rock 'n' roll attitude to horror fiction, and cyberpunk author John Shirley. Schow and Shirley gave Eric a surname, 'Draven', a direct tribute to Edgar Allan Poe's inspirational poem 'The Raven', and made him into an alternative rocker. Brandon Lee (slender but powerful son of martial arts legend Bruce), the young actor who played Eric Draven, had to learn guitar to reinforce the Goth-rock connection. It's a tribute to the film's bleak potency that, when Lee died in a bizarre on-set accident, it seemed somehow appallingly appropriate.

Brandon Lee's demise assured both the star and his cinematic swansong macabre legendary status. His mysterious death (he was shot dead with a prop pistol supposedly loaded with blanks – an end disturbingly reminiscent of his father's) was the culmination of a series of misfortunes that beset the film, which cast and crew members had begun to describe as 'cursed'. With the proceeds from his first film, the 1986 *Legacy of Rage,* Lee had invested in a vintage Cadillac hearse. He surrounded his body with ice to prepare for the role of Eric, in order to find out what it would be like to be buried. Friends recall how he talked in whispers of his premonition that, like his father, he would die prematurely.

When Tim Burton was in pre-production on *Batman*, he turned for advice to a hirsute Englishman named Alan Moore. 'He asked me how I would handle the filming of *Batman*,' Moore told *Uncut* magazine. 'I told him the most important thing to get right was the city, to make it a strange collage of different architectural styles.'

After a disappointing big-screen adaptation, Todd McFarlane's demonic comic book Spawn *was the basis of a much better adult cartoon series.*

Subsequently, Gotham City became the real star of Burton's *Batman*. Such an acute creative sense has made Alan Moore one of the best-respected figures in the history of comics. His breakthrough came in 1983, when DC commissioned him to invigorate their bayou-bound plant monster tale, *Saga of the Swamp Thing*. He hit his stride with a story arc appropriately entitled 'American Gothic', introducing wit, pathos and genuine horror into a title on the verge of cancellation. It was a hit both with readers and critics, *Rolling Stone* magazine hailing it as 'perhaps the brainiest and scariest horror narrative of the eighties'.

Moore's masterpiece is *From Hell*, an epic that took him a full decade (late 1980s to late 1990s) to complete. It explores the Ripper slayings of 1888, meticulously reconstructing the historical, cultural and esoteric background to the seminal Victorian case of serial murder. London, 'the City of Dreadful Night', with all her occult secrets and lost folklore, is the central character. The film adaptation, starring Johnny Depp, proved a richly squalid exercise in gaslight Gothic.

Moore believes that the whole ethos of the twentieth century was born around the brief period of these terrible killings: 'You've got the French incursions into Indochina that would lead to the Vietnam war. You've got the invention of the machine gun. You've got the invention of the motor car. You've got the beginnings of modern art. The beginnings of modern writing. The 1880s are the twentieth century in microcosm, and if you had to choose one event, then the Jack the Ripper murders are the 1880s in microcosm. I was almost trying to imply that this was the seed event of the entire twentieth century.'

Much of the most compelling background to *From Hell* comes from Moore's extensive knowledge of the occult. What is perhaps a greater influence, however, is his occult experience. In a significantly eerie encounter, Moore has described how he was once sitting in a drab London café when he was approached by a man in a scruffy suit and trenchcoat, who winked at him before disappearing elsewhere. Unremarkable perhaps, except that the man was John Constantine – whom until then Moore had believed only existed in his imagination and in the pages of *Swamp Thing*. Some occultists maintain true sorcery occurs where the boundaries between fiction and reality became vague and flexible.

Constantine, originally just a walk-on part in *Saga of the Swamp Thing*, literally took on a life of his own. A blue-collar occultist who relies on his instinct, balls and street smarts, John Constantine resembles a hipper version of the TV detective Columbo, given a punk past and a passion for cheap whiskey and chain-smoking. In 1988 the character was given his own title, *Hellblazer*, which saw the cynical Englishman battling angels, devils and the demons of his own past in a cool, countercultural blend of gritty horror and social satire. There are plans to bring the character to the big screen, in a picture entitled *Constantine* to avoid confusion with Clive Barker's *Hellraiser* movies. (The comic was

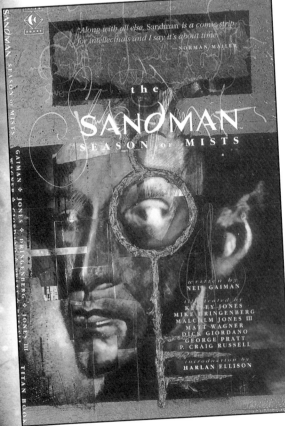

Neil Gaiman's acclaimed comic
The Sandman. Gaiman and artist
Dave McKean have a strong Goth
following, with McKean's art gracing
Goth album covers.

initially slated as *Hellraiser* before its creators became aware that Barker's 1987 film was in production.)

Hellblazer was one of the debut titles for DC's new imprint for mature readers, Vertigo – a sign that the Comics Code Authority – long regarded with contempt owing to its contradiction of First Amendment rights to freedom of speech – was beginning to be ignored completely. (In May 2001 Marvel renounced the Code and announced their intention to adopt a policy of self-regulation, effectively pulling the last of the Code's teeth.) Despite the corporate backing of Time Warner, the Vertigo line became synonymous with boldly experimental titles with Gothic themes, including *House of Secrets* (not to be confused with its DC predecessor, a haunted house saga where vengeful spirits pass judgement from the bowels of a strange old mansion), *Weird War Tales*, and the post-modern horror anthology *Flinch*.

Vertigo's most popular title, *The Sandman*, was also its most Gothic. Written by Neil Gaiman, whose taste in apparel dubbed him 'the Man in Black', *The Sandman* is based on the premise is that there exist seven entities known as 'the Endless'. They are personifications of elemental forces at the essence of existence – in this case: Dream, Death, Despair, Destruction, Desire, Delirium, and Destiny. Gaiman's chief protagonist is Dream, in the form of Morpheus, or the Sandman, though his sister Death also figures heavily (and has herself merited several spin-off titles). Both appear to be denizens of the contemporary Goth subculture. Morpheus is a pale, sombre, introspective, with long, back-combed, raven-black hair and a coat to match; his sister is a perky Goth babe who sports a large silver ankh (the Ancient Egyptian hooded or looped cross and paradoxically a symbol of immortality) as her emblem. The idea of portraying the Grim Reaper as a cheerily-philosophical, sexy young woman is typical of the bold way Gaiman weaves ancient myth, classical literature, Gothic horror and contemporary realism together with seamless skill. *The Sandman* made Gaiman the first comics writer to win the World Fantasy Award, and *The Dictionary of Literary Biography* lists him as one of the ten most important postmodern writers in America (although he's English – as were many of the artists and writers who presided over the rise of the graphic novel). It was Neil Gaiman who introduced the Goth subculture to the potential of comics as a medium.

Gaiman told Hy Bender, author of *The Sandman Companion*, that he originally conceived of the *Sandman* character having an Oriental look, swathed in a black kimono. According to the author, once the character had been realised by artist Sam Kieth, however, Sandman inker Mike Dringenberg observed, '"Hey, [he] looks like Peter Murphy from Bauhaus."' Cover artist Dave McKean and Gaiman 'got some Bauhaus videos and immediately saw that Mike was right; and Dave ended up making the central image on the cover of *Sandman* [number one] a Peter Murphy-like face. Others have noted that, like the Crow, Morpheus also bears a resemblance to Cure lead singer Robert Smith. Morpheus' sister Death is an interesting example of a fictional figure drawing from, and feeding back into, the Goth scene. Visualising Death fell to Dringenberg, working on Gaiman's brief that she should be incongruously happy, sexy and down-to-earth. Dringenberg told Bender his chief inspiration was a Salt Lake City Goth waitress, named Cinnamon, who had 'real star quality in her presence and bearing'. A beautiful, slender ex-ballerina, she 'would draw spiderwebs on her face one week, adopt an Egyptian fashion the next week, and style her eyes like a raccoon's the following week.'

In another spooky case of life imitating art, McKean recalls seeing a girl powerfully reminiscent of Death walking down the aisle on a flight he'd undertaken on which one of the passengers had died…

Goth writer Caitlin R. Kiernan – who has scripted several *Sandman* spin-off comics, such as *The Dreaming* – has identified a number of Goth parallels and roots in the Death character. 'The Eye of Horus [make-up] goes straight back to Siouxsie Sue who was doing it way back in the early 1980s,' says Kiernan, 'and Death's look in general owes something to [Goth-band bassist] Patricia Morrison. As for the ankh, it originally made its way into Goth culture via Tony Scott's 1983 film, *The Hunger* – which also features Eye of Horus makeup in a brief flashback scene.'

Comic-books written by Goths, and aimed primarily at a Goth audience, have become a small but vibrant industry. Among the better titles are *Gloom Cookie*, an archly-observed soap opera set in the Goth subculture which bills itself as 'Tales of social treachery, unrequited love and monsters under the bed.' *Lenore*, by the evocatively-named Roman Dirge, is a Poe-tinged title full of black humour. Lenore is the name of the lost (meaning dead) girl in 'The Raven', but in this case she's an *un*dead little girl. The title's humour is created by the contrast between her cuteness and casual cruelty – admittedly one joke endlessly replayed, but nevertheless not without its charms. The light-hearted *Oh My Goth!* was created by the multi-talented Voltaire (named after the anti-religious eighteenth-century philosopher). When not penning his comic, Voltaire creates spooky stop-motion animations for MTV, and has begun a recording career, with albums like *The Devil's Bris* (its advertising promising, 'twelve songs of love, loss, revenge, and dismemberment sure to bring a smile to even the darkest of souls.').

Gloom Cookie and *Lenore* were issued by Slave Labor, whose prime performer was to be *Johnny the Homicidal Maniac*. *Johnny* is very difficult to describe to the uninitiated – a sure sign of originality. Consciously or otherwise, the lead character is a satire on the Goth revenge fantasy at the heart of *The Crow*. Like the Crow, Johnny commits acts of savage barbarity with apparent impunity. However, he's not motivated by noble revenge, but by hatred of the stupidity, dull conformity and pettiness of mainstream America, alongside a growing sense of alienation – not just from society, but reality.

It's a scenario that could be both mean-spirited and adolescent in less skilled hands, but author, Jhonen Vasquez, handles it with intelligence, scalpel-sharp wit and disarming affection toward the Goth subculture that clearly informs his work. If a future researcher wishes to know what that subculture, its attitudes and its sense of humour were like in turn-of-the-millennium America, *Johnny the Homicidal Maniac* and its sundry spin-offs – like *I Feel Sick* – would be a good place to start. A saga of sadistic torture-murders that's laugh-out-loud funny, *Johnny the Homicidal Maniac* lays claim to that highest of Gothic accolades – it's in exquisitely bad taste.

Jhonen Vasquez's affectionately satirical arch-Goth 'Anne Gwish' – from the pages of
Johnny the Homicidal Maniac – *morosely celebrates her ' individuality'.*

Chapter VII

The Flowers of Evil Are in Full Bloom:

Gothic Music

Throughout history, creative minds have found themselves drawn to the morbid and melancholy – for some reason, much European art is of an eerie or unsettling nature. The crossover between classical music and the Gothic aesthetic has been a rather neglected study – which is a glaring omission, as even a cursory glance reveals a form steeped in the grim and grandiose. How would generations of Phantoms of the Opera have serenaded the night without the score of Johann Sebastian Bach's ominous organ piece, the 'Toccata in D Minor'?

One of the better sources on the roots of macabre music is *The Penguin Encyclopaedia of Horror and the Supernatural* – due in no small part to the book's editor, Jack Sullivan, whose twin areas of expertise are classical music and the history of the ghost story. Any musical phantom who tired of Bach might consult Sullivan. He would be directed to the twentieth-century American composer William Albright, best remembered for reviving the jaunty ragtime piano tunes of Scott Joplin. Albright's own definitively eerie organ music includes his 1971 masterpiece, *Organbook II*, which begins with the threatening 'Night Procession', builds into the apocalyptic 'Toccata Satanique', then spirals down into the 'Last Rites'. Or our phantom may prefer Albright's one-time tutor, French composer, Olivier Messiaen. Messiaen's most disturbing work is his 1964 composition, *Et Expecto Ressurectionem Mortuorum* ('And I Await the Resurrection of the Dead'). 'This terrifying evocation of "the voice that will awaken the dead" even awoke the New York Philharmonic matinee subscribers several years ago during a cataclysmic performance conducted by Messiaen's most renowned student,

Siouxsie Sue in 1977 at the Roxy Club wearing a Wehrmacht swastika badge.

Pierre Boulez,' according to Sullivan, 'an occasion that produced the most disorderly exit of Philharmonic patrons during Boulez's controversial tenure. The shrieking brass and shattering tam-tams ring in the ears and mind long after this piece has ended, making it a must for anyone interested in the music of terror.'

Another notable Messiaen composition is the seventh movement of his *Turangalila Symphony* (1946-8), inspired by Edgar Allan Poe's Gothic tale 'The Pit and the Pendulum'. Just as in the literary and cinematic media, Poe has proved to be highly influential in classical music, and numerous composers have tried to realise his maelstroms of madness and melancholy. These include the Russian, Sergei Rachmaninoff, who composed an evocation of Poe's poem 'The Bells' in 1913; Englishman Joseph Holbrooke also adapted 'The Bells' (1903), alongside the poems 'The Raven' (1900), 'Ulalume' (1901), and 'Annabel Lee' (1905), rendering them as heartbreaking, unsettling tone poems. Over the years, many highly-strung, gloomy artists – notably the French poet Baudelaire – have seen something of themselves in the hard-drinking, hypersensitive Poe. In the final years of his life, the French composer, Claude Debussy, became preoccupied with Poe – particularly his doomed, neurasthenic character Roderick Usher – and resolved to adapt 'The Fall of the House of Usher' into an opera. As his health failed and he became reclusive, Debussy began to lose himself in Poe's fiction. 'I have got into the way of thinking of nothing else but Roderick Usher and "The Devil in the Belfry"', he wrote (the second story being one of Poe's more sardonic tales, where the Devil visits a quaint Dutch town and causes great consternation by making the church clock strike thirteen). 'I fall asleep with them, and awake either in the gloomy sadness of the former or the sneers of the latter.'

The Hungarian, Franz Liszt also became famous for his macabre compositions. In particular, he was fascinated by the mythical medieval scholar Faust, who sold his soul to the devil Mephistopheles. This preoccupation led him to compose his 1861 *Faust Symphonie* and no less than three demonic pieces of ballroom dance music, which he called 'Mephisto Waltzes' (the inspiration for the name of Mephisto Walz [sic], the influential American Goth band founded in 1986). Popular rumour of the day had it that Liszt was in league with Satan, who, it was said, inspired his

The Kronos Quartet formed in order to perform George Crumb's Black Angels. *They later collaborated with Philip Glass on a new soundtrack for the 1931* Dracula.

disturbing compositions.

It was a rumour that gained credibility during his 1882 visit to Venice, as a guest of the famous composer Richard Wagner. Liszt was busy working on an oratorio when a powerful premonition convinced him to abandon it and begin *La lugubre gondola*, about the Venetian vessels being used as floating hearses. Only two months after its completion, Wagner died, and was borne away in just such a fashion. Death figured prominently in Liszt's work, appearing most strikingly in his 1865 *Todtentanz* ('Dance of the Dead', or 'Danse Macabre'). Its musical origins are to be found in the 'Dies Irae' ('Day of Wrath'), the medieval hymn traditionally chanted to ease the passage of the souls of the dead.

Liszt was not the only famous composer attracted to the Faust myth, or the only noted musician who composed 'Dances of Death'. The Austrian Gustav Mahler, the Frenchman Camille Saint-Saens and the Russian Dmitri Shostakovich all drew inspiration from the Danse Macabre paintings and murals of cavorting corpses popular in late medieval and Renaissance Europe. Lizst was inspired by just such a fresco which he found in Florence. His biographer, James Huneker, described how it depicted Death as 'a fearsome woman, with hair streaming wildly, with clawed hands. She is bat-winged, and her clothing is stiff with mire. She swings a scythe, eager to end the joy and delight of the world'

As far as Jack Sullivan is concerned, however, one French composer towers above his contemporaries in the field of macabre music. 'If there is a Gothic horror tradition in music roughly parallel to that in literature, then Hector Berlioz is its Horace Walpole, Sheridan Le Fanu and Edgar Allan Poe all in one. His revolutionary *Symphonie Fantastique* [1830] not only strikes an innovative note of satanic terror but also builds to it from a mood of deceptive calm,' writes Sullivan. Berlioz himself described the composition's theme as follows: 'A young musician of morbid sensibility and ardent imagination takes opium in a fit of despair over his love, and dreams of his beloved, who has become for him a melody, like a fixed idea which he finds and hears everywhere.' In his opium dream, the musician imagines he has killed his lover and is led away to be executed for the crime, then sees her taking part in the demonic orgies of the witches' sabbat.

According to Sullivan, 'nothing had been heard in music before to quite prepare Berlioz's audience for the awesome tolling bell of his "Witches Sabbath", the startlingly realistic musical depiction of a head being lopped off by a guillotine, the ghoulish brass intonement of the ancient Dies Irae from the Mass of the Dead, or the eerie scratchings, scrapings, and rumblings in the strings that forecast "special effects" composers like Krzysztof Penderecki and John Williams. Indeed, Berlioz's grotesque *Symphonie* launched a tradition of terror that continued in the spectral offerings of Liszt (who attended the premiere), Mussorgsky, Bartok, Crumb and many others.'

Of this tradition, George Crumb's work represents an experimental, almost atonal, extreme of musical romanticism, harshly minimalist and darkly evocative. *Black Angels* (subtitled 'Thirteen images from the dark land') is perhaps his darkest hour, featuring a 'Danse Macabre' and a section entitled 'Devil-Music', which employs 'the Devil's tritone' (a dissonant chord progression traditionally forbidden by the Church as unholy). Crumb combines some arcane ideas, such as using strains of the 'Dies Irae' or chanted mystical number sequences from medieval magic, with *avant-garde* techniques like amplifying the stringed instruments on the

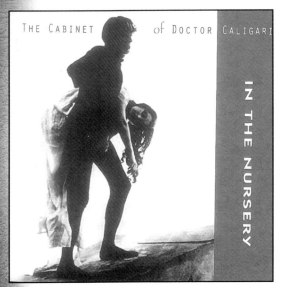

louder sequences to 'the threshold of pain'.

The Polish composer Krzysztof Penderecki is often mentioned in the same breath as Crumb, sharing a tendency to test the boundaries between music and noise to unsettling effect. He burst onto the neo-classical music scene in 1960 with his *Threnody for the Victims of Hiroshima* (a 'threnody' is a dirge or lament). The Pole chose the title after composing the piece, and, as Jack Sullivan observes, 'These nightmarish sounds can conjure any number of horrors, either interior or "real".' Sullivan describes the piece as 'a virtual anthology of 1960s musical special effects . . . The louder passages are not so much played as screamed.'

Such techniques, combining traditional instruments with noise-making apparatus to create disturbing sounds, will be familiar to aficionados of the sinister experimentalists on the fringes of the independent music scene – some of these figures, like Coil and Einstürzende Neubauten, having a dedicated Goth following. Indeed, one of the recent trends in Gothic music has been the rediscovery of classical music, both traditional and *avant-garde*, by a range of influential Goth bands.

Both Crumb and Penderecki have also had an impact on the world of Gothic cinema. Themes by both composers were utilised in the groundbreaking soundtrack to *The Exorcist* (1973). The innovation lay in the way sound effects from the film were woven experimentally into the music. Penderecki fitted Friedkin's brief for a soundtrack that 'swung between very loud, piercing, oppressive noises, and absolute, total dead silence'. His compositions also dominate the soundtrack to Stanley Kubrick's 1980 adaptation of Stephen King's *The Shining* (which also features elements from eerie works by Berlioz, Bartok and Gyorgy Ligeti).

Several 'industrial' performers have contributed original material to Gothic horror films: Coil composed the original soundtrack for Clive Barker's *Hellraiser* (1987), although it proved too 'experimental' for the producers and was replaced by a more traditional score by Christopher Young. Electronic duo In the Nursery have enjoyed a fertile relationship with celluloid: they composed the theme to the trailer for *Interview with the Vampire* (1994), as well as an ongoing series of albums they describe as 'optical music' to accompany screenings of silent films – most notably the 1919 expressionist classic, *The Cabinet of Dr Caligari*.

After World War II, the most morbid or eerie themes in music surfaced in the 1950s-born phenomenon of rock 'n' roll. Rock's roots lay in black culture, via the blues, although it also had origins in 'white-trash' music like hillbilly and country. Nevertheless, the obvious influence of black music led white racists to voice concerns that youth was at risk of being corrupted by 'jungle music', whose strange rhythms would encourage promiscuity and rebellion. They were not entirely wrong. Even among those willing to tolerate a sanitised (i.e. white) version of rock 'n' roll – such as record executives and radio schedulers – a line was drawn. So saccharine love songs were encouraged, but darker sexual themes were most certainly not. But it is the artists who dared to challenge these taboos, and those surrounding the subject of death, who merit our attention here.

In 'Bela Lugosi's Dead and I Don't Feel So Good Either', his essay for the Boston Institute of Contemporary Art's *Gothic* exhibition catalogue, James Hannaham identifies Screamin' Jay Hawkins as the likely progenitor of Goth rock. The blues had always had a defining element of misery, and more than a passing acquaintance with death and the Devil. What Hawkins

Screamin' Jay Hawkins, the godfather of horror rock, with cranial sidekick Henry.

brought to it was shameless showmanship, boundless energy – and a cranium called Henry. Hawkins' background had prepared him for a colourful future. Abandoned by his mother at an early age, he was brought up by a local Red Indian tribe, after which he pursued a career in the military, was wounded several times in Korea, and won a number of belts as a boxer. After all this, the wild world of rock 'n' roll must have seemed pretty sedate.

At least it would have, had Hawkins followed the path most of his contemporaries were forging in the new medium. Instead, the black bluesman wanted something to lift him above his rivals. He found it by developing an outrageous stage persona as a rocking vaudeville

Britain's second-rate shock 'n' roll merchant, Screaming Lord Sutch.

witchdoctor, who travelled to venues in a hearse, emerged to perform from a burning coffin, frightened the audience with pyrotechnic effects, and serenaded his cigarette-smoking side-kick, Henry the skull. The germ of this cartoon Gothic aesthetic was born when he recorded the 1956 single, 'I Put a Spell on You', a possessive love ballad with supernatural overtones. Hawkins couldn't seem to get it right, until someone suggested they bring some liquor into the studio in order to loosen things up. Subsequent takes became increasingly intoxicated until Hawkins and his band, the Hawks, barely able to stand, cut the classic version – Screamin' Jay hollering, growling and cackling over a frenzy of brass and guitars. In the process, he fully unleashed the song's weird, sinister subtext.

DJ Alan Freed – legendary for inventing the term rock 'n' roll – encouraged Hawkins to capitalise on the single by creating his spooky black magic stageshow. Other DJs lost their jobs for playing the single, which had swiftly been banned by stores and radio stations worldwide, while many more quietly dropped it from their playlists. Despite this – or, more probably, because of it – 'I Put a Spell on You' became a bestseller, albeit one that never featured on any official chart. Unbelievably, the reason given for the boycott was the recording's 'cannibalistic' nature.

In the decades to come, numerous charismatic performers would cover 'I Put a Spell on You' – from Nina Simone to Diamanda Galas via Nick Cave – none, however, really touched the black magic of the original. Perhaps a Marilyn Manson version came closest, recorded for the soundtrack of *Lost Highway*, the 1997 quasi-Gothic, surrealist-*noir* movie directed by David Lynch.

The British answer to Screamin' Jay Hawkins came in the form of Screaming Lord Sutch, who burst onto the rock scene in 1960 with the single 'Big Black Coffin' – which his label retitled ''Til the Following Night' to avoid offence. It wasn't only Sutch's 'Screaming' prefix that sounded suspiciously close to America's coolest ghoul, but his act, which featured the lead singer emerging from a coffin and included a cover version of 'I Put a Spell on You'. The one thing David Sutch lacked was talent. A hyperactive exhibitionist, in addition to his band, the Savages, Sutch seized the stage with his political party, the Monster Raving Loonies, founded in 1963 to parody the British electoral process. Both his band and his politics quickly moved from goofy novelty to idiotic irritation, though Lord Sutch was nothing if not tenacious. He was apparently oblivious to a string of pop chart and ballot box humiliations, until depression, and suicide by hanging, finally brought down the curtain on the formerly irrepressible eccentric in June 1999.

He came closest to success in 1963 with his single 'Jack the Ripper', detailing the misdeeds of the infamous prostitute-slaying Victorian killer. Compared to his usual clumsily camp rock 'n' roll – a typical example was re-recording 'Venus in Blue Jeans' as 'Monster in Black Tights' – 'Jack the Ripper' is a faintly chilling effort. British music paper *Melody Maker* thought it was 'nauseating trash', as did the BBC, who banned it from their playlists. Sutch was undeterred, making the song the highlight of his stageshow, where, attired in a top hat and brandishing a knife, he pursued a band member dressed as a Victorian whore. The effects could get quite messy, and Sutch was not above employing sloppy butcher's shop offal to liven up the show. A number of guitar legends began their careers as long-suffering Savages – Jeff Beck, Jimmy Page, Ritchie Blackmore – and most agreed that the tigerskin loincloths Sutch insisted they wear were more humiliating than being transvestite victims of the Ripper.

Posthumous legend has visualised the enigmatic Ripper in a top hat, an assumption based on the popular conviction that the killer was a sadistic upper class gent. British rhythm and blues vocalist Don Craine, on the other hand, adopted another item of Victorian headgear, the deerstalker, as his gimmick. 'People assumed it had something to do with Sherlock Holmes, but it didn't,' he told me in a retrospective interview. 'It's because the only time Jack the Ripper was actually spotted and nearly caught, he was wearing a deerstalker. I love that sort of thing. Not going around murdering prostitutes, I hasten to add – I love prostitutes!'

Craine was a founding member of the Downliners Sect, part of the Beatles-led 'beat boom' with its distinctive English take on rock 'n' roll. The Downliners' career ambitions were hampered, as their name suggests, by a downbeat approach. They weren't entirely on their own. Another Beatles-style beat combo tried to distinguish themselves with the name the Undertakers, arriving at gigs in a hearse, dressed in full undertakers' attire, and taking the stage to the tune of 'The Funeral March'. Record companies were horrified at the display. The band shortened their name to the Takers and abandoned their morbid image, but still sank without trace. The Downliners Sect's taste transgressions, however, were not so easily erased, particularly those of their notorious 1965 EP, *The Sect Sing Sick Songs*.

The release earned the band a blanket radio ban, pretty much sinking their fledgling career – 'but we did get invited to some wild and weird parties because of that record,' Craine reflects philosophically. A collection of blackly humorous rhythm and blues ballads with murderous twists in the tail, perhaps the most disarmingly offensive was 'I Want My Baby Back', about someone prepared to go to any lengths to be reunited with his dead love. 'We didn't state necrophilia,' Craine maintains, 'only implied it as the final verse was sung from inside a coffin, which we replicated by using an orange box for the lid creaking shut.' In many ways, *The Sect Sing Sick Songs* represents a milestone in Goth history, a deliberate attempt to coin a Gothic rhythm and blues sound.

'We were heavily into Victorian Gothic and horror movies and the EP was a way of transferring that onto record,' explains Craine. 'It wasn't our top horror release though. That's the single "Glendora", about a guy who falls in love with a shop-window dummy, then watches in horror as the assistants gradually pull her arms and legs off.'

Meanwhile, Craine's band created another minor footnote in rock history, when they recorded a song called 'Why Don't You Smile Now?' on the 1966 Downliners album, *The Rock Sects In*. It was the first recorded collaborative effort of two young songwriters, Lou Reed and John Cale, who went on to form the Velvet Underground – one of the most influential bands in postmodern rock music.

Alan Clayson, author of *Death Discs*, has been acclaimed by UK music paper, *NME*, as occupying a 'premiere position on rock's Lunatic Fringe'. His book represents one of the few attempts to chart the macabre in modern popular music, and, while factually suspect in parts, contains enough ghoulish esoterica to trace the early roots of Goth rock. 'The Rolling Stones had been there long ago when "the blitzkrieg raged and the bodies stank" in 1969's "Sympathy For The Devil",' wrote Clayson, 'though diabolism had been present in the title and cover of the previous year's *Their Satanic Majesties Request . . .*'

The Stones dipped their toes into dark waters a full decade before 'Goth' began to grow inside the punk womb. While, in the 1960s, they all too often found themselves in the shadow of the Beatles, the Stones cultivated a tougher, sleazier image – to the extent that even sympathetic voices accused lead singer, Mick Jagger, and his band of invoking dark forces towards the end of the 1960s. 'Decent English citizens loathed them,' observes Stanley Booth, author of *The True Adventures of the Rolling Stones*. 'Mick, knowing that he and his colleagues were, although quite naughty, not satanic, used the Stones' reputation in a mocking, dark-comedic fashion to further his own ends.'

Their Satanic Majesties Request was essentially the band's response to *Sgt Pepper's Lonely Hearts Club Band*, the Beatles' colourful, smash-hit 1967 foray into flower power and psychedelia. By comparison, *Their Satanic Majesties* was a pretty bad trip, rather bleak and unsettling. It wasn't the band's first flirtation with the dark side – their 1966 single 'Paint It Black' remains a masterpiece of exquisite gloom, subsequently covered by Goth bands such as Inkubus Sukkubus and Mephisto Walz. 'Sympathy for the Devil', their 1968 hymn to Lucifer, also inspired a whole EP of covers by mock totalitarian East European industrial band Laibach, and a version by Swedish Goth-metal trio Tiamat. The Sisters of Mercy, while eager to avoid overtly Gothic affectations, also made the 1969 Stones number 'Gimme Shelter' – with its apocalyptic promise, 'Rape, murder, it's just a shot away' – a familiar feature of their live shows in the 1980s.

By the turn of the decade, a series of tragedies and setbacks encouraged the band to take an increasingly conservative tack. Not least were the death of guitarist, Brian Jones in 1969, and a free concert the Stones organised in Altamont, California which degenerated into a near war zone in the same year. Their 1971 release, *Sticky Fingers*, featured a cover designed by pop art legend Andy Warhol, in the form of a jeans crotch, where the flies could be undone to expose the underpants beneath. It provoked predictable if somewhat tired outrage, and while the album featured a couple of darkly decadent cuts in 'Sister Morphine' and 'Dead Flowers', it was the band's last truly significant moment before sliding into creative irrelevance.

A few of the exponents of 1960s psychedelia escaped the blanket love-bombing of the hippie revolution long enough to record some intriguingly sinister albums. American horror

Texan psychedelic horror-rocker Roky Erickson (with beard), backed by his band the Aliens.

author H. P. Lovecraft's 'Dream Cycle' – where a sense of awe and adventure are just as palpable as the sense of fear – inspired the US band that took his name, emphasising the 'cosmic' aspects of the writer's unearthly aesthetic. *Uncut* magazine later dubbed H. P. Lovecraft (the band) 'West Coast Gothic psychedelicats', describing their music as 'part *Twilight Zone*, part Gothic Acid Trip, and part baroque folk with its harpsichords, tympani and recorders.' The oddball American outfit Coven introduced satanic themes, including the performance of a Black Mass, to hippie folk-rock – in a similar vein to British prog-rock contemporaries, Black Widow. Their elaborate *Sacrifice* stageshow, featuring nudity and occult rituals, caused a minor sensation in the UK tabloid press in 1969-70 (particularly when the nubile 'sacrificial victim' got carried away in the section of the show where she pretended to whip lead singer, Kip Trevor, drawing blood from the alarmed vocalist).

The 13th Floor Elevators have been credited as the godfathers of musical psychedelia, with their advocacy of mind-altering drugs and musical blend of feverish guitar and surreal lyrics. According to vocalist, Roky Erickson, however, the Texan band's name was an obscure voodoo reference. A 1969 bust for marijuana resulted in Erickson's incarceration in a mental institution when he rashly pleaded insanity. He endured three years of electro-shock and drug therapy, and his already manic stylings just got stranger. His subsequent material in the 1970s and 1980s, backed by bands called the Aliens or the Missing Links (formed with fellow asylum inmates) – and later covered by bands ranging from the Jesus and Mary Chain to the Entombed – contained decidedly 'out-there' themes. The self-proclaimed 'Martian' was a big pulp-horror and science fiction fan, and tracks like 'Creature with the Atom Brain' paid tribute to obscure 1950s movies. Others meanwhile, like 'I Think of Demons' and 'Red Temple Prayer', concern more personal horrors – such as two-headed dogs and malevolent psychiatrists leering at the troubled Texan from the dark corners of his damaged psyche. All was delivered in Erickson's distinctive 'Rokyspeak', occupying a twilight zone between authentic weirdness and hallucinatory horror.

In the mid-1960s, a band emerged which made Jagger's set look restrained by comparison. The Velvet Underground's guitarist, Sterling Morrison, once described his group as 'the original alternative band. Not because we wanted to be, but because we were shunned into it.' Certainly, this black-clad crew were shunned by all but a hard core of New York fans. For

The Velvet Underground – featuring Lou Reed (foreground), John Cale (right) and Nico (centre) – introduced dark tones of sexual perversity to rock 'n' roll.

the bias of the times was towards a lighter, groovier sound than the Velvets' challenging rumble of chaos and decay, described by the *New York World Journal* as 'the product of a secret marriage between Bob Dylan and the Marquis de Sade'. A few wise men, however, would soon celebrate this unholy union.

In 1965, an exasperated New York club owner warned the band that if they played their ominous 'Black Angel's Death Song' just one more time they would be fired. The Velvets duly opened their next set with the song and were shown the door. Fortunately, Andy Warhol, New

York's king of the pop art scene, took a shine to this unfashionably gloomy band, and was instrumental in securing the Velvets a recording deal. Critics remain divided over Warhol, some seeing his work as brilliantly innovative, others dismissing it as fraudulent and simple-minded. Gore Vidal once memorably observed that Warhol was 'the only genius with an IQ of 60', but he did have a genius for bringing the right people together and making things happen. In the case of the Velvet Underground he introduced the band to Nico, a beautiful, mysterious European model and actress, whose whispered Teutonic vocals provided a perfect counterpoint to their barely repressed mania. As critic David Antrim observed in a 1966 feature in *Art News*, 'Nico is astonishing – the macabre face – so beautifully resembling a memento mori, the marvellous death-like voice coming from the lovely blonde head.'

Warhol recruited the band for his Exploding Plastic Inevitable performance art show, their musical explorations of madness, violence, drug addiction and sexual perversion complementing its contemporary vision. Art school student, Brian Eno – later responsible for the innovative electronic elements of early Roxy Music, and a pioneer of ambient music – was excited by the unsettling moods conjured by the band, and 'the idea that rock music could be part of the cutting edge of culture as we knew it, not just about music but art in general. That was the . . . message of the Velvets.'

The people who formed the original alternative bands were art and film students, fashion designers or ex-music journalists, bringing an intellectual edge to the fringes of popular music. The Velvet Underground's bass/keyboard/viola player, John Cale, is an early example of a musician with a background in *avant-garde* musical experimentation rather than rock 'n' roll, who sought to use popular music as a fresh canvas for his proto-Goth expression.

A 1966 article for *The Chicago Daily News* observed, 'The flowers of evil are in full bloom with The Exploding Plastic Inevitable', making a connection between the Velvets and Charles Baudelaire's *Les Fleurs du mal*. The critic for *Los Angeles Magazine* described a Velvet Underground performance that same year as 'Screeching rock 'n' roll – reminded viewers of nothing so much as Berlin in the 1930s.' Pre-War Berlin, the last bastion of stylish twentieth-century decadence, would become an increasingly important ghostly presence, a lost metropolis overshadowing the alternative rock scene of the 1970s. Nico compared the atmosphere of her early live gigs at New York's Dom club to the Blue Angel, the notorious Berlin nightclub immortalised in the film of the same name.

Warhol lost interest in the band after contributing the famous banana cover for their 1967 debut, *The Velvet Underground and Nico*, and Nico herself – never a full member – flew the nest soon afterwards. Thereafter, with a certain chaotic inevitability, the band began to disintegrate. *White Light/White Heat* was recorded the following year, featuring the devastating epic of urban degeneracy, 'Sister Ray', and the Cale-narrated, 'The Gift', a horror story about a frustrated lover who mails himself to the object of his affections but dies on delivery. The plain black sleeve of the original pressing was emblazoned with a skull, only visible if the cover was tilted to a certain angle (the concept was credited to Warhol, and constituted his final contribution to the band). Cale left in 1968, turning over full artistic control to Lou Reed. After Reed's departure in 1970, the band limped on unconvincingly before folding the following year (although they did re-form two decades on).

While never a commercial or critical success at the time, the Velvet Underground left a

huge creative legacy that would gradually grow in influence over the following decades. America's influential *Trouser Press* magazine later declared the band's 'sex-drugs-noise-literature-decadence-obsession template responsible for more offbeat groups than any institution other than art college.'

Some have cited the haunting early solo work recorded by Nico after she left the Velvet Underground, in particular *The Marble Index* (1969) and *The End* (1974), as the first true Goth albums. Certainly the moods evoked by the sparse arrangements and ghostly harmonium playing – which writer, Dave Thompson, describes as 'the flickering grotesqueries of her gaslight intricacies' – are Gothic in atmosphere. Her recordings were, again according to Thompson, 'essentially a cathartic ritual, best experienced with the shutters pulled tight and the gaslight casting eerie shadows on the wall.' By 1981 the enigmatic singer noted how many girls were beginning to dress like her, in flowing black skirts and pointed riding boots, these early Goth girls nicknamed 'Nico-teens'. Little wonder, then, that Goth-rock pioneers, Bauhaus, fell over themselves to perform a cover version of the Vellvet's strung-out drug anthem, 'I'm Waiting for the Man', with this lost legend, herself in the grip of a debilitating, long-term heroin habit. 'Nico was gothic,' confirms Bauhaus singer, Pete Murphy, 'but she was Mary Shelley gothic to everyone else's Hammer horror film gothic. They both did *Frankenstein*, but Nico's was real.'

Nico described *The Marble Index* as having 'to do with my going to Berlin in 1946 when I was a little girl and seeing the entire city destroyed. I like the fallen empire, the image of the fallen empire.' The word 'decadence' alludes to degenerate pleasure, but also to the inevitable decay that follows that pleasure, and the melancholy beauty of fallen empires is a common image in decadent art. So it was with Nico, on both counts. Her dim memories of ruined Berlin, previously the world's most sinful city, are distilled into *The Marble Index* via her distinctive Teutonic vocals.

After the quirky folk-rock of her 1968 solo debut, *Chelsea Girl*, *The Marble Index* marked Nico's descent into the territory that this troubled performer made her own. Authentically strange and mesmeric, the spectral sound of her harmonium and coldly morose vocals wove an eerie black spell that alienated many, but established her as a cult performer. Nico's live performances were similarly unpredictable and gloomy. She rejected an enigmatic introduction as a 'member of the Secret Society' at a 1979 New York gig, preferring to be introduced as 'maybe the Phantom of the Opera'. According to a fan in attendance, she even dismissed her music, in her Germanic drawl, as 'dirge laike funerawl museek'.

But enough people were drawn in by the chilly atmosphere to sustain her precarious existence and erratic recording career. The climax of her first cycle of dirges from the dark side came in 1974, with, appropriately, *The End*. The title track was a haunting cover of the Doors' surreal saga of patricide and incest, recorded as a tribute to Jim Morrison, the Doors vocalist and poet who had died three years before. Morrison was one of the numerous rock legends with whom Nico had been romantically linked, describing him as her 'soul mate'. Both shared an unhealthily comfortable relationship with death. 'Life was a bore to her,' said Alan Wise, who managed Nico in the 1980s, 'she used to say she was only two minutes from death.' Back in 1967, according to Doors producer, Paul Rothchild, Morrison 'took Nico up in a tower, both naked, and Jim, stoned out of his mind, walked along the edge of the parapet. Hundreds of feet down. Here's this rock star at the peak of his career risking his life to prove to this girl that life is nothing.'

Jim Morrison – the Lizard King. His flair for psychodrama and surreal imagery raised his band, the Doors, to a new level of intensity.

The Doors are my personal choice for the most influential proto-Gothic performers of the 1960s. Formed on America's West Coast in the middle of the decade, the Doors earned a residency at LA's infamous Whisky-A-Go-Go club by 1966. The lynchpins of the band were keyboardist Ray Manzarek and vocalist Jim Morrison. Manzarek persuaded Morrison – a poet broadly in the Romantic and Decadent tradition, influenced by the flamboyant Byron, maudlin Poe and sinful Baudelaire – to abandon his planned career in *avant-garde* film-making, and set his strange and often disturbed verse to music. From the start, the connections to decadent art were floating beneath the surface, with the band treating Whisky-A-Go-Go patrons to Kurt Weill and Bertolt Brecht's 'Alabama Song' (Weill and Brecht both had artistic roots in 1920s Berlin).

The band's reputation as kings of sensuous psychedelic rock derived largely from Manzarek's swirling keyboard arpeggios. But it was Morrison's often improvised lyrics and fallen angel charisma that gave the Doors their charge of erotic danger. At a time when many hippies were boycotting animal products and sermonising the virtues of universal love, Morrison took the stage in calf's leather trousers to deliver the macabre romanticism of 'The End', or the deceptively titled 'Peace Frog': a song that describes America literally drowned in blood. In a piece entitled 'Four Doors to the Future: Gothic Rock is their Thing' – possibly the first ever use of the term – the correspondent for the Massachusetts-based *Williams College News* reviewed a 1967 Doors performance. He described Morrison as 'malevolent, satanic, electric, and on fire,' and the audience as 'scared, and rightly so. The Doors are not pleasant, amusing hippies proffering a grin and a flower; they wield a knife with a cold and terrifying edge.' For Morrison styled himself 'the Lizard King' – the reptile coiled at the core of the flower children's Garden of Eden.

'Morrison's twin obsessions were the libertine cults of Dionysus and the kind of ancient fertility religions that ensured their followers' survival and prosperity by choosing a monarch (usually young, cute, male and virile) who would be sacrificed (usually by young, cute, nubile females) after seven years or some suitably mystic period,' wrote Mick Farren in *The Black Leather Jacket*. 'Morrison's writing makes it clear that this was the role he wanted, if not for his total being, then certainly his stage persona: "We are obsessed with heroes who live for us and whom we punish." This wasn't merely a bleak observation, it was Morrison's job description and career goal.' Perhaps the first rock star to articulate the sinister subtext of the role concealed beneath the glamour, appreciating that the fans who worshipped their idols with such hysterical, almost religious fervour subconsciously also craved their martyrdom, Morrison achieved this 'goal' with his early death in 1971.

The Doors' most atmospherically Gothic release, 'Riders on the Storm', appeared as a kind of epitaph, on the last album Morrison recorded with the band. While on the surface an urbane admonition to make the most of life, a nomadic murderer lurks menacingly in the song's background ('There's a killer on the road. / His mind is squirming like a toad'). The well-crafted 1986 horror thriller, *The Hitcher*, which starred Rutger Hauer as serial killer, John Ryder, was scripted by Eric Red (who was also responsible for the script of classic vampire-road movie *Near Dark*). 'I always loved the Doors' song, "Riders on the Storm", with its filmic image of a hitchhiking killer, and felt it would be a great start for a movie,' Red told Buried.com. 'Credit the inspiration to *The Hitcher* to Jim Morrison and Ray Manzarek. I even set the opening sequence in a storm because of the rain sound effects on the song.' It's another movie, however, that subtly highlights the Gothic aspects of the Morrison myth. The 1987 vampire picture, *The Lost Boys*, left most critics unmoved, and is certainly far from perfect – the vampire-hunting comic-store proprietors, the Frog Brothers are an annoying distraction, and the 'surprise' ending is a damp squib. Indeed, *Near Dark*, made the same year, is a much better movie. Yet *The Lost Boys* overcame its limitations to become a cult hit with its black leather-clad youth audience.

It achieved this in two ways. The first was in creating a convincing pack of vampires as Goth-punk bikers, revelling in their supernatural status, which made the film an important icon of the nascent modern vampire counterculture. 'Sleep all day. Party all night. Never grow old. It's fun to be a vampire,' ran the promotional copy. If *The Hitcher* evoked 'Riders on the Storm', then *The Lost Boys* must have loomed large in Poppy Z. Brite's imagination when she conceived her groundbreaking Goth-punk vampire novel, *Lost Souls*.

The film's second strength is its subtle use of pop-culture reference. The title is borrowed from the children's story *Peter Pan*, in which the 'Lost Boys' were a gang of boys who never grew old in Never Never Land. More potent, however, are sly references to Jim Morrison, most overtly in a cover of the Doors track 'People Are Strange' by Echo and the Bunnymen for the soundtrack, produced by Ray Manzarek. The spirit of the Lizard King also looms over the production more subtly – most notably in the large poster that dominates the vampire's subterranean lair.

According to Gary Lachman in *Turn Off Your Mind*, Jim Morrison 'did dabble in a few standard occult exercises. For his marriage to Patricia Kennealy on Midsummer Night 1970,

The Lost Boys *(1987) – bloodsuckers with Jim Morrison posters on their wall, and Doors songs on the soundtrack: 'It's fun to be a vampire.'*

the couple had a Wicca ceremony. Led by a high priestess of a coven, Jim and Patricia prayed and invoked the Moon goddess, then cut their arms and mixed some of their blood with wine and drank it, before stepping over a broomstick. The taste stayed. During rehearsals for *LA Woman* [Morrison's final recorded album, upon which he sings the ominous line, 'A cold girl will kill you in a darkened room'], Morrison got into an affair with Ingrid Thompson, a Viking-like beauty from Scandinavia. Both were heavily into coke at the time, and one night, after going through nearly a film can's worth, Ingrid remarked to Jim that she sometimes drank blood. Jim insisted they have some immediately. After some hesitation, Ingrid managed to slice her palm. Jim caught the blood in a champagne glass. They made love, smearing themselves, then danced. In the morning, when he woke up caked with blood, he was scared.'

Morrison died of drug-induced heart failure (purportedly heroin, administered by his similarly doomed wife) while on sabbatical in Paris, within a few weeks of completing *LA Woman*. Or so the official version goes . . . Persistent rumours maintain that the Lizard King had successfully shed his skin one last time, escaping the constraints of fame – even the attentions of the Grim Reaper – with a final flick of the tail. A few days before his death Morrison had visited Paris' famous Père-Lachaise cemetery, commenting that this was where he wanted to be buried. After his death no autopsy was performed, and the doctor who pronounced him dead refused to talk to friends or the media. The secrecy surrounding Morrison's sealed coffin caused Manzarek to demand, 'How do we even know he was in the

The 'billion dollar bill' from the original packaging of Alice Cooper's Billion Dollar Babies *(1973).*
The reverse side sardonically mocked the violence in US society.

coffin? How do you know it wasn't 150 lbs of fucking sand?' And Doors drummer John Densmore remarked, 'the grave is too short!', when he first saw the Pere Lachaise grave site.

Bizarre rumours about the singer continue to circulate. In 1974, a performer calling himself the Phantom surfaced, who sang in a voice so similar to that of Morrison that it sent chills down the spine of his closest friends. The Phantom was invited to play at a Morrison memorial gig in LA that year, singing 'Riders on the Storm' accompanied by Ray Manzarek. 'He was a weird guy,' recalls the keyboardist. 'He dressed in black and would only wear silver jewellery.' While many Anne Rice fans may be incensed at the suggestion, the real Jim Morrison – whether he's still alive or undead – would have made perfect casting in his reptilian prime, as her vampire-cum-rock star, Lestat.

A drinking buddy of Jim Morrison in his last year of life, Alice Cooper is often airbrushed from the Gothic rock tradition by Goths themselves (with the honourable exception of early Goth-rock band Alien Sex Fiend). Cooper's adoption of homogenised hard rock in the 1980s ensured that most rock subcultures disowned him, the more forgiving heavy metal canon adopting him almost by default. However, Alice Cooper as a band – the moniker originally referring to both the group and its vocalist – were once praised by *Rolling Stone* for their 'nicely wrought mainstream punk raunch and snidely clever lyrics'. And Johnny Rotten successfully auditioned for the Sex Pistols with a (doubtless dreadful) rendition of Cooper's hormonal adolescent anthem 'I'm Eighteen', in 1975.

The band members' outrageous attire defined them as 'glam' (or, in the US, 'glitter') rockers, though the band's experiments in gender-bending were intentionally more grotesque than glamorous, with *Rolling Stone* reviewer Ben Gersen dismissing Alice in favour of 'a more

credible transvestite' from across the Atlantic, one David Bowie. Jayne County (formerly Wayne County), glitter and punk rock's definitive gender-bender, has latterly bitched that Alice Cooper 'had to stop wearing ladies' sling-back shoes and false eyelashes and dresses and get into horror. People could understand horror and blood and dead babies, but they couldn't understand male/female sexuality, androgyny or, as little American boys would say, fag music.' Indeed, 1970s America could accept a star whose lyrics endorsed necrophilia more readily than it could tolerate one who was sexually ambiguous.

Alice Cooper, the band, had its genesis in unfashionable Phoenix, Arizona in the 1960s. 'If we had been from San Francisco or LA, it would have been easier for us,' pondered guitarist Michael Bruce. 'But playing in a long-haired, psychedelic band that dressed all flashy made us an easy target in Arizona. So, very early on, we learned how to deal with a hostile reaction, not to mention a considerable amount of violence.' Early incarnations of the band were heavily influenced by the British invasion led by the Beatles, reflected in monikers like the Earwigs and the Spiders, before the group re-named themselves the Nazz ('hipsterspeak' slang for Jesus), their last pre-Alice title.

On his spectacular Welcome to My Nightmare *tour, horror-rocker Alice Cooper serenades a murdered woman with the gentle ballad 'Only Women Bleed'.*

While they may have borrowed musical leads from English artists such as the Beatles and Pink Floyd, these rough-edged Americans absorbed none of their peacenik ethos, feeding off the frustration of the hippie era's twilight (the frontman was later fond of boasting that they had 'put the stake through the heart of the love generation'). At a 1968 seance, led by the mother of their road manager, a purported medium, the Ouija board revealed that lead singer, Vincent Furnier, had been a woman named Alice Cooper in a previous life. The band adopted the name, later adding the detail that Alice Cooper had also been a sixteenth-century English witch for sinister effect.

Subversive musical maestro, Frank Zappa, signed the band to his Straight label, impressed at the way the quartet emptied venues with their chaotic riffing, deranged dress sense and edgy 'don't give a shit' attitude. 'Even hippies hated us, and it's hard to get a hippie to hate anything,' Cooper later reflected of the band's beginnings. 'But the next time we played, there were maybe 1,000 people there. It became the "in" thing in LA to come see Alice Cooper and then walk out.' They were already turning into something closer to a theatrical experience than a conventional rock band, as lead singer Furnier began experimenting with the weird make-up that would later become his trademark, and indulging in increasingly provocative on-stage behaviour – creating blizzards of feathers with split pillows, baiting the audience, smearing himself in food – anything to get a reaction.

At the Toronto Peace Festival in 1969, where Alice Cooper played on a bill featuring equally unlikely peaceniks the Doors, a chicken was thrown onto the stage, launching a legend in the process. 'I'm from Detroit, I'm not a farm kid,' Furnier later explained. 'I figured a chicken had wings, it'll fly away. So I took the chicken and threw it and it didn't fly. It went into the audience. Blood everywhere. The next day, everybody's reading, "Alice Cooper rips chicken's head off, drinks blood." Zappa called me. He said, "Whatever you did, keep doing it."' So the singer later embellished the story, claiming the front rows had been reserved for wheelchair users, and it was they who had disembowelled the ill-fated fowl.

It quickly became apparent that Furnier – spindly, awkward and nasally over-endowed – was becoming the band's chief attraction, a malevolent perpetual adolescent. With him taking the band's moniker as his stagename, it wasn't long before both audiences and the press assumed that he, rather than the band, *was* Alice Cooper.

Alice Cooper recorded two offbeat albums for Zappa – *Pretties for You* and *Easy Action* – that both proved to be false starts. They discovered their collective voice on their 1971 debut for Warner Bros, *Love It To Death* – regarded by many as Alice Cooper's best, and also as the first 'death rock' album ever recorded. The highlight of this record is the atmospheric voodoo-zombie chant 'Black Juju' (which was later covered by Lydia Lunch, with ex-Birthday Party guitarist, Rowland S. Howard, in 1993).

As the ghoulish showmanship attracted fans, live shows became increasingly elaborate, and albums were released as springboards for the next epic tour. A straitjacket was employed to accompany the performance of 'The Ballad of Dwight Fry' from *Love It To Death*, then an electric chair for the 1971 *Killer* album tour, then a gallows, and, finally, a guillotine – all employed to punish frontman Alice. The singer, morally unfettered, would commit crimes – usually mutilating dolls to the strain of droll ditties like 'Dead Babies' – before he was apprehended and executed. As the props became more elaborate, so did the supporting cast, as Alice, once escorted to his doom by a lynch mob of fellow band members, was now dispatched by a buxom executioneress in dominatrix wear, or disciplined by nurses in PVC uniforms that would look more at home in a wet dream than a hospital. This crime-and-punishment scenario gave the performance a certain moral aspect, though it was fatally compromised when Alice was resurrected, Jesus-style, for the inevitable encore.

By 1974, the show had swallowed the band whole. Furnier toured solo on the *Welcome To My Nightmare* tour the following year, dispensing with the original band and officially adopting the Alice Cooper moniker as his own. In the process, Alice degenerated into bloated excess, as *Sesame Street*-style monsters loomed over the audience and the singer chased dancing teeth with a giant toothbrush. The album and tour were Cooper's most vaudevillian effort to date, featuring the singer on the sleeve *sans* make-up with a top hat and cane. In creating the greatest horrorshow on earth, Grand Guignol ringmaster Alice Cooper, sacrificed much of the hard edge of the band's chaotic early years. Reassured that it was merely camp showmanship, no more dangerous than the ghost train at Disneyland, America embraced her strangest son and Alice became a familiar face on his beloved TV.

The singer also made personal sacrifices for his art. The potion required for the 'Jekyll and Hyde' transformation from shy preacher's son to demonic, snake-wielding exhibitionist was beer – up to two cases a day, later chased down by whisky. By 1978, he was obliged to recognise his possession by the demon drink, and admit himself to a New York sanatorium. In true showbiz style, Cooper used the experience as inspiration for a concept album, *From the Inside*, a mixture of voyeuristic soul-bearing and exploitational sensationalism, even licensing a Marvel comic based on the concept.

Happily for Alice, in the 1980s he finally exorcised the demon drink and the newly acquired cocaine habit that were slowly killing him. Less happily, from a creative point of view, the exorcism was achieved via a rediscovery of his Christian faith (both his father and father-in-law were ministers). The singer successfully re-invented himself as a heavy metal godfather with a social conscience – insistent that recent albums, like *Dragontown*, are Christian morality tales that delve into darkness and depravity only to condemn it. Most unforgiveably bizarre was his gradual transformation into a full-time celebrity, a process that began back in the mid-1970s when he went golfing with Bing Crosby and appeared on *Celebrity Squares* for the first time. This, according to his apologists, is his most subversive role yet, but his recent tendency to chide contemporary bands for tastelessness or moral bankruptcy make Alice look more like just one more mainstream 'personality' with a shady past.

'I used to celebrate moral decay, the decadence of it,' he admitted, in a recent interview. 'I can look back on what I did then and what I'm doing now and they're two different things. But at the time I was the poster boy for moral decay, you know.' The modern poster boy who troubles Alice most is Marilyn Manson – not least due to parallels drawn between the two in the media, though Manson satirises America in a much more knowing way than Cooper's Gothic camp. When Alice criticises Marilyn – somehow taking the *Antichrist Superstar* album as a personal insult, claiming that the album was 'pointed right at me' – he seems to have forgotten how authority figures used him as a scapegoat in the 1970s.

In 1973, Leo Abse, a British Member of Parliament, and self-appointed 'decency campaigner' Mary Whitehouse had called for the refusal of an entry visa to prevent Cooper's *Billion Dollar Babies* tour reaching the UK – 'completely overlooking the fact that Cooper has no plans for a British tour in the immediate future and has not even applied for an entry permit,' noted the *NME* at the time. In words redolent of those levelled at Manson's Dead to the World shows, more than twenty years later, Abse fumed, 'They tell me Alice is absolutely sick,' not having bothered to check out what he wanted to ban. 'And I agree with them. I regard his act as an incitement to infanticide for his sub-teenage audience. He is deliberately trying to involve these kids in sadomasochism. He is peddling the culture of the concentration camp. Pop is one thing. Anthems of necrophilia are another.'

The camp excesses of the early 1970s glam rock scene in Britain were an altogether different kind of decadence. 'The genius of glam was that it was all *about* stardom,' wrote Barney Hoskyns in *Glam!* 'It said flaunt it if you've got it, and if you haven't got it fake it – make it up with make-up, cover your face with stardust, reinvent yourself as a Martian androgyne. Glam was prefab, anti-craft, allied to artifice and the trash aesthetic. Its plasticity and cartoonish bisexuality were all about giving pop back to "the kids" . . . It was simple, flash, throwaway, and from 1970 till 1974 it injected more fun into the pop-culture bloodstream than people knew what to do with . . .'

'Glam swept the nation in ways that were at once innocent and morally subversive. It called into question received notions of truth and authenticity, especially in the area of sexuality. It blurred the divide between straights and queers, inviting girls and boys to

David Bowie's apocalyptic, neo-Gothic Diamond Dogs *(1974). On the original sleeve design, Bowie's canine genitals were clearly visible before neutering by his record label.*

experiment with roles in a genderless utopia of eyeliner and seven-inch platform boots. And it flirted openly with a decadence pitched somewhere between *Cabaret* and *Clockwork Orange*' (both films were cult favourites with punks and early Goths. *Cabaret* is a musical based on Christopher Isherwood's memories of decadent 1930s Berlin, while *A Clockwork Orange* depicts juvenile delinquency in a nightmare near-future viewed from the early 1970s).

The music press had problems taking glam seriously, its blend of flamboyant gender-bending and outrageous camp machismo seen as no more than kitsch trash. The most credible performer of the glam era was David Bowie, whose 1972 *Rise and Fall of Ziggy Stardust and the Spiders From Mars* album transformed him into a superstar overnight.

Ziggy was a persona adopted by Bowie – the ultimate glam star, an androgynous rocker alienated by the excesses of fame, whose rise and fall mirrored the end of a world undergoing some unspecified apocalypse. The concept explored the same ideas that had preoccupied Jim

Morrison, of how the pressures of stardom and the demands of fanatical audiences pulled stars apart, making martyrs of music's messiahs. Bowie, like Morrison, discovered that exploring these pressures meant courting them, a process that proved ultimately fatal for the Lizard King. But Bowie's strength lay in his ability to shed his skin – although his discarding of the Ziggy persona did little to halt the disintegration of his own personality.

While Morrison had used pagan tales of sacrificial god-kings as his personal mythic vehicles, Bowie was drawn to the same cursed chalice that the Rolling Stones had picked up and dropped very quickly in the 1960s. As early as 1970, Bowie made oblique reference to notorious black magician Aleister Crowley, 'the Great Beast'. On his album *The Man Who Sold the World*, Bowie included the infamous Crowleyan maxim, 'do what you will' in the song 'After All'. 'The Width of a Circle' was a less ambivalent occultic saga, depicting a journey into 'the burning pit of fear', where the protagonist experiences a homoerotic encounter with a demon. *The Man Who Sold the World* was his strangest, heaviest recording to date, with bizarre themes of madness and the Crowleyesque struggle to evolve into a higher form of life etched into its grooves. Songs like the title track and 'All the Madmen' (with its crazed end-chant of 'oeuvre le chien') became cult favourites among those who would form the darker strands of the punk movement and the embryonic Goth scene at the end of the 1970s. Bowie's 1971 follow-up, *Hunky Dory*, while far more accessible in style, contained his most overt Crowley reference in the song 'Quicksand': 'I'm closer to the Golden Dawn [the Order of the Golden Dawn, of which the Great Beast was a member] / Immersed in Crowley's uniform of imagery.'

Diamond Dogs, released in 1974, was described by rock journalist Charles Shaar Murray as 'the final nightmare of the glitter apocalypse'. Its apocalyptic unifying concept was variously inspired by Harlan Ellison's bleak science fiction novel *A Boy and His Dog*, William S. Burroughs' dystopian fantasy *The Wild Boys*, and George Orwell's dark political allegory *1984* – though taken to vivid extremes suggested by a grotesque dog-Bowie hybrid on the cover, and an opening narrative where the singer introduces us to Hunger City, where 'the last few corpses lay rotting on the slimy thoroughfare' and 'fleas the size of rats sucked on rats the size of cats.'

'Most of the songs are obscure tangles of perversion, degradation, fear and self-pity,' complained the review in *Rolling Stone*. 'Are they masturbatory fantasies, guilt-ridden projections, terrified premonitions, or is it all Alice Cooper exploitation?' The album's most Gothic offering was the angst-ridden 'We Are the Dead', boasting a keyboard line that sounds as if it was ripped straight from a horror movie (according to leading Goth DJ and historian Pete Scathe, Bowie described *Diamond Dogs* as 'Gothic' in character – another claim to the coining of the term 'Gothic rock').

In the years that followed, Bowie, like the Stones, learned that those who play with black magic invite black magic to play with them. But while Jagger, the perennial dabbler, only touched upon the Great Beast Aleister Crowley's legacy, Bowie became briefly immersed and found it commensurately difficult to escape the orbit. As he would later reflect in a 1995 interview, by the mid-1970s his 'overriding interest was in cabbala and Crowleyism. That whole dark and rather fearsome netherworld of the wrong side of the brain.'

The Great Beast's quest to become an unholy messiah, to explore the taboo territories beyond decadence, has fascinated rock performers who sense parallels between the profane worship he craved and that enjoyed by the rock god. But while the seemingly indestructible occultist endured his leap into the abyss, the slight figure of David Bowie looked destined to extinction. Crowley had gasped in ironic mock horror at the 'cocaine-crazed sexual lunatics' of Los Angeles in 1914 – in 1975, Bowie was visibly falling apart in the city he described as 'a vile piss-pot', amidst a blizzard of black magic and white powder.

Huddled behind perpetually drawn curtains, he drew magic symbols on the walls, burned black candles, reputedly stored his own urine in a fridge, so that it wouldn't fall into the hands of those who might employ it to place a curse on him, and was convinced that two witches, posing as fans, planned to use him to father the Antichrist. In his most terrifying moment,

An undead David Bowie and Catherine Deneuve stalk a nightclub in Goth cult movie
The Hunger *(1983), while Bauhaus play in the background.*

Bowie saw the face of Satan beneath the boiling waters of his swimming pool. 'I drew gateways into different dimensions,' the performer later confided, 'and I'm quite sure that, for myself, I really walked into other worlds and saw what was on the other side.'

In a desperate attempt to survive, Bowie had to shed the skin of the Thin White Duke – the persona he had adopted to explore the idea of the rock star as quasi-fascist dictator. It was a transformation few performers could have got away with, and it tested the tolerance of the press and public to breaking point. For, while never a true innovator, Bowie was adept at interpreting *outre* music and imagery in a fashion that made them palatable to mass audiences, even basing his stage sets and lighting at the time on the designs of Nazi architect Albert

Speer. In his supposedly omnipotent Thin White Duke mode, however, one English journalist described him as 'chalk-skinned, bloodless and apparently dying, if not undead. He looked like a cross between a stick insect and Dracula.' Interestingly, an older, wiser Bowie has recently signed to play the vampire count in an Italian TV production of *Dracula*, due to air in late 2002.

In 1976 Bowie, like Crowley four decades earlier, headed for Berlin, meeting descendants of Hitler's SS men who disavowed their fathers' Nazi pasts – putting his fascist fascination into perspective and bringing it to an end. For he had been drawn by healthier interests, escaping the increasingly stale Anglo-American glam rock scene. As he would later reflect, he and his camp followers were tired of all the ersatz decadence, 'very miffed that people who'd obviously never seen [Fritz Lang's 1926 expressionist science fiction classic] *Metropolis* and had never heard of Christopher Isherwood [the writer famous for chronicling decadent Berlin in the 1920s] were actually becoming glam rockers.' He chose instead to immerse himself in the burgeoning 'Krautrock' movement. Krautrock was the affectionate term coined for German bands – like Kraftwerk, Neu and Faust – who were leading the way in recording a new form of pop music (which some dubbed 'anti-pop') that substituted technology for organic, guitar-based sounds. Bowie would never deny the profound influence Krautrock had on him, although he defined what he was trying to do as 'expressionist' as opposed to the minimalism of the pure German sound. While he was in Berlin, Bowie also used the derelict UFA film studios, that had once produced expressionist classics such as *Metropolis* and *The Cabinet of Dr Caligari*, as rehearsal space.

In Germany, Bowie rebuilt his shattered health and repaired his sanity, recording three albums almost as a form of therapy. *Low*, *'Heroes'* and *Lodger*, now referred to as his Berlin trilogy, were Bowie at his most daringly creative, taking pop as far as he could into the unknown without losing the large cult audience he had built up since *Ziggy*. His collaborators were his long-time producer, Tony Visconti, and the doyen of ambient electronica, Brian Eno. But Bowie's recuperation was gradual, and sinister apparitions seemed to dog the recordings. While suffused with the gloomily decadent spirit of Berlin, *Low* was actually recorded in a French chateau – the Chateau d'Herouville (though completed in Hansa studios, overlooking the Berlin wall, which, according to Bowie had formerly been 'a Weimar ballroom, utilised by the Gestapo during the thirties for their own little musical soirees'). The chateau contained two studios named after its most distinguished ex-residents, Frederic Chopin – the nineteenth-century Polish composer best known for 'The Funeral March' – and his lover, the writer, George Sand. Both were rumoured to haunt the building. Bowie declined to sleep in the master bedroom because it felt unnaturally cold; Visconti took the room, later telling *Uncut*, 'It felt like it was haunted as all fuck . . . Eno claimed he was awakened early every morning by someone shaking his shoulder. When he opened his eyes, no-one was there.' Guitarist Ricky Gardiner recalls that Eno stayed in what had been Chopin's room, and suffered from a chronic cough. 'Chopin died of consumption,' noted Gardiner. 'You may make what you like of that!'

The critics weren't sure what to make of *Low* on its release in 1977. Many were disturbed. British rock journalist and longtime Bowie fan Charles Shaar Murray, was appalled, describing it in *NME* as reflecting 'futility and the death wish glorified, an elaborate embalming job for

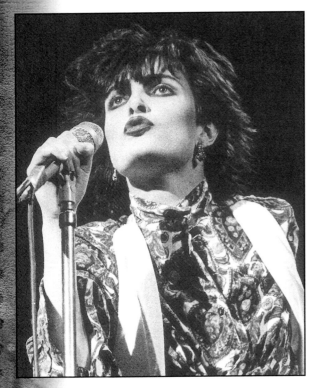

Siouxsie Sue in 1978, when her band the Banshees headed the post-punk 'Cold Wave'.

a suicide's grave . . . decadent in the sense that it glamorises and glorifies passive decay.' In a sense Murray was right, but he failed to spot the album's redemptive qualities. *Low* is unquestionably grim and strange – synthesisers and distorted snare-drums blend to unnerving effect with more traditional instruments, from xylophones to guitars – while Bowie's world-weary lyrics often degenerate into urbane wallpaper. But it is the sound of an artist immersing himself in Berlin's tragic heritage to rebuild his own fractured soul.

'Heroes' was equally experimental and often equally downbeat, but more energetic and self-assured. Those who had responded to *Low* felt even more at home with its Teutonic pop experimentalism. 1980s bands who are now familiar favourites on the Goth dancefloor – New Order, Gary Numan, Depeche Mode – all cut their creative teeth on 'Heroes', paving the way for gloomy yet commercial synth-pop. *Uncut* would describe it retrospectively and reverentially as 'Embracing everything from Wagnerian electronica to disco romanticism, the vocal tunes . . . crackle with a lusty intensity, while the ambient sound-paintings bathe in deep Gothic shadows.'

Lodger, released in 1979, represented the end of both Bowie's Berlin residency, and, as far as many hardcore fans were concerned, his most creative period. Siouxsie Sue spoke for many when she described the album as 'the first of many to disappoint'. A less outright rejection came from *Rolling Stone* magazine, which dubbed *Lodger* 'a footnote to *"Heroes"*, an act of marking time.' Nevertheless, the Berlin trilogy was a landmark on the alternative music map, assuring Bowie's later status as an influence on the Goth scene. 'Nothing else sounded like those albums,' he boasted to *Uncut* in 2001. 'Nothing else came close. If I never made another album it really wouldn't matter now, my complete being is within those three. They are my DNA.'

However, his 1980 follow-up, *Scary Monsters*, was well received by the press, and a good deal more easily digestible than his Berlin trilogy, without ever being throwaway or trite. The title track, 'Scary Monsters (and Super Creeps)' is a blend of disordered guitar riffing and almost oriental rhythms that tells the tale of a sinister girl who 'opened strange doors that we'd never close again'. The album was also a favourite of themed 'Bowie Nights' at London venues like Billy's and Blitz, where the short-lived 'new romantic' movement paved the way for the transition between punk and Goth. (Several of the Blitz nightclub's most extravagant figures appeared in the strangely expressionistic promotional video for the first of the album's hit singles, 'Ashes to Ashes'.) From hereon, however, it was downhill creatively for Bowie, who made the transition from pioneering artist to mainstream rock institution in the decade that followed.

Punk rock hit the UK like a thunderbolt in 1976, and the shockwaves were still being felt across the globe years later. For many, punk was a grassroots explosion of frustration and disgust at the bloated, stagnant state of culture in the depressed mid-1970s. But punk began as an experiment by art school and fashion graduates, fans of the highly contrived images of Bowie and Roxy Music – as a mass media prank, it would soon demonstrate the way in which teenage rebelliousness, even chaos, could be packaged and marketed.

The writing was on the toilet wall for the movement when standard bearers, the Sex Pistols, disintegrated in early 1978. The group's bassist, Sid Vicious, the scrawny, talentless hooligan, whom manager Malcolm McLaren had groomed to embody punk, died of a heroin overdose on 5 February 1979, while on bail for the murder of his girlfriend. Sid had, in the words of his infamous performance in *The Great Rock 'n' Roll Swindle*, done it his way. It was an apt epitaph for punk – whether as an act of squalid stupidity or twisted martyrdom – and the movement began fragmenting as rapidly as it had emerged. In one last breathtakingly cynical act, the original Sex Pistols reformed in 1996 for a farcical yet lucrative tour – proving that manufactured rebellion could be repackaged and remarketed as nostalgia.

Siouxsie Sue, original punkette and Sex Pistols camp member, made her debut as a performer at the now legendary 1976 punk festival at London's 100 Club. As the singer (in the loosest sense) of the original Siouxsie and the Banshees, she delivered an atonal improvisation around The Lord's Prayer, accompanied by Sid Vicious on drums, Marco Pirroni on guitar and Steve Severin on bass. Only Siouxsie and Severin would remain in the classic Banshees line-up, while Pirroni went on to join Adam and the Ants (whose edgy early material, dubbed 'punk *noir*', explored the sadomasochistic chic later central to the Goth aesthetic) and Vicious replaced the Pistols' original bassist. Initially, Siouxsie was a female counterpart to Sid's archetypal male punk, but as punk rock's creative energy dissipated into a haze of self-destruction, the Banshees were already following a musical direction all of their own.

Paul Woods was a young Banshees fan, and describes the band's early sound as 'characterised by John Mackay's clanging, metallic guitar and Kenny Morris' thudding, semi-militaristic drums – with Siouxsie's strident caterwauling over the top. It was unlike anything else at the time, including punk, in that it had no discernible blues element and it came as close as you could get to an "industrial" sound with a guitar/bass/ drums line-up . . . older rock fans found them completely unpalatable and oppressive' – reflected in the dismissive words of *Rolling Stone*, who dubbed the band 'uniformly ghoulish, self-indulgent and monotonous'.

'The original punks were more fashion people – into the early aspects like bondage gear and Vivienne Westwood clothes,' says David Edmond, who would later design T-shirts and merchandise for London's first Goth club. 'As you get towards 1980, when the more politicised people came along, the original punks got bored and split into various new directions and factions.' While the rock press expected punk, which had once prided itself on its inarticulate fury, to carry a 'message', on Britain's deprived housing estates disaffected youth began to take grassroots punk in socially unacceptable directions – adopting Nazi imagery, without any of the irony once attached to it by Siouxsie Sue. For early champions of political correctness had blanched at a bare-breasted Siouxsie taking the stage at a Sex Pistols gig, flaunting a swastika. As a consequence of this and the icy ambiguities of some of her lyrics ('Too many Jews for my liking' ran one line of 'Love in a Void' – in marked contrast to the sympathetic lament of the later 'Israel'), Siouxsie and the Banshees remained on an unofficial

Adam Ant on stage with his manager Jordan (foreground) in the punk era. Exploiting taboos like S&M, Adam and the Ants were originally bad-boy untouchables.

blacklist for more than a year. They were finally signed to the UK's Polydor label in 1978, by which time most of the other first generation punk bands were on their second album.

Criticisms of lyrical nihilism and musical cacophony were difficult to sustain by the time of the band's early to mid 1980s material, when Siouxsie casually described the Banshees' new direction as 'Gothic'. From the 1980 album, *Kaleidoscope*, onwards, elements of Eastern exoticism and eerie romanticism began stealing into their sound, the 1981 *Juju* containing compositions entitled 'Voodoo Dolly', 'Hallowe'en' and the haunting hit 'Spellbound'. Their 1984 album *Hyaena* represents the climax of the Banshees' Gothic period, described in *Cult Rockers* by authors, Wayne Jancik and Tad Lathrop, as 'a nightmare ride through lusting spawn, sucking leeches, drooling vultures, and frenzied vipers, worms, and jackals on a landscape of corrosion and rot.' Such purple hyperbole aside, it's difficult to see how the band could later disavow the 'Goth' tag, when the album contained sultry, sinister material such as 'Belladonna' or 'Bring Me the Head of the Preacher Man'.

Other social undesirables on the edge of punk included seedy 'Men in black' the Stranglers, a garage band whose early material had strong undertones of psychedelia and Gothic horror – they called their 1979 album *The Raven*, after Edgar Allan Poe's famous poem. But despite such references and a tendency to dress in black, the Stranglers – with their reputation for sexism and thuggishness – were too crude to merit the sophisticated 'Gothic' tag. However, Tim Kennedy, a fan, insisted in a review of the group's official biography that they inspired a 'generation [who] grew up that played strange dark music – ultimately "goth" was probably the Stranglers' doing.'

Adam Ant completes his transformation from perverse punk to pop idol, adopting a 'dandy highwayman' persona to plunder the pop charts in the early 1980s.

Aspects of their music certainly reveal strong Gothic sensibilities – particularly keyboard player Dave Greenfield's marvellously creepy organ sound, and the harpsichord-like melody on 'Golden Brown', the eerily decadent ode to heroin, that earned the band their biggest hit in 1981. But far more Gothic, in an overtly traditional sense, was the album that Stranglers vocalist/guitarist, Hugh Cornwell, recorded with Robert Williams, drummer with Captain Beefheart and his Magic Band. Entitled *Nosferatu*, it reflected Cornwell's passion for horror movies, the title track was obviously inspired by the 1922 German vampire classic, and concluded, 'Lifeless eyes with no reflection. / We may die but he'll go on: Nosferatu!' Released in 1979, the album features a suitably spooky sleeve depicting the darkened, plague infested streets of Bremen from the original silent horror film.

Adam and the Ants was the only early punk band to have an authentic interest in sadomasochism as anything more than shock chic, Adam taking the stage in full fetish-wear to sing songs like 'Beat My Guest' and 'Whip in My Valise'. This, alongside outrageous clothing from Vivienne Westwood's Sex boutique – such as a T-shirt emblazoned with the legend 'Cambridge Rapist' (a sex criminal who terrorised Cambridge University for months in the mid-1970s) – marked out the singer as a misogynist, as well as politically suspect, at least as far as the humourless, left-leaning music press was concerned.

The band's 1979 debut album, *Dirk Wears White Sox*, referred to the mannered English film actor, Dirk Bogarde – whose poise and performance in controversial films like *The Night Porter* (where he played a Nazi war criminal in a sadomasochistic relationship with a Jewish girl) made him a hero to the Ants' leader, but an unlikely punk icon. There was an intelligence and wit to the lyrics that combined with the singer's interest in sexual taboos to alienate punk's self-appointed thought police, who associated sexual dominance games with sexism and the hated middle classes (their own social roots – albeit concealed with a bright pink mohican). In response to the rejection, Adam did the unthinkable – abandoning his punk past and heading for the charts with a new pop sound, suggested by Malcolm McLaren, that hitched traditional rock 'n' roll guitar to an overriding tribal drum sound. The resultant 'Antmusic' made the band one of the most interesting, if peripheral, exponents of a movement that briefly dominated London's music and fashion scenes.

As many of London's leading trendsetters tired of punk's bleak anti-fashion ethos, they reacted against it by overdressing in extravagant plumage inspired by the dandies and fops of the past. The movement found a home in London clubs like Blitz (the club that first hosted 'Bowie nights'), and its flamboyantly dressed clientele were briefly known as 'Blitz Kids'. 'I came to London in October 1979,' recalls designer Nigel Wingrove, a Blitz regular. 'It was becoming a "new romantic" club – though back then it was called "the cult with no name". It was a post-punk thing, having gone from punk to the style of dressing all in black, but at Blitz people dressed up like you wouldn't believe.'

In hits such as 'Kings of the Wild Frontier' (1980), 'Stand and Deliver' and 'Prince Charming' (both 1981), Adam Ant elegantly articulated the philosophy of the nineteenth-century dandy that was implicit in the new romantic movement, updated for a late twentieth-century milieu. Unlike the original dandies, the Antpeople eschewed sombre black in favour of a cross-breed of highwayman chic and Red Indian war paint, although the core ethos of becoming an ersatz aristocrat by virtue of outrageous style remained the same (the same ethos of seeing vanity as a virtue became central to the nascent Goth scene soon after). The whips and chains and provocative sick humour of yesteryear were shelved in favour of some of the most innovative, exciting pop music of the decade. As the mainstream embraced Antmusic, however, purists like Goth archivist Mick Mercer yearned for what he described as 'the highly stylised, intellectual, brutal beauty of the early records'.

While Alice Cooper had responded to the British pop invasion of the 1960s by mutating it, the Cramps responded by stubbornly pretending it never happened. This frenzied four-piece was formed in 1974, although as far as vocalist Lux Interior and guitarist 'Poison' Ivy Rorshach were concerned, time had stopped a decade earlier, prior to the impact of the Beatles on US popular music, when Elvis was still king. While Lux was a fan of Alice Cooper's trash-culture rock, his own band fetishised the pop culture of the 1950s and early 1960s, playing in the rockabilly style that combined a traditional hillbilly guitar sound with an up-

tempo rock 'n' roll beat. Nostalgic trash–
Americana was a prevailing theme in the
Cramps' lyrics, with the addition of sordid
sexual innuendo – 'Can Your Pussy Do The
Dog?' – and a speedy tempo quite out of step
with the repressed 1950s.

EC horror comics and sleazy drive-in
monster movies of the era loom large in the
world of the Cramps. Vampira, mother of all
horror hosts, was also lured out of retirement
for a Hallowe'en 1981 Cramps gig – though, in
a flourish worthy of Ed Wood, the lights never
went up and few of the brawling audience
noticed the vamp emerge from her coffin.

But perhaps the Cramps' most obvious
influence is Screamin' Jay Hawkins, the
legendary wild horror-rocker who, like Lux,
came from Ohio (the Cramps shared a
headline bill with their idol in 1984, as did
Nick Cave and the Bad Seeds the following
year – the latter shows resulting in acrimony
between the two intense frontmen).

The classic Cramps line-up was completed
by drummer Nick Knox and guitarist Bryan
Gregory – who refused to play bass – giving
the band two guitarists, no bassist, and a very
distinctive sound by default. Gregory may not
have taken a stage name, but if anything, he
looked more the part than his bandmates – a
1950s rocker as realised for an EC horror
comic. He wore a necklace of bones, as well as
a little bag into which he would put a pinch
of graveyard dirt from every town the band
visited, a feature of his well publicised interest
in the occult. But he recorded only one album
– *Songs the Lord Taught Us* in 1979 – before
leaving under acrimonious circumstances. 'It's
hard to imagine the Cramps without Bryan,
but it's harder to imagine Bryan without the
Cramps,' reflected New York's *East Village Eye*,
'Where does a human reject from a *Vault of*

Lux Interior ('the psycho-sexual Frankenstein
from beyond') with soulmate Poison Ivy
('the ultimate bad girl vixen') of the Cramps.

Horror comic go?'

For his part, Gregory had decided he didn't want to live in the underbelly of the 1950s for the rest of his days. After abortive attempts to break a death rock act called Beast, or to follow his cinematic idol Boris Karloff into horror movies, rumour has it that Gregory began a new life as a practising black magician. He died on 10 January 2001, having reconciled with the lovers Lux and Ivy ten years earlier. Gregory had a point about his former band.

While the Cramps are a one-off, only the dedicated fan really needs more than one album of their distinctive brand of hyperactive horror rock. The Cramps themselves, as obsessive rock 'n' roll purists, have always scorned the horror rock label – 'voodoo rockabilly' being their own description. The death rock tag received similarly short shrift, with Ivy dismissively observing that those bands 'supposedly influenced by us are obsessed with death and we are so much about life.' 'Yeah,' added Lux, 'we're into blood-lust, not death.' They have also disowned psychobilly – a blend of rockabilly, horror imagery and punk energy that characterises English bands like the Meteors, the Krewmen and Demented Are Go!. However, the cult was manifestly spawned by the Cramps – the term psychobilly was coined on a 1976 tour poster – but disinherited by the vocalist for not being 'psycho' at all (whatever Lux may think, British psychobilly fans had a fearsome reputation for violence in the 1980s).

Needless to say, reluctant as the Cramps were to take their place in the death rock canon, they were even more contemptuous of those who suggested a connection between them and the burgeoning Goth-rock movement. Interior was insistent that they had nothing to do with a double-billing with arch-Goths Specimen on a 1984 UK tour. 'I saw them on TV one time and all they did was talk about their make-up for fifteen minutes,' he sneered.

The only concrete connection between the manic, morbid trashiness of the Cramps and the dark melodrama of Goth lies in sharing personnel with another American band, the Gun Club. Formed in Los Angeles in 1980, briefly known as Creeping Ritual, the Gun Club was a vehicle for the haunted vision of vocalist Jeffrey Lee Pierce, until a cerebral blood clot claimed him in 1996. Stylistically, the Gun Club occupied the swampy territory between the overheated trad-rock 'n' roll of the Cramps and the blues-tinted Southern Gothic that became the style of Nick Cave and the Bad Seeds – sharing a similar aggressive streak with the former and the morbid, soul-searching tendencies of the latter. In his band's lifetime, Pierce recruited a succession of musicians who read like a *Who's Who* of 1980s Goth and death rock.

Rob Ritter was briefly the original Gun Club bassist, before leaving to death rock outfit, 45 Grave – one of the West Coast's original death rock acts. Patricia Morrison then plucked bass for Pierce, before heading for Europe and Goth immortality. The Cramps' most credible successor to Bryan Gregory, guitarist Kid Congo Powers, was recruited from the Gun Club, and would also record and tour with the Bad Seeds (German noise-guitarist Blixa Bargeld, a Bad Seed on sabbatical, also served time with Pierce's band). Ritter assumed the appropriate moniker 'Rob Graves'. His untimely demise in 1991 precipitated 45 Grave's split. There would appear to be a moral here – choose your stage name with care if you want to avoid posthumous irony. 45 Grave's vocalist was an LA native who styled herself 'Dinah Cancer'.

While the two terms were originally used interchangeably (and often still are), death rock differed from the emergent Goth rock in more than name. More distinctively American, death rock was more in touch with its rock 'n' roll roots, as opposed to the alternative style favoured by European Goth acts. 'Alternative' has come to signify those bands who dispense with the traditional rock 'n' roll style of blues-based lead guitar, bass and drums. Keyboards, percussion and more exotic instruments often come to the fore in alternative music, as do a range of non-rock influences. In addition, death rock band are more lyrically inspired by trash-culture and B-movie horror, rather than the occultism and silent horror movies favoured by their Goth counterparts.

On the cover of their 1983 debut album, *Sleep in Safety*, 45 Grave were resplendent in

The Misfits — reformed in 1996, though without the presence or the blessing of menacing vocalist and founder member Glenn Danzig.

horror movie make-up, draped in cobwebs and spattered with blood. Doing nothing by halves, they were too self-consciously trashy and fang-in-cheek to be categorised with Europe's Goth contingent, yet far too shamelessly sick and intense to be dismissed as another Broadway-style show in the Alice Cooper-*Welcome to My Nightmare* mode.

According to Ms Cancer, however, 'a lot of people have linked us to the Gothic Scene. I do carry a fondness for dead things. Since I was a teenager, I'd always . . . had a very gripping affair with the darker part of our society . . . I've always been a vampire at heart. Being a little girl and viewing Hammer Horror movies changed me. Just a succubus feeding on energy.'

Dinah's words come from the website of her current project, Penis Flytrap, where she ploughs a similar gory furrow with a line-up featuring bassist Lucifer Fulci (whose stage-name crosses the Italian spaghetti-splatter director with the Devil), drummer Hal Satan and guitarist Elvorian Von Spivey, alongside a charnelhouse of ghoulish go-go dancing chicks, determined to put 'the V in Vamp, the F in Femme Fatale'.

45 Grave never quite attained the legendary cult status that their closest East Coast rivals, the Misfits, achieved. The Misfits were formed in New Jersey in 1977, a product of the US punk scene. But, even in the beginning, there was a brooding, inventive element that separated this lean and hungry band from their contemporaries – most notably, vocalist Glenn Danzig's crooned vocals and heavily distorted electric piano playing. After three strong, if unremarkable, hate and hook-laden releases, the Misfits issued their 1979 *Horror Business* EP. It represented a statement of intent, and boasted the first use of their hooded, skull-faced 'Crimson Ghost' logo – borrowed from the villain in a 1940s movie serial that the band spotted in *Famous Monsters of Filmland* magazine.

The liner notes to their 1996 boxed retrospective were provided by Eerie Von, a musician, photographer and fan, who would collaborate with Danzig on several post-Misfits projects (the four-CD set came in a coffin-shaped box with artwork by comic artist, Dave McKean). 'All that horror business was starting to branch out,' notes Von of how the Misfits were modifying their image. 'The trade-mark "devil lock" hair style [an oily, raven black quiff] was becoming more prominent. [Guitarist] Jerry [Only]'s eye make-up, Glenn's bone shirt and gloves, and of course the black clothes. Everyone looks better in black clothes! They were turning into what we used to call a "ghoul rock" band. Some said "monster rock", "horror rock", and others even said "death rock". It was their own niche . . .'

The Misfits shared a similar twisted, trash culture DNA to the Cramps. 'We came from the sixties sci-fi image,' Jerry Only told *Implosion* magazine in 1997. '[Horror host] Zacherle was there, *Chiller Theatre* was on, things like this. As kids you would go to school, and Saturday there would be a horror show on in the middle of the afternoon. We saw movies like *Horror Hotel* and *The Crawling Eye*. During our teens we used to build the Aurora models [kits based on classic Universal movie monsters] and we still bought the magazines [like *Famous Monsters of Filmland*].' As with the Cramps, these Hollywood Gothic influences suffused the world of the Misfits.

Also like the Cramps, the Misfits met up with the queen of the horror hostesses, Vampira – though, unlike the Cramps, they were respectful enough not to exploit her on stage, instead dedicating a steamy love song to the ageing Gothic icon, wherein Danzig implores this 'mistress to the horror kid' to 'take off your shabby dress.' Like the Cramps, the Misfits used raw, basic 1950s rock 'n' roll as the spine of their supercharged, sepulchral sound.

Unlike the Cramps, however, the Misfits were consistently fearsome fun. In an incongruous atmosphere of menace and melody, they somehow managed to make their lyrical tributes to cheesy, z-grade horror flicks such as *Astro Zombies* authentically thrilling, while offensive death-dirges like the baby-murdering, mother-raping 'Last Caress' are irresistibly psychotic.

Glenn Danzig closed the coffin lid on the Misfits in 1983 – though it's stubbornly refused to stay shut, their retrospective reputation growing to legendary proportions. The singer wanted to explore the more seriously saturnine aspects of his lyrics, which he felt were compromised by the band's reliance on Hollywood Gothic. His new outfit, formed with Eerie Von, was named Samhain (after the Celtic day of the dead, the original Hallowe'en), and abandoned the more accessible aspects of the Misfits in favour of plumbing desolate depths. Samhain offered thrills aplenty, but they too were dissolved in 1987. For those with a taste for more traditional Gothic sounds, where haunted carnival melodies and desolate, baleful vocals combine to ominous effect, Eerie Von remains active – his recent collaboration with Mike Morance best described by the title of their wonderfully creepy 1996 release, *Uneasy Listening*.

In the years immediately prior to the emergence of the Goth scene, many British bands were dubbed 'post-punk'. While those with an eye on the mainstream threw in their lot with the fancy-dress cult of the new romantics, others rejected punk's new unwritten rules - fast, crude rock 'n' roll, anarcho-sloganeering or gutter-level rants – as a creative straitjacket. Bands like Theatre of Hate, Killing Joke and Virgin Prunes were rediscovering influences like the Velvet Underground and the Doors, or even styles like Krautrock, that had been eclipsed by punk's dominance of the late 1970s.

While Theatre of Hate played menacing but conventional rock, the Virgin Prunes were as much a performance art collective as a band, their bizarrely theatrical stage shows earning them cult status. The notoriously volatile Killing Joke became as legendary for their offstage eccentricities as for their potent musical assault. Most notoriously, singer/keyboardist Jaz Coleman's obsession with the occult led him to flee to Iceland in 1982 – convinced it was the only safe haven from the imminent apocalypse, and that the six letters in each part of the US president's name, Ronald Wilson Reagan, signified 666, 'the number of the Beast'. Killing Joke are now hailed as forerunners of modern industrial music with their menacing blend of black humour and musical mania. While none of these bands was 'Goth' *per se*, all reflected the exotic gloominess of the UK underground that would culminate in the birth of the Goth scene.

Robert Smith of the Cure – who took over lead guitar for Siouxsie and the Banshees during their most Gothic phase – recalled the period for *Propaganda* magazine in 1992. 'I felt a special camaraderie with certain bands like the Banshees and Joy Division,' Smith reminisced. 'The first crop of punk bands had faded from the scene, and a new crop came up round '79 and '80, who were much darker and moodier – less anarchic. Bands like Joy Division, us, Gang of Four, Echo and the Bunnymen. The only early punk bands who survived were the ones able to make that transition, like Siouxsie and the Banshees and the Damned.'

Alongside the Banshees, Joy Division is often credited as the first post-punk band to attract the 'Gothic' tag. As early as 1979, music journalist Mary Hannon tentatively linked the two as belonging to a loose post-punk movement, described as 'twentieth century Gothic'. In an interview to promote Joy Division's 1979 debut album, *Unknown Pleasures*, Hannon observed, 'One clue to JD lies in their album's title. Another is the description given by [the band's producer] Martin Hannett, who calls them "dancing music, with gothic overtones." Unintentionally, [guitarist] Bernard Albrecht gave an excellent description of "gothic" in our interview, when describing his favourite film *Nosferatu*. "The atmosphere is really evil, but you feel comfortable inside it."' And it's hard to imagine a more concise summation of the Gothic aesthetic than that.

The band's distinctive brand of innovative but gloomy postmodern rock music was described as 'death disco', its desolate vocals and introspective lyrics contrasting sharply with its compulsive dance beat, a contrast some compared with the dark themes-versus-upbeat rhythms of the Doors. The Joy Division legend grew from just two studio albums – *Unknown Pleasures*, and the 1980 follow-up, *Closer*. Peter Saville, who was responsible for the acclaimed sleeve design on both, sees the band as a product of their desolate environment, the grim

Ian Curtis, the doomed vocalist of Joy Division. His distinctive, disturbing stage performances were dubbed 'epileptic dancing' by one critic.

northern English city of Manchester. 'Manchester is a city of concrete underpasses and a gothic-revival cathedral,' he observed in a 2001 *Mojo* interview. 'For me *Unknown Pleasures* was the concrete underpass, while *Closer* was the gothic cathedral.'

In the early hours of 17 May 1980, the eve of the US tour designed to break Joy Division internationally, vocalist Ian Curtis took his own life, hanging himself while a copy of Iggy Pop's album *The Idiot* span on the turntable. Ian Curtis' suicide was at once poignant and absurd – somehow echoing the tragedy of the Decadent poet Gerard de Nerval, who had been found a century before, hanged with a ribbon he claimed was the Queen of Sheba's garter. Both painfully brittle eccentrics left a final artistic document testifying to inner turmoil as their legacy. With Nerval it was his novel, *Aurelia*, a testament to the obsessive love that precipitated his suicide. Curtis left the world his song 'Love Will Tear Us Apart', which bleakly exposed the romantic entanglements some believe inspired the singer's desperate act, and became an instant classic. (With both Curtis and Nerval, their emotional problems were most likely compounded by neurological or psychological ill health.) As a 2001 cover feature for *Sleazenation* reverentially exclaimed, 'As the lead singer of Joy Division, Ian Curtis fronted the most important band of the post-punk generation. As the dead lead singer of Joy Division, Ian Curtis fronted the greatest rock 'n' roll band of all time.'

His death unquestionably created ripples. In a 1997 article on the birth of what the author calls the 'Doom Generation' for *Details* magazine, David Dorrell – a rock journalist some credit with popularising the term 'Goth' in his *NME* reviews in the early 1980s – told Suzanne Colon, 'By committing suicide, Ian Curtis of Joy Division not only put an end to his own life and that of his band, but allowed a vacuum to occur into which all of these other bands scurried.' Curtis' death proved an act that was impossible to follow. It gave all of Joy Division's danceable dirges an instant – if appallingly grim – credibility, and assured them a place in rock's history books. It also allowed the band's enthusiasts the romantic indulgence of speculating over what might have been, had their idol lived beyond his brief 23-year span.

Crucially, for the press it established the band's 'authenticity'. Just like literary critics who disdained Gothic romances, and film reviewers who mocked the horror movie, most music journalists had little time for bands that operated in the realms of the imagination. Like Edgar Allan Poe, who found posthumous critical acceptance despite writing in the Gothic genre, Ian Curtis side-stepped the issue by focusing on horrors that were psychological rather than supernatural in origin. Madness rather than monsters writhed at the centre of Joy Division's malign universe, its backdrop the bleak, decaying heart of industrial Britain, derelict factories and neglected estates, rather than the sultry degeneracy that inspired Poe. In a 1994 article for *Mojo*, journalist Jon Savage describes the results as 'the definitive Northern Gothic statement: guilt-ridden, romantic, claustrophobic' (all three adjectives could also be applied to Poe's distinctive Southern Gothic).

'Ian's influence seemed to be madness and insanity,' reflected guitarist Albrecht. 'He said that a member of his family had worked in a mental home and she used to tell him things about the people there: people with twenty nipples or two heads, and it made a big

The original cover of 'Bela Lugosi's Dead' *by Bauhaus, featuring a still from* The Sorrows of Satan *(a 1925 silent film that did not feature Lugosi).*

impression on him. Part of the time when Joy Division were forming, he worked in a rehabilitation centre for people with physical and mental difficulties, trying to find work. He was very affected by them.'

By the standards of a literal-minded media, in the field of downbeat music there could be no higher accolade than a depressive's career culminating in suicide. A refreshingly dissenting voice came from Nick Cave in 1983, who rejected comparisons with his newly formed band, the Bad Seeds. 'I never thought Joy Division were particularly depressing,' the Australian singer sniffed dismissively. 'I always found them pretty funny myself, never liked them very much. They were a bit corny, I think.'

Of course, Joy Division's posthumous credibility was fraught with drawbacks – not least for Curtis' erstwhile bandmates, who found themselves on the brink of success tempered with a tragedy they dared not exploit. The remaining members of Joy Division, with the addition of drummer Stephen Morris' girlfriend, Gillian Gilbert, stayed together to form New Order. 'One of the popular conceptions, or misconceptions about Joy Division [was] that we were dark and sombre young men,' Morris later observed wryly. 'But the reality was completely the opposite of that. We weren't great intellectuals. I suppose Ian was really into that, into dark things.' Indeed, it was Curtis' dark obsessions that inspired Joy Division's name – taken from *House of Dolls*, a paperback novel by Karol Cetinsky that featured concentration camp inmates forced to become prostitutes by their Nazi gaolers (also inspiring the early Joy Division song 'No Love Lost'). 'Ian had always been interested in Germany,' his widow Deborah later recalled. 'At our wedding we sang a hymn to the tune of the German national anthem. We went to see *Cabaret* a dozen times.'

Early New Order material inevitably fell under the shadow of Curtis' suicide. But the absence of the original vocalist allowed the band to achieve a less oppressive, more commercial sound. Their style bridged the gap between traditional rock and Teutonic-style synthesised sounds via an infusion of dance influences, and New Order found themselves at an axis between commercial and 'alternative' audiences.

If Joy Division teetered precariously on the brink of mainstream acceptability, New Order lurched enthusiastically over the edge with the 1989 *Technique* album, aligning themselves with the emergent sound of house. By 1990, they were a million miles away from their Gothic roots with the chart-topping 'World in Motion' single, recorded with the England soccer squad to support the team's 1990 World Cup effort. Quiet for many years, but recently reformed, New Order remain only peripherally relevant to the contemporary Goth music scene on the basis of their early output.

One of the few facts upon which most Goth aficionados are agreed is that the first true Goth-rock record was a 1979 twelve-inch single, 'Bela Lugosi's Dead', released by the English four-piece, Bauhaus, a few months after they formed in the drab city of Northampton. Three of the band members were from the inevitable art school backgrounds, while the fourth, frontman Pete Murphy, possessed striking angular features that would help propel the band to prominence, and, ironically, contribute to its collapse.

A rare marriage of Gothic mood and the minimalism of Bauhaus design, in the classic horror film The Black Cat *(1934) starring Bela Lugosi and Boris Karloff.*

Murphy also shared a strong Catholic upbringing with guitarist Daniel Ash, who had himself been taught as a child, 'if you don't go to confession your soul will get blacker and blacker.' Murphy recalls how his own youthful Catholicism made him profoundly 'aware of the mysteries of life, mortality, Heaven, Hell, angels, saints and purgatory.' Popular wisdom has it that a Catholic upbringing never really leaves you, and Catholic imagery loomed large in Bauhaus lyrics like 'Stigmata Martyr', for which Murphy mimed the crucifixion on stage. This melodramatic blasphemy, and the pangs of guilt-ridden angst that plagued the lapsed Murphy afterwards, were important features of the Bauhaus Gothic aesthetic. Incidentally, vacillation between blasphemy, guilt and redemption was also a preoccupation of notorious Decadent writers and lapsed Catholics such as Charles Baudelaire, J. K. Huysmans and Oscar Wilde.

The band's name hints at their art school connections, and referred to the revolutionary design style launched by German architect, Walter Gropius, in 1919 (the band were originally called Bauhaus 1919). It conferred an aura of arty, pretentious mystery on the band, as well as suggesting a connection with the decadence of 1920s Berlin. Bauhaus design was starkly functional, in direct contrast with the decorative complexity usually associated with Gothic style. But in the early days of the movement, the Bauhaus was associated with the expressionist artists who provided the lighting and sets for seminal German horror films, *The Cabinet of Dr Caligari* and *Nosferatu*. The 1934 film *The Black Cat*, which starred Boris Karloff as black-lipsticked Satanist Hjalmar Poelzig, is widely regarded as the definitive use of expressionist imagery by a Hollywood studio – Poelzig's lair visualised as a Bauhaus mansion.

It was stills from films like these that helped to formulate the band's visual image. The final piece of the jigsaw fell into place in the shape of Karloff's *Black Cat* co-star. In Ian Shirley's book *Dark Entries*, Murphy recalls a phone conversation with Ash which must qualify as one of the most pivotal discussions in the history of Goth rock: 'Danny said, "Oh Dave's [David J. – bassist] got this really great chorus, he's got this name Bela Lugosi. Have you heard of Bela Lugosi?" I said yes. We'd been talking about the erotic quality of vampire movies, even if they were the Hammer horror type. There was this conversation about the sexuality and eroticism of Dracula. Danny talked about his fascination with this and the occult connotations. So we carried on that conversation and made it into a song.' It's interesting to note how Hammer films are regarded as somewhat crass by Murphy in comparison with the Universal films of the 1930s. Hammer would later be widely regarded as the very essence of Gothic restraint next to the splatter movies of the 1980s.

Another telephone conversation between Daniel Ash and David J. saw the ideas take shape. 'I said I've got this riff,' recalls Ash, 'it was basically a Gary Glitter song slowed down with some tricks with the chording, it was really haunting. [Glitter was the most kitsch manifestation of glam rock – now disappeared from the public eye, due to a conviction for possessing child pornography – whose stomping hit, 'Do You Want To Touch?', was incorporated into a medley with glam pixie Marc Bolan's 'Telegram Sam' in Bauhaus' live show.] He said that it was really weird I should say that, because he had this lyric about Bela Lugosi. We went to rehearsals, I started playing this riff, Dave automatically just did those bass notes, Kevin started playing that bossa nova beat and Dave gave the lyrics to Pete and he started singing, and that was near enough "Bela" as you hear it.'

Bauhaus' debut, 'Bela Lugosi's Dead', was released in 1979 on the strength of what the independent record label Small Wonder perceived as a parallel between the experimentalism of their material and that of the Velvet Underground, particularly 'Sister Ray'. Cover versions of 'Sister Ray' would provide finales for one of Joy Division's final concerts and also for the debut performance by the Sisters of Mercy.

When Bauhaus threatened to raise glam rock – with all its theatricality, androgyny and artifice – from the grave, they were destined for a rough ride from the press. But theirs was a kind of 'undead glam', draped in cobwebs rather than sprinkled with stardust, and they absorbed the rather more credible influence of ex-Roxy Music man Brian Eno's experimental recording techniques (they also covered his 'Third Uncle' in 1982). Nevertheless, press criticism focused on them as pale echoes of two of British rock journalism's sacred cows:

Bowie's classic 1970s material, and the punk explosion.

As journalists baited the band for supposedly being mere Bowie copyists, they responded with a 1982 cover of his 'Ziggy Stardust' – an act of such audacious contempt that they got away with it, delivering their biggest hit single. The charges that Bauhaus were heavily influenced by David Bowie are true – most alternative bands of the late 1970s to early 1980s were creatively indebted to him in some way, just as Bowie himself had drawn upon everything from the blues to Krautrock. In the same way that Bowie had refined and adapted German electronic experimentalism to his own style of *avant*-pop, so Bauhaus distilled the most sinister and theatrical elements of Bowie before stirring in other diverse and exotic ingredients to create an alchemical brew all of their own.

In *Dark Entries*, Ian Shirley theorises that part of the reason for press hostility to Bauhaus was that journalists thought their theatricality thin and fraudulent next to Joy Division's violently introspective angst. It's an idea given posthumous weight by James Hannaham in his 1997 essay, 'Bela Lugosi's Dead and I Don't Feel So Good Either'. While Hannaham references the seminal Bauhaus hit, the band only enjoy a passing mention compared to Joy Division, whom he

eulogises at length, defining them as 'what Goth could have become'. But Gothic art has always expressed itself in violent crimsons and raven blacks – Curtis and his band used far too many grim greys in their palette to qualify as inheritors of the tradition, rather than peripheral figures.

The Joy Division fan's army surplus minimalism echoed the stark, Krautrock-influenced sounds of the band. But, while they briefly donned all-black clothing, they were not Goths. For Goth rock requires the kind of shamelessly pretentious escapism and playful mock-profundity that characterised Bauhaus. Whatever Goth's detractors might have you believe, while it can be fulfilling to explore melancholia and stare into the darkness, nobody genuinely chooses to be in a state of perpetual suicidal angst.

Ironically, Paul Morley's dismissive review of a 1982 Bauhaus gig captures much of what fans liked about the band, but which always seemed to mystify the press: 'Bauhaus find an idea, dust it off, lick it dearly, stretch it, tear it, drench it in perfume, burn it, colour it darkly, splatter it with luminous

Bauhaus, featuring a bare-torsoed Pete Murphy. Adding macabre atmosphere to a Bowie influence and glam-rock theatricality, they arrived at the basic recipe for Goth.

green dots, take it for a walk through a waxworks of horror, lead it into safe temptation, feed it obscure and diluted hallucinogenic drugs, paint a crazy face on it and then – only then – consider it fit and pretty for the public airing.' They may have been melodramatic, and their self-indulgent surrealism came dangerously close to commercial suicide on occasions, but Bauhaus' self-destructive urges were never more than metaphorical. In other words, in the classic Gothic style they were having a ball, while making gloomy music.

Much of it was self-consciously cryptic in contrast with 'Bela Lugosi's Dead', which is a pretty straightforward Gothic mood piece. Most of the bands that followed in the wake of Bauhaus emulated the mysterious, surreal qualities of their material, rather than the more obvious spookiness of 'Bela', but fans loved the hokey horror movie melodramatics of their debut, and the band never discouraged their Gothic reputation. In 1981 they filmed a promotional video for 'Mask', heavily influenced by German expressionist horror cinema, with Pete Murphy lying 'in state' on an improvised tomb. The following year, Bauhaus invested in a touring vehicle that showcased their more playful side, a used hearse soon dubbed 'the Bauhearsemobile'.

This unorthodox auto is symbolic of Bauhaus: over the top, in questionable taste – but, for aficionados, irresistibly camp, with unexpected narcotic qualities and arch gallows humour. 'We had it [the hearse] done out in black velvet,' bassist David J. told biographer Shirley. 'The smoking compartment in the back had black velvet drapes – we were really living it out at that time – we used to sit in this thing and smoke hashish and listen to our favourite records and drive through the English countryside immersed in this black haze. Occasionally, it used to break down and we'd have to get out and push the fucking thing and we'd be these pallid denizens of the dark in all our garb. For everybody who passed by there was this vision of these four corpse-like creatures pushing this clapped out hearse up the hill.'

The band's most overtly Gothic moment, and the performance that brought them international exposure, also precipitated their end. (It also enabled them to meet their idol, David Bowie, though it was the most fleeting of acquaintances.) Bauhaus were cast to play 'Bela Lugosi's Dead' in the opening scene of contemporary vampire movie, *The Hunger*, in which Bowie starred alongside Catherine Deneuve as a fiendishly fashionable undead couple. The finished product received a lukewarm reception on its release in 1983, most critics dismissing it as a glossy extended

UK Decay's Gothic-tinged punk album For Madmen Only *(1981).*

music video, but it quickly attracted a cult audience seduced by its sinister, slick eroticism.

In a disarmingly frank tribute in *Retrohell*, contributor Brian Doherty recalls that he 'didn't think much of this film, but it made my girlfriend – who didn't like having sex with me – *really* want to have sex with me. [Editor] Darby calls the movie the equivalent of ecstasy for women'. *The Hunger*'s fans were not only women in search of an aphrodisiac. Like *The Lost Boys* it gained a significance for the modern Goth audience, who championed self-indulgent style over content. The reaction of Athan Maroulis, in his liner notes for US label Cleopatra's genre-defining 1996 CD collection, *The Goth Box*, is typical of this audience.

For Maroulis, seeing the movie was a Gothic epiphany: 'As I took my seat, this strange rhythm began to flow from the theatre's blown speakers, introducing me to a wide array of eye candy, splashes and quick edits. Through the smoke, I caught my first glimpse of Bauhaus and things were never the same.' Ironically, as he concedes, by the time Maroulis first heard Bauhaus, they had disbanded. Part of the reason is that while Maroulis and other fans may have *heard* the band, they pretty much only *saw* Pete Murphy. For, as success beckoned, Murphy's striking looks made him the focus of media attention at the expense of the other members. Being all but edited out of the opening sequence of *The Hunger* was pretty much the final straw for the other three, and in July 1983 the band split up.

All went on to other projects: Murphy was briefly one half of experimental duo, Dali's Car (with Japan bassist, Mick Karn), before recording solo material. Daniel Ash and David Haskins formed Tones on Tail, which became Love and Rockets with the addition of David J. in 1985, completing the original Bauhaus line-up minus Murphy. Love and Rockets enjoyed success in the US that exceeded anything Bauhaus – essentially a cult European act – achieved commercially, but never had the same cultural impact. Meanwhile, Athan Maroulis – who left that run-down New York cinema in 1983 inspired by his brief exposure to Bauhaus – went on to form the Goth-rock bands Fahrenheit 451 and Spahn Ranch (named after the Death Valley home of the 'Manson Family'), who preserved the Bauhaus spirit in the USA. Later, as A&R man for Cleopatra Records, he signed many of the bands who would dominate the Goth scene in the 1990s.

While a review of Adam and the Ants' debut album in *Sounds* had dubbed the band 'punk *noir*', Mick Mercer argues that early Antmusic was the spark that lit the Goth flame – inspiring acts like Southern Death Cult, Ritual and Sex Gang Children. The 'punk *noir*' label never caught on as a description of the dark, exotic spirit moving through the post-punk underground of the time, while 'Gothic' would only enter common usage gradually. Indeed, even the question of who first applied the term to the music scene is the subject of some debate.

Alongside Siouxsie – who described the Banshees' 1981 album, *Juju*, as 'Gothic' – a number of suspects have been fingered as the originators of the Gothic label. In a 1994 interview with *Alternative Press* magazine, Ian Astbury, vocalist with the Cult [originally Southern Death Cult], recalled, 'The Goth tag was a bit of a joke. One of the groups coming up at the same time as us was Sex Gang Children, and [lead singer] Andi – he used to dress like a Banshees fan, and I used to call him "the Gothic Goblin" because he was a little guy, and he's dark. He used to like Edith Piaf and this macabre music, and he lived in a building in Brixton called Visigoth Towers . . . and his followers were Goths.'

Blood and Roses' 1986 EP Love Under Will *– its title taken from a maxim of black magician Aleister Crowley, 'the Great Beast 666'.*

Rival claimants include UK Decay, a band with roots in the punk scene who were exploring a more atmospheric approach in the early 1980s, as suggested by their debut EP, *The Black Cat* – the title track inspired by the Poe story of the same name. Their singer, Abbo, dates the coining of the term to a 1981 *Sounds* interview. Many years later, he told Mick Mercer how the interviewer had insisted, '"it's gonna be a movement" and we're going nah, we'll be gone in six months. He said you've got to get a name for it . . . and I remember saying "we're into the whole Gothic thing" . . . and we sat there laughing about how we should have gargoyle shaped records and only play churches. 'Course he put it all in the interview . . . For six months everything went quiet then when the album [*For Madmen Only*] came out everyone was asking "what's this Gothic thing you're into?" And it's a total joke!'

This seems a little disingenuous, as evidenced by Abbo's comments on a 1981 US tour. When asked by a Californian journalist about the difference between UK Decay and a political US punk band like the Dead Kennedys, he responded: 'Our lyrics are now sort of based on sex and death, mystical – "Gothic" is how we describe it in England . . .' Which is as good as any a definition of the Goth aesthetic.

UK Decay was just one of a number of bands veering in a more mystical direction in the wake of punk's degeneration. As Dave Roberts, bassist with Sex Gang Children, told journalist David Dorrell, in 1982: 'It's a stagnant scene so they turn to the dark side to seek answers.' To the kinky black leather and camp black humour of early Antmusic, black magic and black and white horror movies were added – all the ingredients of the basic Goth recipe. With, often literal, battles for the hearts and minds of the nation's youth breaking out in music venues and clubs, some journalists were willing to tolerate these dark fascinations as a preferable alternative to the white power ethos threatening to seep into the lowest common denominator punk scene. But most rock critics wanted something they could regard as 'positive' to come out of the punk revolution.

Chief among them was *NME* correspondent Richard North, who in February 1983, penned a cover feature that opened with the 'Don't dream it, be it' motto from *The Rocky Horror Show,* and identified a growing interest in occultism among the bands of the era. This he termed 'positive punk' – an apparent attempt to downplay the growing preoccupation with taboo sexuality, strange rites and sinister imagery.

North almost gets away with it when he describes the movement as consisting of 'UK Decay (positive punk forefathers), using the dark to contrast and finally emphasise the light; Sex Gang Children taking us into the sub-world of the Crowleyan abyss; while Blood and Roses are pushing the symbols a whole lot further, their guitarist Bob being a serious student of the Art.' Then he veers off into a fairyland where 'The mystical tide we are talking about here refers, if nothing else, to the inner warmth and vital energy that human beings regard as the most favourable state to live in. The new positive punk has tapped into this current.' In fact, what these bands were tapping into was something far colder, darker and more morally ambivalent: the Gothic tradition, which, having successfully manifested itself in the books of Anne Rice and films such as *The Exorcist*, was ready to assert itself in the rock world.

Unsurprisingly, the whole positive punk bandwagon collapsed almost as soon as it was launched, as did the first few bands unwise enough to jump on it. Like UK Decay, British bands Brigandage and Blood and Roses are now remembered (if at all) as lower rungs on the ladder that takes us from Bowie's gloomy glam and the punk *noir* of Siouxsie Sue and Adam Ant to full-blooded Goth. Blood and Roses, however, were too interesting to be deserving of this fate. Manifestly Siouxsie-influenced, but with a by then obligatory Crowley obsession (evident by their use of the Great Beast's maxim 'Love Under Will' for their debut EP), the band also flaunted a horror-movie fixation. Foreshadowing a growing interest in soundtracks among today's fully-fledged Goth bands, Blood and Roses covered instrumental pieces by noted horror director John Carpenter (best known for minor classics like *Hallowe'en* and *The Thing*, for which he composed his own synthesiser soundtracks). They also recorded a 1986 track inspired by *I Spit On Your Grave*. The tale of a woman's brutal revenge on the men who raped her, *I Spit On Your Grave* was one of the most notorious of the 'video nasties'. It was suppressed during a clampdown on horror videos by the UK government.

Such macabre elements notwithstanding, guitarist Bob Short gave the 'Gothic' tag short shrift, telling Mick Mercer that 'doomy imagery' was 'so stupid. People think we're doomy. I don't feel doomy. All this Positive Punk, Gothic Punk, Acid Punk . . . Gothic Punk! Shit! Who wants to sit round in a primordial castle going round sticking their fingers in skulls?' Of course, people have been roaming imaginary castles of the mind for centuries, and would continue to do so long after Short's band had gone the way of all flesh.

Two other acts mentioned in North's positive punk article fared rather better. Sex Gang Children and Southern Death Cult both rose to prominence on the UK's alternative circuit in 1982-3. As one of a number of contenders for the first real Goth band, it's easy to see why the white-faced, melodramatic, pretentious Sex Gang Children, with their Grim Reaper logo, might be nominated as godfathers of Goth. Reputedly recorded by candlelight in full stage make-up in July of 1982, the debut Sex Gang album, the cassette-only *Naked*, was described by *Sounds* as 'screaming out of the darkness with a twisting, sinister suggestion of threatening violence and perverse sensuality.' Sex Gang Children's music was a little over ambitious and hastily conceived, and the eclectic blend of Dave Roberts' droning bass, Rob Stroud's primal drumming, Terry Macleay's feral guitar and Andi Sex Gang's shrill, intense vocals don't always gel, with subtlety lost amidst theatrical chaos. Andi Sex Gang really hit his stride with the 1985

The sound of the Batcave: Ollie Wisdom, of house band Specimen, performs in a club environment that was 'more Gotham City than Aleister Crowley'.

solo album, *Blind!*, however, which some identify as a minor Goth classic – Mick Mercer describing it as 'a murderous Abba' (which is a compliment, apparently). Certainly, *Blind!* is the point at which Sex Gang manages to unearth the pop elements within his more complex orchestrations, highlighting the tempting decadence beneath.

Astbury's band, Southern Death Cult, are less obvious candidates for early Goths. Primarily a vehicle for lead singer, Astbury (then performing as Ian Lindsay), and his fascination with Native American spirituality, they were not immune to the gloom and mysticism of the nascent UK Goth scene, as their name suggests. The same tribal percussion that dominated Adam Ant's pop sound rumbled over Astbury's early recordings, though with a less tongue in cheek playfulness. Its use was characteristic of the developing Goth sound, inasmuch as there was one. Certain characteristics would become recognisable trademarks in the 1980s – deep, icy vocals, tribal beats, mesmeric melodies – but the defining characteristic would remain thematic or visual rather than musical, and a bewildering range of bands who evoked bizarre, melancholy or macabre moods would find themselves dubbed 'Goths'.

In the modern day, both Andi Sex Gang and Southern Death Cult are still with us – albeit in substantially mutated forms. Sex Gang released his third solo album, *The Veil*, in 1999, described by one fan as 'goth-psychedelic-folk crossover: cabaret, melodious meanderings, sleaze personified.' Also in 1999, after a five-year hiatus, the Cult (previously Southern Death Cult) reformed, releasing *Beyond Good and Evil* in 2001, which, despite including a track entitled 'American Gothic', and a tribute to Nico, is testament to how Astbury's band very quickly steered away from Gothic atmosphere into straight hard rock.

It's seldom recognised, but one contributory factor in the negative press attitude to the emerging Goth scene was that most of the bands emerged from the northern and midlands regions of the UK, often referred to dismissively by Londoners as 'the provinces'. On a

Mr and Mrs Fiend of Alien Sex Fiend. Note the cartoonish image (and Nik's Judge Dredd t-shirt), far more integral to Batcave style than any exaggerated morbidity.

practical level, any act based outside of the capital had problems convincing London-based journalists and label scouts to see them perform – especially problematic, for so many of the early Goth bands, who put such an emphasis on the visual elements of their act. On a less concrete level, a subconscious snobbery among many London-based commentators held that if it wasn't happening in London, it simply wasn't happening. Thus, while the Goth cult took a strong hold in unexpected regions such as the northern industrial city of Leeds, London became its epicentre by default.

It found its home in a London club named the Batcave, which opened in the summer of 1982 and hosted the first authentic 'Goth nights' – although the term would not enter common usage until the following year. 'It was run by Ollie Wisdom, who was in Specimen,' Ian Astbury told Suzanne Colon for her 'Gloom Generation' article. 'The club was really mixed; it wasn't just this dark death rock club. Specimen was the house band, and they were very dark, but they were as much German [influenced] as they were [by] the Addams Family. They were like a Death Bowie.' An even more powerful influence was the *Rocky Horror* musical, as ex-regular Marc Morris told me: 'Ollie Wisdom was Frank N. Furter!' Indeed, Morris recalls how the Batcave first popularised the Goth style and subculture he describes as an unholy blend of '*Rocky Horror Show* attitude, the theatricality of Alice Cooper, David Bowie tunes, and horror movie imagery.'

Specimen was a colourful, Bauhaus-influenced four-piece, formed in 1980 in the western English city of Bristol, who found relocating to London a frustrating experience. 'We met many bands in a similar position to ourselves . . . nowhere to play!' guitarist Jon Klein told *Orkus* magazine in a 1997 retrospective. '[Specimen vocalist] Ollie found a club called the Gargoyle that had been open since 1927 that ran as a strip bar during the day but Wednesday nights it would become the Batcave. We'd built up a team of people to deal with many aspects of the club including finding cabaret, bands, decoration and the press. Initially the English music press responded well to our intentions and consequently people knew we were opening the club and a lot of people turned up! We had a 200-metre-long queue on our opening night and this queue would become an integral part of the scene. Travelling up four floors in a tiny elevator, you passed through a coffin gateway into a well-dressed labyrinth featuring a cinema/cabaret theatre, hybrid disco, live music and an atmosphere of midweek mayhem! The success of the club attracted record companies and it seemed we'd broken the circle at last . . .'

While few but the most dedicated fans really rated Specimen musically, visually they offered a cartoonish take on Bauhaus' gloomy glam. Indeed, keyboard player Jonny Melton was recruited at the Batcave on account of his extravagant plumage rather than any musical ability, and he had to be trained to play from scratch to re-emerge as Jonny Slut. There was some truth in the accusation that Specimen were little more than Gothic clothes-horses, even if they were definitely thoroughbreds.

Rivals for the house band spot came in the form of Alien Sex Fiend, who released their debut album, *Who's Been Sleeping in My Brain?*, in 1983. That same year, they toured with Specimen as a Batcave double bill – though Alien Sex Fiend dropped out mid-way to be replaced by Flesh for Lulu, another early Goth favourite. Frontman, Nik Fiend, had been involved in previous bands, including the Earwigs and Mr and Miss Demeanour – both Alice

'Living image of clinical depression', or the joker in the pop playhouse? Robert Smith of the Cure.

Cooper references (the former being the original name of Alice's band, the latter an early album track) that betrayed a heavy creative debt to the pioneering US shock-rocker, whom Alien Sex Fiend would support on tour in 1985. In appearance, Mr Fiend resembled nothing so much as a deranged clown, and this same psychotic circus ethos prevailed in live performances.

Alien Sex Fiend had more to offer musically than Specimen, and while Ollie Wisdom's outfit imploded in 1985, Nik Fiend's Goth-cabaret collective continues to this day. Mick Mercer, part of their cult audience, has often championed the band he exalts as 'wolves with painted rubber teeth', hailing the early adoption of an electronic dance edge to the Fiend repertoire long before other Goth acts started toying with techno.

Irreverence was also a feature of Alien Sex Fiend's lyrics. Nik Fiend recorded the 1987 single 'Where Are Batman and Robin?', on the Riddler label, with DJ Len 'the Wizz' Davies as the Dynamic Duo, and such plastic pop-culture references were typical of the Batcave's creepy carnival atmosphere. It was all a little easier for many potential Goths to take on board, and a lot more fun, than the cryptic intensity of post-punk proto-Goths like Sex Gang Children and Southern Death Cult. By 1983, the Batcave had firmly established the Goth subculture, and some of the capital's brightest young things were reinventing themselves as London's darkest young things. Among them were many of the alternative music scene's most talented performers – rubbing shoulders with a motley crew of the creepy and the curious.

Alongside Siouxsie and Sex Gang Children, Goth groupies could flirt with Lydia Lunch, Marc Almond, Nick Cave and members of the Cure. Robert Smith, lead singer/guitarist with

Nick Cave – with early 1980s crow's nest hair – at the time of forming the Bad Seeds, named after the last record by the Birthday Party and a 1956 film about an evil child.

the Cure, had played with the Banshees from late 1979 through the early 1980s, the period which saw them entering their most Gothic phase. (Ex-Specimen guitarist Jon Klein, would take on guitar duties for Siouxsie's outfit between 1988-95.) The singer's melancholy marionette appearance – white-faced, ugly scar of scarlet lipstick, unruly mushroom cloud of black hair – proved highly influential among many male Goths. Particularly the introspective and angst-ridden, who identified with the persona the authors of *Cult Rockers* describe as 'a kind of living image of clinical depression.'

'We used to go to the Batcave because we got in free and it was a good atmosphere and the people were really nice,' Smith told Suzanne Colon in 1997. 'But the music was awful! That whole romanticism of death! Anybody who's ever experienced death firsthand could tell you there's nothing romantic about it.' The question of which performers have 'experienced death firsthand' (Jim Morrison maybe?) notwithstanding, Smith seems a tad disingenuous.

For one thing, the idea that the Batcave sound systems rang with non-stop hymns to suicide was a lazy media stereotype.

According to Jonny Melton, in discussion with Mick Mercer, 'the Batcave wasn't a doomy, Gothy, droney, grungey sort of place . . . it was more Gotham City than Aleister Crowley.' An ex-regular called Merlina, discussing her Batcave days at uk.people.gothic, remembered it as a haven of '"music as fun" rather than the more "music as art/protest/ something profound" attitude.' Alongside house band, Specimen, and the ubiquitous Bowie records, early 1970s glam favourites like the Sweet and Marc Bolan's T. Rex were dancefloor standbys. Joy Division, perhaps the darkest band of the era, were conspicuous by their absence from the decks – although gloomy sounds came courtesy of Siouxsie and the Banshees, Southern Death Cult and, ironically, the Cure. The Cure have recorded more than their share of downbeat material, especially on the classic 1982 album, *Pornography*, that Goths took to their hearts.

'We've really always done pop songs,' Smith told *Spin* magazine in 1992. 'It's just sometimes they're way too down – sort of desperate.' The Cure had debuted in 1978 with 'Killing an Arab', a jangly evocation of the murder scene from existentialist author Albert Camus' novel, *The Outsider*, that could qualify as a death dirge of sorts. But the Cure's tacit acceptance that they were primarily a pop band – exemplified by quirkily catchy singles like

'The Love Cats' – was always bound to alienate some Goth purists. Sure enough, the band receives a brief and decidedly dismissive mention in Mick Mercer's *Gothic Rock* encyclopaedia. By way of contrast, Richard Davenport-Hines' book *Gothic* hails Robert Smith as Goth's 'greatest singer-lyricist . . . His lyrics appeal to people who feel suffocated in hopelessness or crushed by helplessness. His writing may be sombre, morose and inconsolable, but in other moods he is consummately shallow, as a pop musician must be.' The Cure occupy the middle ground between the dark alternative and mainstream music – rarely if ever found on Gothic compilation albums, but frequently found in many a Goth's album collection. A more irreverent assessment comes from Nigel Wingrove's recollections of the Batcave, when he intimates that the Cure were 'always a bit too chubby to be threatening'.

Certainly never too chubby to be threatening, Nick Cave, the lean, volatile vocalist who began his career in the Boys Next Door, an Australian punk band specialising in Alice Cooper covers, had come to London in 1980 with the Birthday Party. The Birthday Party quickly established a reputation as a powerful presence on the capital's alternative scene with their incendiary live performances – stripped-down, hyperactive, chaotic explorations of the crow-black depths of the human soul. Their 1981 single, 'Release the Bats' (whose title was later borrowed for a Goth club in Long Beach, California), seemed to encapsulate the Batcave's allure, with its manic 'Sex, horror, sex, bat, sex, horror, sex, vampire' mantra, as did 'Kiss Me Black', from the 1982 *Junkyard* album, with its rhyming of 'incubus', 'succubus' and 'sarcophagus'.

Closer to the angry Australian's troubled heart, perhaps, were his frequent descents into lyrical madness, reminiscent of the fevered fiction of Southern Gothic authors like Flannery O'Connor and Cormac McCarthy, where insanity and inbreeding in the USA's Deep South replace the supernatural elements of traditional Gothic literature. In tracks such as the disturbed 'Deep in the Woods' (from the Birthday Party's 1982 *Bad Seed* EP) love degenerates into obsession, hatred, mayhem and murder against a backdrop of rural squalor. (Cave cemented this connection to the Southern Gothic tradition with his 1989 novel, *And the Ass Saw the Angel*, hailed by *Elle* magazine as having 'a visionary feel – all underpinned by Bible-black humour,' with 'enough visions, portents and religious lunacy to qualify as the second-greatest story ever told.')

During the 1980s, Cave's meditations on violent passion would bring him onto a collision course with the liberal sensibilities of the music press, as some writers began to feel that his imagery crossed the boundaries between Gothic fantasy and unacceptable misogyny. Indeed, the editor of *NME* reputedly forbade coverage of Cave on the basis that he believed the Australian 'promoted evil'. Cave would later confess that the recording that caused most offence – 'Deep in the Woods', about the murder of a girl from the killer's point of view, is the only song he regrets writing.

The collapse of the Birthday Party in 1983 coincided with Cave frequenting the Batcave, which the Australian described as 'better than most of the clubs in London anyway. At least it's dark and sort of filthy, whereas most of the clubs really make an attempt to be ritzy.' The venue proved a fertile recruiting ground for collaborators on other artistic projects – such as a stage version of the archetypally decadent *Salomé* story – and for putting together his new band, the Bad Seeds (named after *The Bad Seed*, a 1956 movie, controversial in its day, about a sweet little girl who also happens to be a homicidal psychopath – a theme Cave visited in his 1996 song 'Curse of Millhaven'). In this new incarnation, the drug-fuelled frenzy of the Birthday Party was toned down, though the material remained as achingly raw as ever. In a series of critically acclaimed albums, Cave searched for rock 'n' roll's heart of darkness via deconstructed blues, gospel and country ballads, twisted by the singer's distinctive blend of debauchery and delirium. The self-destructiveness was all too real, however, and by the late 1980s the press was more interested in his excessive lifestyle than the disturbed yet beautiful music he was producing.

The crunch came in a 1988 interview with *NME* journalist Jack Barron, whom Cave attacked, both verbally and physically, calling him a 'filthy little prick' for focusing on his

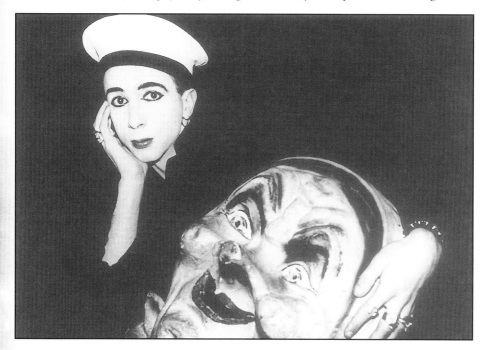

Decadent camp personified, in the impish form of modern torch singer Marc Almond.

destructive personal habits rather than his art. In the interview, Cave also joined the fickle queue of ex-Batcave regulars who disowned the scene, stating, 'I'd hate to go down in history as the number one Goth, the man who spawned a thousand Goth bands with stacked hairstyles, no personality, pale sick people – I really don't want to be responsible for that sort of thing at all.' To be fair, the singer was attacking those who simply emulated their idols, in particular emphasising that his own career of substance abuse was not to be treated as a role model by impressionable young musicians.

Many critics still rate the early Bad Seeds material as Cave's finest, but I personally prefer his early to mid-1990s period – *Henry's Dream* (1992), *Let Love In* (1994) and *Murder Ballads* (1996) – for its sordid American Gothic fantasies. The last album, as its title suggests, was

Cave's most unremittingly bloody and brutal, and it appears to have exorcised most of his demons. 'My interest in the drama of crime and violence is diminishing,' Cave observed. 'It's a dead end, no pun intended. This record closes a chapter for me.' Subsequent material, while still alluringly tenebrous, has a personal, redemptive, even tender quality absent from earlier efforts. Cave is fond of biblical imagery, characterising this gentler, more reflective material as 'New Testament'. It has garnered him almost universal acclaim, but I, for one, rather miss the blood, fire and retribution of the 'Old Testament' Nick.

Impish Englishman Marc Almond, the essence of dark camp, had become a Batcave regular after completing the improbable journey from outrageous art school performance artist to chart-topping pop star. He stormed the UK charts in 1981, as half of the electro-pop duo Soft Cell, with the surprise hit single 'Tainted Love' (recently covered by Marilyn Manson, whose promotional video parodies hip-hop culture with a scene of breakdancing Goth kids). It was singularly appropriate song for this pop perversity, whose evocation of deviance simultaneously compelled and repelled his audience.

Throughout his career, Almond has specialised in reinterpreting classic songs with his own distinctive decadent spin. In 1988, he realised a fond ambition of duetting with his heroine Nico, sharing vocal duties on his 'Gothic torch song', 'Your Kisses Burn'. The 'torch song' a smoky nightclub term for a melancholy ballad of lost love, has become a speciality in the Almond repertoire. (Nico's death shortly after the duet was imbued with similarly camp pathos; she died of head injuries after suffering a stroke while cycling in Ibiza.)

Back in 1983, as Almond observes in his autobiography *Tainted Life*, 'the fashion that year was Goth – black clothes, black lipstick, black lace, black hair – you name it so long as it was black. Pale faces, bone jewellery – anything deathly was the order of the day.' Never one to miss out, Almond became known for wearing decadent black velvet and fetishistic black leather. He also recalls being recruited by two acquaintances for a nocturnal visit to London's legendary Highgate Cemetery, scene of a vampire scare during the previous decade.

To the singer's dismay, his companion Richard – who lived in a black house decorated with skulls – was intent on being more than a mere tourist, and was seeking trophies. While the trio didn't encounter any vampires, the morbid souvenir-hunter still broke open a coffin. 'Suddenly I was hit by the smell of formaldehyde,' recalls an uncomfortable Almond. 'I felt nauseous. Inside, revealed in the glare of torchlight, was a body. Flesh and hair still on the skull. That image remains with me even today. My face contorted in disgust and fear. Richard lifted the shrouded arm and moved the jawbone. It was like a scene from *Texas Chainsaw Massacre*.'

On a less malodorous note, that same year Almond recorded the album *Torment and Toreros*, with the Mambas, his impromptu backing band of the time. He describes it as his most Gothic release, an 'album for pale black-clad lost youths to plan their suicides to in their purple-painted bedrooms.' Alongside flamenco-styled torch songs like 'Black Heart' and 'Torment' is a cover of 'Gloomy Sunday', the most notorious suicide ballad ever written – a painful evocation of 'the black coach of sorrow'. Originally penned by a Hungarian named Rezső Seress in 1936, the song caused a wave of suicides upon its release – a phenomenon that accompanied its many translated versions, leading to a blanket radio ban in a number of countries, including the US, where jazz and blues diva Billie Holliday first popularised it in the 1940s. American Goth legends, Christian Death, later recorded a version on their 1986 *Atrocities* album.

The most direct artefact of Almond's Batcave days is, however, a duet with Andi Sex Gang, on one of two compilations released to showcase the club's music scene. Both were released in 1983 – *Young Limbs and Numb Hymns* was an official Batcave album, while *The Whip*, with its sadomasochistic theme, was masterminded by Sex Gang Children bassist Dave Roberts, and featured a rogues gallery of Batcave denizens. Both have subsequently been re-released in CD form with contemporary Goth acts to bolster the line-ups, the Sex Gang/Almond duet, 'Hungry Years', regarded as a highlight among the disappointing original recordings.

However, 'Shockwork', Test Department's contribution to *Young Limbs and Numb Hymns*, gives a hint of the increasing significance of industrial music on the Goth scene in the years to come, and 'Tenterhooks', Dave Vanian's solo track on *The Whip*, offers a rare example of the Damned's lead singer in full Gothic flow, as composer of a spooky instrumental that seems to have come from the soundtrack of a kitschy but atmospheric horror flick. (As an added oddity, the album also features 'Just Call Me Sky' by Naz Nomad and the Nightmares – a joke band of homicidal hippies, including Vanian as Naz himself, garbed in wigs and kaftans.) But, overall, the albums are musical morgues of proto-Goth also-rans and 'positive punk' no-hopers, from the last gasp of UK Decay (playing here as Meat of Youth) to the ill-fated Brigandage.

The Batcave offered Goth an early stylistic touchstone, with its dark, somewhat squalid, carnivalesque ethos. Instead of establishing any definitive 'Goth sound', it showcased a mischievous musical *potpourri* of gloomy pop, glittery glam and decadent experimentalism that often lacked the black romanticism and bite that the Gothic aesthetic demands.

A more credible, albeit unofficial Batcave project (although those involved would probably disdain such a description) was the degenerate cabaret revue masterminded by Lydia Lunch, consisting of the New Yorker herself, Marc Almond, Nick Cave and fellow Australian, Clint Ruin (also known as wilfully perverse musical multi-stylist Jim Thirlwell – who recorded under variations of the tasteful title You've Got Foetus on Your Breath). Lunch's sheer volume of work, musically and in other media, make it nigh on impossible to classify her. She emerged from New York's 'No Wave' noise-rock scene in the late 1970s, as the young vocalist of Teenage Jesus and the Jerks, her later projects ranging from the violent funk of the band, Eight-Eyed Spy, to the confrontational spoken word duet of *Rude Hieroglyphics* – though all of it is characterised by an aggressively caustic attitude. Thirlwell is similarly prolific and diverse – experimenting with styles ranging from industrial to rockabilly – and shares Lunch's attraction to the dark side, his music defined by *The Virgin Encyclopedia of Indie and New Wave* as 'a harrowing aural netherworld of death, lust, disease and spiritual decay'.

Temporarily known as the Immaculate Consumptive, Lunch, Cave, Almond and Ruin toured the US over the Hallowe'en holiday of 1983 – a period when all four performers were going through particularly turbulent times. The shows were predictably unpredictable. According to Almond, they were drawn together by their kindred 'reputations or notoriety', and by 'our loves of the same things: truth, love, filth as beauty. All of us use misery – to use Clint's term – as positive negativism. Meaning we're very miserable people, but in a positive way! We are the most cheerful miseries I know!' Ruin himself offered, 'The imagery the four of us use is really desolate, hellish, brown' – a muddying of the blood reds and midnight blacks of classic Goth. Instead of graveyard romanticism, they drew upon 'the urban despair and that sort of thing from the bowels of whatever. But out of that misery, out of the intensity of its experience something positive this way comes!'

The results of this brief, chaotic episode became a legendary footnote in Goth lore. 'The Consumptive tour is a logical flowering of their various collaborations' wrote *NME* correspondent Chris Bohn. 'It sees them working through an hour-long set either solo or in assorted combinations. The hectic pace is dictated by the Revox unit containing most all the musical backing, with the four continually consummating this unholy mating on the Marc Almond composition "Body Unknown", which features Cave on primordial screams, Almond on vocals, Ruin on drums and Lydia on guitar.

'This extraordinary spectacle is like taking a ghost train through a hell in which four malevolently funny demons keep popping out of the darkness to amuse the unfortunate passenger with a series of rehearsed shocks to the system.' Lunch harangued God and Ruin trashed the stage as if possessed, while Almond opened emotional wounds and Cave picked his way through the resulting detritus to deliver a soulful musical elegy. It was a fitting climax to Goth's first phase. Or perhaps an epitaph . . .

Keyboard player Jonny Slut, whose image came to symbolise his band, Specimen, and the early Goth look.

For by 1984, Goth was well and truly *out*, the press heaping derision on rock's creatures of the night. The most significant nail in the Batcave's coffin was, perhaps, an April 1984 feature in the UK's *Smash Hits* magazine about a night out at the Goth mecca. The feature itself is fairly positive (aside from a snide photo caption, identifying enthusiastically heterosexual Nick Cave as Marc Almond's 'ghoulfriend'). But the club's very presence in such a pin-up publication – aimed squarely at the pubescent teenybop market – suggested that the air of subversion and sin that Ollie Wisdom of Specimen originally envisaged was reaching dangerously low levels.

In the years that followed, the Goth culture would find itself subjected to the same blend of mockery and disdain that had already been applied to Bauhaus. Only the most dedicated bearers of the Goth banner remained faithful. The likes of the Cure, Cave, Almond and Lunch consigned their Batcave years to history, preserving their credibility in the eyes of the media. During the second half of the 1980s, the British music press declared open season on those who would not abandon Goth – alternating between indifference and firing off salvoes of contempt.

Chapter VIII

A More Sinister Beauty: Gothic Style

English film-maker and art director Nigel Wingrove began a cultural quest to inject new power into the archetype of the Gothic *femme fatale* in 1989, with the release of his *Visions of Ecstasy* – a short art film featuring a comely Saint Teresa writhing in sexual frenzy at the foot of a crucified Christ. It was banned by the UK government on grounds of 'potential blasphemy'. Notably, the film also featured a soundtrack by Siouxsie and the Banshees bassist Steve Severin. Undeterred by the ban, Wingrove launched the first of a series of video labels – variously known as Redemption, Salvation, Jezebel and Purgatory – that would push the boundaries of what was acceptable under Britain's oppressive censorship rules. The films themselves range from cult Gothic horror and sleaze to softcore surrealism, and include *Salome* (1973) and *The Forbidden* (1978), a couple of early experimental short films by Clive Barker. *The Forbidden* was inspired, as were so many of Barker's horror stories, by the Faust legend, while *Salome* is based on the tale of the biblical vamp.

The Redemption logo, was inspired by Wingrove's stint as a designer for *Skin Two* – the stylish fetish magazine which was instrumental in making the sexual underground trendy in the 1990s. 'The black-winged, pale-skinned angel I used for the Redemption logo evolved from the "rubber nun" image I'd developed for *Skin Two* – though they didn't use it as they thought it was a bit much. It worked for Redemption because everything about the films we were selling – sleazy, horrific, magical – was encapsulated by this image of an eyeless vamp.' The Redemption style, which – with its cast of vampire bitches and killer nympho-nuns – married elements of fetishism, blasphemy and bloodshed, has had both a cultural and commercial influence.

Most directly, Wingrove's design work for Cradle of Filth – the British band who brought

For better or for worse... tattered wedding dresses are a familiar sight at the Slimelight, the 90s equivalent of the Batcave.

Gothic aesthetics to the savage sounds of black metal – was instrumental in propelling them from underground obscurity to the front covers of magazines. 'We'd obviously hit a nerve,' acknowledges the designer. 'I started photographing these blood-drenched models back in 1992 for my *Redeemer* magazine, and back then I can't think of anyone else who was doing it. Cradle of Filth used some of the shots from that *Redeemer* "fashion shoot" and it became one of their best-selling T-shirt images [entitled 'Vestal Masturbation', the image depicts a busty, semi-naked nun in the throes of sexual ecstasy]. I knew I'd caught onto something with this imagery that was just too Gothic and morbid for *Skin Two*. I'd wanted to turn *Redeemer* into a kind of "*Death Vogue*". Now there's that kind of extreme *femme fatale* imagery all over the place, and while I certainly wouldn't take credit for all of it, I'm not aware of anyone who was shooting that kind of thing before 1992.

'The *femme fatale* has become incredibly popular across the board – from *Buffy* and *Xena* on TV to the proliferation of comics featuring these type of women, like *Lady Death* or *Purgatori*. They're young male sexual-fantasy figures on the one hand, but they're *femmes fatales* because they also kill men. It's now commonly believed that in the 1890s it was male fear of female sexuality that made the *femme fatale* such a popular figure. Perhaps in the 1990s, masculine anxieties about the increasing social and political power of women brought the *femme fatale* to the fore again. On the other hand,' he adds pragmatically, 'the attraction could just be that women can still act in an outrageously violent, non-politically-correct fashion that is no longer acceptable in male heroes.'

Nigel Wingrove is a veteran of London's legendary punk rock scene of the late 1970s. Conventional wisdom now has it that Goth was born as punk's morbidly romantic younger sister. Indeed, one of Goth's seminal icons most certainly emerged from the punk scene.

Siouxsie Sue was the archetype of the heavily made-up, confrontationally androgynous punk girl in the 1976 punk rock explosion, a female counterpart to Sex Pistols camp follower (later band member), Sid Vicious. Sid would later become legendary not for his nominal bass-playing, but for the way the emaciated, spike-headed nihilist embodied the punk ethos and inspired imitation by a thousand wanna-be Sids. While Siouxsie's musical talents are not so easily dismissed – she remains the alternative scene's divine diva to this day, performing with husband and ex-Banshee,

Budgie, as the Creatures – it was her image that first drew attention to this arresting artiste.

She also gave birth to the prototype for the late twentieth century Goth chick – although the Banshees rejected the Goth label even more emphatically than they had punk. After their 1996 break-up, Severin informed *Ghastly* magazine that 'spawning the dread "goth" movement' was not 'high on the list' of the Banshees' achievements. Siouxsie's image was in a state of constant flux – from her early days as a confrontational, swastika-wearing bitch to her later incarnation as a living China doll – but nevertheless maintained a fidelity to the concept of the *femme fatale*. From cruel Cleopatra to demonic dominatrix, her kinky kaleidoscope of styles made her, according to *The Village Voice*, 'the most influential female Brit pop star' of the 1980s.

It's a measure of her impact on the Goth subculture that a whole entry is devoted to 'Siouxsie Clones' in *Retro Hell*. Significantly, contributor, Pleasant Gehman, notes that girls began imitating Siouxsie's style before her first single, 'Hong Kong Garden', hit the stores in 1978. Siouxsie, however, adopted the influential look that launched thousands of Goth-chick 'clones' at the beginning of the 1980s. Gehman describes 'a mass copying of her trademark long, crimped punky hair, pale white make-up with heavy dark-lidded eyes, and severe, Roaring Twenties mouth drawn on. These main features seemed to flatter every possible facial type, and it was an exotic, alternative look that was still very sexy . . . girls with day jobs could copy it and still get away with being subversive.'

Perhaps Siouxsie's closest stateside equivalent is Lydia Lunch. Both adapted the *femme fatale* persona to their own ends, not least to exorcise the demons of their strange or abusive upbringings. Siouxsie described her unusual family situation – with an alcoholic father and rebellious older sister – as 'scandalous' by contemporary standards. 'My earliest memory is pretending to be dead,' she told *The Face* in 1980. 'My mum used to keep stepping over me while I was laying on the kitchen floor. I was five. I once took a bottle of pills to make it more realistic.'

Even bleaker, 'Candyman', a track from the Banshees' 1986 album, *Tinderbox*, is, in Siouxsie's words, an attempt to 'put across the unspeakability of child abuse'. Told from the point of view of the abuser rather than the victim, the lyrical narrative has fed (apparently unfounded) conjecture that it relives the singer's real-life childhood nightmare. Lydia Lunch's childhood was also filled with unequivocally ferocious demons, as a result of the sexual abuse she suffered at the hands of her father – the exorcism of this trauma forming the basis of her 1985 spoken-word piece, 'Daddy Dearest'.

This harrowingly raw act of soul bearing is emblematic of Lunch's more overtly aggressive, more American approach, as is her use of a broader range of media. Lunch is as well known for her spoken word performances, shock-erotica prose and appearances in the art-porn flicks of 'cinema of transgression' director Richard Kern, as for her diverse musical output. And while Siouxsie had a seductive element to her ambivalent sexuality, Lunch has always been more brashly confrontational, even rapacious. Consequently, while still a potent force on the darker fringes of the underground, Lydia Lunch has never had the profound visual impact on the Goth scene that made sultry Siouxsie clones such a perennial presence.

Nevertheless, in 1983, when Goth was briefly flavour of the month in London, Lunch was

Siouxsie Sue in bewitching garb, the year after the release of Hyaena *(1984) – the Banshees' most overtly Gothic album.*

at the forefront of the movement. In his autobiography, *Tainted Life*, Marc Almond recalls first meeting the woman he describes as having 'helped invent Goth. Small, red-lipped and voluptuous in bosom-baring black lace, she was the kind of woman that has always both fascinated and terrified me.' Her Barons Court flat sounds as if it was every inch the archetypal Goth lair: 'The decor was as I imagined it would be,' writes Almond. 'Heavy, frayed curtains in deep red, closed – always closed. The whole room deep blood red. A single white light bulb swinging in the middle, creating living shadows in the musty gloom. Once I grew accustomed to the lack of light, Lydia's taste in ornaments began to grab my attention – a line of leering devil masks, a stuffed deer head, antlers, magic symbols, cushions of animal fur, animals' skulls, pieces of bone that held some mystic significance. In the corner of the table was a vase of dried flowers; on the floor was a pile of *Penthouse* magazines. A drape curtain divided off the bedroom, in which I saw everything laid out in ritualistic order. All around the room sat dolls – broken dolls, misfits, crippled orphans. Further inspection revealed stuffed lizards, rubber bats, spidery things, religious paraphernalia, and a gruesome collection of weapons – a spiked ball and chain, flick knives, cleavers and axes – all rusted and chipped from an unthinkable past. In the middle of the room was the seducer's bed – red and black – where no doubt wicked deeds were carried out. Jesus and the Laughing Cavalier stared down from the walls, and a leopard skin clung for dear life to the peeling wallpaper. Lydia sat me down and proudly showed me her extensive collection of pickled amphibians, condemned to float in clouded jam jars. Lovely!'

The prototype male Goth is perhaps more difficult to define – not least because the style quickly evolved into one of gender ambiguity, with the male of the species courting ridicule (and worse) by wearing more make-up than his girlfriend.

Pete Murphy, vocalist and frontman of Bauhaus, had an unearthly stage presence. His persona clearly owed something to the silent German expressionist horror movie: redolent of Cesare, the eerie sleepwalking killer of *The Cabinet of Dr Caligari*, though animated with the urgency of *Nosferatu*'s Graf Orlock. Somehow androgynous yet still essentially male, the heavily made-up Murphy, with his stage-prop coffin, resembled a sexualised horror star rather than a rock singer, his magnetism imbued with a heavy dose of sepulchral chic.

'I'm enhancing my looks because I want to look a certain way, not because I want to look beautiful,' Murphy explained to *In the City* fanzine. His stark monochrome look – razor-sharp cheekbones beneath a slick crest of raven-black hair – influenced a generation of gender-ambiguous Goths. 'Within six months of starting, Bauhaus started getting the black-wearing audience and seeing the kids dressing up like us,' guitarist Daniel Ash later recalled. 'We used to call them the androgynous space demons.' Just as Bowie had draped a camp hand around platinum-blond guitarist Mick Ronson and performed an outrageous 'electric blowjob' on his fretboard, in the 1970s, *Ziggy Stardust*-era, so Murphy and Ash added an extra charge to their live act with flirtatious horseplay, Murphy often garbed in revealing black hosiery.

The mainstream also sat up and took notice – Maxell cassette tapes employing Murphy as their model for a high-profile TV and billboard advertising campaign in 1983. For this commercial gig the singer donned a sharp suit, resembling an impeccably dressed, albeit otherworldly businessman almost literally blown away by the power of Maxell as he sits impassively in a postmodern living room. This surreal moment, while the peak of Murphy's public profile, precipitated the break-up of Bauhaus shortly afterwards. But the band's enduring appeal was later underlined by the 'Gothic Chronicle' *Propaganda* magazine, in their Fall 1996 Bauhaus photo-spread – though, evidently unable to convince the singer to revisit his past, they had to feature a 'Murphy clone'. Two years after the shoot, when the band finally reformed, Goth had become a stateside phenomenon, when their initial Californian performances sold out in under fifteen minutes.

When the burgeoning Goth cult found its first home in London's legendary Batcave, clothing designer David Edmond helped develop its look by designing merchandise for the club and its house band, Specimen. 'There were one or two people around at the start of the 1980s using that kind of [Gothic] imagery,' Edmond told me, 'There was a girl called Morticia who had a stall in Carnaby Street. She was the first person who had a clothing unit that sold nothing but Gothic clothes and jewellery. And she really lived the lifestyle. There was also Laurie Vanian, who was going out with Dave Vanian of the Damned.' The couple had actually married in September 1977. 'I wore black lace and magenta satin,' Laurie told Carol Clerk in *The Book of the Damned*, the band's official biography. 'David's mother made us a wedding cake and put two black roses on it.' All three – Laurie, Dave and Morticia – were like Charles Addams cartoons come to life.

'Then bands like Specimen and Alien Sex Fiend began utilising that graveyard imagery.

Post-punk performer, cutting-edge raconteur and erotic cult movie star – New York's 'black widow', Lydia Lunch.

At the time I went to work for [Chelsea alternative fashion store] Boy it was very much at the end of the new romantic thing, and we were selling bits of new romantic and bits of punk. We wanted something new to put forward as a big movement. We started working with the Batcave and Specimen, doing their T-shirts and so forth. The people at the Batcave were initially a mixture of punks, new romantics, the curious, the dispossessed. They gradually became more and more Gothic, until the club was dominated by the Gothic look. It was very organic.'

Citing Damned vocalist Dave Vanian (as in 'Transyl-Vanian'), as a proto-Goth is complicated by the fact that his band, the Damned, was the first British punk group to release a record ('New Rose' in 1976) and were originally closer to an energetic pub-rock band than

Frank N. Furter (Tim Curry), the 'sweet transvestite from Transexual, Transylvania' in
The Rocky Horror Show – *whose ethos of 'Don't dream it, be it' made him a Goth icon.*

anything at all Gothic. However, Vanian, previously employed as a gravedigger, is described on the band's website as 'part Bela Lugosi, part Nosferatu'. Erotic horror author Cecilia Tan wrote an article entitled 'Vampire Chic' for *Blue Blood*, the American journal of countercultural erotica, identifying Vanian as 'undoubtedly one of the first to dive headlong into vampire chic, to the point of appearing in other eighteenth century trappings, such as a laced shirt with a candelabra on stage.'

In 1979, the band had recorded 'Plan 9 Channel 7' on their *Machine Gun Etiquette* album – a lyrical tribute to horror hostess Vampira and her bittersweet relationship with James Dean. Released in 1981, *The Black Album* swung further in a Gothic direction, with its horror-inspired lyrical content: 'Wait for the Blackout' is about a contemporary vampire and 'Dr Jekyll and Mr Hyde' takes the point of view of literature's most celebrated split personality; '13th Floor Vendetta' was inspired by Vincent Price's classic camp horror movie, *The Abominable Dr Phibes*.

The Damned's occasional Gothic flourishes reached a peak in the 1980s. The tour supporting their 1982 *Strawberries* album featured a Gothic stage set on an ecclesiastical theme, complete with stained glass windows and a trio of 'Naughty Nuns' as backing singers. Vanian declared the show to have been what he'd been working towards for years – and, as both of the band's original songwriters had left, his sensibilities came to rule the roost. The 1985 album, *Phantasmagoria*, featured creepy cuts such as 'Sanctum Sanctorum' and the hit single 'Grimly Fiendish', while the rest of the band emulated the lead singer's undead-dandy image. As Patricia Morrison later observed to British Goth magazine, *Meltdown*, '*Phantasmagoria* spawned a zillion Vanian look-a-likes.' In recent years, Vanian has adopted an image closer to a vaguely sinister, be-quiffed lounge-crooner than the Hammer horror of his glory years, but the Gothic taint remains. The Damned's original drummer, the quaintly named Rat Scabies, even upped sticks for Nosferatu – arguably the UK's most unreconstructed traditional Goth act – making a guest appearance on their 1997 album, *Lord of the Flies*.

Patricia Morrison now plays bass for the Damned, and has also become the new 'Mrs Vanian' in a Las Vegas wedding ceremony. Mick Mercer, in his *Gothic Rock*, hails Morrison as the 'Goddess of Goth', and she holds a position in female Goth iconography second only to Siouxsie Sue. An admiring Natasha Scharf, editor of *Meltdown* magazine, describes Morrison as 'the original Morticia Addams. Forget Siouxsie and Gitane [DeMone, the decadent blonde diva of Christian Death], Patricia was gothing it up in low-key clubs around America while Ms Sioux was still brandishing swastikas at art school and Ms DeMone was just dreaming of Christian Death.' Certainly, by the late 1980s, Morrison's image – big, back-combed hair, velvet dress and stilettos – reflected a very definite aesthetic move away from the punk look toward a pulchritudinous heroine from a period Gothic-horror movie. Morrison has served her time on the Goth circuit, playing in seminal acts such as the Gun Club, the Sisters of Mercy, and more recently, Dave Vanian's Phantom Chords – a side-project for the Damned mainman, whose blend of tongue-in-cheek spookiness and rock 'n' roll guitar has been described by fans as 'gothabilly'.

Morrison's former Sisters of Mercy bandmate, frontman Andrew Eldritch, has conducted a notoriously

Dave Vanian, lead singer of the Damned – the first punk performer to adopt vampire chic in the late 1970s, his image embraced by the entire band in the mid-1980s.

abrasive relationship with the Goth scene. Regardless of whether he likes it or not, however, the aloof, spiderishly-slender Edritch exerted a similarly potent influence on the male Goth image of the late 1980s. In his study, *Gothic*, Richard Davenport-Hines credits the singer, in a manner that would doubtless make him spit blood, as 'superbly photogenic because, although like other middle-class escapees he resembled a nervous stick, he reinvented himself as a broody goth fop.'

Donna Ricci is a young woman modelling a modern variation on the classic Goth look. Recruited as a photographic model by Neil Gaiman and Dave McKean for the cover of their *Death* comic, Ricci subsequently founded her own agency, Wicked Talent, exclusively featuring 'gothic, vampire, pierced, punk, tattooed, bald or rockabilly models', and plans to open her own vampire-themed nightclub. 'It is an uprising trend that a darker and more ethereal aesthetic is being sought in marketing and advertising,' she told *Bite Me* magazine in a 2001 feature entitled 'The Rise of the Gothic Supermodel'. 'Mainstream versions of the gothic subculture are in Calvin Klein ads, Levis commercials and major make-up companies. The entire club scenes for the movie *8mm* were local goth club kids and they are also often used in *Buffy*, *Angel* and many music videos. My personal career has increased with CD covers, calendars and fashion catalogues. I have no doubt that a more sinister beauty is not only accepted, but now sought after in today's fashion world.'

In *Men in Black*, his study of the colour black in the history of fashion, author John Harvey observes that youth culture, and Goth culture in particular, wears the colour as a mark of aloofness, of being outside of society, 'playing all-black clothes against a white or whitened face . . . seem to echo at a distance the dandy's Hamletizing [brooding and gloomy intensity] . . . Goth black seems again to say, as black has at various points in the past, I am important.' Harvey may have been enlightened further if he read an article entitled 'Five Reasons Why I Wear Black', in the USA's journal of 'sex, death, rock 'n' roll', *Horror Garage*. The piece is by horror and science fiction writer John Shirley (though he prefers the term *noir* fiction, as in pitch-black), who co-wrote the script

Patricia Morrison has been the bassist with Goth bands ranging from the Sisters of Mercy to the Damned. Her image provided a style template for Goth chicks second only to Siouxsie Sue.

for the *Crow* movie with splatterpunk pioneer, David Schow.

According to Shirley, black serves partially as a tribal colour for disaffected youth, 'but then there are those dressed all in black who scuffle and mosh with me at Ministry and Sisters of Mercy concerts who are saying, *This is my tribe but my tribe is the untribed, the unacknowledged Diaspora. I am the defective.*' He contends that it is more than 'just the black banner of romanticized alienation' or 'post-punk fashion classicism . . . I wear black because I'm in mourning. And I write *noir* for the same reason.'

Nineteenth-century dandies like Charles Baudelaire adopted black attire to symbolise the 'last splendour of heroism in decadence' – a mark of contempt for a grey world and of grief for the death of the Romantic spirit. Unlike the Parisian poet, however, Shirley is not in mourning for the declining nobility of the human spirit, but for the general bleakness of life.

His 'five reasons' are tragedies, personal and general, from his own traumatic, drug-addicted past to the brutality meted out to children in war. One can't help but feel that Shirley overdoes the 'Hamletizing' a little, especially when he claims Goths serve a 'shamanistic' role in society – 'to protest, to mourn; to amplify and relay mourning and anger for the collective mind.' But it's difficult to argue when he concludes, 'Somebody has to play the dirge.'

Many Goths wear black simply because it looks good, as evidenced by the perennial search by mainstream fashion pundits for 'the new black'. But black, beyond the classic 'little black dress', can still be a statement of subversive style, almost a denial of fashion. 'I remember the first time my mother saw me wearing black lipstick,' writes Cecilia Tan in her essay 'Vampire Chic'. 'She said "You look dead." I took it as a compliment.' After a few pointers on achieving the Lily Munster or Bride of Frankenstein look, Tan concludes that the Gothic 'ensemble is easily completed with a long black coat or cloak, suitable for stalking the night with, or other attire as befits a creature of the shadows. So go, now, my children, and never let it be said that a vampire does not cut a well-dressed figure.'

Donna Ricci, 'Gothic Supermodel' – as lauded by Bite Me *magazine. Her image also graces the cover of Neil Gaiman's* Death *comic, for which she was the model.*

Chapter IX

DARK ANGELS OF SIN:
Modern Gothic
Sensibility & Sensuality

The prevailing trends of the Goth counterculture were encapsulated, in 1998, by the heading of a magazine feature: 'Vampires, Pagans, Sub/Dom culture: the connection?' The journal in question was *Bloodstone*, a UK publication that proudly proclaimed itself 'The Magazine for Vampires'.

While aiming a magazine at a mythical readership might seem like commercial suicide (with little chance of returning from beyond the grave), *Bloodstone* enjoyed a successful run. It became the flagship for a series of impressive vampiric projects – most notably the spectacular trilogy of Vampyria shows that were staged in London, climaxing in 1999. These events featured performances from vampirically inclined metal and Goth bands, Cradle of Filth and Inkubus Sukkubus, and erotic 'blood rituals' where fake plasma spilled over the scantily clad forms of cult actress Eileen Daly (star of low-budget Brit vampire film, *Razorblade Smile*) and leading fetish-glamour model Theresa May. There was also the chance to buy your very own custom-fitted fangs. Vampyria was presided over by *Bloodstone* editor (and self-styled 'king of the vampires') Louis Ravensfield. Sadly, however, this undead entrepreneur's empire fell in the year following the final show, with *Bloodstone* ceasing publication in early 2000.

While the magazine was an impressively bold affair, the feature on links between vampirism, the pagan revival and sexual fetishism concluded somewhat weakly that all three subjects had something to do with the pursuit of personal power, promising further research on the matter. It's tempting to forgive the anonymous author, as, to put it bluntly, there are

Two horny little devils enjoying the Carvival of Souls –
the Goth and fetish festival organised by specialist record label Nightbreed.

no obvious connections beyond the fact that they have become dominant Gothic themes.

Contemporary Goth attitudes to this unholy trinity of paganism, vampirism and sexual fetishism coalesce in the traditionalist Goth-rock act Two Witches. Godfathers of the Finnish scene, they cultivate a sultry, yet sinister image – lead singer Jyrki Witch, describing the band's chief themes to *Black Monday* magazine as 'sex and passion'. In true Gothic style, these themes are explored through the eyes of the undead, Jyrki explaining that the allure of the vampire for Two Witches rests upon the 'mystical aspects; life without end, the power of seduction and all that sexual fetishism (the colour red, bloody kisses, blood itself, bites…).'

The 'two witches' of the band's name are represented by staged photos of a pair of predatory looking Goth girls entwined in an erotic embrace, smouldering in black PVC and lingerie. On their 1999 album, *Eternal Passion*, the song 'Dark Angels of Sin' eulogises these fetishistic babes as 'those beautiful demons', and, '(I Don't Need Your) Holy Land' assures us that Jyrki would 'rather be a pagan and live in sin and lust than buy your stupid stories of heaven and hell.' 'Sin and lust' may be a feature of the occult, but in the politically-correct neo-pagan scene, you're far more likely to encounter patchwork dungarees and unshaven armpits than the bondage wear and whips that feature in Two Witches' lyrics and on their album covers.

Like many Goths, Two Witches are united in the insistence they are not Satanists – allowing them to play up their sinister aspects, while rejecting the label of 'Evil'. It's all a little disingenuous, not least because Christian fundamentalists make remarkably few such accusations against Goth bands (although it's true that Christian Death have been targeted because of their overtly blasphemous name and imagery).

Among the most serious musical exponents of neo-paganism are the English Goth band, Inkubus Sukkubus. 'Despite the blanket pagan denial of Satan, I think a lot of pagans are interested in the figure just because he's such a colourful character,' guitarist Tony McKormack conceded to me in 1995. 'We're firmly pagan because we're more interested in the ecological, natural side of things . . . Our version of it is an understanding of reality, an earth-based faith. Three members of the band are shamen, while [vocalist] Candia and I are Wiccan . . . To some extent we come from a darker side than many Wiccans are comfortable with, which is just to do with our personalities.' That dark side is expressed in their many songs about vampires – the incubi and succubi who lend the band their name being sexually-rapacious demons who prey on the human lifeforce.

Their music, which blends Wiccan-influenced folk rhythms with traditional Goth rock, is a vehicle for apparently sincere pagan beliefs. 'We try to raise a certain amount of psychic force when we play and a lot of people say that they can feel it,' claims McKormack. 'We chant the Isis [Egyptian goddess of fertility]-Astarte [Mesopotamian goddess of love and war] goddess mantra on stage. As to actually performing a ritual on stage, I feel that would be a

little corny . . . [though] we do magical workings to further the band.'

Midnight Configuration represent a bridge between traditional Goth rock and the electronic and sample-dominated sounds of the millennial era, a style some have dubbed 'black industrial'. Their 2000 album, *Dark Hours of the Southern Cross*, is unashamedly demonic, the words 'Luciferian defiance of the grace of God' emblazoned upon the sleeve. Midnight Configuration leader, Trevor Bamford – a pivotal figure on the English Goth scene, whose Nightbreed label has released CDs by Two Witches and Inkubus Sukkubus – told me of his band's self-styled 'evilution'. 'Satanic or demonic thought and imagery has been associated with the heavy metal scene in the past. And Goths consider themselves, for various reasons, to be a "cut above" metal fans,' he admits. 'As for myself, I just felt I was being naturally drawn to this area. Perhaps it's a coming of age thing after putting so many years into the dark music scene.'

Sexual fetishism is an altogether easier Gothic obsession to explain, although the term begs further definition. To the modern mind, fetishism is generally thought of as the sexual preferences abbreviated as 'BDSM': bondage, domination, sadism and masochism. In practice, however, the playful perversions on display at the modern fetish club are often less extreme, fixated on rubber, leather and PVC-wear – as well as voyeurism and exhibitionism, among those who go along to see and be obscene. In the late twentieth century, the sexual underground began to overlap with youth counterculture, providing an iconography of forbidden pleasures with which to shock the older generation.

It was punk, in the mid-1970s, that put fetishism at the top of the countercultural sexual agenda. Scene insider Nils Stevenson, in *Vacant*, his 'diary of the Punk years', observes how 'the style of most of them [the original punks]

Artwork by Inkubus Sukkubus founder Tony McCormack depicting the sex demons that lent the band its name.

Demonic manifestations and the spirit of an ancient pagan past are popular themes in modern fetish clubs.

combines elements of Glam, *Clockwork Orange*, *Cabaret* and *The Rocky Horror Show*.' But bondage-wear was the dominant influence on the clothes designed by Sex Pistols manager Malcolm McLaren and partner Vivienne Westwood, whose SEX boutique in London was the birthplace of punk. The affinity seldom went beyond shock chic, however. The safety pin through the cheek that became emblematic of the movement was a statement of confrontational nihilism, rather than sexual deviance. For many of the early punks, sadomasochism represented the guilty secrets of respectable society put on display. In *Vacant*, Stevenson remembers staying with a dominatrix called Linda, who 'lived opposite Scotland Yard, a stone's throw from Buckingham Palace and not far from the Houses of Parliament. At her work premises in Earl's Court she entertains celebrities, and she is much admired in the Sex Pistols' camp for her anecdotes about whipping the rich and famous. She is, with delicious irony, paid to enslave our enslavers.'

The SEX boutique also sold T-shirts with graphic homosexual imagery, but the intent was ambivalent. Appreciated as sanctuaries for social outcasts, gay clubs had provided drinking holes for the shock troops of early punk. In a 1997 interview for *Vacant*, original punk, Simon Barker, observes, 'the only clubs that accepted the way we dressed were gay clubs. Unfortunately at that time it was the height of fashion to be gay, or at least bisexual . . . As a result the doormen became stricter and stricter on who they let in. Fashion-wise we were a little too avant-garde, i.e. before fashion, even for gay clubs . . . This led us to discover a little-known lesbian club in Soho called Louise's frequented by prostitutes and, on our first night there, ladies' Wimbledon tennis players. It was there in Louise's that the hard core of the Punk scene met by night.'

But the original punks were not quite the scions of tolerance this implies. Some, like Siouxsie, wore swastikas in a spirit of provocation, or possibly hoping to evoke the spirit of decadent 1920s Berlin. 'It took a long time to live down that Nazi thing,' Banshees bassist, Steve Severin, would later ruefully reflect. Most, however, like that other icon of punk, Sid Vicious, saw nothing beyond the symbol's shock value. If one image of punk is of a brotherhood of freaks defying convention in the company of sexual outcasts, the other is the 1979 video to 'My Way', after punk had become a mass-market commodity – with poster-boy Sid drawling, 'You cunt, I'm not a queer.'

Adam and the Ants, among the last bands to emerge from the original punk explosion, were perhaps the only 1970s British punk band with an authentic interest in sadomasochism as anything more than shock chic. Band flyers, posters and sleeves were literally dominated by fetishistic images of stiletto-heeled dominatrices and gagged bondage babes, while Adam sometimes took the stage in full fetish gear, complete with leather 'gimp' mask. The lead Ant had even written a thesis on the fetish scene at art college – and his first cover story for *Sounds* dubbed him, 'The Face That Launched a Thousand Whips'. However, despite rumours to the contrary, even this kinkiest of punks maintained in a 1977 fanzine interview that he was 'not personally into S/M, I mean I never smacked the arse of anybody. It's the power, it's the imagery . . . which I find magnetic. It's not done viciously, if you read S/M mags and spank mags or anything like that, it's done with an essence of humour . . . War-dress and stuff, that just appeals to my imagination.'

It was the post-punk generation that really began to explore the pleasures of the sexual underground. Tony Mitchell was a London-based rock journalist working primarily for *Sounds*, the music paper that gave most of the attention a begrudging rock press bestowed on the early 1980s Goth scene. 'While I was still a music journalist I was invited to become involved in the first ever public fetish club, which was called Skin Two,' Mitchell told me in early 2000. 'It opened on the 31st January 1983 in a little place in Soho [in the West End of London]. I was invited because I was already fairly well "out" about my interest in that area. My girlfriend and I were both music journalists, and we were both happy to give this splendid new club our support. That's how I became involved in what was really London's first semi-public fetish community.'

The club went on to found a magazine one year later, with Mitchell taking the editorial helm a year after that. *Skin Two* went from strength to strength, and is now the flagship publication for the international fetish scene. Though criticised for being too glossy and glamorous to portray realistically the various schools of sexual deviance, few could deny the vast impact *Skin Two* had on the style and fashion of late twentieth-century pop-culture. Meanwhile, the post-punk underground continues to co-opt and crossbreed with the sexual underground – in the style of such proto-Goth babes, as Siouxsie Sue and Lydia Lunch, who created their powerful dominatrix personae years ago. Corsets, bondage-wear and black leather have become favoured evening-wear for female Goths. Goth diva, Gitane DeMone, a member

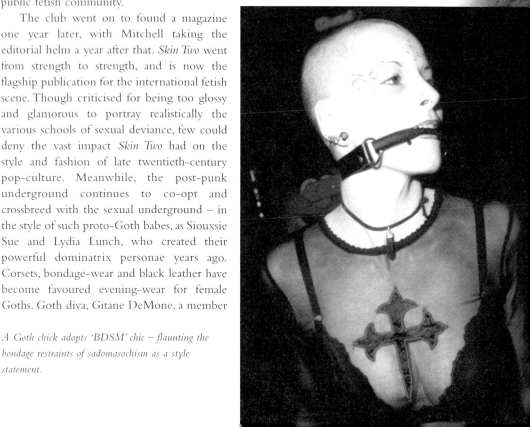

A Goth chick adopts 'BDSM' chic – flaunting the bondage restraints of sadomasochism as a style statement.

of Christian Death during the late 1980s, explained her passion for fetish-wear to *Propaganda* magazine in 1994. 'I find wearing rubber to be really sophisticated and sexy,' she affirmed. 'It creates an atmosphere, a surreal mood – sort of what I like to do in my music. It's all about fantasy, which is why early Christian Death was so great. It helped a lot of our fans live out their fantasies vicariously.'

'Fetishism' – the term most often used today to denote sexual deviance – derives from the religious term 'fetish', which means the worship of an object as an embodiment of the sacred or divine. Sexual fetishism may therefore translate as finding erotic stimulation in something of little, if any, sexual attraction to most people. This could mean anything from getting turned on by surgical-support stockings to a compulsion to fuck cracks in the road. These days, however, the term has been co-opted by those who are sexually adventurous, rather than obsessive, or even by clubbers who like to wear leather and rubber as a clichéd uniform.

It's a tribute to the popularity of these trappings that many self-consciously cool people now label themselves 'fetishists' – a tag that would have stigmatised them as mentally ill only a few decades ago. Some insiders are a little dubious of this development, such as New York photographer Eric Kroll, who since the 1970s, has catered for the sophisticated end of the erotica market with his artful yet daring work. 'Fetishism is about obsession, not fads or curiosity,' he told me in 1998. 'I'm not putting down fetish fashion or anything like that, but it only touches the edge of the unique focus and fixation on one thing that marks true fetishism. At any given time there will only ever be a tiny percentage of the population

The modern fetish club scene is more about role playing and dressing up than sexual obsession – hence this feisty leopardess with her echoes of Catwoman.

with that level of obsession, and that will never change.'

The study of sexual fetishism as a phenomenon began in the late nineteenth century, most notably with the work of psychologists Sigmund Freud and Richard von Krafft-Ebing. Both continue to enjoy mixed reputations – some lauding them for opening serious debate on taboo topics, others condemning the pair for projecting their own obsessions onto the private lives of others. Author, musician and ex-*Fetish Times* editor, Mark Ramsden, particularly condemns the legacy of Krafft-Ebing. As the author of several light-hearted thrillers set in the occult and fetish scene (an approving review in London's *Time Out* magazine promised readers would 'laugh along till your piercings ache'), he's also responsible for serious journalistic works such as his book *Radical Desire* – designed to rescue fetishism from the stigma of abnormality.

The book is in part an attempt 'to attack the legacy of Krafft-Ebing', Ramsden told me in 1999. 'He invented the ideas of "sadism" and "masochism", but he put things into an almost criminal perspective, and it's inaccurate because different people . . . like different things at different times. You don't have to be [serial killer] Fred West to enjoy fetishism. But that's the way it is in the public mind because "experts" like Krafft-Ebing put it into psychopathological terms. We've got to get rid of . . . all of these stern German professors who're ruining all our fun. Even Shakespeare was familiar with "a lover's pinch which hurts and yet is desired." Everybody knows the phrase "slap and tickle" – it's part of everyone's sexuality.'

But Ramsden may be overstating his case, overestimating the popular hostility to fetishism, while forgetting that many are attracted to it precisely because of its forbidden nature. The conflict between acceptance and retaining some kind of outlaw status is familiar to *Skin Two* editor Tony Mitchell, his magazine often accused of over-glamorising the scene. 'On the one hand, they [fetishists] want to be accepted in the sense that they don't want to be discriminated against or attacked in the streets for dressing in rubber or whatever,' Mitchell explained to me. 'They want to go to certain clubs where there's some kind of community and enjoy certain activities without being raided by the police. At the same time, part of what makes it exciting is the feeling that you are part of the underground, that you are not in the majority or mainstream. So it's a balancing act. We move out into the open in one area, but something more underground, scary or dangerous comes to balance it. It comes with the territory.'

Whether fetish scene aficionados like it or not, that territory was first mapped out by Krafft-Ebing in the late 1800s. To be fair to the German academic, he chose the names of Gothic or Decadent authors, rather than those of criminals, to describe specific forms of algophilia or algolagnia (pleasure from pain), the most controversial sexual perversion. 'Since the Marquis de Sade had given his name to the type of sexual pleasure derived from inflicting pain,' writes historian and novelist Reay Tannahill, in *Sex in History*, 'it seemed reasonable to Krafft-Ebing to name the alternative pleasure of being hurt, humiliated, or dominated, after its most distinguished advocate, the Ritter Leopold von Sacher-Masoch, a fellow Austrian of some academic distinction who in 1870 had begun publishing novels and short stories on the theme of men who needed to have women inflict pain on them. The most famous of Sacher-Masoch's stories was *Venus in Furs*, which established once and for all the essential weapons in the masochistic armoury. Wanda, cruel, imperious, and fur-clad, entices her lover Severin into a trap, has him tied up, and then appears before him with a whip in her hand. Furs, whips and satanic (but always aristocratic) beauties were a recurring theme in Sacher-Masoch's work.'

Having a sexual practice named after him was apparently much to Sacher-Masoch's distaste. But it was later celebrated by the highly influential Velvet Underground, when they recorded an eponymous tribute to 'Venus in Furs' on their 1967 debut album (the band had taken their name from a paperback sexual expose. 'There were whips and chains on the cover,' remembered guitarist Sterling Morrison, 'but it was basically about wife-swapping in suburbia'). Siouxsie Sue would also make potent use of the dominatrix image, while the second original Banshee styled himself 'Steve Severin'.

Today, sadomasochism is no longer confined to the *boudoir*, but struts its stuff in the trendiest clubs in town. Arguably, the cutting edge of such clubs is London's Torture Garden, which borrows its name from a notorious 1898 Decadent novel by Octave Mirbeau. Described with ambivalent approval by Oscar Wilde as 'revolting . . . a sort of grey adder,' suggesting its mesmeric repellence, Mirbeau's *Torture Garden* describes a sadistic Englishwoman who indoctrinates a jaded Frenchman in an Oriental garden setting. Here, torture is practised as an art form, elaborate blood-stained instruments and broken bodies lying decoratively arranged among the exotic flora.

This same idea finds expression, in a less extreme fashion, at the Torture Garden, which first opened its doors in 1990. In acts that often deliberately blur the line between art installations, sex shows and religious rites, performance artists are branded, pierced, crucified and suspended from curious devices. 'Torture Garden is more underground than a lot of the fetish and SM clubs,' said founder David Wood when we spoke in 1996. 'The Torture Garden crowd are more alternative, and more likely to have alternative lifestyles in their everyday lives. We tend to attract a lot of Goths, the industrial piercing scene, techno-dance freaks and people into the ritual magical aspects of fetishism, alongside the suburbanites. Torture Garden is a little darker and more cutting-edge than most other fetish clubs.'

Ironically, the success of clubs like Torture Garden have had in bringing sexual fetishism out into the open has proved to be a problem, as Wood observed. 'The scene's definitely going through a crisis at the moment,' he reflected. 'It used to be that going out to a club in rubber dress was a big thing, quite outrageous. Now it wouldn't even turn a head – it's lost a certain something, become almost ordinary. The scene's become rather over-exposed and over-analysed. There's a risk of getting to a point where you'll end up looking around and not knowing where to go next, because it's all been done and nothing's new. That's a danger, because it's all very much about novelty, being on the edge and being different.'

The rising profile and acceptance of sexual fetishism has shadowed the increasing tolerance of homosexuality. Indeed, in contrast to punk, which chiefly adopted bondage gear for its offensiveness to mainstream sensibilities, it was the gay community who first paraded publicly in fetish-wear – leather, chains and whips becoming a familiar sight at the celebratory gay 'Mardi Gras' which sprang up in many major cities.

Since the 1980s, chart-topping alternative acts have also performed songs about S&M – like Depeche Mode's 'Master and Servant' and the Cure's 'Torture', numbers which still haunt Goth dancefloors today. Singer Marc Almond used to frequent S&M clubs in the early 1980s. He also collaborated with Banshee Steve Severin on the sadomasochistic song 'Torment', for his darkly kinky 1983 album, *Torment and Toreros* ('Beat me and burn me / And I'll love you more, and more, and more'). The highly-strung Almond visited the offices of the *Record Mirror* in full S&M regalia to whip their reviewer, Jim Reid, who had the temerity to question the sincerity of the singer's sadomasochistic fixation and damn the album as 'neither outrageous nor daring'.

Today, performers in the increasing crossover between the Goth and fetish scenes regard sexual experimentation as a path to liberation and self-discovery. The USA's Sleep Chamber have been pushing the boundaries back since the early 1980s with their blend of occultic and sadomasochistic ritualism. Sleep Chamber lead singer John Zewizz's fascination with sexuality, particularly where it intersects with mysticism and deviance, is manifested live by the Barbitchuettes – a coterie of lace and leather clad female dancers who bring the music's aesthetic to life with their improvised erotic gyrations.

Controversy-seeking Spanish stalwarts Gothic Sex, who formed in 1988, describe their main themes as 'religion, perversion, false morality, cruelty, absurd violence', stirring in preoccupations with 'sex, gore and sadomasochism' for good measure – with a melodic ethos of Gothic Romanticism underlying their visceral metallic edge. Live, Gothic Sex's themes quite literally take flesh. Referring to their 1994 'Death' tour, the band's website describes a

Lord Gothic of Spanish fetish-rockers Gothic Sex.

stageshow involving 'murder, mutilation, flagellation, suicide, depravation [sic] and ultraviolence, using elements like pig heads, cow hearts, [and] entrails that could hurt the audience['s] sensibility since they just can't step aside like in a movie, [potentially] getting hit by blood or meat anytime in the show.'

Dominating the rock 'n' roll dungeon, however, are America's Genitorturers, whose extreme sadomasochistic stage show – half industrial-rock performance, half De Sadean nightmare – has attracted breathless plaudits and official bans across the globe. While the band's raucous, rock-based sound has led the more guitar-unfriendly Goths to dismiss them as heavy-metal shock merchants, the band's sheer vitality and dedication to the sadomasochistic aesthetic has attracted a following from all corners of the dark alternative scene. Gen, the band's statuesque, ice-blonde singer and mistress of ceremonies, presides over a musical rite where 'slaves' are flogged, penises are nailed to ladders or sewn up inside the scrotum, and rowdy hecklers are sodomised with police batons. 'It changes and affects people,' Gen told me in 1994. 'Some find it very liberating, others vomit.'

The stylistic blueprint for the male Goth rock star – like the Damned's Dave Vanian or Bauhaus' Pete Murphy – owes much to the foremost of *Bloodstone* magazine's unholy trinity:

vampirism. (Mick Mercer describes being singled out by Murphy and grabbed by the lapels at an early gig as being in 'the grip of the sodding vampire mate!')

Anne Rice's 1976 novel, *Interview with the Vampire*, had propelled the undead into the best-seller lists, and back to the forefront of popular culture, with its explicit sexual subtexts: not least that of homosexuality, which proved very popular among both the gay male and straight female readerships. As David J. Skal says in *V is for Vampire*, the book brought about 'the mass rehabilitation of the vampiric image'. Its potent blend of homosexuality and blood contagion was also published almost a decade before AIDS became an issue, complicating the relationship between the modern vampire cult and the era's most feared disease, that many claim echoes the fear of syphilis in the Victorian era of *Dracula*. Gay genre enthusiast, Skal – who notes, 'the characteristic of AIDS itself weirdly echoed the classic motifs of vampire legends' – writes in his encyclopaedia of the undead that the disease is 'the undeniable subtext of the explosive growth of vampire entertainments in all media during the last decade; to the conscious mind, the reality of AIDS can be almost too much to bear, but on the plane of fantasy, the threat of AIDS death can be bargained with – defanged as it were.'

But the success of the first of Rice's *Vampire Chronicles* clearly had nothing to do with the pervasive disease. Rice's new cult readers yearned to immerse themselves in her world, a desire they began to indulge in numerous vampire balls and masquerades inspired by her characters, with costumes and settings that evoked the elegant, historical settings of her undead saga. This is when the trickle of vampire books, both fiction and non-fiction, began growing into a flood that would engulf whole bookshelves in the 'occult' and 'horror' categories.

Bernhardt J. Hurwood's 1981 book *Vampires* hangs uncomfortably between fact and fable, representing something of a turning point. It begins in the time-honoured fashion, investigating the legends and historical reports previously exhumed from the archives by Montague Summers, but halfway through Chapter Four, events take an unexpected turn. Here the author introduces us to a 'sangroid' of his acquaintance – this being the term by which, he tells us, modern vampires prefer to be known. Much of the rest of the book is concerned with the lives and loves of these supernatural bloodsuckers who, Hurwood matter-of-factly proclaims, live among us.

Recalling the civil rights era and presaging political correctness, the author insists that vampires are 'the ultimate minority group'. They are, he says, a misunderstood bunch, anxious to live in harmony with their human prey, but have 'received an exceedingly "bad press" over the centuries'. Indeed, in comparison to most humans, we are told, the polite, civic-minded vampires 'look like angels' (although some travelled for a while with Charles Manson's murderous hippie 'Family', regretting not having stopped them before they committed their infamous 1969 massacres).

By the time the author gets around to spouting quasi-scientific nonsense – calculating the chances of a vampire attack as '3,200 to 1', and describing cordial relations between the vampire community and their mortal neighbours in southern California – the suspicion that he is having fun at the expense of his more gullible readers becomes overwhelming. 'They even went so far as to establish a night softball series,' he assures us of the undead's good-neighbour drive.

Whatever one feels about Hurwood's sangroids (who sound like an embarrassing medical complaint), one thing he unquestionably gets wrong is the assertion that few people wish to

Fetish fashion is underpinned by Goth glamour: posing for the international demi-monde, *millennial queens of the night mix traditional styles with futuristic fabrics.*

become vampires. This is disproved by the numerous books and journalistic features that followed, all purporting to draw back the veil on the world of 'real' vampires: Norine Dresser's *American Vampires* (1989); Rosemary Ellen Guiley's *Vampires Among Us* (1991); Carol Page's *Bloodlust* (1991); Tony Thorne's *Children of the Night* (1999); Katherine Ramsland's *Piercing the Darkness* (1999).

In *Vampires Among Us*, the Reverend Sean Manchester, a self-styled Dr Van Helsinng, tells author Guiley that the new wave of vampire clubs are particularly dangerous. 'Look at the new members sections and see what they are saying,' he notes. 'Would they like to become vampires? Would they indeed! This is the folklore equivalent to opening the door and inviting the vampire in. You don't have to physically open a door. The mental door is the real door. Then the vampire can come in anytime he wants.'

(In London during 1970, the Reverend Manchester was central to a true-life Gothic episode that seized the imagination of the British public. With garb and demeanour reminiscent of a vampire hunter in a Hammer horror film, Manchester appeared on Thames TV's *Today* show to describe how he planned to exterminate a vampire in Highgate Cemetery the following night. The 'vampire' was eventually found – though not by Manchester – in the shape of an amateur cine club, which had been making a horror movie entitled *Vampires at Night*. But this didn't deter the self-appointed vampire hunters who plagued the cemetery in the Reverend's wake, joined in turn by amateur occultists who favoured it as a venue for impromptu ceremonies. Things came to a head in 1974 when an architect parked his car near the cemetery one night, only to find a decapitated corpse reclining in the passenger seat next morning.)

But people are evidently not listening to this oddball opponent of darkness, as the millennial years have seen a flood of acolytes eager to invite the undead into their lives. Katherine Ramsland's *Piercing The Darkness* brings us full circle in this sense, with Ramsland – Anne Rice's official biographer – examining a young writer's attempt to do what Rice's protagonist had only achieved in fiction: to conduct an 'interview with the vampire'. *Piercing the Darkness* centres on an investigation into the case of would-be journalist Susan Walsh, who disappeared while researching a piece on 'the vampire underground' for New York's *Village Voice* newspaper in July 1996. She believed that she had uncovered a sinister conspiracy of blood drinkers, lurking in the shadows of America's daylight world – a creepy crew which robbed blood banks and engaged in plasma-fuelled orgies. In the light of this, Walsh's mysterious disappearance seemed like the opening sequence from a horror film, proving too good a story for many members of the media to resist, and her saga entered urban folklore.

More sceptical voices noted that struggling single mother, Susan Walsh, took lithium (usually prescribed for manic-depression), drank heavily, and also worked at the sleazier end of the New York vice industry. Walsh may have been right to worry – and more than one acquaintance commented on

An ad promoting the second of the Vampyria festivals in London, 1998 – as seen in Bloodstone, *'the magazine for vampires'.*

her increasing paranoia – but the dangers she faced may well have been more depressingly familiar than demonic. While journalism supposedly brought her into contact with New York's nocturnal legions, her other trade necessitated encounters with more mundane predators in the shape of organised crime, outlaw bikers and junkies. Many credible alternative theories concerning her disappearance were presented but these did not necessarily make good newspaper or magazine copy. A similar dilemma faces those who devote books to the modern vampire phenomenon. On the face of it, the idea that vampires exist and mingle among us is irresistible. The only problem is, to put it baldly, that vampires *do not* exist.

Deprived of authentic creatures of the night, authors found themselves interviewing a loose grouping of role-playing enthusiasts, Goth-club regulars and fringe characters with a few too many bats in their belfry. (One thing Ramsland does get right is the significance of a role-playing game, *Vampire: The Masquerade*, describing it as 'responsible for the increased popularity of vampires in general'. Since it debuted in 1991, the game has eclipsed the success of its Tolkienesque progenitor *Dungeons and Dragons*, due to the appeal of its richly detailed Gothic setting. Many of Ramsland's counterparts in the journalistic vampire-hunting game have uncritically swallowed *Vampire* role-playing fed to them as fact by their 'undead' interviewees – a tribute both to the game's depth and the self-professed experts' gullibility.)

These interviews are interesting from a sociological viewpoint, but books like Dresser's and Guiley's would not have had the same appeal had they been more honestly entitled *American Eccentrics* or *Goths Among Us*. Consciously or otherwise, the authors were complicit in promoting the Gothic mystique of their interview subjects, and publicising the growing vampire underground. Along the way, some writers went through a series of logical somersaults to vindicate their uncritical approach. Typical is Rosemary Ellen Guiley, who in *Vampires Among Us*, presents us with the concept of 'Vampire Reality', thus justifying her contentious title.

'Can we answer the question "Do vampires exist?"' Guiley posits in her conclusion. 'Yes' is her slightly equivocal answer. 'Vampires do exist because we believe in them. Vampires exist in subjective reality, the internal landscape of our consciousness. Vampires have the capability of existing in objective reality – the external world – when conditions are right. When Vampire Reality is created.' Which is all well and good, but leaves us with vampires who enjoy an existence similar to that of Santa Claus – or, indeed, the fairy Tinker Bell in *Peter Pan*, who will perish if we stop believing in her. Clearly, if we're hoping to find anything approximating a *real* vampire, we're going to have to stop looking for a supernatural being.

In *Vampires Among Us*, the most convincing candidates Rosemary Ellen Guiley finds are Londoner Damien and her German boyfriend, Damon. As the title of the chapter in which they appear – 'Dancing with Satan' – implies, this couple consider themselves to be the spawn of the Devil. This, as Guiley notes, is unusual, as most members of the related Goth and vampire scenes are at pains to disassociate themselves from all things satanic – possibly because the general public is already mistrustful enough, without invoking further reasons for persecution. Indeed, many 'real' vampires emphasise their sensitivity and sense of persecution to the point where the idea of them as predators is negated entirely.

Even Damien and Damon, despite their alleged demonic origins, drink orange and tomato juice cocktails as an alternative to blood. They live in fear of hostile social workers, or having their welfare payments suspended, rather than stake-wielding vampire hunters or the sign of the cross. 'We sit on the tube [London's underground rail network] and we're the ones being attacked, which in the modern day I find very strange,' Damien told Guiley. 'It's supposed to be the other way around!' Indeed . . .

There's something curiously disarming about this batty couple, a harmless but wilfully eccentric pair, who seem to have been carried away by the early 1980s Goth scene. But one can't help feeling that these particular vampires lack bite. Indeed, the vast majority of Guiley's interviewees seem pretty toothless.

A Gothic blend of blasphemy, sexual fetishism and bloodlust courtesy of New York's new Goth divas, the Nuns.

Tony Thorne's *Children of the Night* were comparatively more aggressive – but even then, he observed, most were 'courteous, even gentle'. By the time the book was published in 1999, the internet had become a significant focus for bringing together fringe groups, such as those interested in vampirism, into virtual 'communities'. (While the internet has proved to be a wonderful resource, its distance and anonymity also allow extravagant threats to be launched across cyberspace. Most of the aggression and bravado aimed towards Thorne seems to have come from this direction – hardly the grandiose menace of the classic vampire.) The most substantial of these operations is the Temple of the Vampire, which Thorne quotes at his book's conclusion:

'I am a vampire,' begins the Temple's creed. 'I worship my ego and I worship my life, for I am the only God that is. I am proud that I am a predatory animal and I honour my animal instincts. I exalt my rational mind and hold no belief that is in defiance of reason. I recognise the difference between the worlds of truth and fantasy. I acknowledge the fact that survival is the highest law. I acknowledge the Powers of Darkness to be hidden natural laws through which I work my magic. I know that my beliefs in Ritual are fantasy but the magic is real, and I respect and acknowledge the results of my magic. I realise there is no heaven as there is no hell, and I view death as the destroyer of life. Therefore I will make the most of life here and now. I am a Vampire. Bow down before me.'

Under the heading 'Vampires Exist', the organisation's website defines its historic status: 'The Temple is the only authentic international church in the world devoted to and uniquely authorised by the Vampire religion and its immortal Leaders, legally registered since December 1989 with the US federal government.' The 'immortal Leaders' referred to are presumably the Undead Gods the Temple claims as its patrons (though this clashes somewhat with their 'only God that is' ethos). Stripped of such quasi-theological trappings, and their equally vague but emphatic claims to be real vampires, the Temple's material echoes the pragmatic occultism of the USA's Church of Satan – the Temple's mysterious head being a member of both organisations.

There are many similarities between what motivates some to declare themselves Satanists and others to claim to be vampires: both are Gothic roles that set the adherent apart from the mundane world, deliberately alienating them from mainstream society. Both roles are implicitly misanthropic. The membership of a satanic order is akin to symbolically turning in your membership card of the human race, becoming as close to most people's idea of a monster as possible without crossing the boundary into sociopathic behaviour. Those who claim to be afflicted by the curse of the vampire are making a similar gesture, but the role requires the sociopathic activity of blood-drinking.

However, aspirational vampires effectively defang themselves by identifying with a mythical creature risen from the grave, implicitly attacking their own credibility. You can literally become a Satanist in a way that you cannot *be* a vampire. Perversely, many would-be vampires go even further in compromising their lifestyle, disavowing blood-drinking altogether – adopting a controversial role only to try to redeem it by portraying themselves as misunderstood, saddled with the condition against their will.

In an essay written for the London Vampyre Group's *Chronicles* magazine, entitled 'Sex, Blood and Immortality', an author with the odd moniker of Spaced Ace opines, 'the attraction of the Vampire is, of course, 99 per cent sexual. This is odd, considering the ferocious, hypnotic, utterly selfish and ruthless aspect of the creature. Mouldering corpses and cobweb infested coffins are hardly ideal love nests.' The vampire's appeal, concludes Ace, is because they 'must surely be the ultimate master or mistress. Dark vaults, crumbling castles, the helplessness of being a prisoner under someone else's domination have all the elements of S&M. And to cap it all, one's lifeblood, the very substance of existence, is drunk by the vampire.'

Of course, these elements are not confined to vampirism but central to the Gothic aesthetic overall. Sadomasochism and blood fetishism have long been points of controversy in the developing vampire subculture. Ever since the 1980s, when vampire clubs and societies first began to emerge, actual blood-drinking and affiliated sadomasochistic aspects have long been condemned. The UK's Vampyre Society, founded in 1987, is a classic case in question – the unorthodox spelling is used to distinguish between those who actually believe in the existence of vampires and those who merely enjoy indulging in the fantasy, styling themselves 'vampyres'.

Vampyre Society founder Carol Bohanon typified the attitude, disavowing sadomasochism and blood fetishism as anathema to her organisation. 'It doesn't happen within our group,' she insisted to me, 'it isn't what we're into. If we do get any letters from blood fetishists we politely turn them away.' At the same time, she accepted the erotic element of vampirism, 'but it's more sensuous than sexual.' It's easy to sympathise with this attitude – you don't need to shoot each other to play cowboys and Indians. On the other hand, there's something disingenuous in the suggestion that you can enjoy the vampire legend as long as you don't confront what is, for many, its dark heart, its deviant sexual charge.

This debate became more intense as the vampire subculture established itself throughout the 1990s, the period in which 'real vampires' started coming out of the coffin. By the time the Vampyre Society sadly folded in 1998, the undead had never been livelier. That same year two glossy vampire magazines were launched in the UK, representing the twin poles of the subculture. While *Bite Me* touted itself as a 'Magazine for Night People', *Bloodstone* proudly styled itself a 'Magazine for Vampires'. Similarly, *Bite Me* carried a disclaimer in their classified section stressing the magazine did 'not endorse blood drinking, blood fetishism or occult activities', while *Bloodstone* harangued those vampire organisations it believed were discriminating against blood fetishists. Critics of *Bloodstone*, with its unabashed interest in the sexual side of vampirism, accused it of being little more than blood-soaked porn for Gothic perverts, while critics of *Bite Me* dismissed it as anaemic fare that lacked the courage of its convictions.

In *V is for Vampire*, David J. Skal includes cross-referenced entries for blood fetishism and sadomasochism which claim the interest among vampire aficionados may have been inspired by Anne Rice writing both vampire fiction and kinky erotica. It doesn't seem to occur to him that an interest in the erotic aspects of the vampire myth naturally lead to the pain, pleasure and power games of sadomasochism. Perhaps this reflects Skal's own hostility to the fetish. He dismisses the way it 'is often romanticised by its practitioners as a renegade activity,' whereas, to Skal's mind, 'it is a depressingly status-quo fantasyland where real-world power imbalances are erotically celebrated and thereby reinforced and perpetuated.'

But Skal is fighting a losing corner with regard to Goth subculture, where sexual fetishism and its trappings are widely accepted as the marks of an outlaw libido. Sadomasochistic activities, where the skin is broken and blood spilled, have long been part of the Gothic tradition. They have achieved such prominence over the past decade that they have a generic name: 'blood play' or 'blood sports', though 'haemosexuality', the alternative coined by cultural historian Christopher Frayling, is more catchy. According to a 1997 feature on vampirism in *Bizarre* magazine, 'Vampire dominatrixes are all the rage in big-city brothels.'

The sex vampire, in all her sapphic bloodlust, from designer Nigel Wingrove's Femme
Fatale series. Incongruously, this design was reproduced on a set of coffee mugs.

One such dominatrix, a New Yorker named Christine, is quoted as claiming, 'You can get a lot of money for blood play. It's the next taboo. Once some guys have lived out their fantasies in a commercial dungeon, they want to up the odds. Need to. And this is one of the ways to make it extra forbidden. They are literally giving you their life force.'

While *Bite Me* is still going strong and *Bloodstone* has gone into terminal torpor, the blood-fetish debate is far from resolved. But those who favour the more visceral, transgressive approach are very much with us, as evidenced by the 2001 British TV documentary, *American Vampires*, which interviewed blood fetishists across the USA. In New York, a 21-year-old 'vampire' who calls himself Ghost described his pastime as a sexual act: 'I am very intimate with my blood-drinking. It generally tends to be something to enhance sex – maybe a bite in the thigh area, close to an arterial vein.' The connection with sadomasochism was evident in the case of Ghost, who appeared on camera prior to performing at a popular vampire club called the Realm of Darkness, where he planned to undertake a 'full stigmatic crucifixion'. This, according to Ghost, involved five stages – whipping, nails through the palms, nails through the feet, a crown of thorns, and a slash across the chest. For the grand finale, the young transgressive performer planned to pierce his mouth, cheeks and ears in order to give the impression of having his face sewn up.

On the West Coast, a twenty-year-old girl named Amanda from the Los Angeles suburb of Riverside talked about being a spigot (or tap) girl, a title bestowed upon her by the local blood-drinking community to honour her frequent 'donations'. Cameras followed her to the Near Dark Pub in Hollywood, a hang-out for LA's vampire enthusiasts where, according to Amanda, 'Everybody gathers, drinks, has fun, and also drinks blood.' Sure enough, a young Oriental named Sue followed her to a secluded place outside the bar, where she lapped away at a trickle of Amanda's blood. There is something akin to an erotic assignation here, reminiscent of the way customers slope off to quiet corners of more conventional clubs to exchange bodily fluids. But there's also something disturbingly clinical in the way Sue sterilised her willing victim's shoulder with a swab before making a neat little incision with a hypodermic needle.

Amanda says she's been 'donating' in this fashion since she was fifteen, when she graduated to the vampire scene from the Goth community. Unsurprisingly, many Goths are quick to distance themselves from such potentially dangerous activities, labelling such ersatz creatures of the night as pathological kooks. Indeed, many Goths disdainfully dismiss self-styled 'vampires' as an entirely different subculture, rather than a subgroup, offshoot or radical extreme of the Goth scene.

Such prejudices were legitimised in many eyes in early 2002, when a German couple were arrested for the brutal murder of a friend. Manuela and Daniel Ruda bludgeoned and stabbed one of Daniel's workmates to death in their Witten apartment, surrounded by the skulls, coffins and other Gothic paraphernalia collected by these self-styled vampiric Satanists. At the subsequent trial it became clear that their motive was not drinking their victim's blood – or, indeed, the Satanic sacrifice they claimed – so much as a perverse desire for notoriety, as the pair posed, flashed demonic hand signals and kissed for the benefit of the cameras.

That they were no more 'real Satanists' than they were 'real vampires' became clear when they tried to blame instructions from the Devil himself for their crime. (The Church of Satan, the most credible of the world's satanic organisations, does not believe in such literal demonic manifestations, while responsibility for one's own actions is a central part of its credo.) But the world's media preferred to report the Rudas' fancifully melodramatic version of events – complete with meetings with 'authentic vampires' in London – as fact. The presiding judge displayed more sense, ordering that the pair be sent to a secure psychiatric ward to receive therapy, adding that neither should be thought of as 'evil', and that they were 'humans not monsters'. Similarly, the sheer amount of media attention the couple commanded is a reflection of the level to which the crime was an aberration, far from typical of either the Gothic, satanic or vampiric subcultures. The Rudas were symptoms of the modern craving for fame at any cost, rather than manifestations of the Gothic appetites they claimed to serve.

Pierced Goth princess: the Goth scene and the fetish underground merge, at the Carnival of Souls.

Nevertheless, whether indulged obsessively, symbolically or merely in a spirit of play, vampirism, sadomasochism, sex magic and other melodramatic forms of sexuality have become an inherent part of the Goth scene. Several Goth and fetish clubs are now interchangeable, or even share themed nights – like the Carnival of Souls festival in the northern English town of Derby, organised by Nightbreed supremo Trevor Bamford. 'I think one of the principles of "Gothic-ness" is a love of dark sensuality, which in turn touches upon the more creative side of brooding sexuality,' enthuses Bamford. 'The fetish scene essentially glorifies the innate sexual power of objects and substances (i.e. rubber etc.) and seeks to reach the same area of dark brooding eroticism. The two kind of meet in this area.'

This is nothing new. This book's survey of Gothic literature identifies the Marquis de Sade as both the forefather of fetish and the godfather of the Gothic novel. American author Mark Edmundson has subtitled his thesis on modern American Gothic, *Nightmare on Main Street*, as 'Angels, Sadomasochism and the Culture of Gothic'. According to Edmondson, 'you cannot have Gothic without a cruel hero-villain; without a cringing victim; and without a terrible place, some locale, hidden from public view, in which the drama can unfold . . . S&M is where Gothic, in a sense, wants to go.'

But Gothic has been around for centuries – it's just come out of the closet. In the 21st century, alternative sexuality – long a characteristic of the Gothic cultural underworld – has increasingly become the norm in much of mainstream culture. The trappings of fetishism are now a familiar sight in advertising campaigns and music videos, as well as trendy clubs and on the fashion catwalk. The dominatrix, the dominant Gothic female archetype, has become a positive icon of predatory feminine sexuality.

Under the pseudonyms of Ann Rampling and A. N. Roquelaure, vampire novelist Anne Rice has also enjoyed success writing erotic fiction with a strong sadomasochistic flavour. The early 1990s also saw a minor revolution in the British literary market, when a number of erotic imprints aimed specifically at women – most notably Black Lace – became surprise successes, selling over three million copies worldwide. Many of the features of these books – historical settings, light fetishism and dark anti-heroes – were staples of the original Gothic novels so popular in the early 1800s, mostly written by and for women, now revisited with libidos and bodices fully unlaced.

The unforgettable gargoyle gang-bang from Michael Ninn's award-winning porn movie Shock *(1996).*

The epicentre of the Gothic sexual revolution is perhaps America's self-styled 'Trade Mag of Cool', *Blue Blood*, edited by Amelia G and her partner, Forest Black. 'It's counterculture erotica,' Amelia – who did her honours thesis on 'Vampires as a Paradigm for Human Sexuality' – told me when we spoke in 1999. 'It's intended for a pan-sexual audience, not any specific orientation. The Gothic influence is really strong, as is the vampire kink, but also just unusual sexualities with a punk or rock feel, like fetishism or body modification.' *Blue Blood* is a sexual celebration of the counterculture, with classy photo-shoots of punks, Goths and rockers engaged in sexual activity alongside fetish fiction and offbeat pornography reviews.

Over the past few years, while porn has continued a slow but steady rise in both profitability and respectability, the darker side of sexuality has taken the adult industry by storm. This is evidenced by the hardcore movies, such as *Ritual*, *Forever Night* and *Shock*, directed by the man *Adult Video News* calls 'the Orson Welles of porn', Michael Ninn. Ninn's films are distinguished by unusually high production values and sophisticated storylines for the porn genre, and a lavish visual style that is often heavily Gothic. 'As a director, darkness can be a more expressive vehicle,' he told me in 2001. 'It's certainly true that good sex always takes place in bad places.' Like the scene in *Shock* where the heroine is ravished by two gargoyles that come to life. Or pretty much every scene in *Forever Night*, his brooding tribute to the Gothic genre, where the frantic couplings feature dildo-wielding demons and fog-shrouded graveyards, and the hero is cursed to walk the earth for eternity for cursing the Almighty – like a hardcore adaptation of Maturin's 1820 novel *Melmoth the Wanderer*.

The purest expressions of Gothic sexuality come naturally from within the Goth scene itself. Sadly, Christa Faust's *Necromantic* on-line project has folded. (I suspect her offer to stroke 'your biggest sex organ (your brain!)' was a little progressive for many porn-surfers.) But other Gothic internet dens of iniquity continue to thrive: *Barely Evil* bills itself as 'the new naughty site to bring you little devil dolls, tasty witches, Gothic babes, kinky troublemakers, very bad young punk girls, sweet sexy Satan babes, and wicked fantasy!'; *Gothic Sluts* is pretty self-explanatory, promising 'Supermodels of Gothic Fetish Erotica' such as Countess Lilith Stabs, Jade Blue Eclipse, and Mistress Persephone. 'We started this site because we were sick of seeing mainstream people trying to cash in on our scene with pictures of boring normal girls with french fry-looking fangs,' explains the site's introduction. Naked Goth girls with crimson hair and tattoos caress spiders and skulls, while pierced princesses spread their stocking-clad legs for the camera, artfully draped over tombs or suggestively licking what look suspiciously like human bones. These Goth cuties are most definitely deadlier than their male counterparts.

Gothic Sluts features a substantial input from *Blue Blood* founders Ms G and Mr Black. In 1999, I asked Amelia G why she thought the kind of Gothic erotica she produced has been enjoying such widespread popularity of late. 'I think some of it's end of the century decadence – and that has to be a good thing!' she enthused, though, as this book testifies, the dark aesthetic transcends dates and trends. 'For me, I had bondage and SM fantasies – more bondage than SM – pretty much since I passed puberty. I was into it at a young age. I took some flack for it at college before it became trendy . . . I think it's a good thing if people are exposed to new, different ways of making love. I think it makes people happier. I think it makes life a more varied and interesting experience.'

Countercultural and Gothic erotica from Blue Blood *magazine.*

CHAPTER X

DARK SHADOWS OVERWHELM US: GOTH ROCK

Just as glam rock crossed the Atlantic to the US in the 1970s to mutate into glitter rock, so Goth was exported to the Americans in the early 1980s – their local variety dubbed 'death rock'. As Don Bolles describes in *Retro Hell*, LA soon developed a host of Goth-friendly clubs, beginning with Fetish and culminating in the likes of Scream, Helter Skelter, Sanctuary, the Crypt and Zombie Zoo.

The most influential band linked to this scene was Christian Death, who like their British counterparts Bauhaus, were founded in 1979. The chief architect behind the band's concept was LA resident Rozz Williams, then only sixteen – a restless, brilliant talent who burned as briefly as he did bright. (Rozz Williams was not the singer's real name – portentously, he borrowed his pseudonym from a favourite gravestone in the local cemetery.) The band's name – in part a corruption of Christian Dior – also reflected the singer's rejection of his religious upbringing, and, as Christian Death progressed through their various incarnations, the anti-religious theme remained constant. The band would later claim to be attacking not the teachings of Jesus, but of those in the Church who have perverted his creed to their own ends. Their name and cruciform logo were based on the observation that Christianity, purportedly the religion of love, takes as its symbol the device used to execute its messiah.

The inherent controversy of the band's moniker was a different brand of shock tactic to those employed by the death rock scene. Indeed, the 'Goth' tag is far more appropriate here. While the likes of 45 Grave (who were supported by Christian Death for their first live performance) were looking to low budget horror movie-makers like Roger Corman and Ed Wood for inspiration, Christian Death's lyrics revealed influences from Poe and Baudelaire.

This latter day Medusa exemplifies cyber-Goth style as the
traditional Goth arts of hair and body adornment are taken to new creative heights.

In the afterlife: after the death of Rozz Williams, the Christian Death name and ethos continue with Valor Kand, and his female collaborator Maitri.

Similarly, the atmospheric sound of Christian Death was more akin to the post-punk experimentalism of their English contemporaries than to the evil rock 'n' roll of the Misfits. Even in appearance, Williams' long, raven-dyed hair, silver jewellery, fishnet stockings and black evening gowns put him in the same camp as the eerily androgynous European Goths, rather than the every-day-is-Hallowe'en style of his fellow Americans. Williams' vocal stylings also exhibited the baritone tendencies favoured by Goth bands – indeed, his voice sometimes sounded more English than American. The fact that Williams claimed to have been largely unaware of the growing European scene makes the parallels all the more striking.

Like much that is brilliant, however, what was to come was fraught with confusion and controversy. The confusion began in earnest when the Christian Death fragmented not long after their debut. This was their first incarnation, but there were more to come – Christian Death rose again when Williams was joined by guitarist and vocalist Valor Kand, a former member of Pompei 99, yet another Californian dark 'alternative' band.

Shortly after the new Christian Death came together, the band relocated to France, allowing Williams to absorb the atmosphere of Paris, the city that had been home to so many of his Decadent heroes a century before. They recorded *Catastrophe Ballet* at Rockfield Studios in Wales (the same studio that had played host to Bauhaus for their albums *The Sky's Gone Out* and *Burning from the Inside*). This 1984 album showcased a more delicate, multi-layered sound, its harsh beauty confirming Christian Death's cult reputation among the growing Goth audience. The band's return to the US resulted in *Ashes* (1985), the pinnacle of the classic Christian Death line-up, where Kand's pretentious mysticism and Williams' poisonous poetry mesh to ominous effect. It was also Williams' last official recording with this version of Christian Death.

The split was initially amicable, with Williams keen to explore new directions. By this point, however, Christian Death were becoming a credible money-spinner. In the late 1980s, in the company of chanteuse Eva O, who had sung backing vocals on their early material (the two had also married in 1988), the band's founder began to perform once more under the name Christian Death. This incensed the Kand camp, who insisted Williams had bequeathed the name to them. Fans became confused by two rival Christian Deaths touring in the early 1990s and a plethora of different releases, Kand's obsession with esoteric religion and mysticism appearing impenetrable to those who knew Christian Death solely from the Williams incarnation. The rivalry split the unusually fanatical Christian Death fanbase, just as it had split the band.

Many of Williams' recordings at this time smacked of desperation, but among them were some true gems – like the epic *Path of Sorrows* (1993), which the singer described as his favourite Christian Death album. 'I called Rozz,' Kand explained to *Terrorizer* magazine in 2000, 'and he said he needed the money. I couldn't argue because he had joint ownership of the name but it just wasn't fair practice.' Kand's response was to continue to record his own grandiosely pessimistic Christian Death albums, attempting to stamp his own creative mark on the band for good. With inflammatory material and censor-baiting packaging to match (such as an image of Jesus injecting himself with heroin for the 1988 album *Sex and Drugs and Jesus Christ*, or the swastikas on *All the Hate* the following year), Kand pretentiously and provocatively showcased his views on sex, death and religion.

Confusion was dispelled in the worst possible fashion when Rozz Williams took his own life, hanging himself in his bedroom on 1 April 1998. Friends expressed mystification at the singer's motives. Even a cursory glance at his artistic legacy, however, reveals a very troubled soul, whose creative gift came with an awful price – the ability to see the darkness of the world with painful clarity. Like so many of his Decadent heroes, the singer found solace in narcotics, and the same heroin addiction that helped to inspire convincingly horrific spoken-word performances such as *Whorse's Mouth* (1996) must have been eating away at his spirit.

In addition to his harrowing spoken-word performances, Williams recorded with Gitane Demone, another former member of Pompei 99. Demone has made a speciality of torrid torch songs – most notably on *Dream Home Heartache* (1995) which plays like a lounge band from Hell, and whose title track is a cover of the song by English art-glam band Roxy Music. Eva O has also recorded solo material – most notably the album reflecting her bizarre conversion to Christianity, *Demons Fall for an Angel's Kiss* (1994), which was originally going to be called *An Angel Falls for a Demon's Kiss*, until she saw the light courtesy of a book by evangelist Billy Graham! She had seen precious little light in the Shadow Project: the five-piece formed by her husband Williams upon leaving Christian Death. 'We made a home of hell, LSD trips and darkness 24 hours a day,' O told an interviewer, post-conversion.

Numerous significant Goth bands have emerged from the Christian Death crucible: Mephisto Walz, formed by Kand's former guitarist, Bari-Bari, created a luxuriantly moody sound that one reviewer described as 'fit to be played at a ghostly masquerade ball'. Completing the classic Mephisto Walz line-up, Christianna's melancholic vocals provided an angelic counterpoint to Bari-Bari's subtly infernal melodies. While Bari-Bari shied away from the Gothic clichés, dismissing 'satanic and vampyre poetry' as 'a subject that was meant more for serious fiction writers, not bands dressed up gothic for their big night at some club,' the demonic connotations of the band's name were far from coincidental – inspired by the classic drama about a deal with the Devil, *Faust*, by the German poet, Goethe. 'After returning to LA I started to re-read the text over and over again and obtained several translations of it,'

Bari-Bari told Australia's *Aether Sanctum* magazine. 'What impression did it make? I think it is the ultimate story of the good and evil that lies in each of us.'

Multi-instrumentalist William Faith was once an integral part of Mephisto Walz, before he was recruited for the Williams-led incarnation of Christian Death in 1992, and the albums *The Path of Sorrows* and *The Rage of Angels*. Previously, under the name Bill E. Bones, Faith had been a founder member of Wreckage, alongside Tony Lestat in 1989. Lestat described Wreckage as '"punk" with a classic horror film feel', which pretty much describes the death rock field in which Wreckage are key players. Faith affectionately recalls the band as possessed of 'some sort of broodish [sic] romance', but finally found his muse in the shape of Monica Richards, former vocalist with Strange Boutique.

Faith and the Muse, as they are known, have arty aspirations to explore mythology and history in their music and highly theatrical stageshows. Richards – who creates the artwork for their record covers, heavily influenced by Austrian symbolist artist Gustav Klimt – described the band's ethos to *Naked Truth* as 'a journey through every hidden part of the human psyche: dramatic, theatrical, turbulent, yet dreamy . . . a recalling of ancient cultures and ideas . . . an invocation of dream and love.' Richards' seductive mezzo-soprano and Faith's evocative guitar, layered with keyboards, classical strings and woodwind, create a tapestry of many moods. Some of these are Gothic in the modern sense, like the gloomy 'Dead Leaf Echo', others in the eighteenth-century sense of mock-medieval. 'Everyone has their own definition of what the term "Gothic" means,' Faith reflected to the *Twilight Realm* webzine. 'I attach it to the literary and architectural traditions – as such, I am quite endeared to the term.'

William Faith's late friend and former collaborator, Rozz Williams, was always more ambivalent about his position as a Gothic icon, but for someone who once stated 'I've never done anything Goth in my life!', the founder of Christian Death had a huge impact upon the Stateside Goth scene.

'People tell me I'm an influence, but I don't want to take too much responsibility,' Rozz Williams said, speaking about the Goth scene to *Alternative Press* four years prior to his death. 'Now, it's so strange, it's become a way of life for so many people. How do these people maintain it? "Wake up, put in my fangs, do my hair, make it down to the graveyard before it closes . . ."' It's very characteristic of the whole scene to find yet another musician disowning their Goth audience. Just as Ian Astbury of Southern Death Cult fingered Andi Sex Gang, rather than himself, as the 'true' Goth, so Williams identified the Sisters of Mercy, rather than Christian Death, as the pivotal Goth band of the 1980s. Needless to say, Sisters lead singer, Andrew Eldritch, would most certainly not have agreed, which was characteristic of a late 1980s crisis in the British Goth scene that many thought would condemn the cult to history.

Founded in 1980, the Sisters originally had Eldritch in the drummer's seat. But as he was, by his own admission, 'a very bad drummer', a drum machine was drafted in. This device, nicknamed 'Doktor Avalanche', helped to create the Sisters of Mercy's distinctive sound, which began as downbeat rock with a barbed synthetic edge, inviting uncomplimentary Joy Division comparisons, before evolving its own identity. The good Doktor was also, unsympathetic commentators have observed, the only member of the band willing to tolerate vocalist Eldritch's notorious 'artistic temperament'.

One year after recording their 1985 debut album, *First and Last and Always*, in typical Sisters style the line-up dissolved in a cacophony of accusation and counter-accusation. Guitarist Wayne Hussey and bassist Craig Adams initially intended forming a rival act to Eldritch's called the Sisterhood, but when their erstwhile vocalist got wind of this, he recorded a single under that very same name, forcing the duo to adopt the Mission as their new moniker. Acrimony in the Sisters camp was not confined to internal feuding. After a brief honeymoon, the press began identifying Eldritch's outfit as a 'Goth' band – this being tantamount to a term of abuse in the mid-1980s.

Eldritch reacted violently against being dubbed a Goth, developing contempt not only for the rock press, but also for the dedicated Goth following that the Sisters were beginning to attract. Their next album, however, did little to dissuade either the press or the fans. *Floodland* was released in 1987 and became an almost instantaneous classic. If Joy Division's spiralling claustrophobia was the most obvious point of comparison at the Sisters' inception, they soon developed an expansive exoticism and self-conscious rock-god decadence. Yet the extent to which both bands could be defined as 'Gothic' was born out of a similar milieu. Both hailed from England's depressed north, and the same imagery dominated their lyrical landscapes: the threatening darkness of a crumbling, post-industrial world, rendered mythic – even sensual – by a streak of perverse romanticism.

By way of contrast, whereas Ian Curtis was characterised by a kind of raw vulnerability, Andrew Eldritch remained an aloof spectator, able to savour the degeneracy and decay like some reptilian aristocrat, immune to its toxic siren song of destruction. This was

Andrew Eldritch – the mercurial figure at the dark heart of the Sisters of Mercy.

Wayne Hussey of the Mission, whose epic, self-indulgent rock-romanticism made them a favourite with Goths in the late 1980s.

encapsulated in the Sisters' urbane, hypnotic sound, with its jagged, danceable guitar hooks and arabesque backing vocals. These were held together by Eldritch's icy, coffin-deep baritone, which if such an amorphous entity can be said to exist, proved highly influential to the 'Goth sound' that followed in their wake (much to the singer's dismay).

The Sisters of Mercy had previously toured with the Gun Club, who had given Eldritch a long black coat, and for *Floodland* he also helped himself to their bassist, Patricia Morrison. The two sparked off each other to startling effect on material like 'This Corrosion'. They also looked like the archetypal Goth couple – Eldritch razor-sharp and razor-thin with collar-length, crow-black hair and shades, Morrison back-combed and pixie-booted – representing the missing link between the pale faces and lace of the Goth subculture and the black-leather chic of the biker-rocker aesthetic. (Though both were evasive as to whether they actually were 'a couple'.)

Eldritch endeavoured to outdistance the Goth tag in the late 1980s with a series of sartorial shifts, most notably on the lavish 1988 video for their Arabic epic 'Dominion', for which he cut his hair and lost the long black coat in favour of a white linen suit and beard. Another 'Goth accessory' disposed of by Eldritch was Patricia Morrison, who left in 1989 under something of a cloud. Asked ten years later, in an interview with *Meltdown* magazine, if she ever thought of re-establishing contact with Eldritch, the bassist responded, 'I'd rather stick needles in my eyes', adding, 'Andy is only ever as good as the songwriters surrounding him' (a contentious claim, as Eldritch has remained the dominant voice and creative force behind the band). She also dismisses the 1990 follow-up to *Floodland*, *Vision Thing*, as 'a commercial and artistic failure', while this more driven, stripped-down version of the Sisters sound is my own personal favourite. It's indicative, however, of Eldritch's petulant persona that it has a habit of eclipsing his artistic achievements.

While even he surely couldn't deny that the Sisters are definitively dark, even decadent, it's possible to sympathise with Eldritch's rejection of the 'Gothic' label. Coffin-and-cobweb clichés are absent from his world. His lyrics may be cryptic, but crypts are not on the Eldritch agenda (though the stagename 'Eldritch' is an adjective beloved of H. P. Lovecraft, meaning weird and arcane). Occultism and the macabre are not Sisters territory so much as acidly oblique comments on politics, psychology and modern culture. 'Yet,' Eldritch growls, 'I have only to wear black socks to be stigmatised as the demon overlord.'

Like Rozz Williams, Andrew Eldritch preferred to be seen as part of a tradition of dark 'alternative' rock – both citing the Velvet Underground and the Doors as primary influences. But like Christian Death, the Sisters of Mercy were reluctantly at the eye of a Gothic storm – even if they tried to shake off the tag when the media declared it terminally uncool.

The last English band of the 1980s to be classified as 'Goth rock' – and often referred to in the same breath as the Sisters of Mercy and the Mission – was the Fields of the Nephilim. It was 'the Nephs', as they affectionately became known, who best qualified for that fond Goth epithet, 'Gothic as fuck'.

Formed in 1983 in the sleepy town of Stevenage, their first album, *Dawnrazor* (1987), was a truly breathtaking recording that combined the Mission's sense of epic scale with the Sisters' sense of saturnine,

Caroline Blind, of Sunshine Blind – allegedly dropped from Philadelphia's Dark Harvest festival at the insistence of Andrew Eldritch, for being 'too Gothic'.

enigmatic foreboding. Vocalist and chief lyricist, Carl McCoy, was unafraid of entertaining the arcane forces that often threatened to break through the Sisters' soundscapes, but never truly manifested themselves. While Eldritch took his band name from a song by melancholic Canadian singer-songwriter Leonard Cohen, and Hussey claimed in old-school rock 'n' roll style to have been inspired to dub his band the Mission by the guitar amps of that name, McCoy drew his band moniker from biblical lore. As he explained to *Cornerstone* magazine in 1989, 'The Nephilim was something I'd known about since I was really young [McCoy, like several influential Goths, endured a rigid religious upbringing]. If you're familiar with the first book of the Bible, Genesis, you see the sons of God seduce some of the women on the earth and they produce a race of people known as the Nephilim. According to legend they taught man about war, astrology, and magic.'

This Hebrew myth is also linked to the heretical Apochryphal Gospels, where the leader of the Nephilim, known as Semjaza, is sometimes equated with Satan – though McCoy shows the characteristic Goth reluctance to invoke the Prince of Darkness. He is less squeamish about referring to to H. P. Lovecraft's fictional Cthulhu Mythos (McCoy has described the Neph classic 'The Watchman' as a musical invocation of the monstrous god

Cthulhu). Aleister Crowley also makes an inevitable appearance: the song 'Moonchild' is a reference to one of the Great Beast's most notorious magical rites, and his only published novel, while 'Submission' contains a vocal sample allegedly culled from the notorious black magician himself. (The band led the way in sampling, later to be a standard feature of modern Goth rock.)

Macabre sounds and dialogue were also borrowed from horror movies like *The Evil Dead* and *The Texas Chainsaw Massacre*, but these weren't the band's only connection with grim

Fields of the Nephilim. Vocalist Carl McCoy in 1990 cyberpunk film Hardware, *directed by McCoy's friend Richard Stanley – who also directed the band's best videos.*

Americana. While early Goth acts like the Cult had played games of Crowley and Indians, the Fields of the Nephilim took inspiration from the Native Americans' Wild Western opponents. They borrowed their distinctive visual image – of battered long coats and broad-brimmed hats, covered in dust (or talcum powder) – from the 1960s spaghetti-Western genre originated by Italian director Sergio Leone. Spaghetti Westerns are about as Gothic as the Western genre gets – bleak, misanthropic, death-fixated dramas, whose gun-slinging, snake-eyed anti-heroes are almost supernatural in their skill. But most influential were the soundtracks composed by Ennio Morricone, whose rhythmic machismo and twangs of tension came to symbolise the genre. *Dawnrazor* opens with 'The Harmonica Man', composed by Morricone for Leone's *Once Upon a Time in the West*, although the Italian soundtrack composer's influence can be felt throughout the band's canon. This unlikely cocktail – of Cthulhu, Crowley and Clint Eastwood – really shouldn't gel, but it's an integral part of the imaginative power of the Fields of the Nephilim.

Among the band's fervent fans is Goth-fantasy author, Storm Constantine, who also used the Nephilim legend in her fiction. Constantine supplied the notes for the 1993 Nephilim compilation, *Revelations*, where she describes their music as 'evoking both a harrowing tension of apocalyptic despair and an uplifting aurora borealis of hope.' By the time she wrote this line it was an affectionate eulogy, as the Fields of the Nephilim had folded two years before, after only two more studio albums: *The Nephilim* (1988), the band at their peak, and *Elyzium* (1990), which saw their power waning. McCoy formed a new band with the familiar-sounding name of Nefilim, but alienated many admirers by introducing furious heavy-metal thrash to the familiar Gothic themes.

Part of the importance of the Goth rock bands of the late 1980s, particularly the Fields of the Nephilim, lay in lending a masculine aspect to the Goth scene. In an aesthetic long associated with androgyny, gender-bending and bisexuality, such dark machismo provided a

Classically-trained Greek American singer Diamanda Galas, who, in her confrontational style, has re-interpreted everything from Baudelaire to the blues.

credible role model for those who identified with the Gothic ethos but found its foppish effeminacy less appealing. Despite this, the Gothic aesthetic remains more than comfortable with its feminine side. Indeed, no contemporary musical subculture can compete with Goth in presenting positive, powerful roles for women – as embodied in the Gothic diva's aura of predatory femininity.

Classically trained Greek–American singer Diamanda Galas paid tribute to the Decadent poet, Charles Baudelaire, with her debut 1982 recording, *The Litanies of Satan* (the 'B' side – 'Wild Women with Steak Knives' – gives a clue as to her spiky approach). She followed with a nerve-shredding trilogy – *The Divine Punishment* (1986), *Saint of the Pit* (1986) and *You Must Be Certain of the Devil* (1988) – collectively known as *The Masque of the Red Death*.

The title is taken from Edgar Allan Poe's short story about a medieval plague – though in Galas' case she is referring to the AIDS virus that killed her brother and to the decidedly 'un-Christian' attitude taken to the illness by many members of the Church. 'It may in places sound like Gothic Horror,' according to the Mute Records press release, 'a fact that Galas is well aware of, embracing [film director Roger] Corman as readily as Poe, but the really black joke is just how close that is to the reality of the witch-hunting American heartland.' In many ways the definitive difficult diva, Galas' unforgettable performances are as much artistic ordeals as entertainment – though she commanded respect from both Goth and 'high art' audiences for her electrifying, ear-splitting output, inspired by the expressionistic German Schrei ('shriek') operatic style, whereby the voice is utilised as a harrowing musical instrument rather than as a vehicle for oratorio. On her more recent material, she has put her formidable vocal cords to work in the blues, torch-song, and even in the gospel tradition, all given a barbed edge by her fierce delivery.

Dead Can Dance, based around the core duo of Lisa Gerrard and Brendan Perry, were one of the most diverse and important cult acts of the 1980s, whose influence is often underestimated. The band's name encouraged interest from Goths, and even death metal bands cited the ambient duo as a primal influence. 'Unfortunately, a lot of people missed the symbolism of what we were trying to convey, and simply assumed Dead Can Dance was some innocuous Death Rock reference. To the contrary, our music was about giving life, not taking it,' mused Perry to *Propaganda* magazine. 'I realise that retailers and the media like to categorise bands and have been struggling to pigeonhole us – from new age to gothic to classical, whatever.'

The Batcave's resident diva Danielle Dax, as 'the wolf girl', on this French poster for The Company of Wolves *(1984) – adapted from the Gothic fairytales of Angela Carter.*

For once, the familiar musician's plea of being beyond classification rings true. Dead Can Dance have made an epic musical journey, from Arabic influences on *Within the Realm of a Dying Sun* (1987) to Renaissance melodies on albums like *Aion* (1990), all mixing traditional techniques with modern technology. Perry's bemusement at their association with the Gothic aesthetic doesn't ring quite so true, however. Many of their most moving moments evoke melancholia and mystery, like 'Arcane', where 'dark shadows overwhelm us and we become blind.' The duo borrowed the title for their second album, *Spleen and Ideal*, from the first part of French poet Charles Baudelaire's Decadent masterwork, *The Flowers of Evil*, and two of his verses provide lyrics for the follow-up, *Within the Realm of a Dying Sun*, its sleeve depicting a shrouded figure reaching disconsolately for a crypt.

Miranda Sex Garden were discovered busking by Barry Adamson in a London underground station (Adamson, an early Bad Seed, has recorded a number of acclaimed jazz-*noir* albums, such as 1998's

As Above So Below – as close as we're likely to get to Gothic be-bop). Originally a trio of female music students, they so impressed Adamson with their singing of medieval madrigals that he helped them to secure a deal with 4AD Records (the British label had loomed large in the 1980s – indeed, 4AD issued Bauhaus' debut album, *In the Flat Field*, way back in 1980, and subsequently signed the Birthday Party and French Goth legends, Xymox).

Lisa Gerrard and Brendan Perry, aka Dead Can Dance. Despite their discomfort with the 'Gothic' tag, their eclecticism influenced the more progressive Goth bands.

Beginning with relatively faithful renditions of Renaissance ballads on *Madra* (1991), Miranda Sex Garden spread their creative wings on the 1992 follow-up, *Suspiria* (its title borrowed from the stylishly surreal 1977 film by Dario Argento, Italy's master of garish Gothic horror). By now, they had recruited a band to bring a modern musical spin to their radiant vocals – an approach *Trouser Press* approvingly described as 'an intriguing, challenging art felon, dancing eccentrically near the fringes of Goth' – happily pilfering influences from whatever catches their magpie eyes. Those critics still inclined to dismiss Miranda Sex Garden as staid wallflowers were silenced by their fetishistic follow-up, *Fairytales of Slavery*, which the girls performed at fetish clubs, under the name of the Waltzing Maggots, where according to *The Virgin Encyclopedia of Indie and New Wave*, founder Katherine Blake performed 'half naked in Nazi regalia (finally destroying utterly their early press reputation for Victorian primness).'

In 1996 Blake returned to Miranda Sex Garden's historical roots, forming another outfit with eleven other female singers called the Medieval Baebes. She found fertile ground in which her Goth sympathies could flourish. As Baebe Rachel Van Asch revealed to *Bite Me* magazine: 'Our first ever gig was in an overgrown sprawling necropolis. We performed in front of a derelict chapel in the centre of the graveyard. We lit flaming torches along the twisting overgrown paths to guide our guests to us. I think we made a bit of an error of judgement when we chose to sing an extract from [Verdi's opera] *Macbeth* . . . "Come Ye Spirits" because the spirits were surely roused that night. Total chaos ensued . . .' Indeed, equipment went missing, two of the assembled revellers had to be taken to hospital, one Baebe's house was broken into while she performed, while another was, bizarrely, stung on the nose by a nocturnal bee.

Italy's Ataraxia also echo Europe's spiritual past with their entrancing female vocals, explaining on their website that they have 'grown up in Medieval burgs and we carry on the "oral tradition" of those times.' Multilingual and multi-talented, Ataraxia's sound is dominated by the beguiling voice of Francesca Nicoli. Nicoli has been compared to 1980s British pop princess Kate Bush, who herself unorthodox and bewitching, could be described as a proto-Goth diva. Bush's 1978 debut, an interpretation of Emily Brontë's 1847 Gothic romance novel, *Wuthering Heights*, was covered by Ataraxia on their 1996 album, *Il Fantasma Dell'Opera*.

The more light-hearted, upbeat tendency among Goth divas in the 1990s gave rise to the

Girl power, fifteenth century style, with dreamy revivalists the Medieval Baebes.

'perkygoth' persona – a reaction to the familiar charges that Goths are all sulky, pretentious depressives – which emphasised the colourful, fairy-tale aspects of the Gothic aesthetic. It was pioneered by the Scottish duo of Rose McDowall and Jill Bryson: garishly glamorous post-punk princesses who performed as Strawberry Switchblade on the British alternative music scene in the mid-1980s. In recent years, 'perkygoth' has been embodied in another female duo, that of the similarly-named Switchblade Symphony. This popular San Francisco Goth band, founded in 1989, centred on 'spooky little girls' singer Tina Root and keyboard player Susan Wallace. It was as if, while the 1980s Goth chick had been inspired by *Addams Family* matriarch Morticia, in the following decade her mischievous yet doleful daughter, Wednesday, had grown up into the female role model of choice. 'What if the Brothers Grimm had decided to set their gruesome little tales to music?' asked *Propaganda*'s Eric Fischer rhetorically. The answer was Switchblade Symphony, whose 'music has all the delirium and gothic horror of some demon-possessed, antique music box.'

'I've always chosen to see the good side instead of the bad,' Root explained to *Implosion* magazine, 'and I've always been into fantasy and fairytales and cartoons. But they always have to balance out with a sense of darkness. Because anything that's beautiful but isn't dark is kind of cheesy. There has to be a demented side to it.' This contrast of cuteness, kitsch and creepiness caught the imagination of the Goth audience, as did the diverse musical approach implicit in their name.

Switchblade Symphony broke up in 1999. To fill the vacuum, a new duo of femme fatales emerged. Diva Destrucion, a much more sepulchrally traditional Goth act, were collectively Debra Fogarty and Severina Sol, and their inspiration was as black as one can get. Fogarty told Girlmedia.com she began Diva Destruction 'in order to vent pain that had no other outlet. I once lost a dear friend to suicide . . . She took her life because she couldn't end her cycle of abusive relationships. Many of my bitter lyrics, such as in "Cruelty Games", stab back at betrayal, masochism, and emotional torture. My lyrics explore the depths of cruelty in human nature and how people destroy each other emotionally.'

Musically, they credit Siouxsie and the Banshees and classical composer Beethoven as influences on their blend of heavy guitars, sinister electronics and lush vocals. 'We have created a very theatrical and dramatic stage show that includes a suicide shrine complete with hanging noose, suicide note, candles, and dead roses,' Fogarty told the Gothland.com site. Only time will tell whether Diva Destruction's unashamedly dark melodramatics will be the shape of things to come in the 21st century . . .

The story of the alternative scene in the 1990s is dominated by the rise of what we call industrial music. The Goth scene had already embraced industrial wholeheartedly in the latter part of the 1980s, owing largely to parallels between the two, particularly

21st century Goth girls: New York City band the Nuns.

Trent Reznor – the melancholic maestro behind industrial rock phenomenon Nine Inch Nails.

their shared interest in the darker aspects of life – though Goth typically looks back with black nostalgia, while industrial is characterised by pessimism towards both the present and the future. Similarly, while Goth expresses itself in morbid metaphor and fearful fantasy, industrial wallows in life's harshest realities.

Yet industrial music was once an underground scene, existing way below the strata of the acceptable. This may come as a surprise to today's fledgling industrial fans, for whom it all began with Nine Inch Nails. As NIN mainman Trent Reznor observed, in the mid-1990s, 'There's a scene that's been flourishing for the past five years or more. Underground, club-orientated danceable music has been labelled "industrial" due to the lack of coming up with a new name. What was originally called industrial music was about twenty years ago, Throbbing Gristle and Test Department. We have very little to do with it other than there is noise in my music and there is noise in theirs.'

Throbbing Gristle are broadly agreed to have been the first industrial act, beginning as a side-project of the creative collective called Coum Transmissions. Coum had been inciting the artistic community with truly shocking performances of sex, self-mutilation and impenetrable pretension since 1969. Thirty years later, main man Genesis P-Orridge fondly recalled to UK paper *The Independent* that he used to 'do things like stick severed chickens' heads over my penis and then try to masturbate them, whilst pouring maggots all over it' (P-Orridge cited 'the psychic hygiene of the species' as his motivation, while Conservative MP, Nicholas Fairbairn, described him and his cohorts as 'wreckers of civilisation').

In 1976 P-Orridge formed Throbbing Gristle (slang for an erection – often shortened to TG), which was similarly designed to challenge concepts of what pop music, or music itself, was about. Concerts were often chaotic assaults on the audience, consisting of noise and disconcerting, free-form rants. One typical Throbbing Gristle 'song' is 'Hamburger Lady', which consists of P-Orridge reading the medical report of a woman who has suffered severe burns, after sunbathing in baking foil, accompanied by the electronically altered sound of a hunting horn. The object was not to entertain, but to provoke.

Throbbing Gristle's *avant-garde* outrage was too much for even the most broadminded of talent scouts, and so they started their own label: Industrial Records, named to comment on the way that a creative form like music had become merely an industry. 'Industrial Records began as an investigation,' wrote P-Orridge in the notes for a 1984 retrospective album. 'The four members of TG wanted to investigate to what extent you could mutate and collage sound, present complex non-entertaining noises to a popular culture situation . . . Our records were documents of attitudes and experiences and observations by us and other determinedly individual outsiders.'

The British music press began by labelling Throbbing Gristle and others working in this field of unsettling noise – such as English electronic experimentalists Cabaret Voltaire and American taboo-buster Monte Cazazza – as 'New Musick'. But this tag ended in the dustbin of history alongside 'positive punk', as the term 'industrial music', inspired by P-Orridge's label, entered common usage. According to V. Vale, editor of *The Industrial Culture Handbook* (1983), 'There is no strict unifying aesthetic, except that all things gross, atrocious, horrific, demented, and unjust are examined with black-humour eyes' – the area where Gothic and industrial aesthetics overlap.

As a growing number of people were beginning to accept, or even appreciate, Industrial Records' output, P-Orridge called a halt, sending a postcard to all interested parties in 1981 declaring, 'Throbbing Gristle: The Mission is Terminated'. As far as many purists are concerned, industrial music ceased to be at this point. The movement reached its climax at the 'Fetish Night Out' at London's Lyceum Ballroom, where TG performed on British soil for the last time on a bill with fellow industrial pioneers Non, Z'ev, Cabaret Voltaire and Clock DVA. The gig – including a 20-minute S&M-orientated piece entitled 'Discipline' – was recorded and later released as an album (*Once Upon a Time* in 1984) with liner notes describing how, outside the hall, 'a ragin' preacher protested about the contents of proceedings indoors. He bleated over his public address system, brandishing [sic] the participants and collected audience as "evil".' In the years that followed Genesis P-Orridge continued to promote taboo sexuality and fetishism on the underground – notably via the influential Re/Search book, *Modern Primitives* (1989), featuring an interview with P-Orridge and his wife Paula alongside graphic photos of their extensive body-piercings, tattoos and ritually applied scars.

The influence of TG refused to die, and the main man himself has ambivalent feelings about his hideous progeny. 'It had backfired to an extent,' he told Jon Savage in a recent interview, 'it had become impossible to distinguish between gratuitousness and seriousness. We'd left a rather unhealthy residue of people and ideas, albeit because people had chosen to misunderstand what we were saying. It got into this thing of who could shock each other the most, SPK doing videos of dead bodies, [or] Whitehouse for example, who I instantly and totally despised. Making a hole for these kind of people was scary.'

Other acts which fell under the spreading industrial banner in the 1980s are not so easy to dismiss – some of them still figure in Gothic record collections. Genesis himself formed Thee Temple Ov Psychick Youth (sic), an art movement-cum-1960s-psychotherapy-cult crossed with an occult order, with P-Orridge's new band, Psychic TV, as its self-styled 'propaganda unit'. During the 1980s, both these entities worked behind the scenes of youth culture, playing no small part in popularising the art of body piercing, and utilising acid-house music as a form of mind-altering ritual before it swept British mainstream culture. The PTV

The imperious Daniela Modolo, of apocalyptic folk band Von Thronstahl. Their orchestral anthems of pan-European nationalism have led to accusations of fascism.

package was an incongruous blend of psychedelia, death's-head skulls, pop and perversion, its sheer weirdness leading to an ill-founded police investigation of P-Orridge in 1992 (for 'satanic abuse') and a period of self-imposed exile. (Despite claims that both operated as collectives, the organisation and the band collapsed in his absence.)

Of the industrial bands that arose from the ashes of Throbbing Gristle, the most overtly Gothic were Coil, formed by ex-TG member Peter 'Sleazy' Christopherson. Preoccupied with taboos and the occult, Coil produced truly grim electronic journeys into hell and dark sonic invocations. Their Gothic credentials were confirmed when Clive Barker commissioned them to compose the soundtrack for his debut feature film, *Hellraiser*, in 1987. Coil's compositions proved too harrowing for the studio bosses, however, and Christopherson's crew were forced to title the recordings *Unreleased Themes from Hellraiser* – still regarded as among their best material.

Early material by David Tibet's Current 93 – *Nature Unveiled* (1984) and *Dog's Blood Rising* (1986) – joins Coil's output as among the most unsettling electronic music ever recorded. Tibet, who has made a career out of confounding expectations, then went on to release an album of acoustic folk music entitled *Swastikas for Noddy* (1987). 'I went through a period where I was just obsessed by [the children's story-book character] Noddy,' he explained to *Terrorizer*. 'I took some acid once and I saw Noddy crucified over the North London skyline being laughed at by elves. And the next morning I was really disturbed by that and started collecting everything to do with Noddy.'

Tibet's music has remained intensely odd and curiously personal ever since, reflecting a twisted sense of humour and the emotions of a man who says he's spent much of his life 'desperately unhappy'. It begged a new category, and many began describing Current 93 as 'apocalyptic folk'. Other bands that have shared Tibet's musical eclecticism and ominous outlook – such as Death in June, Sol Invictus and Nurse with Wound – have been variously labelled as apocalyptic folk, death industrial and dark ambient (sometimes cutely abbreviated as 'damnbient'). This incestuous subculture is often impenetrable or threatening – with accusations of black magic or fascism hounding many artists, because of their preoccupation with sinister imagery and taboo symbolism.

While the totalitarian overtones and abrasiveness of industrial imagery contrast sharply with Goth's cultivated, decadent mystique, by the end of the 1990s the two cults cross-bred. Test Department and Cabaret Voltaire had already enjoyed a sympathetic hearing at the Batcave in the early 1980s, while legendary German industrial metal-bangers, Einstürzende Neubauten, supported early über-Goths, Specimen, on their 1983 US tour – though, as guitarist, Jon Klein, later explained to *Orkus* magazine, some industrial musicians were more heavy-duty in their approach than synthesised dance-pioneers like Cabaret Voltaire (who had themselves begun as a more caustic concern, especially on the morbid 1981 album *Red Mecca*). 'They used jackhammers on the stage which was directly above our dressing room, causing the ceiling to completely crumble into the 40 cups of tequila and orange on the table,' he recalls of Neubauten's performance. 'They then managed to set fire to the stage which got quite out of control – none of the fire extinguishers in the theatre worked so we were pissing on the fire and using lager, and all in all it was a memorable night!' (Neubauten frontman, Blixa Bargeld, also took on a dual role as noise-guitarist of Nick Cave and the Bad Seeds.)

On the other side of the Atlantic, caustic chaos came in the form of Canada's leading industrial band, Skinny Puppy. Angry noise merchants, the sheer bile beneath their basic rhythmic skeleton and Throbbing Gristle-style barrage ensured that only the most dedicated cultist actually *enjoyed* Skinny Puppy. The closest the Canadians came to a dancefloor-friendly release was with *Rabies*, their 1989 collaboration with Cuban-born musician, Al Jourgensen. Something of a one-man industrial revolution, Jourgensen is best known for his Chicago-based outfit, Ministry, whose 1985 single, 'Every Day is Hallowe'en', took America's alternative club scene by storm with its Gothic overtones.

Ministry's style has been termed 'death disco' (a tag derived from Public Image Ltd. and formerly applied to Joy Division): descriptive of the way Jourgensen and accomplice Paul Barker bolted heavy metal guitars and a compelling beat onto an industrial chassis, to create a vehicle that didn't so much cross genre boundaries as crush them flat. Ministry generated an audio horror movie of epic proportions, one that lacked all of Goth's cultivated facade but, in the style of *The Texas Chainsaw*

Ministry's 1992 breakthrough album, Psalm 69.

Midnight Configuration, with Nightbreed label founder Trevor Bamford at the centre.
Bamford uses modern musical technology to conjure the dark Gothic aesthetic.

Massacre, was drenched in the blood and sickness that lies beneath. An evil sense of humour, epic substance abuse and a hellraising cowboy-biker image all fuelled the engine that ravished the alternative music scene with the 1988 album, *The Land of Rape and Honey*. By 1992, Ministry looked set for world domination with the release of the *Psalm 69* album, though industrial purists regarded their industrial-metal-dance crossover with suspicion. The follow-up, *Filth Pig*, did not surface for four years, largely due to Jourgensen's love of narcotics, and this silence was regarded as a sign that his juggernaut had run out of juice.

By this time, however, Trent Reznor and his project, Nine Inch Nails, were breaching the barrier between underground and dance styles, changing the landscape of contemporary music forever. 'Jourgensen has always brought a catchiness to his songs that Einstürzende Neubauten or Test Department or Throbbing Gristle, the classic industrial bands, don't,' claimed Reznor of his predecessor. 'I find a lot of [that music] unlistenable, [but] Ministry is like fucking good songs arranged in a way that could kick your ass.'

While Reznor exceeded the limits of his industrial ancestors by creating popular music with computerised technology, he took the stage looking very much the leather-clad Goth, complete with black lipstick and eyeliner. Reznor also brought a personal vulnerability to industrial music's defiant inhumanity. The result was multi-platinum-selling albums that won awards and topped polls in categories as diverse as heavy metal and dance.

Decay and collapse motivated his 1994 masterpiece, *The Downward Spiral*. 'I've done everything I ever wanted to and I'm still pretty miserable,' confessed Reznor – and he evidently wasn't on his own, as *The Downward Spiral*, a blizzard of suicidal self-loathing, charmed critics and fans alike. In 1994 Reznor was voted 'Artist of the Year' by *Musician* magazine, scooped 'Best Band', 'Best Album' and 'Best Live Act' in the *Alternative Press* polls, and was named one of the top ten entertainers of the year in *Entertainment Weekly*. The list goes on, astounding for an artist so preoccupied by trauma and decay. But Nine Inch Nails always were, Reznor has maintained, a pop band – albeit the first, as he observed of his 1992 track 'Wish', to win a Grammy for a song with the term 'fist fuck' in the lyrics.

Over the last decade, Goth bands such as Rosetta Stone have embraced the industrial elements popularised by NIN. France's Corpus Delicti moved into industrial territory with the CD *Syn:Drom*, while English arch-Goth Trevor Bamford describes his band Midnight Configuration as 'black industrial'. Contrary to all expectations, British artists Gary Numan and Depeche Mode have also been reinvented as the forefathers of 'cybergoth'.

After soaring into the UK album and singles charts in 1979 with his grim, futuristic sound, Numan's career had gone into freefall in the late 1980s. However, consistent name-checking by Trent Reznor, among others, brought Numan to the attention of a whole new generation a decade later. It culminated in the 2000 release of *Pure*, which received favourable critical comparisons with Reznor's *The Downward Spiral* – Numan freely confessing in turn that NIN was a big influence on his revitalised sound, this 'perfect circle' further represented by guitars creeping into the Numan mix while the Gothic performers who grew up on his music employed his former dark electronic approach.

Depeche Mode are perhaps the unlikeliest godfathers of Goth, although their contemporary influence is even greater than that of Numan. At the time of his debut album, *Replicas*, under the name Tubeway Army, Numan looked saturnine and strange with his bleached blond hair, black clothes, nail varnish and eye-liner, while the enigmatic, downbeat futurism of his first hit single, 'Are "Friends" Electric?', certainly fits the cybergoth ethos. By way of contrast, Depeche Mode looked, by their own admission, 'like dodgy New Romantics' at their 1980s peak, and started their career playing very lightweight synth-pop. However, according to songwriter, Martin Gore, who took over compositional duties in the mid-1980s, their new style was out to 'subtly corrupt the world'. *Terrorizer* agreed, noting how Depeche Mode's 'doom pop' reached its Gothic peak on the 1990 album *Violator*. 'Marilyn Manson, NIN, Paradise Lost – the Mode could eat them all for breakfast,' insists the magazine's Goth correspondent, Damien. 'It's pop but it's pitch black.'

And so the current Goth scene eagerly embraces the new technology and the possibilities it offers – particularly that of exploring dark territory while simultaneously enjoying commercial success. If the Sisters of Mercy seemed mildly innovative for anchoring their rock sound with a drum machine in the early 1980s, by the end of the 1990s it was becoming difficult to find a new Goth band where samplers and synths hadn't replaced guitars and drums. Goth planned to enter the 21st century looking forward.

As far as many Goths are concerned, heavy metal is the crass, crude, macho antithesis of everything that their music represents. The term is tantamount to an insult, used to dismiss

Black Sabbath *(1969) – sometimes called the first Gothic rock album – with the poster for the 1963 Mario Bava horror film that gave the heavy metal band their name.*

any aggressive-sounding or guitar-based band out of hand. However, a few bold souls have identified Black Sabbath's eponymous 1969 debut album as the first ever 'Goth-rock' record. Its title track describes a satanic rite, complete with driving-rain and tolling bell sound effects, while the cover focuses on a black-cloaked, spectral-looking girl in a graveyard, shot through a sickly pale ochre filter. The gatefold sleeve opens to reveal a prose poem framed within an inverted cross: 'Still falls the rain, the veils of darkness shroud the blackened trees, which, contorted by some unseen violence, shed their tired leaves, and bend their boughs toward a grey earth of severed bird wings.' A tad ham-fisted, perhaps – but unquestionably 'Gothic as fuck'.

Black Sabbath's closest American equivalents, Blue Oyster Cult, sometimes used noted fantasy authors, such as Gothic horror-cyberpunk writer John Shirley, as lyricists. Although their occasional tendency to lapse into radio-friendly, soft-rock balladry would seem to brand them as terminally unhip, it also brought them their 1976 hit single 'Don't Fear the Reaper' – a haunting, suicidal serenade to Death himself. There were raised eyebrows aplenty when Lydia Lunch and Clint Ruin covered the song in 1991, but this morbid mini-masterpiece has subsequently been covered by acts as diverse as English electro-rockers Apollo 440, pop-Goths HIM (whose tattooed, top-hatted front-man Ville Valo is a parochial rock god in his native Finland), and arty American Goth duo Thanatos.

English band, Iron Maiden, made forays into Gothic territory, such as loose adaptations of *The Phantom of the Opera*, Poe's 'The Murders in the Rue Morgue' and Coleridge's eerie poem 'The Rime of the Ancient Mariner'. Original black metal band Venom had traces of a Gothic sensibility ('I drink the vomit of priests, make love to the dying whore,' began the blurb on the back of their 1982 *Black Metal* album), but it was almost eclipsed by punk-style shock squalor and an ugly streak of misogyny. Danish metal vocalist King Diamond issued a series of concept albums which told Gothic horror tales with sound effects and song – such as the haunted house saga, *Abigail* (1986), or *Conspiracy* (1989), where a devilish doctor sedates the protagonist before burning him alive in a coffin. Only a handful of the more broadminded Goths ever confessed to a weakness for such histrionic horror-rock – perhaps most significantly, respected American Goth duo, Midnight Syndicate (whose spooky symphonies make them bestsellers at Hallowe'en), have credited both Black Sabbath and King Diamond as seminal influences.

By the early 1990s, however, the more inventive and ambitious heavy metal bands began welcoming a diverse range of new sounds into their work. Among these fresh factors were female vocals, keyboards, classical flourishes, even poetry. The most credible 1990s metal was moving in an unmistakably Gothic direction, tempering testosterone with a welcome dose of sensitivity.

Previously, only death rock veteran Glenn Danzig, the unmistakably masculine ex-Misfit, had occupied the no man's land between Goth and heavy metal. In 1988, his band, Samhain, had become the eponymous Danzig, the diminutive, muscle-bound vocalist adding blues as black as Mississippi mud to bombastic, Black Sabbath-style riffs to create a demonic gumbo too rich for many rock palates. The press derided him as an 'Evil Elvis' for his creepy crooned vocals and infernal lyrics – but this was the basic recipe for Gothic metal, a black oasis of creativity. While Danzig's machismo has not endeared him to Goth audiences, even the most adamantly anti-guitar snobs may find themselves won over by his *Black Aria* – a 1992 quasi-classical solo album of instrumentals depicting Satan's fall from grace.

Gothic metal, as a musical style, truly began in the early 1990s in the north of England. Three bands – Anathema, Paradise Lost, and My Dying Bride – represent the core of the movement. All three had roots in frenetically abrasive death metal, but they

As the Flower Withers – *the 1992 debut album by British Gothic metal act* My Dying Bride *(right), featuring a cover by cult artist Dave McKean.*

were also influenced by what Paradise Lost vocalist, Nick Holmes, described as 'the really bleak, dark sound' of Dead Can Dance. They were characterised by romantic melancholy rather than aggression, and all found a home with the northern English Peaceville label where they pioneered a new style which many music journalists characteristically stereotyped as 'doom metal'. (Both Paradise Lost and My Dying Bride also employed Dave McKean – the cult comic artist so highly regarded on the Goth scene – to create sleeve art.)

Paradise Lost's 1991 second album title, *Gothic*, was surely a statement of intent. 1993 saw Anathema release their debut album *Serenades*, while My Dying Bride unleashed their second, *Turn Loose the Swans*, which many fans regard as their finest collection of sweeping

*Eclectic Italian metal band Lacuna Coil, whose ethereal rock-romanticism has
won them favour among many Goths.*

melancholia and gloomy grandiosity. All three bands deserve to be taken more seriously by the international Goth fraternity than the 'metal' tag might suggest. As vocalist Nick Holmes puts it, 'there was always a fine line between Iron Maiden and the Sisters of Mercy.'

Other European nations began contributing to the burgeoning Gothic metal movement: Sweden's Cemetery had released one unremarkable death metal album before their criminally underrated Goth-metal epic, 1993's *Godless Beauty*. Cemetery mastermind Mathias Lodmalm followed it up the following year with the equally impressive *Black Vanity* – in both cases, in contrast to the orchestral embellishments adopted by the English, the Swedes bolstered their atmospheric hard rock with horror-movie samples. Dutch band the Gathering also erupted from death-metal roots, but secured the services of female vocalist Anneke von Giersbergen for their third album, *Mandylion* (1995). Once again, their introspective atmosphere owed a creative debt to Dead Can Dance, and established them as a leading band in their native Holland.

Italy's Lacuna Coil ('empty spiral') featured female vocalist Cristina Scabbia, who like Ataraxia's Francesca Nicoli, has attracted complimentary comparisons with Kate Bush. Superficially similar in style to the maudlin experimental rock of the Gathering, Lacuna Coil have remained more faithful to their metal roots by retaining Andrea Ferro on vocals – his rough tones providing an aggressive counterpoint to Scabbia's seductiveness: gruff majesty set against melodic yearning. Portugal's Moonspell (another of the European bandmates on Century Media, which has established itself as the home of intelligent, atmospheric European rock) were formed from the ashes of death metal act Morbid God, in 1992, adding a keyboard player and – inspired by the ubiquitous Dead Can Dance – traditional melodies from the Middle East and their native land. Their 1995 debut album, *Wolfheart*, caused a minor sensation on the European underground with its epic metallic hymns to a forgotten, blood-hungry goddesses of fertility, ancient wars in the band's Iberian homeland, a 'werewolf masquerade' and a love song to 'Vampiria' (sic). Moonspell reinforced their position as heralds of the Gothic metal movement with *Irreligious*, which included verse by the obscure Portugese Decadent poet, Fernando Pessoa, and a demonic address from 'the angel who dresses in red', Mephisto.

'In the end we almost ended up doing something that was almost anti-Moonspell to get away from it,' disillusioned singer Fernando Ribiero told *Terrorizer*. 'We have never been so tired of an image as we were when this whole Gothic Metal thing blew up, because it brought so many bad bands, and lots of cheesy music, and when you mix dark and cheesy, it's the worst thing you can do!' All the Gothic metal bands covered here subsequently recorded albums designed to challenge these preconceptions, drawing on the inspiration of Depeche Mode and Nine Inch Nails.

By the mid-1990s, a new wave of black metal had replaced death metal as the extreme style of choice on the heavy metal underground. With its occultic obsessions, this style inevitably has Gothic overtones – although the influence of Venom usually ensures they are buried under furious guitar and antisocial attitudes. As the genre matured, however, so did some of black metal's more accomplished exponents, although only the more open-minded or younger people who first embraced Goth culture in the 1990s, warmed to such developments. (Although mainland Europe is a more fertile breeding ground for performers who add heavy metal guitars to the Gothic sensibility – British Goth-metal bands like Paradise Lost enjoy a better reputation away from home.)

Scandinavia quickly established itself as the heartland of the black metal revival, with some of the most overtly Gothic material produced by Swedish bands like Tiamat. The trio's 1999 release, *Skeleton Skeletron*, had critics comparing the vocals of singer-songwriter Johan Edlund with those of Sisters supremo Andrew Eldritch, alongside musical comparisons to Nick Cave and the Bad Seeds – remarkable for a metal band. Fellow Swedes Katatonia have also nonplussed metal purists, while attracting the attention of broad-minded Goths with *Brave*

Murder Day (1996), which owes as much creatively to the Cure and the Fields of the Nephilim as it does to more traditional metal influences. 'Heavy music with a dark and morose edge,' is as far as Katatonia guitarist Anders Nystrom is willing to go in categorising the band's recent output, which has simultaneously seen them becoming more mellow and more maudlin.

One band who have yet to mellow, but whose success has attracted charges of 'selling out'

British black metal band Cradle of Filth – with frontman Dani Filth, enthroned – won success by introducing a decadent horror aesthetic to their savage guitar sound.

from the black metal faithful, are Britain's Cradle of Filth. Retaining black metal's distinctive angry guitars and tortured vocals, they have also made good use of strong, although sometimes clichéd, Gothic imagery, ever since their 1994 debut album *The Principle of Evil Made Flesh* – initially courtesy of designer Nigel Wingrove, whose distinctive blend of blasphemy, blood and breasts helped to get the band noticed. It also helped to get ex-Filth drummer, Nick Barker, arrested in 1998 for wearing the band's notorious 'Jesus is a Cunt' T-shirt.

Musically, Cradle of Filth clearly want to bridge the gap between atmospheric Gothic romance and metal mayhem, citing brutal black metal bands, Bathory and Celtic Frost, alongside literary luminaries Lord Byron, J. Sheridan LeFanu, Bram Stoker and Charles Baudelaire as influences. Over the years, the band's outspoken vocalist, Dani Filth, has employed keyboard veterans from Gothic metal pioneers, Anathema and My Dying Bride, to strengthen his proposed marriage of satanic savagery and Goth sophistication – without achieving the sublime synthesis of power and mood of either at their best.

Horror movie legend Ingrid Pitt was also employed to provide voiceovers on *Cruelty and the Beast*, their concept album inspired by the life and crimes of the sixteenth-century Transylvanian Countess, Erzebet Bathori. Their 2000 album, *Midian*, its title track inspired by Clive Barker's novel *Cabal* (filmed disappointingly as *Nightbreed* in 1990), utilised the vocal talents of actor Doug Bradley – who attained cult status in Barker's series of *Hellraiser* movies as Pinhead, leader of the sadomasochistic Cenobites. Most recently, Dani Filth has starred in *Cradle of Fear* – a British-made, low-budget horror movie, featuring cameos from his band-mates. The film is an anthology of four stories, wrapped in a linking narrative concerning a cannibalistic psycho hell-bent on visiting vengeance on his enemies, despite being incarcerated in a sanitorium. *Cradle of Fear* is a self-conscious tribute to the horror anthologies made in the 1970s by British studio Amicus – which now enjoy cult status – such as *Asylum*. Unrepentantly gory and somewhat camp, it is aimed at a cult audience.

Cradle of Filth frontman Dani resembles an impishly evil version of the Crow, in low-budget Brit horror flick Cradle of Fear *(2002).*

America, meanwhile, has made a comparatively limited contribution to the Gothic metal crossover. This is, at least in part, a reflection of the cultural status of heavy metal. Ever since the 1970s, courtesy of Kiss, it's been the USA's semi-respectable soundtrack to teen rebellion, and is therefore less likely to crossbreed with such a self-consciously underground style. Nevertheless, Type O Negative, a New York quartet, are just as controversial in their own way as Cradle of Filth. The band themselves don't embrace the 'Gothic metal' tag, preferring homegrown categories like 'gothadelic' as a reflection of their penchant for covering upbeat rock classics – like the Beatles' 'Day Tripper' – in such a downbeat tone as to render them suicidally miserable. The self-styled 'Drab Four' have bewildered their many critics, while delighting converts to their unique blend of black humour and even blacker depression.

Type O Negative were always going to be a contentious proposition – not least because of their imposing frontman, Peter Steele, an intimidatingly large, sarcastically self-deprecating original, whose dry, dirty one-liners and morbid machismo challenge those who insist the

Peter Steele – of New York's 'drab four', Type O Negative – finds a novel, if sacrilegious, use for a crucifix.

archetypal Goth is a po-faced androgyne. Steele's background with Carnivore – a notorious New York hardcore metal outfit, who seemed to regard political incorrectness as a mission statement – didn't help his case either. But the surprise success of Type O Negative's third album, *Bloody Kisses* (1993), obliged Goths to take notice. 'Black No. 1' (its title a reference to a hair-dye favoured by Goths), subtitled 'Little Miss Scare-All', surely qualifies as one of the pre-eminent Goth anthems of the 1990s, eulogising an archetypal Goth chick in a tone of affectionate parody: 'She's got a date at midnight / With Nosferatu,' sings Steele in his sepulchral baritone, 'Oh baby, Lily Munster/ Ain't got nothing on you.' Though Steele has his tongue firmly in his cheek here, there is real sincerity in some of his bombastically bleak compositions – particularly on the 1999 album, *World Coming Down*, with tracks like the morose meditation on cocaine addiction, 'White Slavery'.

Rob Zombie is another artist whose metallic roots have divorced him from the Goth scene, despite some decidedly Gothic preoccupations. His sleazy, comic-book version of the dark side was too loud and lurid for the underground's more dignified denizens, but it has proved to be a contagious hit with a horde of fans. The eponymous Zombie made his debut as lead singer with White Zombie (whose name was taken from a 1932 Bela Lugosi movie) in the mid-1990s, with albums like *Astro-Creep 2000* (1995) combining B-movie horror samples, creepy pop art-style visuals (by Zombie himself) and a grindhouse guitar groove. The album went double platinum, but White Zombie's chief draw was the lead singer who, with his bellicose beard, dreadlocks and undead pallor, looks like a supercharged version of Charles Manson revamped for a drive-in monster movie (Zombie sampled the notorious killer's ranting on the 1991 album, *La Sexorcisto: Devil Music Vol 1*).

In 1999, he was commissioned to design a walk-through horror maze for the Universal Studios theme park, confirming his status as successor to Alice Cooper as America's clown prince of darkness. Zombie admitted, 'ever since I was a little kid I wanted to be Alice' – and fulfilled a lifelong ambition by duetting with him on 'The Hand of Death', for an *X-Files* episode in 1996. The success of his horror maze, and acclaimed production work on a number of rock videos, convinced Universal to commission Zombie to write and direct a movie entitled *The House of 1000 Corpses*. The results, however, showed that this Zombie didn't lack teeth, and the film currently remains in limbo – proving a little too much for the studio, which sheepishly confessed that the finished product had 'a visceral tone and intensity that we did not imagine from the printed page.'

Few topics are as hotly debated in the

Marilyn Manson – routinely dubbed a 'Goth superstar' by the mass media, but vehemently disowned by many within the Goth subculture.

Goth subculture as the issue of which bands are, or most definitely are *not*, authentically Gothic. This debate, alongside the dismissive attitude towards the subculture (and therefore the audiences) displayed by many of the most influential Goth bands means that music, while being the backbone of modern Gothic culture, has become a divisive factor. Marilyn Manson emerged from the Florida underground, but his rise to international stardom in the late 1990s, caused a rift from his Gothic roots. Most post-teen Goths began to regard Manson and his band as somehow bogus, a troublesome cuckoo in the Gothic nest. For his part, the singer began eyeing the Goth scene with the archly ironic disdain for which he was notorious – depicting it squalidly in his 1998 shock-rock confessional, *The Long Hard Road Out of Hell*, in which only he himself is subjected to greater indignities than the band's black-clad Goth following, who are bound, spat upon and subjected to sexual humiliation. Manson also depicts New Orleans, America's Gothic mecca, in less than flattering terms, calling it a soul-stealing 'cesspool', which turned Marilyn Manson and his compatriots into 'walking clichés, parodies of ourselves.' A divorce was inevitable, as Manson's material made the journey from Goth and industrial to the rock and metal sections of the world's CD emporia. It's undeniable, however, that the band's early visuals and imagery – creepy carnivals and poisonous playfulness – have leaked into the Goth underground, whether purists like it or not.

Antichrist Superstar, recorded in New Orleans, was the 1996 album that transformed Marilyn Manson from a cult band into an international phenomenon. It was also Manson's most overtly Gothic release, overflowing with Crowley references, fallen angels, occultic symbolism, drug-fuelled despair and dark introspection, all wrapped in the blistering industrial cocoon of Trent Reznor's production. Ironically, it was also the album that put the seal on Manson's divorce from the Goth scene, its aggressive guitar sound giving ammunition to those who dismissed the band as 'heavy metal'. Perhaps most damning, as far as the guardians of Goth's underground status were concerned, were the *Rolling Stone* covers and MTV appearances that followed, the result of Manson's calculated promotion to the mainstream. His growing youth following, the 'Spooky Kids', were callow embarrassments to the subculture's carefully cultivated ethos of sophistication. Manson's own pronouncements on inflammatory topics such as sex, drugs and violence were also regarded as somehow indicative of Goths, most of whom had little interest in or sympathy for him. His 1998 follow-up, *Mechanical Animals*, was on the surface his least Gothic outing, though beneath its futuristic synth-pop veneer lurked themes of altered states, esoteric symbolism and painful self-discovery – with the obvious influences of David Bowie's decadent glam rock and Gary Numan's pessimistic synth-pop.

Martino Diablo has been involved with Goth 'crossover' acts such as Atrophy of Faith, Deadboy Craved, Necromantik and – his current and most exciting incarnation – Katscan. Most have worn their diverse influences on their sleeves – musical demolition derbies where synth-pop, heavy metal and techno have collided to entertaining effect. Indeed, not even the taboo Marilyn Manson is exempt from their myriad influences. 'It's so funny how upset people get about Marilyn Manson and other crossover bands or artists,' Diablo told *Meltdown* magazine in 2000. 'It's that whole thing you get in music scenes that consider themselves to be underground in some way, then when an artist sells more than 1,000 copies of an album they are branded a sell-out.'

Richard C. – the Nightbreed label's A&R man, as well as a member, at various times, of Goth groups Midnight Configuration, Upside Jesus and 'techno-folk Goth-noise' band Serotonin – has also witnessed this inverse snobbery. 'Mainstream popular approval often seems to alienate Goths,' he told me in 2001, 'as Goths are generally narcissistic, opinionated, intelligent and fucked-up individuals – but I love 'em! One can never categorise their music without someone complaining!'

It's now harder to cite music that hasn't been dubbed 'Gothic', or adopted by the Goth

Martino Diablo, self-proclaimed 'electropunk scum', of Katscan. Diablo is a high-tech Dr Frankenstein, creating his musical identity from diverse stolen parts.

scene at some point, than to identify music that has. But surely the redneck world of country and western, for example, is the very antithesis of effete Goth? Except that perennially depressed country's recent resurgence has featured respected acts like the Handsome Family, whose gloomy introspection has led many to dub them 'Gothic country'. How about reggae, a laidback sound whose evocation of Caribbean sunshine is a million miles from the chilly graveyards of Goth's clichéd spiritual home? Even here, according to Ian Shirley in *Dark Entries*, his biography of Goth pioneers Bauhaus, 'Bauhaus had taken the technique, structure, space and sound used in reggae and managed to combine it with their own ideas in order to formulate the band's influential approach.' This improbable reggae-Goth crossbreed is perhaps most evident on the Bauhaus track, 'Exquisite Corpse' – originally a game played by many famous surrealist artists, using pen and paper to make nonsense-figure drawings, it also lent its name to the novel by Poppy Z. Brite – and in the dub influence lurking in the rhythmic shadows of 'Bela Lugosi's Dead'.

This bewildering diversity has been taken on board by those catering to the Goth marketplace. Cheeky Monkey is an English record distributor and mail order firm affiliated with the organisers of the biannual Whitby Gothic Weekend (Whitby is the small Yorkshire fishing town where Dracula landed in Bram Stoker's 1897 novel). The festival has run since 1994 and is an important date in the Goth calendar. Cheeky Monkey's catalogue divides almost evenly into 'alternative, goth & credible' and '80s, pop & cheese' – reflecting a subjective approach founded on

Lisa Ross of orchestral Goth rockers Brother Orchid. Their debut album, Winter Shadow, *was inspired by the eighteenth century's Hellfire Club.*

humour and irony rather than a taste for darkness.

As a cultural barometer, UK Goth label Nightbreed has issued sampler CDs, featuring bands on its own label as well as friends and fellow travellers. By the third album, the series title, *The Gothic Sounds of Nightbreed*, had a question mark added after the word 'Gothic'. The suggested alternative in Richard C.'s liner notes is 'dark alternative'. He told me that 'the general negative attitude towards all things "Gothic" has led to a splintering of the Goth scene.' He continued to describe how from the early days, when Alien Sex Fiend were calling themselves 'positive punk', until nowadays, when Andrew Eldritch's contract prohibits the use of the word 'Gothic' in any publicity, people have tried to escape the confines of what is referred to in the sleeve-notes as the 'G-Tag'. No-one wants to be categorised – particularly in a scene which promotes individualism and experimentation – nor constrained by a word that every individual interprets differently. This has led to the almost comic proliferation of prefixes and suffixes to the word 'Goth': Rock, Punk, Industrial, Metal, Techno, Electro and so on, creating a host of sub-categories, ironically comprehensible only to those pigeon-holed by the very 'G-Tag' they seek to escape. Richard's current personal favourite, suggested by the band, Katscan, is 'Goth-hop'!

So what of traditional Goth rock, in its British birthplace in the 1990s? 'Towards the end of the 1980s the entire British mass media turned against the Gothic scene very quickly and very viciously,' recalls Trevor Bamford, then in a Goth band called Every New Dead Ghost. 'Suddenly, if you were a band tarred with the "Gothic" tag you could absolutely forget all the usual help that up-and-coming bands got at that time. That, in real terms, meant no John Peel radio sessions, no kind of press coverage at all, not even a mention in gig guides! . . . definitely no chance of TV coverage . . . it is actually only [in] our country – the UK – that things became so extreme. In places like Germany, in particular, there was no discrimination against artists who were connected to the Gothic genre. To the German press, all art was entitled to a fair shake of the stick. Whereas over here, it was near impossible to do anything at all!'

If anything, Goth became a stronger beast as a result of its years in the wilderness. Germany was fast becoming the international home of the Goth scene. It has always been particularly fertile soil for the Gothic aesthetic – many regard German composer E. T. A. Hoffmann's adult fairy tales of the early 1800s as the first horror stories; the book that inspired the 1816 Villa Diodati ghost-story competition that spawned *Frankenstein* was a translated German anthology entitled *Tales of the Dead*; the original horror movies were the silent expressionist classics of the 1920s. Going back even further, the original Goths sprang from the region before striking out in the third century BC!

German Goth rockers included the guitar-oriented Dreadful Shadows, or House of Usher (formed in 1990 by Gothic novelist Jorg Kleudgen, whose vocals invoked the spirit of Joy Division's Ian Curtis). The Merry Thoughts, Germany's answer to the Sisters of Mercy, had a sound so close to Eldritch's outfit that reviews frequently cited their material as the best Sisters songs the Sisters never recorded. (Their excellent 1993 ode to the ultimate *femme fatale*, 'Pale Empress', still fills Goth dancefloors.)

German stalwarts Girls Under Glass, began in 1987, described to Australia's Infectious Unease radio show, by guitarist Axel Ermes, as 'a kind of slow version of Sisters of Mercy,

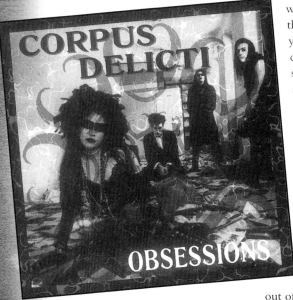

with keyboards, drum-machine (not faster than 80 bpm!), guitar and vocals.' Over the years, Girls Under Glass have perfected a catalogue of pop-Goth-rock and danceable synth-pop, inspired, according to Ermes, by sources as diverse as the cyberpunk movie *Blade Runner*, the Gothic horror fiction of H. P. Lovecraft and Stephen King, 'and last but not least personal experiences, the weather, naked girls in handcuffs.'

Garden of Delight (G.O.D.) were founded in Germany in 1991 by Artaud Franzmann, alongside an Italian named Pisacane and a drum machine called the Watchtower. Franzmann described the G.O.D. sound to *Cynfeirdd* magazine as 'very romantic indeed. Dark and distorted, malicious and foreign, born out of the depths of a sick soul.' G.O.D. are a fine example of those bands who used the template abandoned by England's Goth-rock pioneers of the 1980s as a springboard to explore the bizarre dimensions only hinted at in their guitar invocations. Nephilim influences are also obvious in parts, although the German takes his Crowley and Lovecraft flavoured occult themes even further than Carl McCoy – indeed, Franzmann vowed that Garden of Delight would record only seven albums, containing seven tracks each, over a period of seven years, as part of a mystic progression. Just as Crowley believed publishing limited editions of his work was a potent ritual act in itself, so Franzmann's occult art, his music, centres around the mystical figure of '7'.

Love is Colder than Death have been described as a German Dead Can Dance. Formed in 1990, the quartet is schizophrenic in style, oscillating between lush, organic melody and cold, metallic moments – according to their label, Metropolis, 'the voices of the Dark Ages whispering across the centuries.'

Project Pitchfork, formed in 1989, are among the foremost exponents of the danceable Teutonic electro style referred to as darkwave, or EBM (Electronic Body Music), that came to dominate many Goth clubs in the late 1990s. While Project Pitchfork combine brooding lyrics with classical undertones, the defining characteristics of EBM are hoarse Germanic vocals and the driving electronic dance beat that steered the Goth club scene away from the stately 'taffy-pulling' of the 1980s towards the more energetic approach found in most dance clubs and raves.

Love Like Blood are a more traditional German Goth-rock act, whose early material bore comparison with the Fields of the Nephilim. Formed in 1988, and centred around the Eysel brothers, singer Yorck and bassist Gunnar, they recently released their *Chronology of a Love Affair* album, dedicated 'to ourselves, to Gothic music and its scene in general.' Its sixteen tracks chart the development of the music with covers of all of the major exponents and influences, from Joy Division, Bauhaus and Killing Joke (from whose song the band took their name) to Gothic metal acts like Tiamat and Type O Negative – though, perversely, the Eysels have reservations about the scene, Gunnar claiming, 'I don't take Goth as seriously as maybe our fans do.'

The continental Goth scene has long been dominated by Dutch band Clan of Xymox – late additions to English label 4AD's Goth-friendly roster of ethereal and ambient acts. Xymox's sundry pop-Goth adventures into darkness – which evoke the Cure as often as their 4AD labelmates – are a refuge from bitter existence for the band as well as their audiences. 'I try to escape from reality as much as possible. I really don't like reality,' founder, and only permanent member, Ronny Moorings has admitted. 'I just like songs with that dark mood.'

The French Goth scene spawned Corpus Delicti in 1992. Influenced by Bauhaus, their Gothic characteristics are more overt than those of their more self-conscious inspiration. As with the German bands, this inventive French act developed its own distinctive voice – one with a Gallic accent, very effective for evoking French Decadence. Their 1995 album, *Obsessions*, moved even sceptical commentators like *Trouser Press* magazine to concede that vocalist Sebastian's French Pete Murphy impersonations had 'that crucial swoon factor'.

In the USA, the main factor in the 1990s Goth-rock revival was the foundation of California-based Cleopatra Records in 1992, by fan and entrepreneur Brian Perera. Cleopatra have helped numerous excellent new European acts like Corpus Delicti reach an American audience, while making seminal recordings by the likes of Specimen available to the CD generation for the first time. Cleopatra's main rival is Sam Rosenthal's Projekt Records. Like Nightbreed, Rosenthal's company began as a labour of love that released his own group's material and that of affiliated bands. Rosenthal's band, Black Tape for a Blue Girl, played a style he described as 'darkwave' rather than Goth – luxuriantly maudlin music that eschews any rock trappings in favour of an acoustic or electronic-based approach. Rosenthal was attempting to coin a term that captured the brooding musical melancholia he favoured. European Goths, however, adopted the term as a catch-all for EBM, or dark-tinged techno, evoking the smell of sweat and PVC on the club dancefloor rather than Projekt's aroma of incense smoke and dead flowers.

Projekt's first release, in 1989, was the third album by Black Tape for a Blue Girl, *Ashes in the Bitter Air*, which *Alternative Press* described as the sound of a 'precariously desperate soul hanging beneath hope by a frayed thread.' 'As we postmodernists shuffle off our mortal coil,' observed a review in the *LA Weekly*, 'our demise will undoubtedly be scored to one of the many 4AD releases that have defined bad-mood music in the late eighties. Until now, we've had to import our choler and phlegm from that fine English label, but Black Tape for a Blue Girl do a reasonable approximation of the 4AD vibe.' During the 1990s, while Cleopatra bought the rights to the Gothic elements of 4AD's back catalogue, Projekt stole their title as the Goth mecca for ambient and ethereal music. Lycia, Projekt's first outside signing, were hailed approvingly by Type O Negative's notoriously downbeat Peter Steele as 'the most depressing thing I've ever heard in my life'.

London After Midnight had a more traditional take on the Gothic aesthetic, outspoken founder Sean Brennan initially motivated by the desire to bring a little sophistication and darkness to LA's traditionally glam and metal-dominated rock scene. 'At the time every musician in LA was into Guns N' Roses and I hated that garbage,' he told *Meltdown* magazine.

In 1990 his androgynous male glamour pusses – all eye-liner, lipstick and shiny stiletto-heels, posing in midnight black with feisty pouts – were the first act to play Helter Skelter, the club that would become the home of Hollywood Goth.

London After Midnight shows are Gothic spectaculars, featuring home-made horror props such as a 40-foot spider's web. Despite such cobweb and candelabra visuals, Brennan dismisses those Goths who refuse to evolve 'past the Sisters, past the 1980s'. Brennan, a vegan, also claims 'the whole vampire thing is incredibly boring and we've never been a part of it' – a reaction, no doubt, to early suggestions that London After Midnight were part of the blood-drinking fraternity (though naming the band after the first Hollywood vampire epic can't

British Goth rockers Killing Miranda, *whose* Blessed Deviant *album includes the necrophiliac love ballad 'Burn Sinister' (sung from the corpse's perspective).*

have done much to dissuade).

On the other side of the US, the 1990s New York Goth scene's most outrageous denizens were the Empire Hideous, the deranged death rock legend founded in 1988 by superlatively strange singer Myke Hideous. Their reputation rested solidly on the band's sanity-shaking live performances before a backdrop of skulls and smoke, described in press releases as 'a mad doctor extracting guts from a Hallowe'en pumpkin, an invalid confined to a wheelchair stroking his long dead kitty cat Spooky, his re-enactment of Christ getting whipped (for real!) in time to the *Jesus Christ Superstar* cover "The 39 Lashes", sucking the blood from lifelike babies, and having his face pierced with hypodermic needles.' *Lollipop* magazine hailed their 1994 release, *Only Time Will Tell*, as 'Noble, anthemic songs that communicate a brooding desire, a vague desperation . . . This is the music of leather manacles and slow bleeding.' The Empire Hideous fell briefly when Myke briefly joined re-formed death rock legends, the Misfits, in 1998, replacing

Myke Hideous, undisputed ruler of New York's Empire Hideous, takes the trappings of horror rock to their logical extreme.

former lead Glen Danzig, though they have since reformed in early 2002.

The Shroud first appeared on Hallowe'en 1991, descending from campy vampire roots into a more broad-based Gothic outfit. Lead singer Lydia Fortner told me that the band 'began as the Shroudettes (three Goth gals up front) – it was more stereotypically death rock, and we were definitely Anne Rice fans. Our stage names had last names like de Lioncourt and Lestat . . . I wanted to do something more serious, so we became the Shroud and got way more arty, using musical quotes from Chopin and Stravinsky in some instances' (though those songs didn't get recorded, unfortunately). Fortner explained to *Propaganda* magazine in 1992 that she wanted both their songs and presentation to reflect her more esoteric influences, 'such as Gothic and Victorian literature, the symbolism of the alchemical arts, and mysticism of the medieval Christian heresies. As a whole, we wanted to have a more mystical and medieval outlook.' The pensive acoustic moments and soaring, melancholy vocals of what Lydia Fortner describes as 'dark, evocative brood rock' create the Shroud's anachronistic private world.

In England, Nosferatu released their debut EP, *Hellhound*, in 1991. 'We're taking the Gothic label a lot more seriously than a lot of our peer bands,' guitarist, founder member and band hearse-driver Damien DeVille told me. 'A lot of them used punk for an inspiration, but we're much too young for that. We're more into backing choir sounds, things like that, and the demonic power that builds up from it.' Nosferatu offer plenty for unrepentant Goths to get their teeth into: classic Hammer-horror themes, gloriously over-the-top Gothic imagery and a guitar-based sound, haunted by spooky samples. Nosferatu are 'Gothic as fuck' – a guilty graveyard pleasure for some, but too much for those who regard the traditional Gothic aesthetic as an outdated cliché.

But the most successful of the 1990s British Goth rock bands was Rosetta Stone (named after the black slab that bore the first translated ancient Egyptian hieroglyphics). Formed as a duo by Porl King and Karl North, who came together in 1987, while sales of their 1991 *Eye for the Main Chance* debut album, and accompanying singles 'Leave Me for Dead' and

Archetypal cybergoths Goteki: this cartoon, by the band's sample-maestro Dr A (left) also features vocalist Mr Sneakybat (centre) and keyboardist Crash 303.

'The Witch', were very encouraging, the band hit a brick wall as far as promotion was concerned as a result of accepting what they called 'the Goth dollar'.

Industrial influences then came to dominate Rosetta Stone's work, but it was also evident that the band had hit the glass ceiling erected to restrict the success of Goth bands. By the time they played their last performance as a duo, on Hallowe'en 1998, it was difficult to find a Goth band who were *not* flaunting industrial influences. Nosferatu stood out from their more credible British rivals for 'the Goth dollar' – most notably Suspiria and Children on Stun – by refusing to be seduced by stylistic fads or new musical technology. Instead, they remained faithful to the undiluted Gothic aesthetic of the past 250 years, and, perhaps significantly, were one of the few 1990s British Goth bands to survive into the 21st century.

The final years of the twentieth century saw the rise of the cybergoth. Industrial music has provided the masculine animus to Goth's more feminine anima, in the way that an arranged marriage between Goth and metal never quite has. 'I view Industrial and Gothic to be two sides to the same coin – the yin and yang, the male and female,' writes Alicia Porter in her on-line *Study of Gothic Subculture*. 'Gothic expresses the emotional, beautiful, supernatural, feminine, poetic, theatrical side and Industrial embodies the masculine, angry, aggressive, noisy, scientific, technological, political side. Industrial music often uses electronics, synthesizers, samples from movies or political speeches, loops, and distorted vocals. It tends to be male dominated in those who make the music and those who enjoy it.'

According to the *Cybergothic Nexus* site, cybergoth's genesis dates from no earlier than 1995 – though traces of its roots can be found as far back as the early 1980s Batcave heyday of Alien Sex Fiend, whose colourful irreverence and early adoption of electro-dance stylings predated cybergoth by at least a decade. However, the advent of an affiliated subculture, which threatens to dominate its Gothic parent, is very much an end of millennium phenomenon. 'The ideals surrounding, and fascination with, such topics as computers, the internet, technology, cybernetic/bionic augmentation and artificial intelligence have all been borrowed from the cyber side,' reads the *Nexus* site. 'From the goth side, cybergoth has borrowed its sense of apathy (mostly towards issues cyberpunks would be enraged about), questioning of mortality especially with regards to augmentation and AI [artificial intelligence] (not the usual goth obsession with death, but more with what constitutes life) . . .'

There was much crossover between the futuristic chic of 'cybergoths' and the ironic kitsch of 'perkygoths'. British Goth funsters Sneaky Bat Machine became the embodiment of the new crossbreed, their frontman, Mr Sneakybat, describing their material in a 1998 interview with Scottish Goth 'zine *Naked Truth* as 'outrageously cheesy, but in a postmodern ironic nineties "Ooh look at me I aren't I bloody clever" kind of way.' This attitude was summed up by their 1999 album, *Disco 4 the Dead*, which Sneakybat described as 'Gothic yet space age, cartoony but twisted.' In 2001 the band changed their name to Goteki, a reflection of their increasing endorsement of dance music and kitch Japanese pop culture. It also reflects a growing recent trend among many Goths who find authentic industrial music too dark, or difficult to dance to.

According to Goteki, when founder Sneaky's 'not obsessing about Goteki world domination plans, he tends to be obsessing over some other facet of the information age, basking in the comforting glow of radioactive screens.' Nightbreed supremo Trevor Bamford spoke to me about the growth of the cyber-strand in Goth culture in early 2001: 'Our whole society is becoming more computerised and familiar with technology. It's obvious that this cultural influence will find its way into music and music-making. So on the one hand we have a general move in the Gothic scene towards all things electronic, while on the other we have new people coming into the scene with different perspectives on things. A fair few have come into the "cyber" scene from club and dance culture, which is fuelled by drugs amongst other things. So essentially we have at the moment this crossover situation. I think, paradoxically, that this tendency in the scene represents both a progression and a surrender to the mainstream at once. My only concern is that the problem with drug-based cultures is that there is a very real danger of burn out. The days of wine and roses never last forever!'

This new generation of Goths has also been busy rewriting the genre's history with almost Stalinist thoroughness. The Goth rock bands of the 1980s have been all but erased from the story in many minds, their place taken by the darker synth-pop bands that dominated the charts during this decade. By the year 2000, more new bands were emulating Depeche Mode's 'doom pop' stylings than were drawing on almost any other single influence. Typical of this new generation are British 'industrialpoptechno' act Chaos Engine, founded in 1994 as a NIN-style solo project by Lee H., who describes his music as 'Nine Inch Nails, [guitar-based techno-terrorists] Pitchshifter, [indie darlings] Garbage and Depeche Mode being locked in an elevator together, while the lights flicker and an air balloon inflates in one corner,' symbolising the band's danceable blend of self-effacing contagion, where opposites attract and breed mayhem.

Leechwoman, founded in 1994, are regarded as one of Britain's leading old-school industrial bands, although they also enjoy a significant cybergoth following. Live, they create a breathtakingly primal wall of guitar noise, sparking with a combination of music technology and angle-grinders, gas canisters and washing-machine parts. The rising stars of the UK Goth scene, however, are VNV Nation, founded in London in 1989 by the Irish duo of Ronan Harris and Justin Morey. They won the prestigious DAC (German Alternative Chart) Award for their 1999 album *Empires*, making the kind of thoughtful, gloomy EBM music that the Germans made their own during the previous decade. VNV Nation utilise the technology popularised by the techno scene to create music with an epic vision and soulful romanticism. 'The project preserves that which it seeks to express; the notion of Europe, modern and classical, clashing,' according to the band's website. 'Mythology and Technology in uneasy fusion . . . Cold energetic electronics and orchestral passion.'

Chief rivals for the electro-Goth crown Apoptygma Berzerk (APB) were founded in Norway in 1989 by Stephan Groth, who describes their music as the aural equivalent of the films of David Lynch: 'Easy and bright on the outside, but mystical and weird under the surface.' A more appropriate cultural comparison, at least in terms of APB's lyrics, might be *The X-Files* – rather than the vampires and spectres of traditional Gothic, the lyrics conjure mysterious, post-modern landscapes menaced by government conspiracies and alien visitations. Musically inspired by Depeche Mode, Apoptygma Berzerk have developed a sound some have described as 'Gothic techno'. Their founder remains respectful, however, even protective, of the much-maligned Goth scene. 'I think that it is very important for me to be

on the frontline and to make the scene continue and develop and to keep it alive,' Groth told *Meltdown*. 'I won't think of black as negative – never!' If Groth embodies any of the Gothic archetypes, however, it is the mad scientist presiding over a bank of blinking lights, switches and dials, rather than the black-clad, Byronic vampire.

So significant has been the recent electro-dance domination of the Goth underground in its British birthplace that some have begun referring to 'post-Goth', as if Gothic rock were no more. But, as ever, rumours of its demise have been much exaggerated. Indeed, the end of the twentieth century could even be seen as a Renaissance for the Goth pioneers of yesteryear. Death rock legends the Misfits re-formed in 1996; Goth-rock stalwarts the Fields of the Nephilim and Bauhaus re-formed in 1998, though neither have been forthcoming with any new original material; the Sisters of Mercy re-established themselves as a live entity after a period of relative silence, while Wayne Hussey took the Mission back on the road at the end of the decade, after a tour supporting Gary Numan. 'It wasn't until we started playing live [again] that I realised how vibrant the Goth movement is right now,' Hussey told me. 'We were playing shows to people of sixteen years and up – we're playing to people who were playing with Barbie Dolls last time we toured . . . It became obvious to me that kids are serious about this – it's been around a long, long time and I can't see it going away.'

Indeed, a new generation of bands is

A 'perkygoth' at the Carnival of Souls festival, displaying the playful influence of Japanese cartoons (anime) on this futuristic mutation of the Gothic aesthetic.

emerging with its feet planted firmly in the graveyard soil of the Gothic aesthetic, but with the vision to find new directions. US band Element want to see the fashionable dance elements of the Goth scene recede, allowing the darkness back into the light: 'This is the dark, twisted side of electro, in a genre I prefer to call "electro-death", for electronic death rock.' Fear Cult are described by *Aether Sanctum* as 'Goth with a capital "G" . . . Cold and sterile . . . [their music] paints a picture of a world devoid of light,' while leader Matt Riser says Fear Cult are dedicated to exploring 'the vicious realms of love, death and the darkness of life.' Back in the UK, Trevor Bamford's 'black industrial' band, Midnight Configuration, have embraced modern studio technology to invoke familiar demons from the fiction of H. P. Lovecraft and the strangest passages of the Bible. Critics remain divided about Bamford's unmistakably demonic vocals, now distorted to a rumble that makes Carl McCoy and Andrew Eldritch sound like a couple of soprano choirboys – a reverberating echo of primeval Gothic.

At the end of 2001, however, Bamford announced that his Nightbreed would cease business as a Goth-rock distribution and retail company, though it lives on as a record label. In part, this was because the internet, which so many cybergoths saw as a liberating development, was having a negative impact on the underground music scene: people were increasingly downloading music for free, rather than buying it on CD. But his motives weren't entirely commercial. While careful not to attack any particular artist's means of expression, he admitted to me that he 'got sick and tired of the whole "cybergoth/woolyhead" ethic and attitude.' While insisting that the traditional Gothic aesthetic has 'never really gone away', Bamford contends, 'it's been obscured by "candyfloss"'! I feel, and always have, that "Goth values", to coin a term, will always be with us in one form or another as they are part and parcel of the human condition – inasmuch as, to a great number of people, the dark, the melancholic, the romantic and the shamelessly sinful will always attract.'

Certainly, the Gothic tradition has weathered more serious challenges than day-glo dilution during its long history. Years, decades, centuries of suspicion and ridicule by the forces of conformity have just made the Gothic aesthetic all the more enduring. When Goth musician, and one-time Cleopatra promotions man, Athan Maroulis suggests, 'we may even have a Goth president one day!', in his liner-notes to Cleopatra's 1996 *Goth Box*, he's obviously being tongue-in-cheek. Nevertheless, Maroulis – who, since experiencing Bauhaus in a New York cinema in 1983, has played a very active role in promoting the Goth scene – makes an impassioned point. Goth has too long taken the defensive, apologised for its existence, attempted to placate its many detractors.

In our increasingly dumbed-down culture, it remains the only youth cult with a literary and artistic tradition all of its own – outliving the trappings of youthful self-indulgence to become a viable lifestyle and aesthetic. It has not only tolerated social diversity and deviance, but celebrated it long before fashion made such attitudes popular. As our grey world becomes more homogenised and commercialised, Goth extols the esoteric and unusual. Its playfulness, theatricality and love of the arcane represent a direct affront to a dull consumerist culture and a rigid work ethic. To those who suggest a preoccupation with sex and death is somehow weird, I'd counter that not being fascinated by both life-affirming eroticism and the inevitable fate that awaits us all is far weirder still. And what could be more captivating than the point at which these opposing poles of existence collide?

Or, in the words of Mr Maroulis' rather pithier conclusion, '"GOTH'S UNDEAD!", so fuck you if you don't get it, we don't want you to.' I'll raise a glass of the red stuff to that . . .

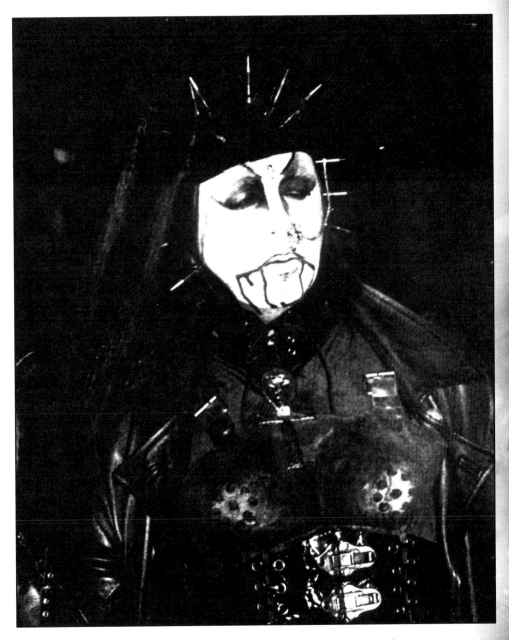

The Gothic aesthetic may mutate and evolve, but the same love of mystery and grotesquerie remains its dark essence.

SOURCES

By its very nature, researching a book such as *Goth Chic* involved consulting a bewilderingly diverse variety of sources. Chief among those books that proved useful were: Almond, Marc *Tainted Life* (UK, Pan Books, 2000); Anger, Kenneth *Hollywood Babylon* (US, Dell Books, 1981); Barton, Blanche *The Secret Life of a Satanist* (UK, Mondo Books, 1992); Bloom, Clive (ed.) *Gothic Horror* (UK, Macmillan Press, 1998); Brottman, Mikita *Hollywood Hex* (UK, Creation Books, 1998); Bruce, Michael with Billy James *No More Mr Nice Guy* (UK, SAF Publishing, 1996); Clayson, Alan *Death Discs* (UK, Sanctuary Publishing, 1997); Core, Philip *Camp* (UK, Plexus Publishing, 1984); Daniels, Les *Fear* (UK, Granada, 1977); Darby, *Retro Hell* (US, Little, Brown and Company, 1997); Davenport-Hines, Richard *Gothic* (UK, Fourth Estate, 1998); Dijkstra, Bram *Idols of Perversity* (US, Oxford University Press, 1986); Edwards, Ted *X-Files Confidential* (UK, Little, Brown & Company, 1997); Farren, Mick *The Black Leather Jacket* (UK, Plexus Publishing, 1985); Ford, Simon *The Wreckers of Civilisation* (UK, Black Dog Publishing, 1999); Frayling, Christopher *Nightmare: The Birth of Horror* (UK, BBC Books, 1996); Gagne, Paul *The Zombies That Ate Pittsburgh* (US, Dodd, Mead and Co., 1987); Gaunt, William, *The Aesthetic Adventure* (UK, Jonathan Cape, 1945); Gordon, Mel, *The Grand Guignol* (US, Amok Press, 1988); Gray, Jennie *Horace Walpole and William Beckford* (UK, Gargoyle's Head Press, 1994); Grunenberg, Christoph *Gothic* (US, MIT Press, 1997); Guiley, Rosemary Ellen *Vampires Among Us* (US, Pocket Books, 1991); Hardy, Phil *The Aurum Film Encyclopedia: Horror* (UK, Aurum, 1985); Hurwood, Berhardt J. *Vampires* (US, Omnibus Press, 1981); Huxley, Martin *Nine Inch Nails* (US, St Martin's Griffin, 1997); Jancik, Wayne and Tad Lathrop *Cult Rockers* (US, Fireside, 1995); Johnston, Ian *The Wild, Wild World of the Cramps* (UK, Omnibus Press, 1990); Jones, Stephen (compiler), *Clive Barker's A-Z of Horror* (UK, BBC Books, 1997); Jones, Stephen (ed.) *The Hellraiser Chronicles* (UK, Titan Books, 1992); Jones, Stephen and Kim Newman (eds.) *Horror 100 Best Books* (UK, Xanadu, 1988); Jones, Stephen *The Illustrated Vampire Movie Guide* (UK, Titan Books, 1993); Kendrick, Walter *The Thrill of Fear* (US, Grove Press, 1991); King, Stephen *Danse Macabre* (UK, Warner Books, 1993); Kuryluk, Ewa *Salome and Judas in the Cave of Sex* (US, Northwestern University Press, 1987); Larkin, Colin (Ed.) *The Virgin Encyclopaedia of Indie and New Wave* (UK, Virgin, 1998); LaVey, Anton *The Satanic Bible* (US, Avon Books, 1969); Lee, Christopher *Tall, Dark and Gruesome* (UK, Granada Publishing, 1977); Manson, Marilyn with Neil Strauss *The Long Hard Road Out of Hell* (UK, Plexus Publishing, 1998); Mercer, Mick *Gothic Rock* (UK, Pegasus Publishing, 1991); Mercer, Mick *The Hex Files* (UK, B.T. Batsford, 1996); Mulvey-Roberts, Marie (ed.) *The Handbook of Gothic Literature* (UK, MacMillan Press, 1998); Newman, Kim *Nightmare Movies* (UK, Bloomsbury, 1984); Nichols, Stan *Wordsmiths of Wonder* (UK, Orbit, 1993); Norton, Rictor *Mistress of Udolpho* (UK, Leicester University Press, 1999); Pitt, Ingrid *The Ingrid Pitt Bedside Companion for Vampire Lovers* (UK, Batsford, 1998); Praz, Mario *The Romantic Agony* (UK, Oxford University Press, 1951); Peary, Danny *Cult Movie Stars* (US, Simon and Schuster, 1991); Price, Victoria *Vincent Price* (UK, Sidgwick and Jackson, 2000); Ramsden, Mark *Radical Desire* (UK, Serpent's Tail, 2001); Rigby, Jonathan *English Gothic* (UK, Reynolds and Hearn, 2000); Robbins, Ira A. (Ed.) *The Trouser Press Guide to '90s Rock* (US, Fireside, 1997); Rottensteiner, Franz *The Fantasy Book* (UK, Thames & Hudson, 1978); Ruff, Marcel A. *Baudelaire* (UK, University of London Press, 1966); Salisbury, Mark (ed.) *Burton on Burton* (UK, Faber and Faber, 2000); Shirley, Ian *Dark Entries* (UK, SAF Publishing, 1994); Skal, David J. *The Monster Show* (UK, Plexus Publishing, 1994); Skal, David J. *V is for Vampire* (UK, Robson Books, 1996); Stableford, Brian *The Dedalus Book of Femmes Fatale* (UK, Dedalus, 1992); Stableford, Brian *Moral Ruins* (UK, Dedalus, 1990); Stevenson, Nils *Vacant* (UK, Thames and Hudson, 1999); Sullivan, Jack (ed.) *The Penguin Encyclopaedia of Horror and the Supernatural* (UK, Penguin, 1986); Summers, Montague *The Gothic Quest* (UK, Fortune Press, 1938); Tannahill, Reay *Sex in History* (UK, Cardinal, 1990); Thompson, Dave *Beyond the Velvet Underground* (UK, Omnibus, 1989); Thorne, Tony *Children of the Night* (UK, Victor Gollancz, 1999); Tudor, Andrew *Monsters and Mad Scientists* (UK, Basil Blackwell, 1989); Vale, V. and Andrea Juno (eds.) *Modern Primitives* (US, Re/Search, 1989); Winter, Douglas E. *Faces of Fear* (UK, Pan Books, 1990); Woods, Paul Anthony *Ed Gein – Psycho!* (US, St Martin's Griffin, 1995)

I would like to thank the following specialist periodicals in the UK and Europe: *Bats and Red Velvet; Bite Me; Bizarre; Blood Stone; Chronicles; Dark Life; The Dark Side; Fear; House of Hammer; Kaleidoscope; Meltdown; Naked Truth; Orkus; Redeemer; Skin Two; Terrorizer; Udolpho*. In the USA I would like to thank: *Alternative Press; Blue Blood; Carpe Noctem; Fangoria; Ghastly; Horror Garage; Implosion; Iniquities; Morbid Curiosity; New Grave; Propaganda; Scary Monsters; Wicked*.
My thanks to the following websites in the UK: The Dark Side of the Web (http://www.darklinks.com/index.html) has offered links to almost every aspect of Gothic culture since its foundation in 1994. The Old Curiosity Shop (http://www.oldcuriosityshop.net/indexflash.html) deserves a mention – not least because this writer is one of the proprietors, and the curious can sample a few more morsels from the Baddeley *oeuvre* therein (if they haven't had enough already) and in the USA: Deathrock.com (http://www.deathrock.com/main.html) provides an excellent resource for anyone interested in the Gothic music scene in its numerous manifestations.

Thanks to the following photographers, artists, record and film companies, magazines, publishers and photographic agencies: Nigel Wingrove for the cover photograph;

4AD/Sara Leigh Lewis; 20th Century Fox; ABC TV; All Action; American International Pictures; Aquarius; BBC; Beggars Banquet; BFI; Caroline Blind/George Olsson; Byron Films/Blue Dolphin; Cannon Films/Vestron Video; Carnival of Souls Festival/Jim Campbell; Dave Carson; CBS TV; Century Media; Channel 5; Chaosium Inc; Chatto & Windus; Cherry Red Music Publishing; Columbia Pictures; Columbia Tristar International TV; Corgi Books; Creation Books/Lydia Lunch; Dark Angel Productions; Demon Records; Doktor A; Dover Publications; Elektra/Warner; Entertainment Films; EOS/Harper Collins; Epic/Allan Ballard; Epitaph Records; Factory Records; Futura; Diamanda Galas/Tom Caravaglia; Geffen Pictures; Gladstone Publications; Gorse Records; Hammer American International; HBO; Mike Hideous; David Hindley (pp213, 216 and 233); David Hindley and The Stranger (pp2 and 244); ID; Inkubus Sukkubus; ITN Corporation; Kamera Records; Keystone; Matthew Lewis; Lord Sutch Fanclub; Lucanna Martinez; Charles Maturin; MCA/Universal City Studios; Mercury Records; Metrodome; MGM; Moore Video; Marc Morris; Music for Nations; Nems Records Ltd; Nightbreed Recordings/Trevor Bamford; Patricia Morrison/Henrich Beck Poulsen; Palace Pictures; Paramount; Peaceville Records/Vile Music (P.R.S.) UK; Barry Plummer; Pocket Books; Polydor; Pragmatic Pictures; Projekt Recordings; Purgatory Video; Record Collector/Ben Thornberry; Redemption; Restless Records; Roadrunner Records; Arlene Russo; Salvation Films/Nigel Wingrove; Savant Garde Entertainment; Sive Records; SLG Publishing; Smirnoff/Wayne Brown; Sonovabitch Records; Starmaker; Strike Back Records; The Stranger; *Time Out*; Titan Books; Triple Silence; Ts/Munchen, Konzept: Josef K; Universal; Vampira; Vestron; Video Search; Walt Disney Productions; Warner Brothers/Wayne Maser; Annette West Lerman.